STRONG RELIGION

STRONG RELIGION

The Rise of Fundamentalisms around the World

GABRIEL A. ALMOND,
R. SCOTT APPLEBY, AND
EMMANUEL SIVAN

The University of Chicago Press
Chicago and London

GABRIEL A. ALMOND is professor emeritus of political science at Stanford University and the author of numerous works, including *Progress and Its Discontents*.

R. SCOTT APPLEBY is professor of history and the John M. Regan, Jr., director of the Joan B. Kroc Institute for International Peace Studies at the University of Notre Dame. He is author of, among other books, *Religious Fundamentalisms and Global Conflict*.

EMMANUEL SIVAN is professor of history at the Hebrew University of Jerusalem and author of a number of books, including *Interpretations of Islam* and *Radical Islam*.

The University of Chicago Press, Chicago 60637
The University of Chicago Press, Ltd., London
© 2003 by The University of Chicago
All rights reserved. Published 2003
Printed in the United States of America

12 11 10 09 08 07 06   5
ISBN: 0-226-01497-5 (cloth)
ISBN: 0-226-01498-3 (paper)
ISBN: 0-226-01499-1 (electronic)

Library of Congress Cataloging-in-Publication Data

Almond, Gabriel Abraham, 1911–
    Strong religion : the rise of fundamentalisms around the world / Gabriel A.
    Almond, R. Scott Appleby, and Emmanuel Sivan.
        p.   cm.
    Includes bibliographical references and index.
    ISBN 0-226-01497-5 (cloth : alk. paper)—ISBN 0-226-01498-3 (pbk. : alk.
    paper)
    1. Fundamentalism. I. Appleby, R. Scott, 1956– . II. Sivan,
    Emmanuel. III. Title.
    BL238.A28 2003
    200′.9′04—dc21

                                                    2002013665

For Dorothea

CONTENTS

Acknowledgments   *ix*

Introduction   *1*

CHAPTER 1
The Enclave Culture   *23*

CHAPTER 2
Fundamentalism: Genus and Species   *90*

CHAPTER 3
Explaining Fundamentalisms:
Structure, Chance, and Choice   *116*

CHAPTER 4
Wrestling with the World:
Fundamentalist Movements as Emergent Systems   *145*

CHAPTER 5
Testing the Model:
Politics, Ethnicity, and Fundamentalist Strategies   *191*

CHAPTER 6
The Prospects of Fundamentalism   *220*

Appendix to Chapter 2   *245*
Appendix to Chapter 3   *249*
Appendix to Chapter 4   *253*
Notes   *255*
Index   *273*

ACKNOWLEDGMENTS

The authors are happily indebted to the American Academy of Arts and Sciences and to dozens of scholars who contributed essays to The Fundamentalism Project, many of whom were also consulted directly during the preparation of this volume, including Nancy Ammerman, Gideon Aran, Said Arjomand, Raymond Grew, Samuel Heilman, and Harjot Oberoi. Alan Thomas, Randolph Petilos, and Maia Melissa Rigas of the University of Chicago Press supervised and expedited the publication process. Clare Appleby and Jonathan Bischof prepared the index. Barbara Lockwood arranged the authors' meetings in Jerusalem, Palo Alto, and South Bend and coordinated various aspects of the project. Martin E. Marty provided inspiration and intellectual leadership along the way.

"Fundamentalism" is one of the most significant political phenomena of our time. Since the Iranian Revolution, purported fundamentalist movements have risen to the highest levels of power in five countries—in Iran in 1979, in the Sudan in 1993, in Turkey, Afghanistan, and India in 1996, and again in India in 1998 and 1999. There have been even more frequent penetrations by fundamentalist movements into the parliaments, assemblies, and political parties of such countries as Jordan, Israel, Egypt, Morocco, Pakistan, and the United States.

Spurned or driven underground, other fundamentalist movements formed powerful and deadly opposition groups, such as Hamas, the Palestinian Islamist resistance movement; Al Qaeda, the terrorist network organized by the Saudi expatriate, Osama bin Laden; the Sikh extremists who took up arms against moderate Sikhs and the secular government of India; elements of the Jewish Underground, who assassinated Arab mayors, and another group that plotted to destroy Muslim shrines on the Temple Mount/Haram al-Sharif in Jerusalem; guerrillas of the Armed Islamic Group in Algeria (GIA), who indiscriminately massacred villagers and town dwellers in retaliation against the regime; Islamic revolutionaries in Chechnya and Dagestan fighting for independence from Russia; and Christian radicals in the United States who stalked feminist activists and gunned down doctors who performed abortions.

The media used the term "fundamentalism" to describe each of these religiously inspired actors as well as many others. Given the origins of the term in a 1920 edition of the Northern Baptist (U.S.A.) periodical, *The Watchman-Examiner*, whose editor described himself and a group of conservative evangelical Protestants as militants willing to do "battle royal" to preserve the "fundamentals" of the Christian faith from the evolutionists and biblical critics infecting mainline seminaries and colleges, it is ironic that today "fundamentalism" is used most frequently to refer to Islamist movements of varying size, shape, and social and ethnic composition.

The phenomenon of "global fundamentalism" took on unprecedented urgency in the minds of millions of people around the world in the fall of 2001. More than 2,800 people from four dozen nations died on 11 September 2001 in the terrorist attacks that destroyed the World Trade Center and damaged the Pentagon. Shortly thereafter, it became apparent that bin Laden, working through his extensive Al Qaeda network, had engineered the attacks as an act of a jihad, or holy war, against the United States and its allies. As a result of the attacks, the United States and Great Britain, among other nations of the West, finally and fully came to grips with the fact of religious violence in the fundamentalist mode. Now manifested on a truly global scale, the astonishing power of religious fundamentalism became undeniable, even within the policymaking circles accustomed to formulating secular explanations for a range of acts and operations that have been engineered and enacted by self-styled true believers.

We call our book *Strong Religion* because these movements are militant and highly focused antagonists of secularization. They call a halt to the centuries-long retreat of the religious establishments before the secular power. They follow the rule of offense being better than defense, and they often include the extreme option of violence and death. We intend the notion of "strength" to suggest that these are movements to reckon with seriously.

The Western myopia on this subject of religious power has been astounding. Christians of the United States, long accustomed to living in a religiously plural society governed by the principles of religious freedom, separation of church and state, and the rule of law, seemed to have forgotten the death-defying roots of their own tradition. Christians, like Muslims, have considered martyrdom a prime opportunity for holiness and, indeed, a direct ticket to heaven. Consider the early second-century example of Ignatius, bishop of Antioch, whose letters, written while he was traveling under armed guard to his death in Rome, pleaded with fellow Christians not to rescue him from his fate—to be eaten by lions. "What a thrill I shall have from the wild beasts that are ready for me! I hope that they will make short work of me," (Saint) Ignatius exults. "I shall coax them on to eat me up at once and not to hold off, as sometimes happens, through fear. And if they are reluctant, I shall force them to it. Forgive me—I know what is good for me. Now is the moment I am beginning to be a disciple."[1] One need not reach back to the early church fathers, however, to glimpse the self-sacrificing intensity of the religious imagination. Roman Catholic schoolchildren as recently as the early 1960s were still being taught to prepare themselves to die for their faith rather than to renounce Jesus—in this case, the setting was the Cold War and the enemy, the communist "pagans" of the Soviet Union.[2]

When pagan Rome gave way to the "Holy Roman Empire" of medieval Christendom, the tables were turned. Christian crusaders and inquisitors were on the giving end of lethal violence. The religious imagination of millions of contemporary Muslims is shaped in part by the vividly preserved cultural memory of these brutal encounters with the so-called followers of the "Prince of Peace." Thus, President George W. Bush inadvertently confirmed Arab and Muslim suspicions about "Christian statecraft" when he described "Operation Infinite Justice" (as the U.S. military response to the September 11 terrorist attacks was initially named) as a "crusade."

Contemporary U.S. Christians, however, safe to practice their faith openly and, in the main, nonviolently, tend not to think of Christianity as a source of lethal violence. Until recently, they have also failed to recognize the religious nature of much of the political violence elsewhere in the world. Remarkably, Americans expressed surprise upon reading the letter of instruction sent by Mohamed Atta, one of bin Laden's confederates, to his fellow doomed hijackers. Attorney General John Ashcroft called the document's prayers and exhortations to martyrdom "a disturbing and shocking view into the mindset of these terrorists." "Chilling," "eerie," and "haunting," effused Bob Woodward. Like other major news organizations on 28 September 2001, ABC News led with the story, portraying the letter as a minor revelation, a confirmation that the United States faces an unconventional war against an irrational enemy.

Such stunned reactions to evidence that Muslim extremists seem actually to believe in God, pray to Him, and even invoke His assistance are baffling. Even a glance in the direction of world events beyond U.S. borders since the Shi'ite revolution in Iran twenty-four years ago should have prepared the arbiters of U.S. public opinion to anticipate the possibility that the young Muslim suicide hijackers would be willing, even eager, to sacrifice their lives in support of a cause they judged to be sacred. One may recall the televised images of Iranian women sending their young sons across land-mined fields to certain death in the protracted war against Iraq, or the 241 U.S. Marines killed in October 1983 at the hands of Shi'ite self-martyrs who drove an explosive-laden truck into their barracks. Perhaps we Americans assumed that the suicide bombers of Hizbullah, Hamas, and Islamic Jihad of Palestine were an aberration—or a problem for the Israelis and the Middle East alone.

As religious movements concerned with and imitative of earthly power, fundamentalisms are also political movements driven by their own ideologies. In describing fundamentalisms, one expert has written, "modern political science categories do not fit and are irrelevant."[3] While this is something of an overstatement, it alerts us to the need to recognize the dual sources, religious and political, of fundamentalism's dynamism and appeal.

Despite the high visibility of fundamentalist movements in the world today, however, there is a general tendency to underplay religion as an autonomous force in politics, to oversimplify and minimize the complexity of "church-state" relations as they form and reform around the globe. The dominant explanatory view of religion is reductive, treating it as epiphenomenal to economic, political, or psychological realities. Since the Enlightenment, the principle of separation of church and state has been an essential criterion of modernization and the measure of liberty. It leads scholars, journalists, and statesmen to assume that religion is an unequivocally private matter.

The boundary between the sacred and the secular varies from country to country, however. Millions of people structure their daily routines around the spiritual practices enjoined by a religious tradition, and they often do so quite "publicly." Dress, eating habits, gender relations, negotiations of time, space, and social calendar—all unfold beneath a sacred canopy. Whereas secularists reject arguments and claims drawn from religious doctrines or sacred Scripture, the majority in many countries relies on such sources of authority in making political as well as personal decisions. Secularists may have internalized the privatization of belief, but religion continues to perform complex, multiple roles and functions in societies from the United States and Europe, across the Middle East, Africa, and South Asia, to Indonesia.

Denial, nonetheless, reigns in elite circles. Reasons for this form of secular myopia vary, but the dictionary suggests some plausible explanations; it defines "denial" as a process that enables "the mind to reach compromise solutions to problems it is unable to resolve" and as a "defense mechanism" that conceals "the more unpleasant aspects of external reality."[4] The denial of the causal significance of religion rests, at least in part, on an inertial persistence of the culture of "progress"—a survival of Enlightenment expectations of continued cultural secularization, growth of scientific knowledge, technical and institutional creativity, and enhanced welfare, with religion seen only as fading tradition. While this version of an idea of progress no longer reflects reality, it has not been replaced by views more consistent with our understanding of the human situation, as it is being pressed upon us by the discoveries of science and by the costs of industrial and technological development. The mobilization and militance of modern fundamentalist movements cannot be reconciled with the persistence of notions of progress and hence must be denied and explained away.

This is not the first time that Enlightenment expectations have been rebuffed by history. The ideas leading up to the rationalism of the French Revolution were succeeded by the clerico-conservative and authoritarian ideologies of the end of the eighteenth and the first part of the nineteenth centuries—the sober constitutional traditionalism of Edmund Burke, the organicism, clericalism, and hierarchalism of De Maistre and Bonald. The democratic-socialist-internationalist version of the Enlightenment of the later nineteenth century, distorted into totalitarian Bolshevism in the early twentieth century, was followed by ethnonationalist and clerico-authoritarian movements, by fascism and Nazism.

What we call fundamentalism is the third rebuff that history has administered to "modernization" and secularization since the eighteenth century. It is not a homogeneous rebuff. In its Asian and Middle Eastern manifestations it shares ethnonationalism and clerico-authoritarianism with the first and second rebuffs. What is remarkable about the third rebuff is that it is being administered after the great scientific revolutions of the twentieth century—after the unlocking of nuclear power, the development of molecular biology, the replacement of Newtonian cosmology by relativity and quantum theory, and the big bang cosmology. The fundamentalist rebuff comes after "big science." Its pervasiveness and militance raises questions about the boast that science and secular rationalism will fully replace religion and the sense of the sacred as approaches to meaning.

The terrorist attacks of September 11 signified much more, however, than merely another wake-up call to a somnolent U.S. public. They thrust into the international spotlight a web of concerns that have since become the preoccupation of the educated general public in the United States and Europe. Based on the Fundamentalism Project, a decade-long interdisciplinary public policy study of antimodernist, antisecularist militant religious movements on five continents and within seven world religious traditions, *Strong Religion: The Rise of Fundamentalisms around the World* addresses three sets of questions that fall within this web of concerns.

The first set of questions asks, What are the local, regional and global contexts for, and triggers of, the emergence of fiercely antimodernist, antisecular movements from within virtually every major world religion in the twentieth century? Under what conditions have such movements grown and gained momentum? What factors precipitate their hibernation, decline, or disappearance?

The second set of questions asks, What characteristics do these movements share across religious, cultural, and political borders? Once movements and groups that bear only superficial resemblance to fundamentalisms are eliminated from consideration, is it possible, and appropriate, to understand fundamentalism as a singular phenomenon—as a genus containing various species? May we speak, as did the Fundamentalism Project, of fundamentalist "family resemblances," not least of which is a set of shared criticisms of, and common reactions to, the directions taken by secular modernity?

The third set of questions asks, Is fundamentalism truly a global phenomenon? That is, are fundamentalist movements, whatever their places of origin and everyday activity, capable of extending their influence transnationally? To put the question sharply: are fundamentalist movements now capable of, and inclined to, carry the battle against their enemies far beyond their territorial borders so that we can be said to be facing a "third world war," as President Bush termed the conflict against terrorism? Is it a war, further, not only against Islamists but against the fundamentalists in general?

"The fundamentalists." Is it correct to generalize? *Strong Religion* argues, in effect, that while Islam has produced a particularly virulent and potentially global form of radical fundamentalism, other major religious traditions have also given birth to movements that can be fruitfully compared with the Islamist movements (as well as to the original Christian case of the 1920s). Osama bin Laden attempted to demonstrate that the ideology of Islamic fundamentalism is readily exportable. Is this indeed the case? May this be said of fundamentalist movements and ideologies within Judaism, Christianity, Hinduism, and Buddhism—or is it a unique characteristic of Islam as a host religion for fundamentalisms?

Such questions take on a greater salience in the wake of the events of September 11 and the subsequent war against terrorism. At the dawn of the twenty-first century, "denial" may no longer be possible. Educators and policymakers are studying religiously motivated movements at a deeper level of seriousness. Is fundamentalism, by whatever name, necessarily given to violence? In combating radical fundamentalisms, is there a viable alternative to state-sponsored violence, which is considered terrorism by its victims? Are there viable strategies of rapprochement? Others ask, simply, how such movements are to be defeated, neutralized, or where possible, transformed to nonviolent and constructive purposes.

SOURCES, METHODS, AND ORGANIZATION OF THE BOOK

In *Strong Religion* we address such questions by providing a framework for analysis of the rise, growth, and decline of fundamentalist movements. We begin by immersing the reader in a richly textured historical essay, "The Enclave Culture," which provides a clinical, ethnographic picture of fundamentalism drawn from intimate knowledge of the histories, literatures, and cultures of the Abrahamic religions—Judaism, Christianity, and Islam—as they encountered secularization in the course of the late nineteenth and twentieth centuries. Mary Douglas's cultural typology illuminates the "enclaves" that took shape in that encounter—communities whose outside boundaries are tightly closed and where the interior division of influence and labor tends to be egalitarian.[5] We focused on the Abrahamic traditions in this introductory chapter because we wanted to work from original sources in the languages we are able to command.

Chapter 2, "Fundamentalism: Genus and Species," is definitional and classificatory in approach. It compares some twenty religiopolitical movements in seven religious traditions according to their ideological and organizational characteristics, thereby enabling us to distinguish between "pure" and syncretic fundamentalisms and to eliminate from consideration militant religious movements not properly included in the fundamentalist category. The model is based on the analysis in chapter 1 and discussions of definitions and traits of fundamentalism presented in the Fundamentalism Project and elsewhere in the literature on religious militancy.

Chapter 3, "Explaining Fundamentalism: Structure, Chance, and Choice," breaks the problem down into the kinds of questions that we ask of these movements: What structural variables (long-term cultural, economic, and political conditions), what chance factors (e.g., the death of a charismatic leader, the outbreak of war), and what choice variables (such as the creativity of leaders) explain their origins, ideology, organization, strategy, growth, and decline? The approach of this chapter is analytic and reductive.

Chapter 4, "Wrestling with the World: Fundamentalist Movements as Emergent Systems," deals with fundamentalist movements as they function in specific times and environmental contexts. On the one hand, such movements are emergent systems that can be analyzed as such by examining the combination of structural, chance, and choice variables sketched in chapter 3. On the other hand, the elements of chance and human creativity and the synergies among the interacting conditions and actions within a specific context mean that the emergent sum is greater than the parts. In an attempt to reflect this complexity, we isolate four modes in which fundamentalist movements interact with their environments; these constitute four strategies such movements adopt in their interactions with the world outside the enclave: conqueror, transformer, creator, and renouncer. We also explain shifts from one strategy to the other according to the analytic scheme of chapter 3.

Chapter 5, "Politics, Ethnicity, and Fundamentalism," deals with the two most significant structural factors that help determine and condition fundamentalist programs and strategies—the political and ethnoreligious contexts. Here we examine the ways in which public policy and fundamentalist movements interact in democratic and authoritarian societies and in situations of ethnic heterogeneity and conflict.

In chapter 6 we look at the prospects of these movements by anticipating changes in their social and cultural environment. We ask how worldviews, cosmologies, and patterns of activism might change as a consequence of scientific discovery and technical invention, the growth of global markets and democratizing trends, the increasing competition within the religious marketplace, and the success of the state in minimizing the gains and multiplying the losses sustained by religious movements that engage in terrorist violence. Beyond the question of the relative rise or decline of these movements under the impact of these external changes, we examine the possibility that they might adjust their orientation to the world along the spectrum of positions described in chapter 4: world conqueror, transformer, creator, and renouncer.

Our goal is to provide readers with a framework and foundation for understanding not only the crisis surrounding "terrorism" but also the events, trends, and conflicts that will shape the interaction between radical religion and politics for years to come. Related to this interaction are cultural and political issues at the heart of contemporary debates over individual and collective rights and freedoms, civil liberties and civil societies, and the role of justice and morality in international relations.

THE FUNDAMENTALISM PROJECT

Strong Religion draws upon more than seventy-five case studies and comparative essays published in the five-volume Fundamentalism Project of the American Academy of Arts and Sciences. Dozens of other books and hundreds of articles on "fundamentalism" (or on such movements described by another name) have appeared in the last twenty years, and we draw upon many of these studies as well. Finally, we have traveled extensively and draw upon our personal experiences and interviews with fundamentalists, and with their opponents, in the Middle East, North Africa, the United States, Europe, and South Asia.

Since the Fundamentalism Project volumes provide our most detailed databank, it may be useful briefly to describe their overall design and content. The five volumes of the series proceeded inductively, first gathering detailed accounts of individual movements in their particular settings, then describing their impact on the social, economic, and political world around them, then examining their patterns of emergence, growth, and decline, and in the final volume making direct comparisons and offering interpretations and explanations.

The first volume, *Fundamentalisms Observed* (1991), is historical and empirical in emphasis, introducing the reader to a set of discrete movements in fourteen monograph-size case studies. At this early stage, project directors and editors do not provide explicit theoretical justifications for analyzing the disparate movements together as related phenomena beyond noting the striking similarities that remain after substantive differences are taken into account. Rather, the approach is strictly hypothetical: the traits and elements that seem to recur across movements are cataloged for future consideration in the volume's conclusion, "An Interim Report on a Hypothetical Family."

Fundamentalisms Observed makes a powerful case for "family resemblances" shared by the movements under scrutiny. It does so by virtue of the sheer cumulative weight of the separate testimonies by the regional and religious specialists—the historians, anthropologists, sociologists, and political scientists who authored the various case studies. The movements share neither a homeland—they are found on five different continents—nor a common host religion. They emerged from Christianity, Judaism, Sunni and Shi'ite Islam, Hinduism, Sikhism, Buddhism, and neo-Confucianism. Their different doctrines, cosmologies, social composition, sizes, organizational structures, political settings, and scope of influence could—and do—fill a separate encyclopedia. Yet most of the movements were found to share certain traits with one another that are not found in the same combination in other modern social protest movements.

These shared traits included cadres composed of former religious conservatives who chose to separate from their orthodox or traditionalist communities and to redefine the sacred community in terms of its disciplined opposition to nonbelievers and "lukewarm" believers. Convinced of a conspiracy between secularists and liberal religionists, these separatists adopted a set of strategies for fighting back against what they perceived to be a concerted effort by secular states or elements within them to push people of religious consciousness and conscience to the margins of society. Male charismatic or authoritarian leaders emerged from each religious tradition, often in defiance of the conventions and conventional leadership of the tradition in its nineteenth- or twentieth-century incarnations. Acting strategically, these new fundamentalist leaders ransacked the tradition's past, retrieving and restoring politically useful doctrines and practices and creating others in an effort to construct a religiopolitical ideology capable of mobilizing disgruntled youth into militant cadres or into grassroots political organizations. The religious ideologues established new boundaries between "insiders" and "outsiders" and imposed a strict discipline on their followers; in many if not all cases, they were able to elevate their mission to a spiritual plane in which apocalyptic urgency informed even the most mundane tasks of the group.

All of this unfolded in the name of defending and preserving a hallowed identity rooted in religious tradition but now under threat of erosion. *Fundamentalisms Observed* demonstrated, however, that radical Shi'ite Muslims in Lebanon and Iran, militant Sikhs in Punjab, Jewish extremists on the West Bank, Hindu nationalists at Ayodhya, and Christian cultural warriors in the United States—despite being worlds apart from one another geographically, historically, and in the specific content of their beliefs and practices—were establishing "progressive," world-creating, and world-conquering movements that looked to the past for inspiration rather than for a blueprint. Direction and models would come not only from a selective interpretation of the sacred past but also from imitation of what works in the present— including, of course, secular models. Thus the subjects of *Fundamentalisms Observed* became important players in local, regional, and even national politics not as a result of their nostalgia or "backwardness" but for their ability to adapt to modern organizational imperatives, political strategies, communications advances, and economic theories.

The second and third volumes in the series, published in 1993 as companion pieces, explored the extent of influence of putative fundamentalist movements in the various spheres of human existence. *Fundamentalisms and Society* measured the impact of Islamic, Christian, and Jewish fundamentalisms on scientific research and the application of technology in societies in North America and the Middle East. Borrowing disguised as reappropriation characterized fundamentalists' attitudes toward science and technology. Fundamentalists blamed the erosion of religious belief and practice on the irreligious worldviews and materialistic lifestyles accompanying the growth and spread of secular science and technology. But they did not retreat from the secular-scientific world; they strove, rather, to transform or conquer it.

In so doing, however, fundamentalists accepted the underlying premises of the modern scientific worldview, a concession that was most evident in their adoption of empirical criteria for the verification of at least some truth claims. Hence Christian creationists argued with evolutionists about the age of fossil records[6]; Islamist philosophers claimed (medieval) Islamic origins for modern sciences and technologies.[7] Ultra-Orthodox Jews in Israel, falling short of the political power necessary to impose "universalistic obligations" taken from Jewish law, attempted to curtail archaeological exploration and restrict autopsy, abortion, and certain operating technologies. But they also sponsored extensive research into technologies enabling Sabbath observance (e.g., voice-activated microphones for use in the synagogue).[8] Time and again, fundamentalists borrowed modern ideas and developed expertise in mass communications, computer software, and other modern instruments and technologies.

In short, if we are to describe fundamentalists as defenders of "traditional religion" against the encroachments of "secularization," we must also recognize both their ambivalent attitude toward modern science and their simultaneous selective adoption of its methods.

Contributors to *Fundamentalisms and Society* also explored a fundamentalist "family trait"—the defense and consolidation of patriarchy as the divine plan for the moral ordering of society—by surveying the role of women and children in fundamentalist movements of the United States, Latin America, Egypt, Iran, Pakistan, and Japan. Strikingly, women in these disparate settings, the anthropologists and sociologists reported, shared a dedication to the maintenance and valorization of patriarchal social structures. They spoke of "feminism," or "women's liberation," but challenged and recast the secular/Western understanding and practice, rooting their approach to gender relations in Scriptural and traditional sources that commanded subordination to male leadership but also sacralized unambiguous spheres of female authority.[9] Most saw the education and moral formation of children as the most important task of the family and the mother as the central figure in a counter-acculturative educational network that extended beyond the home but never contravened its basic precepts. This characteristic focus on countercultural moral and spiritual formation recurred in studies analyzing fundamentalist educational systems and communications networks in the United States, Guatemala, Israel, Iran, and India.[10]

A striking finding of the second and third volumes taken together was the diminishing returns on fundamentalist investments of time and energy as these investments moved beyond the domestic and into the public political sphere. Because the modern state regulates many aspects of social existence and establishes the basic political and cultural conditions within which social life occurs, fundamentalists feel compelled to provide a compelling religious alternative to the state. Thus, even when fundamentalists attempted to preserve their separateness from secular society, they found themselves participating in a common discourse about modernization, development, political structures, and economic planning.

Fundamentalisms and the State chronicled fundamentalists' participation in politics, lawmaking, and economics up to 1992. Case studies included Christian antiabortion activists in the United States, Protestant unionists and Catholic nationalists in Northern Ireland; Muslim radicals in Iran, Egypt, Pakistan, Saudi Arabia, Sudan, and Turkey; Jewish settlers in Israel; and Hindu and Buddhist nationalists in South Asia. The volume also compared a variety of militant fundamentalists in their use of violence as a political tool.

When fundamentalists played politics to influence the policies of the state, many authors discovered, they were necessarily involved in compromise and accommodation. Political involvement, that is, tends to alter the exclusivist, dogmatic, confrontational mode of the fundamentalist to such a degree that the word *fundamentalism* or its cognates is no longer appropriate.

In some states—Pakistan, Morocco, Israel, India, and the United States, to name a few—religious fundamentalists influenced the terms of political and social discourse, but they found the construction of an Islamic or Christian or Jewish polity to be well out of reach. This appears to be the case even in contemporary postrevolutionary Iran, the premier "fundamentalist" state, where economic exigencies, international politics, and a new generation of Iranian youth, among other forces, have conspired to dissipate Islamic revolutionary energies and have undermined the principles of Khomeinism as the litmus test for practical political decisions.[11]

In chapters 5 and 6 of the present volume, drawing in part on the findings of *Fundamentalisms and the State*, we offer reflections on the limits of fundamentalist politics and terrorist violence. The reflections address a question at the heart of our study: How may we account for the various attitudes, ideologies, and behaviors of fundamentalist movements toward the outside world? Drawing upon the same religious tradition, why do certain fundamentalist movements act aggressively against outsiders, while others are integrationist or accommodationist, still others passive or separatist in relation to the surrounding communities and cultures?

Such questions were taken up initially in *Accounting for Fundamentalisms* (1994), the fourth volume in the series, which explores the dynamic character of religious radicalism as it moves into or away from a fundamentalist mode of relating to the world outside the enclave. What "causes" a modern religious movement to become militant and exclusivist or, by contrast, to join coalitions and lower its defenses? The twenty-eight contributors to the volume explored the conditions under which fundamentalist movements around the world change their ideological and behavioral patterns in ways that resulted in either a greater or lesser engagement with people and forces outside the group or movement.

Each author charted the relationship over time between the organizational characteristics of a particular fundamentalist movement (its structure, size and social composition, recruitment process, mode of governance or decision-making, and means of retaining members and mobilizing resources) and its changing worldviews, ideologies, and programs (the discursive fields fundamentalist leaders construct through the reinterpretation of symbols and ethical traditions via the stories they tell of themselves, of the world, and of their aims).

Considerations of how fundamentalist movements change over time and in response to internal and external dynamics is a major theme of our work as well. We are concerned with the role of charismatic leaders and with contingencies beyond their control that constitute opportunities for growth or occasions for decline. How, for example, would the death of Rabbi Menachem Mendel Schneerson, the charismatic leader thought by his disciples to be the Messiah, affect the organizational dynamics and message of the Lubavitcher Hasidim? How did policies of the Congress Party in India create an opening for the political emergence of Hindu nationalism in its most recent manifestation (e.g., the Vishwa Hindu Parishad and the Bharatiya Janata Party)? What role did radical Sunni Muslims play in the day-to-day operations of the Islamic Salvation Front (FIS) of Algeria? By refining an analytical framework for addressing such questions on a comparative basis, the present volume takes up such matters where *Accounting for Fundamentalisms* left off.

Fundamentalisms Comprehended, the fifth and final volume of the series, features analytic and comparative essays testing the project directors' original characterization of fundamentalism as a "hypothetical family"—a reactive, selective, absolutist, comprehensive mode of antisecular religious activism. Comparisons of fundamentalisms with secular totalizing systems, within religious traditions, and across religious traditions serve to isolate distinctive characteristics of the fundamentalist family. *Fundamentalisms Comprehended* concludes with a four-part essay by the present authors that serves as a capstone statement of the Fundamentalism Project. *Strong Religion: The Rise of Fundamentalisms around the World* presents a revised and elaborated version of this earlier attempt at defining and "explaining" the rise and growth of fundamentalisms.

THE PROBLEMS WITH "FUNDAMENTALISM"

There are numerous problems in applying the word "fundamentalism" beyond its original historical use.[12] First, it may lead some to assume that Protestant fundamentalism, with its emphasis on the inerrancy of the Bible and the imminent Second Coming of Christ, is the template for all other "fundamentalisms." They would therefore expect Scriptural inerrancy to be the defining mark of all such movements; it is not.

Second, some equate "fundamentalism" with violent extremism, thereby rejecting any possible distinction between militants (whose militance may be expressed without recourse to violence) and terrorists. In this mistaken view, that is, "fundamentalist" and "terrorist" are synonymous terms.

Third, mainstream Muslims, Christians, and Jews have objected to the use of "fundamentalism" because it implies that their militant coreligionists are indeed the true believers, the righteous defenders of the faith, when in truth they are skilled only in manipulating sacred texts and traditional teachings to serve political ends. Mainstream believers do not fail to note the irony in the posturing of self-anointed defenders of the faith who have little respect for the integrity of its "fundamentals."

Fundamentalism, in other words, is best understood as a particular configuration of ideology and organizational resources—not, that is, as an "essence" or constitutive trait of any one or all of the host religious traditions. Most adherents of Islam, Christianity, Judaism, Buddhism, Sikhism, and Hinduism consider the extremists in their midst to be an irresponsible minority whose claim to represent the "fundamentals" of the religion is without merit.

Fourth, the extravagant use of the term "fundamentalism" encourages nonspecialists to make facile generalizations, to ignore the details of individual movements and their contexts, and to conflate the vast differences between these movements.

Fifth, it has been said that what we are calling "fundamentalism" is a pattern of belief and behavior (rather than a specific ideology or set of doctrines) shared by some secular as well as religious groups and individuals. Our use of the largely pejorative term "fundamentalism" only for religious movements with which we disagree therefore reflects our liberal religious or secular biases and distorts our findings.

To this fifth objection we respond: Other movements have their "true believers," it is true, and their leaders often make absolute claims on the rank and file, who are sometimes called to sacrifice their livelihoods and possibly their lives in service to the cause. Indeed, it is tempting to speak in this regard of "secular fundamentalism" and see its manifestations in Marxism or Soviet-era state socialism, in the many virulent strains of nationalism evident in the modern world, or in the unqualified extremism of ideologically driven revolutionary or terrorist movements existing across a spectrum from the Shining Path of Peru, to the Baader-Meinhof gang of Germany.

One hesitates to call such secular movements "fundamentalist," however, because they are pseudo-religious rather than authentically religious. They may call upon their followers to make the ultimate sacrifice, but, unlike the monotheistic religions, especially Christianity and Islam, they do not reassure their followers that God or an eternal reward awaits them. The absence of a truly "ultimate" concern is decisive in the dynamics of such groups, just as the belief in a heaven or paradise serves as a framework for and legitimation of self-martyrdom in the monotheistic religions.

A sixth and related objection to the Fundamentalism Project is the application of "fundamentalism" within Asian religions. We are not wholly in disagreement with this objection. Let us put aside for the moment, however, the definition-destabilizing observation that Hinduism and Buddhism are not "religions" in the Western sense of the word and that Hindus and Buddhists do not believe in a personal God. Like Sikhism, another major religion of South Asia that has produced its candidate for the fundamentalist family, these great traditions of belief and practice orient their devotees to a reality (or nonreality) that transcends or renders illusory the mundane

world. And they have produced powerful modern, antisecular, antimodernist, absolutist, boundary-setting, exclusionary, and often violent movements
that bear startling resemblances to fundamentalisms within the Jewish,
Christian, and Islamic worlds.

Indeed, the Hindutva ("Hinduness") movement in India has con-
sciously borrowed elements from the theistic traditions of the West, including the concept of a supernatural founder (the Lord Rama) with his own
sacred (and hotly contested) "birthplace," in order to give Hinduism the
kind of spine that allows Western theistic fundamentalists to get their backs
up when threatened. Sikh radicals exhibit a sense of apocalyptic expectation
more natural in non-Asian cultures, which have a linear sense of time
and unfolding history. Buddhist "warriors" in Sri Lanka, partly imitating
colonial-era Protestant missionary crusaders, have transformed segments of
the *sangha* (community of monks) into an implacable force for religious
and cultural nationalism.

Each of these "synthetic" Asian fundamentalisms, as we call them, tends
to select and canonize a corpus of sacred texts, transforming epics and
poems and other open-ended genres into the stuff of "fundamental," "inerrant" Scriptures. We have therefore examined these movements without
feeling it necessary to include them in the core group of movements that,
strictly speaking, qualify as fundamentalist.

When describing particular movements, then, the term "fundamentalism" is accurately applied only to those Protestant Christians of North
America, who coined the term in the early twentieth century, and their contemporary ideological heirs; Muslim "fundamentalists" are best described
as "Islamists," Jewish "fundamentalists" by specific Jewish designations, and
so on.

Why not, then, abandon the use of the term altogether?

In short, because we believe that many, if not all, of the disparate religious movements studied for this volume do share certain resemblances
that come from belonging to a particular time in world history. These shared
characteristics tell us much about the movements themselves and perhaps
even more about the increasingly secularized and modern world in which
they have formed and gained influence.

As for the term itself, substitutes for "fundamentalism" as a comparative
construct have not been satisfying and can be misleading. Call something
"neo-reformist radical revolutionary Islamism" and you may well point to
features of one movement. But how, then, compare it with others so that
both common and distinctive feature stand out? As Martin E. Marty has
noted, some who attack the word fundamentalism will use words like "capi-

talist," "socialist," "nationalist," "revolutionary, "liberal," "conservative," all of which were born in specific circumstance before they were translated into such general "umbrella" terms. Careful scholars and publics will take care to see exactly how the various fundamentalisms invest their antisecular and antimodernist movements with meanings. But to deny the use of the term "fundamentalist" because it did not exist in other languages a century ago is silly. It did not exist in English either. A new phenomenon was on the scene, and it needed a new name.

When they are carefully defined, comparative constructs help us differentiate patterns of activism. They reflect and systematize the findings of case studies in order to build a cross-cultural vocabulary useful for making structured comparisons of movements and groups. *"Fundamentalism," in this usage, refers to a discernible pattern of religious militance by which self-styled "true believers" attempt to arrest the erosion of religious identity, fortify the borders of the religious community, and create viable alternatives to secular institutions and behaviors.*

FUNDAMENTALISM AS "STRONG RELIGION"

Is extremist violence and intolerance inherent to fundamentalisms? Such behavior, while not inevitable, is a strong tendency in fundamentalist movements. They seek to protect and deepen religious identity—to promote a formidable religious presence—by competing with other religious movements and with secular institutions and philosophies for resources and allegiances. Nothing in this broad purpose requires fundamentalists to violate the basic tenets of pluralist societies. But fundamentalisms equate "strong religion" with "purity" and purity, with uniformity of belief and practice.

From their descriptions of themselves and what drives and animates their group or movement, we can see that one of the most striking "family resemblances" shared by these religious actors—more striking because they hail from disparate religious traditions—is precisely their notion of what constitutes "strong religion."

Strong religion, as fundamentalists understand it, is not beholden to the mainstream religious establishment or to conventional religious authorities, weakened as they are by deadening compromises with secular powers. Nor is it bound by the precedents set by traditional interpreters and commentators on the divine law or sacred texts, who faced fundamentally different challenges and political contexts. "The Qur'an reminds us not to accede to the accepted notions and beliefs of past generations until we have weighed them on the scales of reason, and recommends independence of thought vis-à-vis past generations," wrote the Iranian Shiʿite intellectual Murtaza Mutahhari.[13] Prior to his assassination in 1979 by opponents of the Iranian revolution, Ayatollah Mutahhari warned his fellow revolutionaries not to be "overwhelmed" by the legacy of the great Shiʿite figures of the past and "the grandeur they assume in people's minds."[14]

Similarly, in setting forth his "Biblical Plan of Action" for "America's moral rebirth," the Baptist minister Jerry Falwell warned fellow fundamentalists to look elsewhere than the Christian mainstream for inspiration. "Our elaborate church structures will not cause [God] to change His mind and restrain His judgment," Falwell wrote. "We must allow Him to strip us of all that we put our confidence in, so that we may trust in Him alone."[15]

Fundamentalist leaders arrogate to themselves the right to pick and choose from the legacy of teachings and prescriptions, finding passages and rules that suit their immediate purposes. They may reject all previous interpretations and seek to recover the pristine message of the Messiah or the Prophet. The Egyptian preacher Shukri Ahmad Mustafa, for example, attacked the ulema, discrediting their handbooks and "commentaries upon commentaries" on the Shariʿa. Appearing before an Egyptian court under charges of conspiring to murder Shaykh Muhammad Husayn al-Dhahabi, former cabinet minister for religious affairs and hence a symbol of official Islam, Shukri Mustafa lectured his judges on the need for individual and innovative interpretation of the Qurʾan. The founders of the four schools of Islamic jurisprudence were relevant to their own times, Mustafa acknowledged, but they needed constant supplements and updating. The jurists' writings, furthermore, were not part of divine revelation. Do Muslims really believe, he asked the judges rhetorically, that their views supply something that was lacking in God's revelation? Are the words of these lawyers clearer than God's own word? Years later, after Mustafa's execution in 1978, one of his former disciples put the matter pointedly. "We do not accept the opinions of the early jurists, or their consensus (*ijmaʿ*), or the other idols (*asnam*), like analogy (*qiyas*). How can words of mere humans be a source of divine guidance?"[16]

The comparative point to be registered is not the rejection of law and tradition, per se, but the need to bolster the authority of the contemporary guardians of the faith. For religion to be strong, its leaders must be unassailable in their authority over contemporary belief and praxis.

The hardening and splintering of segments of the Orthodox Jewish community, leading to the emergence of a cohort of fundamentalist-style rabbis in the haredi (ultra-Orthodox) world, provides an example of the narrowing of the religious law through selective application and amplification by a new class of experts. While traditional Jewish society has always been regulated by the normative written word (e.g., the Talmud and its Halakhic codes), the transmission of the traditional Jewish way of life had been mimetic—absorbed from parents and domestic rituals, patterned on conduct observed in neighborhood, synagogue, and school. It was a way of life, lived at a time when people experienced the Jewish tradition not only in prayer and divine service but also in food and drink, dress, sexual relations between husband and wife, the rhythms of work and patterns of rest. Often these mimetic norms conformed to the sacred law, but occasionally they strayed from its letter while nonetheless remaining true to its spirit. Indeed, the Ashkenazic community saw the law as being manifested in both the canonized written corpus (the Talmud and codes) and the social practices of the people.[17]

The dispersion of the modern Jewish community, however, led to the decoupling of the dual tradition of the intellectual and the mimetic, law as taught and law as practiced. Authors of legal commentaries and codes, especially after the trauma of the Holocaust, began to privilege the legal literature over practice, perhaps reflecting an anxiety that orthopraxis was weakening as Jews assimilated into the surrounding society. Eventually, received practice had no longer an inherent validity of its own. One of the most striking phenomena of the contemporary haredi community, Haym Soloveitchik notes, is the rise of the omnipotent religious authority (the range of concerns addressed by the rabbis having been expanded), signified by the explosion of Halakhic works on practical observance. "Much of the traditional religious practice has been undergoing massive reevaluation, and by popular demand, or, at the very least, by unsolicited popular consent," he writes. In Jerusalem, B'nai Br'ak, London, New York, and elsewhere in the haredi world, "religious observance is being both amplified and raised to new, rigorous heights." This transformation, furthermore, "has taken place in the inner sanctum of the haredi world and has left nothing untouched."[18]

Religion must be strong because its enemies are perceived as powerful and potentially overwhelming. Foremost among these enemies is the modern state, which projects itself as omnipresent, omniscient, and omnipotent. How could an entity possessing these three properties avoid becoming the object of a religion and being fervently worshipped, fundamentalists worry, especially when its existence is beyond any doubt? The existing regime therefore becomes the object of both resentment and envy for fundamentalists, and they fashion their own programs and ideologies in an awkward mimesis of the enemy: they see power as indivisible, and they seek power over any-one or anything that even contemplates resisting them—the kind of power, that is, which they see exercised by the regime.

This simultaneous imitation of and resistance to the modern state marks fundamentalisms as specific religious phenomena that have emerged in the wake of the success of modernization, secularization, and the scientific revolution—global trends perceived as intertwined with the rise of the sovereign secular state. The aforementioned "culture of progress" celebrated the spreading confident belief that humanity, through the power of reason, the triumphant discoveries of science, the magnificent inventions of technology, and the secular transformation of traditional institutions, was on a clear course toward the mastery of the evils of the human situation. Religious communities and elites were put on the defensive, retreating into cultural ghettos or adapting to and compromising with the secular world.

Fundamentalist movements are the historical counterattacks mounted from these threatened religious traditions, seeking to hold ground against this spreading secular "contamination" and even to regain ground by taking advantage of the weaknesses of modernization. Fundamentalist ideologues spent much of the twentieth century probing and describing these weaknesses, playing to an audience composed of the so-called victims of secular modernity—the Sikh farmer whose livelihood was taken by the high-tech conglomerates of the Green Revolution; the Iranian merchant displaced by the Shah's rapid modernization program and insulted by its cultural pretensions; the Algerian engineer unable to find employment in an oil-rich economy; the American parents who witnessed U.S. society spinning out of control in the sixties.

Indeed, the resistance to modern forms of secularization is a defining common feature of religious fundamentalisms. Not all religious traditions make clear separations between the sacred and the secular, have the same kinds of religious establishments, posit an "end of days" deliverance by a savior or a messiah, or have clearly formulated doctrines and codes imputed to divine origin. Nor have all religious traditions been confronted in the same way and degree by modernity and secularism. Secular modernity may have been introduced endogenously as in Europe and North America, through the industrial, technological, and scientific revolutions; or it may have been introduced by alien, imperialistic, and exploitative forces as in the Middle East, Asia, Africa, and Latin America. While the understanding of, and reactions against, secularization may vary, however, fundamentalists across religious traditions and regions of the world share an animus against political cultures that would deny religion what they feel to be its central place in ordering society.

In chapter 1, "The Enclave Culture," Emmanuel Sivan evokes this anti-secularist mood by drawing copiously on the sermons, speeches, and writings of Jewish, Christian, and Muslim leaders who denounced (and exploited) the costly and threatening side effects of modernization such as crime, moral decay, political corruption, the breakdown of the family and the community, environmental pollution, and the like. "Fundamentalism" is the form of strong religiosity and political culture these preachers and ideologues helped create in response and retaliation.

CHAPTER 1

The Enclave Culture

[T]his is an age of demons and amoral angels and all sorts of deep fears. Like the first centuries of the Christian era, it's an age of extreme solutions.

Iris Murdoch, *The Message to the Planet*

In Exile

Just after World War I, Dr. Nathan Birnbaum, formerly a Jewish secularist thinker (Zionist, then cultural autonomist) who had recently returned to the faith, took stock of the state of Judaism. It was almost a century after the early proponents of ultra-Orthodoxy such as the Hatam Sofer (d. 1839) had been alarmed to discover an "unheard of phenomenon: the father being still God-fearing and knowledgeable in the Talmud while the son desecrates the Sabbath." Birnbaum assessed the impact of fourteen decades of Jewish Enlightenment and produced a gloomy diagnosis: most Western European Jews have ceased altogether to be *mitzvot* (precepts) observant and are indifferent to divine Providence; the mass immigration from Eastern Europe to the United States brings hundreds of thousands to a land of greed and licentiousness; and they are bound to lose their religion in this *treifene medina* (defiled country), as it was commonly dubbed by Orthodox rabbis. In Eastern Europe, Birnbaum thought, most Jews still observed the Halakah in both ritual and social relations, but there was no mistaking the fact that the curve was on the decline and defections from the faith were on the upswing.

The observant, or haredim, live "in exile among Jews" (*in Galus bei Yidn*), that is, among nominal Jews, Jews by birth only.[1]

Even this diagnosis may have been too sanguine. The great Halakhic authorities of the day—the Hafetz Haim (Rabbi I. M. HaCohen), and Rabbi E. Wasserman—expressed grave doubts as to the quality of observance and belief among Eastern Europe's Jewish plain folk.[2]

In the post–World War II era, with these masses having been annihilated in the Holocaust, Birnbaum's diagnostic formula seemed to haredi activists more poignant than ever. As Rabbi E. Dessler, who had escaped to England (and then to Israel), put it in an incisive pun, virtually all Jews replace the injunction "thou should be *qdoshim* [sacred]" with a newly concocted one, "thou should be qaddishniks," thus reducing their Judaism to the act of saying the prayer for the dead (*qaddish*) on the memorial days of deceased family members.[3] Small wonder that "in exile among Jews" is indeed one of the most common terms the haredim use, in sermons as much as in informal conversation, in order to denote their sense of being a tiny minority, marginal and alienated.

In the fall of 1990 an ultra-Orthodox weekly, *Ha-Mahane ha-Haredi*, was sentenced by an Israeli court to pay heavy punitive damages for calling a left-wing member of Knesset, a long-time critic of the haredim, a Nazi. The haredi press saw this libel verdict as further proof that "we live in exile among Jews," and, irony of ironies, in the Holy Land.[4] The demographic growth of the ultra-Orthodox community and of its political clout in the 1980s and 1990s barely mitigated the gloomy, defensive gloss they tended to put on reality.

At about the same time that Birnbaum coined this term, Rashid Rida, a Syrian-born thinker living in Cairo, pondered the question, "How fares Islam?" He found most so-called believers to be mere "geographical Muslims" *(muslimun jughrafiyun)*, people who belong to the faith merely by virtue of living in an Islamic land and performing certain rituals. Their belief is tepid, and worse still, they acquiesce to the European-inspired laws introduced by their ostensibly Muslim rulers who "forsake what was enjoined upon the believers by Allah. . . . They abolish allegedly distasteful penalties such as cutting off the hands of thieves or stoning adulterers and prostitutes. They replace them by man-made laws and penalties."[5]

Terms like the "eclipse of Islam" were already frequent in Rida's day and age, especially after the breakup of the Ottoman Empire, the abolition of the caliphate (1924), and the imposition of atheistic Communist rule upon Muslim Central Asia. Coining a powerful metaphor to depict this decline was a task left to an Indian Muslim, Maulana Maududi, in the late 1930s, and to an Egyptian, Sayyid Qutb, a decade or so later. They saw a relapse of Islam to a state of *jahiliyya,* that is, to that of pre-Islamic pagan Arabia. Mid-twentieth-century Muslims, like their ancestors thirteen centuries earlier, were a tiny and harassed minority, surrounded by idolaters and the groupies of modernity cults as well as by nominal and hypocritical "believers."[6]

Jahiliyya was an emotion-laden metaphor, redolent of historical connotations. The present-day idols—such as nationalism—were Western-imported but rendered all the more insidious for being cloaked in indigenous garb. In the 1980s another metaphor emerged: "Islam is in exile [*ghurba*] in its own lands," much like it was in Arabia when Muhammad had to flee pagan and hostile Mecca for Medina. As the Hadith has it, "Islam began in exile and will return in exile in the [end of history]. Blessed are the exiled."[7]

Idols more openly inspired by European culture also made blatant inroads. By the late 1950s the Iraqi mullah Muhammad Baqir al-Sadr would voice grave concern over the lure that communism and the Ba'th Party held for youth, including Shi'ite madrasa students. Such jeremiads would soon be echoed in Morocco and Egypt and were no different in a way than those of al-Sadr's Roman Catholic contemporary, Luigi Giussani, also a theology professor. Giussani, the future founder of the Italian Catholic movement Comunione e Liberazione, worried that the nominally Catholic students in Italian high schools and universities were signs of the ultimate victory of the Enlightenment in an increasingly de-Christianized and individualistic Italian society in which some Catholic rituals still subsisted but were increasingly devoid of any real significance. The upshot of this mass defection, Giussani felt, was the marginalization of religiosity. Even a good many of the church's adepts, following theologians like Jacques Maritain and Pierre Teilhard de Chardin, had made their peace with modernity and accepted the autonomy of the world vis-à-vis the faith.[8]

As for those who remained loyal to Islam, their state of mind was expressed by al-Sadr as well as by his Lebanese counterpart, Shaykh Muhammad Husayn Fadlallah. Faced with this seemingly unstoppable decline and defection, Muslims felt despair and humiliation, impotence and disgrace.[9]

After three decades as a missionary in Africa, Archbishop Marcel Lefebvre returned to France in 1962, at the time of decolonization. He discovered to his dismay a similar mood in French Catholic circles. He attributed this to a substantial dwindling of attendance at Mass, a steep decline in new priestly and monastic vocations, and the growing republican liberalism of Catholic political groupings. (These were phenomena no different in nature yet wider in scope than those deplored by Giussani in Italy, which had not known the ravages of the French Revolution.) Troubled by this crisis, Lefebvre was soon to suffer a shock when the Second Vatican Council introduced what he considered the wrong type of response to the crisis. Instead of greater discipline, a closing of the ranks, stronger hierarchy, and a more aggressive stance, the council seemed to be moving toward "a conversion of the Church to the World [of modernity]." Lefebvre deplored the accommodative attitude of the council, an attitude based upon the "heretical" principles of collegiality (power sharing among the bishops), freedom of conscience, and ecumenical dialogue. This was not, he thundered, the remedy needed for an ailing church operating in a "society governed by a liberal and hedonistic mentality."[10]

Even before Birnbaum and Rida wrote their own pessimistic diagnoses of Judaism and Islam, Protestant America was already deeply worried by the late-nineteenth-century expansion of Romanism (a euphemism for "garlic-eating" Catholic immigrants from southern and southeastern Europe). Protestants experienced their own doubts as to the solidity of the Bible-believing bloc early in the twentieth century. The faithful, who took the name Fundamentalists (ca. 1910), detected a takeover of this bloc (especially of its Baptist and Presbyterian parts) from within by liberal modernism. They saw everywhere the hidden hand of modernist Protestants with their devotion to the higher criticism of the Bible, to the German philosophy of the Enlightenment, to the progress-oriented social gospel ("that Godless social-service nonsense"), to accommodation with secularism, and not least, to the discoveries of science.

By the 1960s the heirs to Protestant fundamentalism began to view the danger as much broader, as coming from a more alluring and external force—secularism, later called secular humanism (or scientific humanism), a full-fledged alternative to religion per se. This social force, said to be predicated upon the twin doctrines of atheism and evolution as well as upon an amoral way of life appealing to humanity's baser instincts (permissiveness, promiscuity, pornography, feminism, etc.), seemed to have usurped cultural hegemony. By controlling the media and the educational establishment and wielding influence upon the intrusive federal government, secular humanism was spreading its facile credo into every nook and cranny and drawing in the naive masses.[11]

Die-hard American Bible believers confronted with this "disintegration of our social order," in Jerry Falwell's terms, came to see themselves as outsiders, aliens in their own land. In the words of the popular revival hymn, they were "stranger[s] here, within a foreign land" or, in the words of Recon-structionist thinker Gary North, prisoners of a "new Babylonian captivity." The same metaphors recurred among Catholic Pentecostalists in the United States, who lamented that "[w]e are in a post-Catholic society and in some ways we are Christian exiles in it." The similarity of these statements to Birnbaum's diagnosis of Judaism is evident, as is the adage of Muslim mili-tants: "We are in one ravine [*wadi*], and life is in another." The diagnosis was also shared by European Catholic theologians in the midsixties such as Henri de Lubac and Hans Urs von Balthasar (who inspired Giussani), who noted the marginalization of the old faith by the hegemony of the "atheistic humanism" bred by the Enlightenment.[12]

It is true that at certain moments, after investing in a huge countercul-tural endeavor, American fundamentalists saw a glimmer of hope: we have reversed the tide, we grow and expand, perhaps we are on the way to restor-ing our hegemony. This hope fueled the Moral Majority movement when it was launched in 1979. Tim LaHaye, among its other spokesmen, even performed intricate computations to prove that most Americans are not ac-tually lost, being either silent believers or unwitting hostages of the devious secularist forces of moral decay. Once activated and regenerated, they would provide the troops of the coming majority and remake America into a City on the Hill. Some six years later, however, all hopes had evaporated. A mood of doom and despair returned.

Shi'ite radicalism followed the same curve in a shorter span. Fervent visions of Khomeinist insurrections across the Middle East were deflated in a matter of three years following the Iranian revolution. Sunni radicals proved to be lukewarm, if not hostile, to Khomeini's appeal; even Arab Shi'ite communities, whether cowed by repression or depressed by the pe-ripeties of the revolution, were not ready to follow Iran's lead.

Haredim, who comprise 6 percent of Israeli Jews, also indulge some-times in daydreaming about becoming a majority—or at least the second largest political bloc—due to their high birthrate and the "growing num-bers" (actually no more than several thousand) of secular Jews who make their return (*teshuva*) to the Orthodox fold. For the shorter term, the haredi Jews fantasize that, thanks to the swing votes they control in the Knesset enabling them to make or break government coalitions, they may overhaul legislation and make Israel "Jewish" again.[13] More often than not, however, they exceed the limits of their clout and find themselves rebuffed, as when Israeli prime minister Yitzhak Shamir balked at the prospect of having to pass the "who is a Jew" bill. Rather than run the risk of incurring the wrath of American Jewry, Shamir broke off negotiations with the Agudat Yisrael and established a national unity coalition in December 1988. The "projects" of Orthodox political control having proved to be chimeric; the deep-rooted fear once again resurfaced. A haredi newspaper editorialized:

> Some of us tended to forget that we are in Exile and pretended that we may become kingmakers in this secularist so-called kingdom. We rather have to be afraid of the resurgence of an anti-Orthodox consensus. If we do not close ranks and fight back, antireligious laws will, God forbid, be enacted, and the status quo [in religious matters] will disappear. We will be thrown into a rearguard battle for our very survival as haredi Jews in "religious autonomy," lest our own educational system, our sacred yeshivas, may not be immune from the claws of the powers-that-be.[14]

This combination of loss of hegemony and mass defection represent, in Catholic parlance, "the worst danger to the church since Luther." Archbishop Lefebvre dubbed it a catastrophe more intimidating than the persecution of Catholics under the French Revolution's cult of reason. Haredi rabbis such as the Hazon Ish (d. 1953) and E. M. Schach (d. 2001) considered it the worst calamity in two millennia of life in exile. Sunni and Shi'ite Muslims see it as analogous to the infidels of Mecca falling upon Muhammad's tiny host, and in the Shi'ite case, as reminiscent of the encirclement of Imam Hussein and his few followers by the Umayyad army, ending in the infamous massacre of the late seventh century. Archbishop Lefebvre compared his tiny flock (perhaps seventy to one hundred thousand worldwide) with the seven thousand disciples of the Prophet Elijah in his fight against the prophets of the Baal.[15]

What makes the danger all the graver is its lure and insidiousness. The alternative, secular way of life certainly is alluring. It appeals to the instincts, promising instant gratification, better material conditions, and the experience of "marrying one's own times" in terms of scientific and technological achievement. How easy it is, and how common, to be addicted to it. Religious tradition is likely to be shed lightheartedly, often unwittingly. Tradition succumbs to a pleasant infatuation and dies a sort of sweet death, a painless euthanasia, if you will.

Images of addiction and infatuation crop up incessantly in the fundamentalist diagnosis. Nathan Birnbaum wrote of the "assimilation mania" (*Assimilationgesucht*) from which fellow Jews, especially the enlightened intelligentsia (*maskilim*), "these Jewish rebels," suffered. The Iranian Jalal

Al-e Ahmad (d. 1969) coined the term *West-mania*, or rather, *Westoxication* (*gharbzadagi*), to explain the predicament of intellectual elites (*rowsan-feur*) drawn to modern culture. The Westernized (*faranji-ma'ab*) are in fact West-infatuated (the Arabic equivalent, in Sunni parlance, is *mustaghribun*). The secularists had fallen prey to a fit of insanity, said Jonathan Blanchard, while other Protestant polemicists identified the sexual obsession unleashed by permissiveness as the most enticing facet of the secular-hegemonic way of life. Marcel Lefebvre used the metaphor of AIDS—an insidious malady contracted through permissive behavior—as an apt description of the syndrome afflicting both society and the postconciliar church: a syndrome of pleasurable self-destruction.[16]

The insidiousness of the danger proceeds from its being not only an overt, well-articulated, intellectual challenge but one that operates on a broader front, in every walk of life, appealing to instinct, to the subconscious, to mimetic action. It unwittingly subverts norms of behavior well before consciousness follows suit, molding social and ritual practice even among people who still consider themselves true believers. "The trouble is that the secularized are wholeheartedly secularized, while the orthodox are no more completely orthodox. Their Jewishness is rather mediocre, tepid, operating by rote," remarks a recent pamphlet of self-styled Concerned Yeshiva Students. This holds true not just for the masses, they add, but for the beliefs of many yeshiva students as well.[17]

The result is a state of limbo, the blurring of distinctions (*bilbul tishtush* or *tishtush ha-tehumim*), so frequently deplored in writings of the twentieth-century rabbis or in synagogue sermons.[18] In the Yinglish (Yiddish-English) dialect common to the ultra-Orthodox in the United States one speaks of *mish-mash*, a term that can be found even among Protestant fundamentalists (when they wish, for instance, to excoriate liberal modernists for indifference to the true and crystal-clear instructions of the Gospel). A commonly cited example is the blurring of God-ordained gender distinctions by liberals and humanists alike. Thus in 1999 the Southern Baptist Convention voted to reinforce traditional gender roles. More radical by far was the much-publicized deplorable treatment of women by the Taliban of Afghanistan and Pakistan.[19]

Lack of clarity has many shades and is hence difficult to detect and to pinpoint. No wonder that the Hafetz Haim's Halakhic magnum opus, designed to stem the tide, was entitled *Mishna Berura* (The clear code). The same malady he wanted to combat, confusion and disorientation, is often cited by Protestant Bible believers and by Muslim preachers who see it as the upshot of the eclecticism (*talfiq*) and contrivance (*iltiqat*) so typical of reformist apologetics, which tried hard to accommodate every modern fad within the tradition.[20]

THE ENCLAVE

Exile is an apt metaphor for describing the marginalization of religion in industrialized and developing societies. It is the primary impulse (at least at the leadership level) that lies behind the rise of groups that endeavor to reshape the tradition so as to forestall the danger of being sucked into the vortex of modernity, constantly losing members and ultimately dying a sweet death. "The number of defectors is on the rise, while the distinction maintained in the past between apostates and those faithful [to the Covenant] has gotten blurred."[21] This diagnosis of pre–World War II Eastern European Jewry could be borrowed by the proponents of Christian and Islamic fundamentalism. More than a primary impulse, this metaphor was and still is a pillar of fundamentalist ideology in its various manifestations throughout the last seven or eight decades.

Yet how does this sense of alienation stand vis-à-vis the elements of their ideology? How is the ideology cogently related to their organizational mold and to the behavioral norms that flesh it out? Here a good theory, probably relying on a functional explanatory model, may be needed in order to serve as a guide in the maze of data. Such a theory is all the more vital regarding the major enigma enveloping fundamentalist groups: how and why they survive and even flourish at times. After all, the odds are pretty much against them, as evidenced by the fact that turnover rate is high. Their stringent behavioral demands stand in stark contrast to the "anything goes," hedonistic, open society around them. One can just pick up one's things and quit the religious group and join the easygoing life teeming nearby. The group has rarely any coercive powers to retain members by other than moral pressure. (The exception are terrorist groups such as Al Qaeda, which may execute defectors and collaborators or which may provide lucrative financial incentives, as Osama bin Laden was capable of doing.) Neither do fundamentalists, who pride themselves on their austerity and asceticism, always possess the material means to reward members. Furthermore, in Third World countries the latter may even suffer persecution by the authorities or harassment by rival sects and end up in the hospital, in prison, or on the scaffold.

Here the grid/group theory developed by anthropologist Mary Douglas comes to our aid.[22] This theory proposes that in any social context shared cultural ideas (about time and space, human and physical nature, ethics, etc.) will be structured in such a way that individuals within that social context can negotiate their way through the constraints they experience in daily life in order to make sense of the world in which they live.

In order for a social group to keep together, a cohesive fit must be maintained between ideology, organization, and behavior that combines to create a way of life, or culture. To survive, a group must see to it that, most of the time, most members will conform to the requirements of this culture. Shifts in ideology/cosmology will require shifts in ideology and/or behavior and vice versa.

Underlying the building up and maintenance of a way of life Douglas detects the working of two sorts of constraints (or claims), grid and group. *Group* constraints determine the extent to which people are restricted in their social relations by their commitment to a human group. *Grid* constraints restrict how (rather than with whom) people interact by virtue of their category (gender, race, age, class, etc.).

By combining the group and grid dimensions, Douglas developed a typology designed to facilitate comparative analysis. This typology consists of three major social contexts. Each carries its own "cultural package" that, together with its prescribed mode of behavior (and organization), comprises a way of life.

The three major types of social contexts are the *hierarchy*, the *market*, and the *enclave*.

The hierarchy is high on both grid and group claims. It is more or less assured of its outer group boundary and invests most of its energy in controlling its various and separate compartments and keeping them in smooth interaction. Its overriding fear is that the top-down relationship be broken. The cardinal sins plaguing it are, hence, pride and arrogance.

One should stress that there are several kinds of hierarchy. Not all consist of a simple, centralized command system. There are also hierarchies with multiple peaks of authority and balanced juxtaposition of ordered units taking precedence in alternating spheres of control (a situation typical, for instance, of old monarchies, traditional communities, or small groups and families).

The market is a supple web of free-floating agents. Thus it is low on both group and grid, consisting of individually negotiated social networks with little intervention of the rival claims of group and grid. Its cardinal sin is greed. Blame (and responsibility) are individually assigned, while they are collective in the case of the hierarchy (i.e., the whole group has sinned or one or some of its members have deviated from group norms).[23]

The enclave is low on grid and high on group. It is usually the response to a community's problem with its boundary. Its future seems to be at the mercy of members likely to slip away. For some reason, usually the appeal of the neighboring central community, it cannot stop its members from deserting. Devoid of coercive powers over its members, it cannot punish them; lacking sufficient resources, it cannot reward them. The only control to be deployed in order to shore up the boundary is moral persuasion. The interpretation developed by this type of community thus stands in opposition to outside society. (This is, of course, easier to achieve when an enclave is created not by pull but by push, that is, by exclusion from the central community, as was the case of the Jews in pre-Emancipation Europe.) In other words, the defining relations for the enclave are "inside-outside" (relations between the enclave and what exists beyond its boundary) rather than "upside-downside" (relations between the hierarchy of social categories within the given community).

The previous paragraph reflects rather well the situation of religious traditions in a modern world governed by market networks and corporate hierarchies. And little wonder that most characteristics of fundamentalist groups, which attempt to create and preserve a contending way of life, conform to Douglas's description of what makes up an enclave. Whether in ideology, behavior, or organization, fundamentalist groups are indeed enclavelike, hence distinct from the hegemonic modern groups that menace religion today with sweet death. The fundamentalists may thus keep themselves apart, for as in all enclaves what they fear most is pollution by the malevolent outside and/or leakage of members to it; in other words, group boundary is more important than grid.

Loss of members may be above all due to the appeal of the easygoing, hedonistic groups and, to a lesser extent, to the allure of a top-down (i.e., high-grid, formalized, and routinized) hierarchy. In order to keep together the group of moral dissenters, counterclaims and counterconstraints are staked out by the enclave, be it the biblical one studied by Douglas or the modern variety presented below. These claims exercise moral coercion upon members, with little or no recourse to top-down human authority. Claims and constraints equate morality with knowledge (i.e., cosmology). The cardinal sin typical of such a social context is envy, that is, control by an egalitarian membership (although some grid differences, such as gender and age may be maintained). Blame is, of course, put at the door of outsiders and any agents they have recruited on the inside.

All this does not preclude variations on the mold over time and between groups. One may also encounter combinations of enclave and of other molds, especially hierarchy (of the multiple peak kind).

Beside these three major social contexts, there is a fourth minor one—low group/high grid. It ennobles individuals in a dominated social position, with no control of their lives (i.e., high grid), but also isolated and devoid of a support group (low group). They may be marginals (homeless persons, etc.) or functionaries found in the lower or middle ranks of hierarchies with no sense of identification with the whole—a sense that the "normal" organization man is supposed to have. People in such a context tend to be fatalists (blame is pinned on fate, not on individual responsibility as in the market context); they are passive, the slaves of routine, fragmented in their views of life, suspicious of grand theories as well as of other people but resigned to authority that must be obeyed as a fact of life rather than because it has any moral claim. One could say that this is the territory mapped for the United States in Raymond Carver's short stories of the inarticulate working class.

While market and hierarchy are the dominant social contexts and as such represent major contenders or enemies of the enclave culture, the dominated are an ideal recruitment pool upon which to draw. Holding recruits in the movement, however, requires hard work creating and maintaining that fit between ideology/cosmology (or some form of rationality), organization, and behavior that makes for an enclave culture. "Push"—exclusion from the mainstream society—may explain why new members join a movement, but only "pull"—the advantages of life in the enclave—may account for why they stay. To understand "pull" we must look at the movement's way of life.

At first glance, the description seems to fit the primordial problem of the fundamentalist movement as presented in the preceding section of this essay. Let us now examine in greater detail the culture fundamentalists develop so as to enable their loyal members to steer their way under the constraints of a way of life designed to seal a porous group boundary.

WALL OF VIRTUE

An enclave's outer boundary is leaky due above all to the material and social temptations of the central community, which enjoys prestige, cultural hegemony, and access to governmental sanctions as well as to resources (whether those of the state or of wealthy individuals). Virtually the only thing the beleaguered enclave can offer from its own authority is moral reward.

In some instances, moral rewards may be accompanied and complemented by social or economic benefits. Access to welfare state emoluments, for example, as in the case of the haredim in the United States and in Israel, may reduce this dependence upon moral suasion, as may charity contributions—by the Saudis to Islamic *jama'at* (associations) in Egypt and North Africa, for example, or by ultra-Orthodox benefactors to students in *yeshivot* and *kollelim*. Dependence on moral suasion alone is also mitigated by the employment of haredi or Baptist women by the community (as teachers, for instance); by the establishment of cooperatives by the Italian Catholic movement Comunione e Liberazione; by the tutoring of student members in Muslim jama'at; or, by the granting of soft loans by Islamic banks. Nonetheless, most sanctions are moral in nature, even in these cases.

How does one come to wield such a suasion? Cultural theory posits that the enclave must stress the voluntary character of its members, who are specially chosen (in religious enclaves, elected to salvation by God), and how much the community relies upon their commitment to the "holy cause." The value of each member is highlighted, and distinctions (at least overt and formal ones) between them are minimized as much as possible, a strategy that, as we shall see, shapes the nature of the enclave's authority. Last but not least, the enclave must place the oppressive and morally defiled outside society in sharp contrast to the community of virtuous insiders. A sort of "wall of virtue" is thereby constructed, separating the saved, free, equal (before God or before history), and morally superior enclave from the hitherto tempting central community. Who but the depraved would desire to cross such a boundary and join the defectors and the evil outsiders?

The wall in question may at times be physical as well (as in the case of the fence surrounding Bob Jones University in South Carolina), but even then its significance is primarily moral. It is quite typical that the organ of the Neturei Karta haredi sect is called "The Wall" *(Ha-Homah).*

The most obvious bricks of the wall of virtue are the shorthand terms used within fundamentalist communities in matter-of-fact fashion in everyday conversation, in sermons, and in their press to designate fellow members: Christians, Muslimun (Muslims), Mu'minun (believers), Yidn (Jews), Reb Yisroel (the Jew as an individual). The sense is unmistakable: the real, the true-blue, full-fledged Christians, Muslims, or Jews. All the rest are cut from an inferior cloth; they are lesser affiliates of the same tradition if not outright rejects—apostates and disbelievers. One also speaks of a "Christian home" (or attitude), an "Islamic solution," "Jewish Jews." The adjective is invariably positive, signifying the sole type that is in full accordance with the tradition. References to the scriptural basis of that tradition crop up in synonyms: "Bible believers," "Biblical standard," a "Qur'anic way of life," "Torah-true."

The tradition—as could be expected from the above diagnosis—is presented as shrunken and under siege, nay, even persecuted. The faithful, the Believing Remnant, the Last Outpost, Covenant Keepers are some of the most common self-descriptions in fundamentalist writings in the United States.[24] Anxiety as to the fate of the tradition is interlaced with praise for the virtuous who stick with it. And as all these terms have Old Testament roots, it is no wonder that one finds their Hebrew (and often, original) analogues among haredim: She'rit Yisrael, Shlumei Emunei, Sridim. An exact analogue of the first of these terms, "the remnant of Israel," is used by the disciples of Lefebvre and Giussani to describe their respective movements.[25] That amalgam, anxiety cum virtue, is evident in the very term *haredi* (based on Isaiah 66:5 and Ezra 10:3), which refers to those anxious to obey the Lord's word.[26] The ultranationalist rivals of the haredim plume themselves the Bloc of the Faithful (Gush Emunim) who remain loyal to the Whole Land of Israel idea; their settlement branch is called Covenant (*Omana*).

Shi'ites (and, to a lesser degree, Sunnis) prefer to express this through the Qur'anic term for Muhammad's disciples, "the Oppressed" (*mustad'fun* and some of its synonyms).[27] When the Islamic Republican Party refers to present-day Iranian territory as the "liberated part of the lands of Islam" (*qesmat-e azad shoday-ye mamlekat-e Eslam*), it may be adding a dash of hope.[28] Evident is the sense of being just one segment of a perverted whole (that used to be identified with one's own tradition).

The righteous character of the enclave is brought forth even more sharply by the common Protestant terms of self-reference such as "the saved," "the saints," and "the defenders of the faith," as well as in some less common but quite telling titles such as "salt of the earth," "the leaven in the dough," and "the zealots."[29] Zealots (*qana'im*) is indeed an epithet the haredim take great pride in, though their secularist opponents hurl it as a slur.[30] Marcel Lefebvre, as we have seen, used the same term, the "zealots of Elijah," to refer to his supporters, whom he also dubbed "the leaven of the dough."

Terms like *the saved* would, of course, make no sense in a Jewish, or for that matter, Islamic, context (and the "redeemed" the Gush Emunim speaks about is the land, not the individuals). One should not look for exact equivalents. Each dissident community molds its worldview from the symbolic capital available in its own tradition. Even zealotry is a much more powerful metaphor in Jewish lore, based as it is not only on the story of the prophet Elijah (1 Kings 19:10) but also on the Great Revolt against the Romans (67–70 C.E.).[31] The Muslim militants, who do not share in the reverence for the Old Testament, dub themselves, as a matter of course, the righteous (al-Salihun, al-Rashidun).

What imports, though, is the virtuous significance attached thereto, as well as the implicit notion that it behooves the insiders to keep apart from the defiled outside and to fight it in order to save souls, to win them to obedience to Halakhah and Shari'a. (Hence the common usage, in all three traditions, of holy-war terminology, interspersed, in the American case, with sports metaphors.)

In effect, the outside casts a heavy shadow on the dissidents inside. Dichotomy is the thread running through much of the terminology: light is opposed to darkness (in Hebrew *bnei or* versus *bnei Hosekh;* in Arabic *daw'* versus *zulumat*), truth to falsehood (in Arabic *haqq* versus *batil*), the party of God to the forces of the Great Satan (in Arabic *hizb Allah* versus *a'da' Allah, hizb al-Shaytan;* in Hebrew *ne'emanei ha-Shem* versus *shluhei ha-satan ha-madi'ah*), the wholesome to the unwholesome (in Hebrew *shalem* versus *pagum, qatu'a;* in Arabic *salim* versus *marid*). One could extend the list on and on, but there is no point in boring the reader. These few illustrations are a small sample of dualistic vocabulary that would make sense in all three traditions.[32]

There is no mistaking the leitmotif: the outside is polluted, contagious, dangerous. The outside is all the more harmful as it may look as though it partakes of the same tradition as the inside while being in essence its very negation. In fact, the very raison d'être of the outside lies in subverting the enclave.

The notion of an ever lurking risk goes some way toward accounting for the prevalence of conspiracy theories in fundamentalist thinking. Leaders as much as the rank and file tend to see everywhere the infiltration of some fifth column. This is a sort of mortar joining the bricks of self-image and the image of the outside. For the enclave, nothing is ever as it appears (hence also the predilection for allegorical hermeneutics). The enemy—modernity in its myriad forms—is a wolf in sheep's clothing and a charming one at that. Islamic radicals warn above all against the danger of *munafiqun* (hypocrites), nominal Muslims who conspire to subvert the faith from within. Their danger is graver than that of outside, imperialist plots. In the case of the Lefebvre movement, for instance, such an argument—"the liberal plot of Satan against Church and Papacy alike" carried out by the Second Vatican

Council—became the juridical justification for not obeying pope and council, despite the doctrine of infallibility. The so-called sedevacantists carried this thesis to its logical extreme: as Paul VI, who presided over the council, was not a true pope, its resolutions were null and void, and the throne of St. Peter remains vacant until the election of a truly traditionalist pope.[33] The ineluctable consequence of this obsession with conspiracies is the need for constant vigilance.

But, of course, if the righteous are said to be weak, this is *peccatis nostris*—due to the sins and imperfections of the enclave itself (though these may be to some extent inspired by the evil outside). The dual result is thus the call for further exertion in self-chastisement and improvement, existing in tandem, at times, with purges of the unworthy.

THE NATURE OF THE BEAST

Modernity is the common denominator of the outside forces. These may operate from within the given tradition, as in the case of liberal churches (for Christian fundamentalists); of Reform, Conservative, and even modern Orthodox Jews (for the haredim); of dovish religious Zionists (for Gush Emunim); or of liberal Muslims and most of the conservative Islamic establishment and its religiously tepid adherents (for Sunni and Shi'ite radicals). Modernity is also an external threat, as in the cases of the secularist majority in the United States or in Israel; or, of the Arab, Iranian, and Pakistani secular intelligentsia and parts of the middle class.[34] The raw nerve of all these forces—implicitly in the United States and in Israel, openly in the Islamic world—resides in their being human-centered. The modernity-suffused outside assumes human autonomy as the ultimate end. *Khod-bonyadi* is the Persian term for such a stance, whether as ideology or as lifestyle geared to serve human self-realization, even if by transgressing (or adapting and subverting) God-prescribed (*shari'a*) rules of conduct.

One may draw a parallel with North American fundamentalists' attacks on the social service, self-help, "me generation" notions of the secular humanists, with their reliance upon human judgment and "anything goes" cultural pluralism. The fundamentalists scoff at the humanist argument that one becomes thereby "totally free." Haredim designate secular Jews as "free" (or freethinker, *hofshi, hofshim be-de'ot*) because they "threw off the yoke of Torah and mitzvot." And again one finds analogous terms of opprobrium among North American fundamentalists, with "yoked" ("yoked together") as the ultimate praise for insiders, for the saved.[35]

In the United States, Hugh Hefner, Gloria Steinem, and Jane Fonda are the supreme examples of this ethos of false freedom. Muslim and Jewish pamphleteers take aim at popular entertainers and sports figures—the embodiments of the cult of anthropocentric hedonism. Even Gush Emunim, with its quite modern ethos of (Zionist) settlement and stress on military efficacy, dub their dovish-secular opponents 'Akhshavists, that is, proponents of instant gratification (a mocking allusion to Peace Now [Shalom 'Akhshav]).

The latent significance of modernity is humanity's revolt against God. The outside is predicated, for Shi'ite radicals, upon istikbar, a Qur'anic notion originally singling out "those who, haughty with pride, refuse to accept the Qur'an." It is often employed in tandem, and in pun, with "servants of isti'mar" (imperialism). The Sunnis prefer a modern term, ghatrasa, or arrogance, which consists of rejecting the sovereignty (hakimiyya) of Allah by replacing His laws with ones made by man—a charge much like that made by, among others, Protestant Reconstructionists and their Dominion theologians. And haredi thinkers speak, in the same context, of the hutzpa (arrogance) typical of the worst (and latest) periods of exile. The arrogant ones are yiddische rebellen who are in fact "Jewish heathens." Islamic and Christian polemics against modernity also employ the metaphor of paganism: the contemporary condition of Islam is jahiliyya; the Christian church faces today a paganism reminiscent of the first century as Darwinism, materialism, and other human-centered paradigms loom as idols.[36]

The arrogant rebels who are the quintessential (though not the sole) manifestation of the outside are, let us remember, affiliated with a monotheistic tradition, however formal and tenuous are their links with it. Even secular humanists pay a kind of homage to the Judeo-Christian roots of the American experience. They are usually not believers of, or converts to, another faith (or to outright atheism). Few are the cases—Hamas in the occupied territories, the Mujahidin in Afghanistan, the Kach movement of Meir Kahane, perhaps also Pentecostal Christians in India—in which the outside, or center community, is composed of infidels, old and new. In those cases the enclave would take different forms that are beyond the scope of the present essay. (For a treatment of these cases, see chapter 2 in this volume.)[37]

SHADES OF BLACK AND GRAY

In principle, the outside is black. Yet, as one takes a closer look, this dualistic worldview appears more complex. Time and space, as well as the impact of the specific tradition, produce many shades of black and gray. (The enclave, however, remains a priori and metaphorically white, although a constant effort is required to maintain it lily-white.)[38]

In Judaism, an enclave-like social context existed throughout medieval and early modern times, albeit by push—exclusion by the dominant Gentile community in the lands of the Diaspora—rather than by pull. Jewish pre-Enlightenment enclaves adhered to the Halakhic principle, "A Jew remains a Jew even if he sins," in order to keep as many members as possible within the fold (including, in theory, Jews who converted of their own free will). The guiding principle was the group's responsibility for individual believers, as slack as they might become in the dire straits of exile. Even in a worst-case scenario, they remain part and parcel of *klal Yisrael* (the community of the Jews). This dynamic was in evidence following the outbreak of the second intifada in Israel/Palestine in October 2000. Jews of whatever religious/secular mix felt themselves threatened by Arabs in general, and Palestinians in particular. Speeches by haredi members of the Knesset suddenly began to call for reconciliation among all Jews on matters of religion and state in order for the people to withstand the grave test posed by the new intifada.

With the nineteenth century the perception of danger changed. Exclusion diminished, and conversion was less often the issue (intermarriage was). Yet Jews tended to slip away in droves. Some embraced new ideals (liberalism, socialism, indigenous nationalisms) without necessarily denying their faith; they often merely became indifferent to it. Others tried to modify age-old religious norms completely, thereby virtually "Protestantizing" the faith, as in the case of Reform Judaism. (Marcel Lefebvre made an analogous argument in reacting against the newfangled Catholic ritual in the 1960s.)

The worst part of this new syndrome (*neliza* was the term the Hazon Ish coined for it)[39] was a third deviation, this one in the quality and regularity of mitzvot observance due to changing material conditions. The uprooted life of immigrants in North America, Western Europe, and Australia made the Halakhic precepts harder to follow, as did the requirements of the big-city capitalistic economy into which formerly shtetl Jews were now increasingly integrated in Eastern and Central Europe.

While the emergent ultra-Orthodox were busy shoring up the boundary around the separatist *kehillah* (local community) pioneered by the Hatam Sofer, the Hasidic court, and the transnational politicocultural organization (e.g., Agudat Yisrael, founded 1912), the principle "a Jew remains a Jew" was too ingrained to be abandoned. Not merely because of its Halakic authority and long pedigree but also for its affective value, klal Yisrael is often assimilated to *ahavat Yisrael*, love of the Jews and, hence, responsibility for their fate.[40] One did not easily despair of getting the deserters to return to the fold.

The lenses that this notion offered were now focused differently, however, in order to account for new conditions. Rabbinical authorities endeavored to introduce distinctions. Some of these distinctions were homespun in style, such as the Hafetz Haim speaking—in a manner reminding one of Bob Jones, Sr., decades later—of warm, lukewarm, and cold Jews,[41] the first type being within the enclave, the second in its immediate periphery and likely perhaps to be recuperated, the third being hardcore modernists. Other rabbis, employing a more Halakhic lingo, viewed the "cold Jews" as more variegated: there were both *kofrim le-hach'is* (disbelievers out of spite) and the less aggressive *epikoirsim*, and neither forfeited their Jewishness by (maternal) origin. Alongside these Jews, one distinguished shades of gray: *frumer epikoiros* (observant of many mitzvot but not believing in some essential values), *yehudim beinonim* (of mediocre observance and belief), *amei ha-aratzvot* (observant, yet often transgressing norms out of sheer ignorance), and so forth.[42]

Perceptions fluctuated incessantly with the changing times. Until the late 1950s, Zionism and socialism were tarred the darkest black. In the early days of the state of Israel many haredim feared that even baking matzo or carrying phylacteries in public might be prohibited. Irate rabbis had to contend with the overconfident declarations of Israeli politicians (mostly left of center) that Zionism had definitely replaced traditional Judaism, with the Knesset being a sort of Third Temple.[43] Toward the end of the decade, some authorities observed that the Zionist zeal was fizzling out, and most unbelievers were so not "out of spite" but "out of appetite" (*kofrim le-te'avon*, i.e., hedonistic). Most second-generation Israelis, it was argued, are actually "captive children in the hands of unbelievers" (*tinokot she-nishbu*). That is, they are gray more than black, indifferent and ignorant rather than hostile, typical products of the irreligious education they received at the hands of the first generation. This was said to be even truer of Oriental Jews, who were still suffused by tradition when they migrated but were transformed by schooling or by the temptations of the Israeli city, that modern Babylon.[44]

The above description represents mainline ultra-Orthodoxy and does not do justice to minor variants. There are, for example, extreme separatists such as the Neturei Karta, who view all secular Jews as evildoers (*resha'im*, i.e., black). By contrast, others, whether inspired by the Lubavitcher rebbe or, in the case of Gush Emunim, by Rabbi A. I. Kook, see a sort of kabbalistic "spark of sanctity" in any Jewish soul and thus consider virtually all Jews as recuperable.[45]

Roughly the same trajectory can be charted for Islam. Due to the traumatic shock it suffered during the civil wars of its first century, Islam tended to define very narrowly the conditions making one an outright apostate (*murtadd*) and hence punishable by execution. To fall into this category a Muslim would have to explicitly reject the credo ("There is no God but Allah and Muhammad is his messenger"). Prior to the twentieth century, and in a way even today, such cases were few and far between.

The arguments of a modern agnostic like Salman Rushdie—that he cannot be penalized, as he is not a Muslim but a secular pluralist, and that what one has not affirmed one cannot apostatize[46]—would have sounded as bizarre to a medieval Muslim as they do to present-day radicals of Tehran, Cairo, or Bradford, England. In their eyes, Rushdie is Muslim by (paternal) origin, and having slandered the Prophet in *The Satanic Verses*, he thereby denied the credo (*shahada*). Yet even after the reforming Iranian president Mohammed Khatami abrogated the decree against Rushdie in 1999, the foundation that put a prize on his head maintained it as the new century dawned.

Yet the modern challenge to Islam was rarely as blatant as that. Even Communists in Muslim lands learned fast to play down their atheism. The implicit or half-concealed secularism of other modern ideologies represented an uncanny and insidious challenge precisely because it was indirect and conceived in terms hallowed in Islamic history. Radical Muslim thinkers, from the 1930s on, thus had to develop finer heuristic tools and denounce major modern creeds as latently (but not ineluctably) opposed to the shahada. Topping the list, after communism, was nationalism, be it pan-Arab (*qawmiyya*) or of the nation-state variety (*wataniyya*). Nationalism, for the radicals, was a new type of polytheism (*shirk*) in that it attaches a modern idol, the nation, to Allah, whom the nationalists profess they do not reject. Shirk, of course, equals apostasy. To add confusion to sacrilege, the nationalists used for the national community the same term, *umma*, reserved for the "community of the believers."[47] (Such a "polytheism argument," interestingly enough, was likewise employed by haredim against Zionism.)[48]

As in the case of Judaism it was soon discovered that the polluting danger operated on a broader front. The state disregards the Shari'a and introduces laws borrowed from Europe; it also limits the scope of Shari'a courts in sensitive domains such as personal status. Due to secularized education and fewer, or inefficient, state sanctions, the believers neglect rituals and Islamic social precepts. As Islam, much like Judaism, is predicated upon orthopraxis rather than orthodoxy—molding behavior rather than belief— this was a frightening diagnosis. Moreover, the transgressions took place, frequently and with impunity, in the public eye and not just behind the closed doors of hearth and home. Their contagious threat was thereby multiplied.[49]

The diagnosis led Muslim radicals to reinterpret creatively a minor strand of the tradition, the neo-Hanbali legal school, which already in the fourteenth century posited that application of the Shari'a, and not just professing the credo, was the test of the true Muslim ruler. The neo-Hanbali doctrine was carried, however, well beyond its typically medieval self-imposed boundaries (which excluded armed revolt against a nominally Muslim ruler), thus transcending age-old distinctions. According to the revamped doctrine, "outside" (that is, *ridda*, apostasy) was now present wherever the Shari'a is not applied.[50] From the early 1960s this new principle determined for most radical circles the shades of black. The top echelons of the state, its repressive apparatus, and the official media are to be found at the darker end of the gamut; so is a part of Westoxicated intelligentsia. This end consists of apostates (*murtaddun*), polytheists (*mushrikun*), or plain infidels (*kuffar*). The last term (with its plethora of synonyms, such as *pharaohs*), was reserved primarily for political leaders such as Anwar Sadat, the shah of Iran, Hafiz al-Asad, and Saddam Hussein. These leaders and their henchmen persecuted Muslim radicals and initiated or presided over the massive introduction of non-Shari'a law and irreligious indoctrination. By virtue of the reinterpreted neo-Hanbali doctrine it was now legitimate to take up arms against these leaders. This was a daring novelty, for the leaders still professed Islam.[51]

Secondarily, one would include some dubiously Muslim pre-twentieth-century sects, such as the Ahmadiyya in India and Pakistan or the Baha'is in Iran and Egypt, that not only survived but even flourished through adjustment to the modern economy. Their value was mostly as whipping boys and as means for drawing the boundary. In the campaigns against these sects, the vindication of the principles of tradition and resentment of those who were both strange and successful commingled.

The black shades off into various hues of gray. Most Muslim radicals (with few exceptions; see above) do not consider the bulk of society to be apostate, as it just drifts away, out of hedonistic appetite, the victim of brainwashing by the elites. The man on the street is still Muslim, albeit a bad one, not up to the standards of the enclave. Such bad Muslims must be admonished and, if possible, even coerced by vigilante action, in conformity with the hallowed precept of "command that which is good and prohibit that which is abominable" (*al-amr bi-l-ma'ruf wa-l-nahy 'an-i-l-munkar*).[52] By no means can they be the targets of violent action with extreme prejudice. Rarely would the effort exerted in this direction be defined as jihad.

As one proceeds down the social ladder toward the "ignorant masses" (*al-'amma al-jahila*), the Muslim activists become more comprehending, at times indulgent, though never resigned. The ignorant, those of slack practice and shallow belief, are the most obvious target of outreach work, which can take two major forms. Outreach is either combined with vigilantism or appears as a strategy per se, designed to reprimand but also to educate, emphasizing a more regular observance of rituals as the path leading back to the faith. The latter form, as developed by the Tablighi missionary move-ment, is roughly the Islamic equivalent of the Lubavitcher sect (though with-out the mystical elements typical of this Hasidic group).[53] Nevertheless, the "ignorant masses" are not taken to be part of the enclave. Be it Tablighi or Lubavitcher, they remain, at best, at its periphery.

This perception of a many-shaded outside may account for the fact that many Muslim and Jewish enclaves, although jealous of their separate entity, make frequent sallies out of their boundaries in order to impose their behav-ioral norms. The tactics are manifold, dictated both by ideological bent and by circumstances; they include "creeping" into neighboring areas, recourse to lobbying and to local (or statewide) ad hoc coalitions, and vigilante-type militancy. This is essentially a defensive action, aimed at creating a sort of *cordon sanitaire* (e.g., banning "licentious" advertising posters as an eyesore or as a potential temptation for yeshiva students and jama'at members). Yet in many cases it also expresses sincere concern for the fate of lukewarm (or indifferent) individuals who make up the vast majority of so-called Muslims and Jews in this day and age. The sermons of the Egyptian Shaykh Kishk, distributed commercially in audiocassettes all over the Arab world, are the most eloquent expression of such concern. So too, at a more basic level, are the audiotapes of Rabbi Nissim Yagen of Jerusalem or the famous televised address of Rabbi E. M. Schach to "pork-guzzling kibbutzniks," which decided the fate of the Israeli government coalition in March 1990.

The Jewish (or Muslim) street is thus not merely a defensive perimeter. To create it is also the performance of a religious duty, although how impor-tant a duty is a question answered differently by various groups (and even by the same group at various points in time). The underlying notion com-mon to most enclaves is that the boorish masses must be made to conform to norms, albeit without comprehending them. In so conforming they are at least somewhat improved and may even end up by perceiving the significance of the norms and returning to the fold.[54]

Extreme separatist enclaves (e.g., Neturei Karta and 'Eda Haredit; Jama'at al-Takfir wal-Hijra) are important exceptions to this pattern. For them, "in our days darkness covers the whole earth";[55] the whole of society is renegade. The extreme separatists would make such sallies only rarely, and then only for immediate and defensive aims. They may, for example, desecrate tombs of alleged "holy men" that have been placed in a mosque; or impose norms of "modest" dress and licit music in quarters in which they live; or forbid the driving of cars on Shabbat in their vicinity. There is no concern for the klal or umma of the so-called believers, for one is faced with an "infidel society" (in Arabic al-mujtama' al-kafir), an "evil kingdom" (in Hebrew malchut ha-resha'a be-Yisrael shultanut zola). Doomed to damnation, it can be saved, if at all, either by messianic intervention or by imposing the divine law upon one and all once the elect take power by force.[56] The extremist critique of the less separatist group is not predicated upon the diagnosis of the ills of the center community. The extremists also point out, quite plausibly, that a dangerous feedback relationship is set up by too frequent sallies into the central domain: the more you deal with the surrounding society, the more you tend to perceive it as variegated and develop some empathy toward it. (That very logic, that it is better not to have any commerce with the wicked, crops up among Protestant separatists of the Bob Jones variety, who refuse, for instance, to accept federal grants.)

Lest the qualifications create a skewed picture, one should stress that even enclaves that engage in day-to-day sallies for the sake of a Muslim or Jewish street—and even intervene on questions related to the private domain (e.g., abortion, consumption of pork, homosexuality)—never essentially modify the sharp distinction between inside and outside (even though the latter may not be taken to be uniformly black). It strikes one that mainline haredim in the 1990s no longer used the slur the "evil kingdom" in referring to the state of Israel (and continue to refer to "our state," "our army").[57] Yet never do they call it a "kingdom of grace" (malchut shel hesed, a fair-minded state). That title is reserved for the United States, a goyish and hence by definition alien entity. And it was applied to the United States only after the 1960s, when the evolution of the welfare state, combined with notions of cultural pluralism, gave the ultra-Orthodox access to federal and state funding. The "in exile among Jews" diagnosis is, of course, not challenged in such a situation, for the haredim are still a minority within a minority. Obviously, when Israeli haredim perceive that the conditions for "sallies" are not favorable (as in the late 1980s), they retreat into the cocoon of their enclave. Its survival takes priority over all other concerns.

One would expect Protestant fundamentalists, especially independent Baptist churches, to constitute a totally different case. Shouldn't their insistence upon personal faith and individual salvation predispose them to indifference about the fate of the vast majority of un-Christian Americans? Why care about those not destined to be saved at the moment of rapture? The saved, who are "called to be winners for God's glory,"[58] are indeed a group apart—a notion quite at odds with the traditional Islamic and Jewish positions as well as with the Catholic doctrine of the community of the baptized, the communion of saints (who remain Christian as long as they are not excommunicated). Such a doctrine makes the Italian movement Comunione e Liberazione strive so mightily in the milieu of tepid Christian Democrats or indifferent Socialists. And Archbishop Lefebvre, for all his antiestablishment vituperations, considered the bulk of baptized Catholics as "sheep of the flock of Our Lord Jesus Christ delivered defenseless to the ravishing wolves [of the conciliar church]."[59]

But even our generalization with regard to the Protestants is true only up to a point. It disregards the fundamentalists' vision of America as a nation elected by God, a shining City on the Hill, a Beacon of Light unto the Nations. This mission accounts for its success in its age of pristine purity, the seventeenth century, and its decline in more recent times (especially since the late nineteenth century, when old-time religion last held sway). Despite current moral decay and disarray, America—that linchpin of Christian civilization—can still be "turned around," its moral decline reversed and "made great again," provided that "the Bible [gets] back into American schools," and "Biblical standards" once again dictate social mores.[60]

This upbeat American patriotism is often xenophobic (anti-German in the early twentieth century, anti-Soviet following World War II) and saturated with the rhetoric of manifest destiny. Further, it relies heavily on military and sports metaphors ("marines for Christ," "be a champion for Jesus")[61] redolent of U.S. popular culture. Xenophobic patriotism may lead to the drawing of a populist distinction between perverted individuals on the one hand, and the somewhat wholesome, perhaps still redeemable, mass of ordinary Americans on the other. Hence also the respect for the flag, the "I love America" rallies, as well as the teaching of "American church history" as a time perspective that sets a sort of road map charting present and future.

Combined with a post-tribulationist twist on the premillennial vision, this implicit sense of some responsibility for America's fate was a prime

mover in the direction of fundamentalist political activism in the early eighties.[62] Yet the fact that the essential rhetoric remained the same from the
sixties to the present suggests that, while fundamentalist empathy toward
the mass of unsaved Americans may be dubious, America as an entity is a
cherished object of concern. In such a context a "revolutionary defeatism"—
let the United States go down the drain like the Roman Empire of yore—
can hardly be envisaged.[63]

SPACE: SYMBOLIC AND SOCIAL

"God's greatest call is separation," claimed A. C. Gaebelein in the Prophetic
Bible conference of 1914.[64] The slogan would have made sense for the
founders of Agudat Yisrael (in Katowice, 1912) who gave a European-wide
organizational expression to Hatam Sofer's pioneering effort at the local
level. The enemy from whom one should separate was the liberal Methodist
church in the former case, Zionists and Reform Jews in the latter; in both
cases, the logic was the same. That logic also presided over Hasan al-Banna's
initiative in setting up the Muslim Brotherhood in 1928; he put flesh on
the bones of Rashid Rida's alarmist theories. Al-Banna, an Egyptian, sought
separation from the Islamic establishment with its addiction to apologetics
designed to make religion conform to the requirements of modernity.

But how to separate? Not merely by formal, doctrinal boundary making.
As we deal here with religion as a way of life (in Arabic *nizam shamil, manhaj
hayyat;* in Hebrew *orah hayyim*),[65] it behooves, in the lingo of American fundamentalists, not just to believe in the Bible (or another authoritative text)
but to live it. It is interesting to note that Luigi Giussani, though Catholic,
quotes in such a context none other than the Puritan theologian Jonathan
Edwards: theological study is valueless unless affirmed through concrete
commitment, that is, by molding behavior.

Behavior is indeed paramount in enclaves—including Christian ones
where orthodoxy is supposed to have precedence over praxis. Behavior endows belief with a mimetic and affective dimension.[66] A viable enclave
wields efficient group constraints and should thus be able to have its individual members conform to homogeneous public norms. And their most
immediate product is a separate space.

Space is, to begin with, symbolic, as one could deduce from the distinct
Islamic and Jewish terminology surveyed above. But a quick checklist of
Protestant terms attests that these fundamentalists do not fall behind: "bear
witness," "walk with the Lord," "surrender one's life to the Lord," "soul

harvest" (recruiting new members), "sacrifice" (contributing money or lei-
sure time), "salvational plan (or work)," "faith promises" (contribution to
missions), "excise the cancer" (of deviation, sexual or otherwise). Such metaphors, not to mention those referring to holy war (or crusade), bestow
a special, sacred significance upon behavior approved for members of the
enclave.

The language one has recourse to, immersed as it is in Scriptures—in
the above passage, the King James Bible with its Scofield premillennialist
exegesis—is, in itself, an act of self-assertion.[67] It also provides members
with lenses to view and select reality. Obviously cosmology, in the sense of
assumptions about history, nature, and so forth, would likewise express itself through language and other symbolic means. Vocabulary is not the sole
linguistic aspect involved. One notes Talmudic (Aramaic) and Yiddish terms
among haredim even when modern Hebrew or English syntax is employed;
in the Islamic case, one finds flamboyant Qur'anic rhetoric and the idiom
of the Hadith. Of equal significance is the linguistic stratum mined: one
finds Yiddish or post-Talmudic legal commentary, Yinglish; classical rather
than modern or colloquial Arabic; the classical Arabic component in Persian; and so on.

This brings us to the music preferred in the enclave, albeit not necessarily
enjoined by an authoritative text: late-nineteenth-century hymns among
American fundamentalists; eighteenth- and nineteenth-century Hasidic
chants; Qur'anic psalmodies, traditional Muslim folk music; Gregorian
chants in the Lefebvre movement's rites. All provide clues to the Golden
Age placed on a pedestal, but they particularly imply rejection of the present,
namely, the texture of contemporary pop music, especially rock.[68] The audial
space thereby created at home, at the place of worship and/or assembly, at
the homogeneous residential quarter (if there is one), reinforces the impact
of language.

The same holds true for other distinguishing marks such as body language (compare the bent posture of the haredim and the erect one of Gush
activists); dress codes (white galabia and headgear for Muslim males, veil
for females; pioneering military style in Gush Emunim, black *streiml* and
distinct headgear for haredi males, wig and long-sleeved dress for females;
reintroduction of the cassock for priests of the Lefebvre obedience); and
hairstyle (compare the shaggy haredi beard and the trimmed one of Islamic
militants). Dress, in particular, seems to be a further indicator as to the
historical period held as the model, as do names given to offspring (compare, again, the traditional Jewish ones among haredim, the rare biblical or
sabra-nationalist names in Gush settlements).

Behavior consists, first and foremost, of strict observance of norms of conduct derived from the tenets of the faith. The observance is strict, if not punctilious, because of the gravity of the outside danger. The norms are, of course, voluntarily assumed, as befits a posttraditional world in which age-old rules of conduct (many of which had been rather lenient) dissolved with the demise of solid, territorially anchored communities due to the constant migration typical of the twentieth century, from small town to big city or to suburban sprawl in the United States; the rural exodus in Islamic lands; Maghrebi and Turkish workers moving to Europe; Jewish Eastern Europe to the United States or to Israel. In the Jewish case one should also add the impact of the annihilation of six million Eastern and Central European Jews, most of whom were still observant to some extent. Another demographic phenomenon, not yet studied sufficiently, is the spiraling birthrate in Islamic countries, where about two-thirds of the population is under twenty-five and thus has no memory of what life may have been like before the onslaught of modernity.

The voluntary nature of membership is legitimated by the notion of the elect who throw their lot in with a dissident—that is, a materially and socially unrewarding—community. In turn, the community represents, as we have seen, a deliberate effort to preserve the essence (or fundamentals) of the tradition in an alien, posttraditional setting (within the limits set by an understanding as to what this essence is). This serves as an incentive for conformity predicated on moral suasion.

As a contribution to a sacred group effort, the duties of members of the enclave are frequently depicted in holy-war terms. To wit: the slogan "wage a Battle Royal for the fundamentals" in the United States of the 1920s; the "crusader passport" distributed by Jerry Falwell to his supporters; the terms *jihad*, or *jihad al-nafs* (against the evil in one's soul) applied by Muslim militants to activities as varied as fasting and superogatory prayers or the banning of TV viewing; the term *milhemet qodesh* (holy war, or *milhamta shel Torah*) applied by haredim to the fight for a modest dress code as much as for (or against, as the case may be) participation in elections. The sacralization of the enclave implies, then, the sacrality of all actions, including "sallies," in which it is involved. That may include, of course, the sacralization of politics in general, as in the rhetoric of the Moral Majority in the 1980s as well as of Gush Emunim in Israel.

At the root of it all, strictness is the product of the need for clarity in an age of ambiguity and confusion. Strict behavior is, again, made possible by the fact that so much traditional (and by necessity local) practice had been lost as a result of migration and other demographic dislocations.

The imposition of a set of rules is thus in part a new creation—it is the enclave's attempt to dictate a semblance of order. This new order, in turn, is in a way quite out of sync with the myriad coexisting forms of the tradition as it had once been practiced. And this is a modern set of rules, the strictness of which is understandable, given that it is geared to fighting the prevailing tendency in the center community to compromise with modernity, that is, to bend some age-old rules.

This would account for the pivotal position enjoyed in Sunni militancy by the neo-Hanbali legal school. During its seven-hundred-year history, neo-Hanbalism made the extirpation of novelties (*bid'a*) and of looseness of morals (*fasad*) its guiding principles. The modern interpreters of neo-Hanbalism—some of them converts from other, more accommodationist schools—developed an arsenal of arguments and stratagems for those who would opt for *'aqd* (tying the knot, holding the line) rather than *hall* (untying the knot, rendering licit). *'Aqd* is required, more often than not, by the insidious dangers lurking everywhere.[69]

The same dynamics can be observed in Halakhic norms. If "bar innovations" was the watchword in nineteenth- and early-twentieth-century ultra-Orthodoxy (encapsulated in the Hatam Sofer's adage "Novelty is prohibited by the Torah"), from the time of the Hazon Ish it came to share pride of place with *humra* (extra stringency, *diqduq*, *hiddur*). Wherever possible and even with regard to old customs or matters where no open modern challenge is involved, there is a sort of built-in moral superiority for the stricter alternative. *Frumkeit* (stricter than thou) behavior is made the object of competition among Halakhic authorities and their groupies, especially the yeshiva youth who have become the accepted role models (or core) for the plethora of haredi communities.[70]

One should note in passing that antinomian tendencies—arguably the structural counterpart of the hypernomian—are rare in enclaves. Among Jews this may be due to the enduring lessons of the nihilistic offshoots of the seventeenth-century Shabbatean movement (which ended up embracing Islam or Christianity), although some such tendencies have lately been evident in fringe underground groups in Jerusalem. Among American fundamentalists a powerful brake operating in this direction may be the gut reaction against the permissiveness of the 1960s, which underlies much of the resurgence of independent Baptist churches. In Islam, neo-Hanbalism, present from the inception of the movement under Rashid Rida, set ironclad limits that few groups dare transgress. Prominent among them was Jama'at al-Takfir, the Sunni group that rejected the Shari'a wholesale as the product of time-serving ulama and demanded that communal life be regulated on the basis of the Qur'an alone. Because of the paucity of laws in the Islamic holy book, this would have left enormous leeway for this sect's leader, a self-styled caliph-cum-messiah.[71]

The stringency and the antinovelty stance are not, however, as all-embracing as they may first seem. Strict observance focuses just on certain aspects deemed crucial (or "fundamental") for the time and place. Gush Emunim would make the precept of the settlement of the Land of Israel, as well as other precepts related to this land, the end-all of the 613 mitzvot, for this land is the center both of the universe and of "wholesome, untruncated Judaism." Their extreme messianic fringe would add some of those 292 precepts related to ritual in the Temple, held in abeyance since C.E. 70; others, the majority, tend to be haredi-inspired and put almost equal emphasis on some rituals. The haredim pay particular attention to family and dietary law rituals (mostly in public, and in Hebrew)—as the basis for group solidarity—leaving aside, for instance, civil law. Writing around 1930, the Hazon Ish set forth seven conditions for the survival of the ultra-Orthodox: in each town they should have their own primary school (talmud Torah), kosher slaughterhouse, ritual bath, observance of Shabbat, a synagogue, and autonomy of the community from control by impious Jews. Seventy-odd years later this formula (education and dietary matters and ritual and organizational autonomy) still serves as the basis for haredi communities. Leniency, if not slackness, in legal matters related to the above is the gravest sin the ultra-Orthodox impute to modern Orthodox, Conservative, and Reform Jews, and at times to some of their own persuasion.[72]

Strictness in Shari'a observance relates emphatically to matters of personal status that had been throughout history the de facto core of Islamic law immune from state intervention. From the 1950s, however, even this core was invaded by legislative initiatives of the regimes in Egypt, Iran, Syria, Tunisia, Iraq, and Algeria and brought under the control of civil courts. The implications seemed to Muslim radicals alarming. Threatened were a gender-based division of labor and status, the traditional means of defining "who is a Muslim," and the role of the family as the major socializing agent (especially given the pervasive irruption of the state media and education into the domestic sphere). Lagging behind as objects of the radicals' concern are ritual affairs, but they are important particularly for novices' self-expression. Here an effort is exerted, in tune with neo-Hanbalism, to "decontaminate" practice from "pagan," anthropomorphic (often Sufi) "insidious accretions."[73]

Control of behavior should perhaps have lesser salience in Protestant enclaves due to the stress on inner belief. But in fact it seems about the same. What the Protestants lack, of course, is the firm textual authority of an elaborate jurisprudence like that provided by the Shariʿa for Muslims, the Halakah for Jews, and canon law for Roman Catholics—that is, a sort of formal, objective anchor. Neither do Protestants invest a huge intellectual effort in the study and further development of religious law. In practice, however, members of independent Baptist churches are subject to rigorous controls in some key areas. There are bans on drinking, on profanity, on abortion, and on certain sexual behavior (premarital, extramarital, and homosexual relations). Strong parental authority over children is stressed, as is attendance at prayer and certain other church activities. Censorship of reading, listening, and viewing material is common. Needless to say, at fundamentalist institutions of higher education such as Liberty University in Virginia and Bob Jones University in South Carolina, controls are stricter on the above issues and apply even to dating, mate selection, and so forth. The visit to Bob Jones University in 2000 by presidential candidate George W. Bush both reignited and put on display the traditional anti-Catholicism of the institution.[74]

Novelty is frowned upon in principle, yet monotheistic radicals have proven themselves quite ingenious in accommodating modern realities whenever they deem it vital for the survival of the enclave. This was naturally easier in issues unrelated to "fundamentals" of religious law but feasible in the core domain as well. Sunni radicals elaborated this attitude into a full-fledged doctrine by subscribing to the concept of "opening up the gates of *ijtihad*" (independent legal judgment by jurists), gates closed since the tenth century C.E. This is, significantly enough, the sole idea they borrowed from the Muslim reformists, although they refuse to open the gates as wide as the latter would. Nonetheless, they have regular recourse to this tool on matters as diverse as interest-taking, new technologies, and civil disobedience.[75]

Shiʿite radicals, in whose tradition this ijtihad had never been banned, had a lighter task, further facilitated by the fact that a good part of the Islamic establishment (the *mujtahidun*, madrasa graduates trained in jurisprudence) joined their ranks, often in leadership positions. This is something quite rare in the Sunni milieu, where radical leaders are self-taught laypeople. The learned and self-confident Shiʿite mujtahid is more likely to take innovative risks in cases considered to be of dire necessity than would the Sunni autodidact with his rather narrow vision of jurisprudence. The Hizbullah mentor, Shaykh Muhammad Husayn Fadlallah, went so far as to permit birth control (though not abortion) in the name of the supreme interest (*maslaha*) of the umma, suffering as it does from overpopulation.

He likewise prohibited as "pagan and tribal" the killing of daughters for "crimes of honor" and banned the imposition of a spouse upon women by their male guardian.[76]

The Halakhic case is quite similar to the Shi'ite. Throughout post-Talmudic times innovation was licit, albeit subject to strict rules. The spate of innovations introduced by the Reform-minded in the nineteenth century elicited a principled stance against novelty per se. Yet at the hands of the right authorities, whose doctrinal standing was actually bolstered in the twentieth century, "the right kind" of innovation was always possible. Present-day haredi dispensers of responsa follow here the lead shown by the Hafetz Haim,[77] who allowed more lenient practice for Jewish recruits in the tsarist army or immigrants in the United States, as well as the Hazon Ish, who solved the problems of the first ultra-Orthodox kibbutz. Certainly Gush Emunim rabbis would issue permits for work on Shabbat in case of "manifest necessity" for furthering the settlement of the Land of Israel and for self-defense, notably against the PLO-controlled entity that seemed likely to result from the Rabin-Arafat Accord of September 1993.

Stringency in observance and supererogatory endeavors (minor Jewish fasts, extra prayers on Muslim feast days) are deemed virtuous in both traditions, but not when carried to extremes. Conspicuous and extreme display is frowned upon. Innovations introduced in such a spirit are often flatly rejected. Haredim denounce confirmation rites (*bar mitzvot*) held at the Western Wall as smacking of the "anthropomorphic paganism" of Gush Emunim (and the kindred National Religious Party) circles. Lefebvrists fulminate against the laxity of the clergy with regard to access to sacraments (e.g., in condoning baptism of babies of nonbelieving parents). Egyptian radicals, for all their commitment to the jihad against Israel and for the liberation of Jerusalem, anathemize jama'at who turn in prayer toward Jerusalem (*qiblat al-quds*) instead of to Mecca.

CLAIMS ON TIME/SPACE

Let us not forget that enclaves are usually people living in close physical proximity, face to face. The end product of the imposition of fundamentalist norms is a strong claim on individual members' "operational time" as lived as a group (not individual) resource. There is no distinction between sacred and profane, work-bound and free. Claims are most evident in the way the religious calendar regiments and punctuates the cadence of members' lives in a way sharply divergent from that of the surrounding society. Suffice it

to look at the way the week is organized around Sunday, the Shabbat (beginning Friday evening), or Friday (especially the noon prayer). Moreover, as
Nancy Ammerman has shown in her study of a Connecticut fundamentalist
congregation, between attending prayer, study, and hymnal groups, outreach and committee activity, and so forth, most of the members' afterwork
time is invested in the group and subject to its controls. (And this includes
even "private dates" such as spiritual birthdays or celebrating one's conversion.)[78]

Located in sprawling suburbia, with many members commuting to
work, such a Protestant community does not enjoy a condensed "operational space" (i.e., space as lived) of its own. Because they have to live within
walking distance of the synagogue in order not to desecrate the Shabbat,
the haredim have such operational space, as does a Gush Emunim settlement. The haredi definition of a "good environment" hinges first and foremost upon space near a synagogue of haredi persuasion. Nevertheless, there
are some heavily fundamentalist residential areas where some analogous
Christian rules are introduced, municipal politics permitting, as well as
brand-new spatial guarantees such as "Christian shopping malls" (where
blue movies and "adult" bookshops are forbidden and homosexual vendors
are prohibited).

But even in regular fundamentalist communities the church (or the Scuola di Communità in the Italian Comunione e Liberazione) is the focus of
social life for the majority of members. Its role in their lives is no different
in essence than that of the *ahli* (not subject to government control) mosque
under the auspices of a *jama'a* (religious association), or even a state mosque
that a Muslim association has succeeded in gaining control of, by bribing
or subverting the imam of prayer. This also accounts for the forceful "occupation" of churches in France by Lefebvre disciples in communities in which
there had been minorities. Space, much like time, becomes a group resource,
an object of the enclave's claims.

Thus welded, the enclave becomes an arena of sociability. Individual
members—who may have been, in all three traditions, recruited through
existing networks of friends and acquaintances—find that the bulk of their
social interaction is with fellow members. This is, of course, even more easily
the case with the haredim, who constitute multigenerational communities
existing for decades.

Cutting off some of one's former friendships, owing to divergent lifestyles or new enclave responsibilities, is a leitmotiv in life histories of converts to U.S. Baptist churches, to Comunione e Liberazione in Italy, to students joining jama'at in the dorms of colleges in Gaza, Cairo, and Amman,

and to kibbutznik returnees to the faith in Jerusalem or the West Bank. The
theme of the "friendly church" or its equivalents—a warm and safe haven
in an atomized and anonymous world—is typical not only of Ammerman's
interviewees but of Muslim, haredim, and Comunione e Liberazione members I talked to as well. The Talmud after-work study society called *khavrusa*
(fellowship, companionship), a fixture of the ultra-Orthodox enclave, provides just such a haven. "Fellowship" is also a secondary meaning of the
term *jamaʿa* used for Islamic radical associations.

Enclave solidarity in action is both positive and negative, uniting and
confrontational. Human warmth, generated within, compensates for the
tough norms and tight schedules imposed by the group. A powerful agent
of enclave sociability is endogamy, effectively practiced by the haredim, often for a number of generations, as well as by some of the extreme Islamic
groups like Jamaʿat al-Takfir wa-l-Hijra. Elsewhere this is done by nudging
and other indirect pressures rather than by direct injunction as, for instance,
in the way mate selection is encouraged at Liberty University or at the annual
festival of Comunione e Liberazione, an organization that caters mostly to
singles in their twenties. Marriage is, however, quite often a sore spot: Baptists complain of "unequally yoked" marriages, those in which one spouse
is not saved. Indeed, dominion theologian Gary North has pointed to haredi
in-group marriage strategy as the model for Protestants if they wish to survive.[79] One wonders whether this would be easily applicable, for the haredi
endogamy tends to exclude even baʾalei teshuva (the equivalent of the "recently saved") for fear of contamination by their secularist families; the
"returnees" are exhorted to marry fellow "returnees."

A structural problem, and one plaguing all three traditions, consists of
the fact that the burden of claims (on time, space, behavior) may be too
heavy. How to keep up standards without condemning the enclave to be a
minuscule sect? After all, members wish to ensure, in principle, that as many
as possible will persist in the faith, and beyond sheer survival, perhaps even
create an alternative society.

The solution adopted by some enclaves is to divide the community into
concentric circles: an inner one of ascetic "religious virtuosi" who observe
to the letter a maximum number of norms; and one or several outer circles
where a lesser number of precepts are observed with the same measure of
stringency and where less time or effort is invested in other norms. The
haredim, who possess an explicit doctrine on degrees *(madregot)* in the fulfillment of mitzvot, maintain as inner circles the yeshiva and kollelim students and their rabbis, dedicated to the study of "Torah for its own sake"

(and, by association, also the wives of postgraduate kollelim students who contribute to their upkeep by their work, usually in ultra-Orthodox schools). Sustained in large part by scholarships financed by state allocations and grants from benefactors, the students—usually young males between the ages of sixteen and thirty—live in decent genteel poverty, spending most of their waking hours in the study of Talmud and its exegesis. The purity of their quasi-monastic effort is supposed to impress and set a role model for the bulk of laypeople (*ba'ale batim*) of the community. The latter are gainfully employed but are expected to observe "fundamentals" of law and ritual (e.g., major fasts but not necessarily all minor fasts, all dietary laws but not with the same punctiliousness); they also engage daily in some evening study (e.g., a daily page of the Talmud).[80] In Gush Emunim circles one can distinguish between the "inner sanctum" of settlement members along with a close periphery of "national-haredi" yeshiva students who contribute some time on a regular basis to the settlement effort, and an outer periphery of supporters in urban centers.

A somewhat analogous grading is found in the St. Pius X Fraternity, the legal-cum-organizational framework of the Lefebvre movement. The nucleus was the seminary in Econe, Switzerland, together with four "missionary" seminaries (in Germany, Italy, the United Kingdom, and the United States), in which students were subject to near-ascetic controls. The next layer comprised 260 priests, members of the fraternity in like-minded communities worldwide, assisted by individual monks, nuns, and lay auxiliaries. Loosely affiliated with the fraternity were seven nunneries, free-floating dissident priests and monks, and at the outermost periphery, associations of lay sympathizers, subject to lesser controls yet providing valuable moral and financial support.

In a more diffuse fashion this is the function of Scuola di Communità, Compagnia delle Opere, and Movimento Popolare, the three organizational layers of Comunione e Liberazione. And the same pattern holds for the distinction developed among Pentecostalists between, on the one hand, a sectarian nucleus (covenant communities, ministry teams) held to ideals such as monastic celibacy and, on the other, a cultlike periphery.[81] A certain evolution in the same organizational direction can be observed after the mid-1980s among jama'at in Egypt, Tunisia, and the Gaza Strip: a core group supported by an outreach periphery that sends its children to the group's kindergartens (a novelty in Arab lands) and schools, frequents its mosques (invariably on Friday noon but also on some weekdays), participates in evening study groups, applies for counseling (shar'i, but also familial) to the group's ulama or to self-taught lay authorities. In technical doctrinal jargon, the core's work for the holy war is *fard 'ayn* (individual obligation) and the periphery's work is *fard kifaya* (group obligation).

In a way, both the Muslim Tablighi movement and its Jewish analogue, the Habad, resort to this very principle, although with a much broader, at times differentiated, periphery. So deeply ingrained is this organizational principle that even when the Habad movement split three ways after the death in 1992 of Rabbi Menachem Mendel Schneerson—who left no male heir—the principle was maintained by all three factions. The messianists who denied his death altogether; those who professed to maintain contact with him and hoped for his immediate return to earth; as well as the third faction, which has come to terms with his death, all preserved the layered structure of the organization.

The importance of the core/peripheries mode of organization lies, first, in maintaining an equality of effort (and status) at each level while enlarging the scope of the movement. Equality is crucial, for in enclaves the grid (i.e., constraints due to formal distinctions) has to be minimal, almost zero, in order to preserve its voluntary character. Second, the peripheries mediate between the core and the surrounding society, serving as a defensive envelope and allowing the movement to operate in society without polluting the core in belief or in action.[82]

COSMOLOGY

In their own eyes, the fundamentalists are reasonable people. It is just that, committed to the revelation, they are pitted in a fight against the outside. "Zealots but not extremists" is an adage common to haredi rabbis; it is echoed by Muslim radicals: "We are partisans of a median way *[hall wasat]*, we are devoted to it, not to extremism." Rational yet embattled, it is a self-perception no doubt as sincere as it is deep.[83]

For a type of rationality to survive in its social context it requires cognitive anchors—notions about historical space and time, physical and human nature, knowledge—in a word, a cosmology. Such anchors provide it with indicators as to its place in a wider scheme of things. Cosmology thus sustains and fashions, in a sort of feedback loop, the culture of the enclave, its mode of behavior, authority, and organization. The underlying assumption is that some sort of balance (or consonance) between cosmology and the social context—in this case, the enclave—must be maintained for the enclave to endure.

Historical time is the cosmological element most readily accessible to the analyst in that it relates directly to that primal impulse—the diagnosis—which the enclave feeds on. Its time perspective tends to be somewhat shrunken, collapsed, and condensed. The past is reduced to a few key eras, closely related to the enclave's notion as to what accounts for the glory and decline of the tradition; it is, hence, intensely relevant for the present. The future perspective is likewise rather short; the more radical the enclave, the shorter it is. Its overall bent is pessimistic if not doom-laden.

The specific content, vocabulary, and significance of the time perspective are determined, yet again, by the tradition in question. One should emphasize here that what is meant by "tradition" is neither desiccated book lore nor some marginal past component (or set of long-forgotten precedents). It is a matter of a living tradition, transmitted from generation to generation by clergy, scholars, mystics, and other activists, and one that is part and parcel of the mainstream of that religion. It is not the case of an age-old heresy suddenly raising its head. American fundamentalism is heir to Calvinist postmillennialism, to John Nelson Darby's premillennialism and, at the root of it all, to Puritan concepts of the City on the Hill, the Beacon of Light.

Sunni and Shi'ite radicalism was born out of an unaccommodating attitude toward political power that had always existed within these two strands of Islam. This attitude was much more important in Shi'ite Islam, given its persecuted stance throughout history. But even among Sunnis, who are, on the whole, more accommodative, there has always been a legitimate, vigilante-type alternative that was definitely unaccommodating and was perceived as being within the pale, an integral part of Sunni political lore. Some of this vigilante lore has been covered by historical dust (e.g., the writings of the school of Ibn Hazm in Muslim Spain), but other variants continue to exist to this day (namely, the neo-Hanbali school founded by Ibn Taymiyya in the fourteenth century). When modern Sunni radicals looked in the 1950s for a tradition to build upon, they naturally turned to Ibn Taymiyya. Neither here nor in Shi'ite Islam does the phenomenon in any way represent a case of heresies raising their heads, outside the pale of the legitimate religious discourse. All attempts made by the Egyptian regime to brand radicals as heretics (for example, as Kharijites in the seventh century C.E. or Qarmats in the tenth century C.E.) inevitably failed.

Heresy is likewise definitely not what Jewish radicalism consists of. The ultra-Orthodoxy of the haredim and the Neturei Karta is a successor to a long tradition of Jewish exclusionary life in the Diaspora, a tradition that until the age of Enlightenment and secular nationalism (nay, even up to the Holocaust) was the major living tradition of Judaism, resigned to life outside of history (and outside of politics) as long as God had not performed the miracle of messianic redemption. As for Gush Emunim, they build upon the minor but legitimate tradition of Jewish activist messianism—exerting oneself to hasten the arrival of the Messiah and not just passively waiting for him—a tradition that has played a key role in certain historical moments as late as the seventeenth century (with the mass movement of Shabtai Zvi with its deep roots in the kabbala). These medieval kabbalistic concepts were revamped by Rabbi Zvi Yehuda Kook in the 1950s in order to answer questions raised by the establishment of the state of Israel, in a manner no different in essence than the one used by Sunni thinker Sayyid Qutb to reinterpret Ibn Taymiyya's political theory for the needs of the twentieth century. In a slightly different fashion, this is also what Khomeini did to the Usuli notion of ulama hierarchy and social responsibility.

Finally, the Lefebvre movement is an outgrowth of the so-called traditionalist trend in Catholicism. It is dedicated to the very notion of tradition as laid down in the sixteenth century at the Council of Trent (and reaffirmed at the First Vatican Council). Facing the challenge of Luther's principle of *sola scriptura,* the council consecrated tradition, that is, the doctrinal developments recognized by the church throughout history. The Latin Mass is a vivid symbol of what has been lost in the post–Vatican II era. Fighting for it proceeds from an overall approach to Catholicism that reflects, in Archbishop Lefebvre's words, "an instinctive horror of novelty under any pretext."[84] These movements' strong base in the religious tradition goes far to explain the initial appeal they have for "true believers." That base is also what makes the believers' task of transcending the living tradition, while remaining true to it, so complex and daunting.

This excursus on tradition may help us to better understand the historical perceptions, to which we now return.

Common to most enclaves is a special perspective on the past: members consider themselves to be living at the end of an era drawing to a close. American Protestants, who are usually of a dispensationalist conviction, would see it as a late stage of the church age (which began with Christ's resurrection), a stage when apostasy and heresy threaten Christian civilization with collapse. Some would even suggest an analogy to the underground church of the first century.[85] Haredim view the contemporary period as that tail end of the Exile when, in the words of the Mishna, "insolence will increase . . . the kingdom will become heretical . . . the study hall of scholars will become a state of licentiousness."[86] Shi'ites saw Islam about to revert to the paganism of the Iranian kings of 2,500 years ago (celebrated with pomp and circumstance in Persepolis, 1972) or to the persecution of the partisans of true Islam under the apostate Umayyad caliphs (661–750). The same twin-pronged fear reverberates in the Sunni belief that one witnesses the return of the jahiliyya, which forced Muhammad into exile.

A certain cyclical perception of time is often implied: the tradition had known such dangers in the past. The Muslims refer to the Crusaders and their native collaborators in the twelfth and thirteenth centuries or the Arab and Persian adepts of Greek philosophy in the tenth century; haredim refer to the Hellenized Jews of the second century B.C.E. or to the Shabbateans in the seventeenth century C.E. Yet time is also, and above all, linear: in crucial respects the present danger is unheard of, worse than anything that has happened since the combative early days of the tradition.

The combined effect of the cyclical and the linear has a distinct pessimistic flavor to it. Enclaves tend indeed to be obsessed with binary formulations, revolving around a before/after axis. The watershed mark is the historical moment when decline and decay set in. Some thinkers, more philosophically minded, place it at the Renaissance, humanism, and the European Enlightenment,[87] but the majority (followed by the rank and file) locate it closer to the present: middle (or late) nineteenth century for Protestants and Jews (and Comunione e Liberazione); early (or post–World War I) twentieth century for Muslims. Lefebvre's disciples refer to the separation of church and state in France.

This is no idle speculation. If one wishes to do something about it and not just wax nostalgic about bygone glory, an imminent danger of decline concentrates the mind, condenses the past. Relevant are periods that account for the present menace and/or may provide an ideal to strive for, a model to be reconstituted (allowing, of course, for some adaptation to technological and economic realities). American Protestants speak with great intensity and longing about the United States before industrialization and mass immigration, with its small-town life and traditional family structure. The very architecture of their churches and topics of their posters bespeak attachment to this era, privileged at the expense of all others, preceding or following. A minority of Calvinist-inspired Dominion theologians add to it seventeenth-century Puritan colonies, a society controlled by Christianity, before the disastrous separation of church and state.[88]

For the Catholics, the golden age is either the thirteenth century, with the rise of the religious orders, the consolidation of scholasticism and Thomism in particular, and the high water mark of the medieval papacy; or it is the Counter Reformation, with the Council of Trent representing the right type of response—tradition-bound, disciplinarian—to a major crisis within both church and society. The council inaugurated the last "wholesome" era in the church's history, an era that would end with the disaster of the French Revolution. It is no coincidence that the two popes the Lefebvrists revere are Pius V, a paragon of the Counter Reformation (whose rite they vindicate for the Latin Mass), and Pius X, after whom they name their fraternity, who opposed the separation of church and state in France (1905)—the culmination of the revolutionary anticlericalism—and theological modernism. Comunione e Liberazione likewise cherishes Pius X together with his predecessor Leo XIII as models of social Catholicism, committed to changing the modern outlying society without accommodating it; they show how "to be in the world without being of the world."

In Islam, much like in Protestantism, one finds a divergence between majority and minority versions, both legitimately ensconced within the tradition. Sunnis are focused upon Muhammad and the first four caliphs, supposedly the era when divine law was effectively applied by the state and its norms reigned supreme in civil society. (The Ottoman caliphate, a secondary object of nostalgia, is not held up as a model to which to return, perhaps because for most Sunnis, who are Arabic-speaking, it meant alien rule.) Shi'ites shrink the scope of the relevant past to the times of Muhammad (622–32) and of his sole legitimate heir, Caliph 'Ali (656–60), when the true version of the Law commanded obedience.

The haredi "foundation myth" is, as one could expect, the eighteenth-century shtetl of east Europe, an emblematic expression of a Diasporic, close-knit, Halakah-governed, autonomous community. This is assumed to be the maximum available to Jews under the conditions of exile, created in the first century C.E. "because of our sins," and bound to endure as long as the Lord sees fit. In contradistinction, Gush Emunim are heirs to a minority strand within Judaism that looked for ways to bring about the end of Exile through human agency and reestablish a sovereign entity in the Holy Land.[89] No wonder that the past enthroned by the Gush is the First Commonwealth (thirteenth to sixth centuries B.C.E.) and Second Commonwealth (second century B.C.E. to second century C.E.). Dress codes and topics for children's literature or for sermons vary accordingly between the ultra-Orthodox and the Gush.

This "highlighted" past is experienced with utmost contemporaneity, spoken about in the same way that one talks about figures and events appearing in the major text, the product of the revelation, which carries authority in the enclave. Chronological distance is abolished, as is clear to any observer watching haredim on the ninth of Av as they lament the c.e. 70 destruction of the Temple and the onset of Exile, or Shi'ites weeping in self-flagellation for the murder of Imam Husayn, 'Ali's grandson, on the tenth of Ramadan ('Ashura).

As we shall see, the past has its counterpart in the future, for history is, as fundamentalists put it, "purposeful," governed by an omniscient Providence. The intersection of past and future grants the believer a secret road map, enabling her to comprehend from whence she comes and where she is headed—a "plan of salvation," in Protestant parlance.

The major cognitive function of the plan is to make sense of the Decline, which consists of the spread of man-centered, progress-minded cosmologies from elites to popular culture, with the backing of a new, interventionist state. A prominent landmark in this context is said to be World War I. The war led to the demise of the Ottoman Empire and the abolition of the caliphate (1924), along with the enforced assimilation of Russian Jews under Soviet rule and elsewhere, the disruption of shtetl life, and the decline of the community rabbinate. In a hitherto optimistic, postmillennialist American Protestantism, the mass slaughter on the battlefields and the subsequent materialism of the Roaring Twenties bred a profound cultural pessimism. The sole dissenting note in interpreting this cataclysmic event can be found in the theology of Rabbi A. I. Kook, which inspires Gush Emunim. There the British conquest of Palestine and the Balfour Declaration (1917) were viewed as a hopeful sign of the times, heralding the Age of Redemption (*athalta di-ge'ula*)—a transitory phase from end of Exile to the messianic era.

Subject to divine control and "purposeful," history must produce miracles—and not only at the formative, sacred periods of the faith, as depicted in the Scriptures, but also in later periods up to and including the recent past. In a similar vein haredim celebrate the Allied victory over the Nazis and the escape of leading Halakhic authorities and Hasidic rabbis from Europe during World War II. The Gush as well as many American fundamentalists celebrate the establishment of the state of Israel and the Six Day War. Islamic radicals impute miraculous qualities to the demise of Nasser (1967–70).

The cognitive function of the past is inextricably entwined with its behavioral consequences: the past is a spur to action, especially when the past and present action are situated in conjunction with the future. This is true because the present is viewed as the end of a historical age. Here the symbolic capital provided by the tradition, and room for variations deemed legitimate within its mainstream, play perhaps even greater a role than in the past, when the long-term perspective was seen as a continuation of present realities, more or less in the same manner.

The dominant strand in American fundamentalism is premillennial and dispensationalist, a tradition imported from Ireland in the mid-nineteenth century and coming to prominence in the second decade of the twentieth century. Its message of messianic redemption following an imminent world-wide catastrophe (from which only the saved, "raptured" Christians would escape) reflected and responded to the downbeat, beleaguered mood in the independent Baptist churches. Their bleak diagnosis of the state of the world gained credibility when war in Europe dealt a heavy blow to the illusions of progress. The older and more optimistic postmillennialist tradition lost its hegemony but persisted in certain pockets such as the Reconstructionists. It still saw Redemption about to dawn, culminating eventually in the Second Coming, and called not just to wait for the messianic breakthrough to happen but to help in bringing it about.

Premillennialism is a strong incentive for focusing on personal salvation in the context of the coming Rapture, with the independent church serving as the support group. This theological outlook sets limits on sallies to the outside, which are geared to recruit new members (who may be among the raptured) and to improve the Christian quality of life in the immediate vicinity of the enclave, a sort of protective perimeter. Transforming the entire society tends to be viewed as an impossibility in this day and age. It can only come after the Tribulation is over; but there is no telling when this will be, even though this is definitely the last stage of the church age. Both the Rapture and the subsequent seven years of Tribulation are expected to occur at some indeterminate date. Such notions are hotly contested by the postmillennialists and denounced as passive and defeatist. They take an interest in collective, not just personal, salvation. Imposing Christian norms (i.e., banning abortion) on the whole of society through influence upon (and perhaps ultimately control of) government is, for them, quite feasible. Moreover, it carries the United States farther on the road to redemption.[90] But as we shall see, even premillennialists like Rev. Jerry Falwell can be jolted into social action by the fear that there will be no future generation of Christians to wait for the Lord if secular humanism continues its rampage.

The haredim, though they view themselves as living toward the end of the Age of Exile (*seifa de-galuta*) and within an indeterminate range of the footsteps of the Messiah, stick with the major, passive strand of Jewish messianism: one should always wait for the Messiah as if he were around the corner, yet expect him to come through divine agency alone (*it'aruta dl'eila*).

The haredi Jew is, in consequence, resigned to live outside history (and outside politics), for Jewish sovereignty can only be established when God performs the miracle of redemption and dispatches the Messiah. For all the tribulations characteristic of the end of the Age of Exile, including the Holocaust, they detect no signs that redemption is imminent. The Age of Exile may be rather protracted.[91] Only the Lubavitchers set forth a different cosmic calendar: the final moments of the Age of Exile are approaching, the sole condition that must still be fulfilled being a massive return to the faith *(teshuva)*. Human agency may help prompt the divine.

The pessimistic messianism of the haredim accounts for their denial of any theological significance for the state of Israel. In turn this denial has deep roots in their sense of alienation from its secularist lifestyle—another example of the "feedback loop." The denial likewise implies that it is useless to strive to impose Halakah upon all walks of life; the "state of the Jews" can become a "Jewish state" only when the Messiah comes. The optimistic counterpart in the Jewish context is represented by the Gush Emunim, who believe that one should exert oneself to hasten the arrival of the Messiah. In its more extreme variations, like the Jewish Underground of the early 1980s, this leads to virulent denunciations of passive messianism as sheepish and quietistic, a typical product of the Diasporic way of life; there is no place for such a mode in the great Land of Israel.

Divergence of diagnosis is involved here as much as theological controversy. For the Gush, inspired by the revamping of the activist mode by Rabbi Z. Y. Kook, the establishment of the state of Israel signifies the dawn of redemption. But in order to prove this assessment they had to resort to a theological innovation: there is a transitory phase between the end of Exile and the actual coming of the Messiah. This transitory stage, begun with the Zionist settlement of Palestine and consolidated in 1948, is already situated outside history. As an integral part of the redemption it is sacred, even though secular Jews are in charge (and Halakah is not implemented).

Different road maps make for different readings of unfolding events. The haredim saw the 1973 war, not without schadenfreude, as a punishing blow to Zionist "idolatry" of military might. For the Gush this was a setback on the way to redemption, after the huge step forward taken in 1967; it was accounted for by the insufficient effort made toward the settlement of the recently "liberated" parts of the Holy Land. The founding and rise of the Gush is closely linked with this "setback" and with what they saw as the defeatism prevalent in Israeli society in the wake of the Yom Kippur War. This conforms to a pattern discussed above: a bleak evaluation of the present spurs the development of an enclave. In Gush terms (and in line with their theological optimism) this was an *it'aruta dilteta,* an act catalyzing the process of redemption through human agency.

The fact that the place of messianism is much less prominent in Islamic living tradition endows the future time perspective, among Sunnis and Shi'ites, with a different texture. The messianic element is held in abeyance in almost all Sunni groups (much as it is in Catholicism). The only exception is the Takfir wa'l-Hijra sect in Egypt, which declared its leader, who was later executed, *Mahdi* (messiah). (This is the only case in all three traditions where a messiah is specifically designated. Even among the Lubavitchers the rebbe Schneerson was just rumored to be Him.) This idiosyncratic group, unlike the Reconstructionists or Gush Emunim, was furthermore anti-nomian, rejecting most of the Shari'a as evil. In any case, it is an exception that proves the rule. The messianic element is, on the whole, quite irrelevant to the Sunni discourse on delegitimation as well as to the reading of current events (and this is, again, equally true of Catholic radicals). Sunni radicals hold that the present order must be toppled in "normal" (nonmessianic) historical time and a new legitimate order—ushering in the application of the Shari'a—without awaiting the new messiah (or Mahdi).[92]

In this stance Sunni radicals are true heirs to the Sunni tradition, in which there is indeed a belief in a messiah who will come at the end of time and, after a struggle with the Antichrist, establish the realm of justice upon earth. But not only was this belief quite secondary, it has become in the course of the centuries virtually marginal. The great eleventh-century theologian al-Ghazali passes over it in silence, while the famous philosopher of history Ibn Khaldun (fourteenth-century) subjected it to a scathing critique.

Belief in the apocalypse was typical, though by no means prominent, among Sufis (mystics), and even there the context was in general quietistic—knowing that the Messiah was due to come enabled one to forbear suffering and injustice, sit tight, and do nothing but pray. While in the first two centuries of Islam there were Sunni apocalyptic revolts, this tradition was soon taken over and almost completely monopolized by the Shi'ites (or to be more precise: by the Isma'ili and Imamite branches). The few such Sunni revolts in later times erupted in peripheral Islamic countries (Algeria, Sudan) in an anticolonialist context and were the product of a subculture of marginal mystics and preachers. Such a subculture was soon to be completely erased by modernization, and with it died much of the spirit of apocalyptic activism.[93] Contrary to what the Arab left expected, messianism did not become the mainstay of a revolutionary tradition in the lands of Islam.[94]

None of the fissiparous groups that participated in the violent struggles within Sunni Islam ever raised a messianic banner—not even during the Algerian civil war of the 1990s, the first and second intifadas in Israel/Palestine, or during the terrorist wave that unfurled over Egypt in the mid-nineties.

Messianism is more important for the Shi'ites, especially the majority Imamite sect with its belief in a Hidden (twelfth) Imam "in occultation" since 941 and due to come back upon earth on judgment day and reestablish the rule of the House of 'Ali as well as the perfect application of Islamic law, and, hence, the rule of justice. This is seen as the coming vindication of Shi'ite suffering throughout history.[95]

This is a major Shi'ite myth, whereas the precept of raj'a (return to earth) of the Hidden Imam is accepted by most Shi'ites—with the exception of a few ecumenical thinkers[96] who wish not to hurt Sunni sensibilities—as a fundamental tenet. Yet the notion of a Hidden Imam operated from the early tenth century above all in a quietistic context. After all, the very use of this idea among Twelver (Imamite) Shi'ites was associated with the time of the worst Abbasid persecutions and tended to thwart Shi'ites from virtually suicidal insurrections, recommending them to suffer in silence and bide their time. This was its major function throughout most of Imamite history. Indeed, most of the important Shi'ite revolutionary movements came from the Isma'ili branch (e.g., the Qarmats, for whom the Mahdi was always steeped in an activistic lore with antinomian overtones).

Khomeini did not try his hand at infusing activism into Iranian beliefs in the Mahdi, judging, quite sensibly, that there was no great apocalyptic tension to be energized among the masses. In his major work, *Islamic Government* (1971), he criticizes the many Shi'ites who collaborate with the authorities based upon the premise that man must strive to achieve justice in the here and now, in this world from which the Imam is absent, and not wait "hundreds and perhaps even thousands of years" for the establishment of absolute justice by the Imam upon his return to earth. However, even if Khomeini did not stress the concept of Imam (or the Mahdi), his teaching repeatedly implies the principle that forms the boundary of the time frame in which he worked. (The fifth article of the Iranian constitution states that it will be valid "as long as the Twelfth Imam is absent.") Furthermore, Khomeini served as a *marja' al-taqlid* (source of imitation; highest religious authority) since the early 1960s, and his authority as such was defined as stemming from a delegation of authority for the sake of guardianship (*wilaya 'amma*) on behalf of the Hidden Imam. Only in this way could Khomeini transform the institution of marja' from a strictly religious function into one that is political as well. Some of his adepts who were inclined to literal interpretations would even claim that Khomeini was a mystical emanation issuing directly from the Mahdi and serving as vanguard for the Mahdi's return. It is this concept from which the title applied to Khomeini—but not to his successor, Ali Khamanei—*na'ib al-imam* (vicar of the [Hidden] Imam) is derived. Khomeini did try to emphasize that he was not imbued with the Hidden Imam's spiritual powers (especially not with *'isma*, infallibility), and that since in essence he was not different from other mortals, his rule was strictly functional (*wilaya i'tibariyya*). Nonetheless, the frame of reference and the basis for comparison is the Mahdi: the regime was measured against him, and the time allotted for it to rule was delimited by his eventual return. This was an important pillar of Khomeini's worldview, though not as crucial as *wilayat al-faqih* (guardianship of the jurist). It should therefore come as no surprise that the Hidden Imam's birthday (which falls on the fifteenth of Sha'ban) has always been one of the four major religious holidays in Iran (along with the 'Ashura and the birthdays of 'Ali and Husayn, each of which relate to the "foundation myth"). During this holiday, Khomeini used to extol the "return of the Imam-Mahdi in the End of the Days" in fervid speeches that received wide media coverage.

Eschatology is thus present in Shi'ite mythology but in a different fashion than among Christian Dominion theologians or Gush activists: no fervent expectation of an imminent End of Days, no computations of the expected date based on signs and miracles, no reading of any crisis (such as the Intifada) as part and parcel of the "pangs of redemption," no temptation "to force God's hand" and hasten the Redemption (as in the case of the Jewish Underground). It is true that at the affective level the Shi'ites do retain an eschatological undercurrent, although even in Iran a certain decline can be observed since Khomeini's death. It is mostly in embattled Shi'ite enclaves, such as among the Hizbullah in Lebanon, that one notes from time to time eruptions of messianic rhetoric, followed by computations of the frequency of lunar eclipses as signs of the times (*akhbar al-sa'ah*). Yet on the whole, much like with the Sunnis, the myth of the Shari'a, with its clear-cut orientation toward the past as the panacea for all social ills, reigns supreme among the Shi'ites, especially as the interpreters of the law, the ulama, lead the Shi'ite radicals and, in fact, constitute the revolutionary cadre.

Possessing the secret road map for the future is likely to empower the enclave member, fill him with a sense of orientation, enable him to "decipher" oncoming events. One can identify players in the world (or national) scene by their biblical codes: Russia, for American premillennialists, is the Kingdom of the North (or Gog), Libya is the Kingdom of the South (or

Magog).[97] Similar attempts can be heard in "national-haredi" yeshivot close to the Gush. Code names are pointers to the ultimate behavior and fate of the players. Deciphering them is evidently helpful for decision-making in conditions of uncertainty, that is, in molding risk perception and risk management strategies. As risk is a cultural construct, moral commitments do enter in its evaluation and in the lessons drawn from them.

The enclave tends to see itself as inherently fragile, given the ever-lurking outside. Its future is expected to be different from the present, most probably—in the short run, at least—for the worse (or worse preceding change for the better). The enclave must, hence, fear irreversible, involuntary, and hidden changes about which there is imperfect knowledge and little or no control. An enclave rarely discounts a piece of bad news about future events. And this explains its propensity to indulge in conspiracy theories as well as the shrill tone of its press in reporting current events.

Obsession with risk underlies the haredi view that Jews in the Exilic Age are eternally persecuted by hateful goyish nations, "a lamb surrounded by seventy wolves," harassed (at times oppressed) by obtuse if not hostile "apostate" Jews.[98] Both evil forces are powerful and have already brought catastrophes on the faithful (Holocaust, assimilation) and may perpetrate worse. The strategy must consist of risk avoidance (or risk minimization). There must be as little confrontation as possible (limiting, at times, the scope of the "sallies") and no provocation of the type that had cost the Jews the destruction of the Second Temple and the loss of sovereignty, ushering in the Exilic Age. This concept (known as the Three Oaths) makes the haredi parties, on the whole, adopt dovish attitudes to the Arab-Israeli conflict and denounce the Gush-affiliated Underground and the Temple Mount Faithful. Their prominent rabbis severely condemned their own hotheads, yeshiva students who in the early 1950s dynamited and set fire to shops and restaurants that broke the Shabbat, sold pork, and so forth. Nor is this a recent attitude. The concept of the Three Oaths is embedded in Talmudic literature (Tractate Ketuboth) and represents a major strand of Jewish thought and action all through the medieval and modern periods. It underlies the rejection of Zionism by Hasidic rabbis in the interwar era as a movement that breaks the commitment not to "take off the yoke of exile." Zionism's activism bothered them no less than its secularism. The passivity of these rabbis and their adepts vis-à-vis the Holocaust is to be accounted for, in part, by this same stance.

This is not to say that the haredim today renounce the hope that the Messiah may come at any moment and change this state of affairs (this is why they oppose the custom of the double tombstone, as it is uncertain that the living spouse will die before the Resurrection, which follows the Coming). Yet all that is in principle only. In actual fact, they do not bank on it and are not filled with intimations of the Messiah's approaching arrival.

The Lubavitchers, who do have such intimations, are the exceptions to this rule. Their future perspective is not just shorter, it is optimistic. Risks are of small magnitude or are to be compensated for by a redemption that is just around the corner. Risk taking is justified. Goyish threats are poohpoohed. The Lubavitcher rebbe was rigidly hawkish on holding on to Judea and Samaria, the sacred arena of redemption (although he recognized the state of Israel only de facto).

The imminent messianism of Gush Emunim is placed at the service of sacred entities: the Land of Israel and the state of Israel. What results is a total sacralization of politics, which reminds one of Dominion theologians or of Shi'ite thinkers in postrevolutionary Iran (the state has become sanctified now that it is in the hands of virtuous mullahs). Such a view is alien to haredi thought, in which politics is separate from their own sallies. (Sunnis and most Protestant fundamentalists would concur.) As the Gush is certain of the sanctity of its tools (arms, settlement), assured of oncoming success if only sufficient help from down below would be given to divine Providence, it is consequently quite cavalier about risk taking. The alternative is nothing short of catastrophic: loss of the historical opportunity to hold on forever to core areas of Eretz Yisrael and postponement of the Redemption for lack of determined human prodding. Such doom-laden arguments in the mouths of optimists are not bizarre; they are quite typical of enclaves that, fragile, tend to fluctuate between extremes. But what about incurring the wrath of the United States or Arab retaliation? The Gush responds that this is a reasonable price to pay for avoiding the catastrophe. Hence its opposition to the evacuation of part of Sinai and Golan (1974–75), the evacuation of the whole of Sinai (1979–82) and, above all, its insistence on the massive settlement of Judea and Samaria.

The hegemonic eschatology in North American fundamentalism—premillennial, pretribulationist—is pessimistic as to what awaits humankind, holding hope just for those individuals (144,000, by a literalist biblical accounting) who will be saved by the Rapture on the eve of the seven years of Tribulation preceding the Second Coming. Recruiting more people to the contingent of the saved and keeping them in an unpolluted milieu until the hour comes—this is the prime goal for the meantime, that short-range future that, in typical enclave fashion, is all they care for. Survival is not an easy task given the temptations, conspiracies, and ever insidious immoralities of modern society. Reducing contact with the latter—except for self-defensive sallies—helps diminish, maybe avoid, irreversible risks: defections, damage to the purity of the enclave. In short, this is a haredi-type strategy predicated upon a different symbolic capital.

The Reconstructionists, with their postmillennialism, present the flip side of the coin: the only way to avoid the far greater risk of living amid a de-Christianizing, profane modernity is to take some smaller risks, including launching a bid for power. This is just a short-term risk, much smaller than any damages that are bound to evolve if the current situation persists over the long haul. After all, victory for such a bid for dominion is practically certain: the time is ripe for miraculous divine intervention; redemption is about to unfold the thousand-year reign.

The type of messianism involved is not, however, the only perceptual context that determines the enclave's attitude toward risk taking. Consider the Islamic case. There is no doubt that some Shi'ite groups, such as the Iranian-Lebanese-Tunisian terrorist network brought to trial in France in 1990, as well as segments of the Hizbullah, are immersed in "Mahdi now" cosmology, seeing everywhere the telltale signs of "growing debauchery and chaos"; ready, much like Gush militants, to take risks in order to forestall graver dangers (i.e., "arrogant imperialist dominance") and facilitated by the return of the Mahdi. Yet on the whole Sunni and Shi'ite activists live in a world in which the Last Days are not taken as an operative eventuality during the course of their own lives. Those who resort to violent acts (the Jihad Organization, assassins of Sadat and, more recently, of the president of the Egyptian parliament) do so impelled by fear that the cancerous jahiliyya is spreading fast and is at the point of becoming irreversible. Emergency surgery is thus imperative. No reference to the End of Days is necessary here. (This also seems to be the logic motivating the majority in Hizbullah, logic shaped by anxieties bred out of the jungle life of Lebanon, where state and public order disappeared.) Nevertheless, the same jahiliyya diagnosis, coupled with a hard-nosed assessment of the resilience and repressive ingenuity of the state, drives most Sunni radicals to consider the risks of "holy violence" to be too great, leading to a head-on collision with a ruthless government. Jahiliyya, rather than being smashed, might win an even greater victory. Caught between a rock and a hard place, the radicals opt for retreat into the enclave community, shoring up their social and physical boundaries and from there branching out, as circumstances permit, into educational and welfare extensions and local political work (all based on the mosque as "immune space"), perhaps later, as in the case of the Algerian

Front Islamique du Salut (FIS), into national politics. We arrive, once again, at a haredi-type strategy, but with messianism not even secondary but marginal.

This supple, fluctuating kaleidoscope calls for some caution in the use of labels such as pre- or postmillennial, "messiah now" or "messiah in his own good time," and so forth. None of these labels is ineluctably entwined with a specific diagnosis (optimistic or pessimistic, for instance); none leads inexorably to just one type of risk perception or to a specific course of action. Feedback from reality, be it interpreted allegorically or factually, may elicit varying responses within the same enclave. Thus while most haredim conclude that until the Messiah comes there is no point in striving toward imposition of Halakah as state law in Israel, there are those, perhaps among the impatient young, who argue that given their growing political clout they should do it and thus improve life of klal Yisrael at the End of Exile.[99]

Moreover, feedback from reality may even modify the doctrinal stance regarding the future, albeit within certain parameters deemed by the enclave to be sacred. The growing conviction of Jerry Falwell, Pat Robertson, Randall Terry, and Tim LaHaye in the late seventies as to the possible emergence of a Moral Majority, likely to acquire hegemony in American politics and culture, made them introduce a "postmillennial window"[100] into their premillennialism. They assumed that the arrival of the millennium depended upon their activism. Tribulation would precede Rapture, not follow it. In consequence, one should act immediately in order to better American society, otherwise devastation would be so comprehensive as to hit the saved as well, and anyhow, it might be so cataclysmic as to render reconstruction extremely difficult. Only a daring bid for power, until then thought to be an un-Christian course of action, could save the day.

It is, of course, their scriptural and charismatic authority that empowered Falwell and his consorts to operate this exegetical legerdemain. The same goes for Gush Emunim, shaken as it was in the mid-1980s by its failure to stop through mass protest the evacuation of Yamit in Sinai (1982) and by the dismantling of the Underground (1984). An autonomous outgrowth of the Gush sought to hasten redemption and block further territorial concessions by murdering Palestinian mayors and plotting to blow up the mosque on the Temple Mount. The ensuing soul-searching in the Gush was intense: was it not presumptuous to assume that we know for certain God's messianic timetable? Was it not to commit the sin of arrogance to claim that we can prod Him to perform the miracle of redemption when we deem it most urgent?

Some of the Gush mentors, such as Rabbi Shlomo Aviner, while main-

taining allegiance to the Kook cosmology, reacted to this quandary by introducing new (or, they would claim, hitherto neglected) distinctions. These
distinctions were based, of course, as in Falwell's case, on proof texts—in
this case, mostly midrashic and kabbalistic ones. Aviner argues that Redemption is on the way, the Messiah will eventually come "even though
He may tarry," but man can neither know the timing nor can he hasten it
significantly by initiatives from below. All he can do is help prepare the
terrain by settlement in Judea and Samaria and immersion in the study of
the Torah (hence enhancing the role of the yeshivot), particularly the study
of portions of the Talmud related to the 292 precepts effective in messianic
times. (Aviner's yeshiva, ʿAteret Cohanim, in the Old City of Jerusalem, spe-
cializes in Temple service procedures.) Prepare the terrain so that all will
be ready when the hour cometh, but without alleging one can force God's
hand or fathom His plan. The doctrine is essentially preserved, yet the order
of priorities for action is reshuffled.

In much the same way but requiring no modification in its theological
premises, Comunione e Liberazione has passed from direct involvement in
the internal politics of the Christian Democratic Party to an emphasis on
welfare and educational work. The risks involved in the former strategy (loss
of members unhappy with their too-conservative positions, especially during the referenda on divorce and abortion) were enough to justify the switch
from "dominion"-type activity to "sallies." As Catholics invest relatively little in eschatology, Comunione e Liberazione did not need an adjustment
on this score. Past models (the Counter Reformation, the church's struggle
in late nineteenth century) were supple enough to remain.

So much for cosmological time. It is more arduous to examine attitudes
related to cosmological space. By that I mean space as learned, not as directly
experienced (the latter dubbed "operational"). In such a context, physical realities crucial for operational space—for example, contiguous areas
around mosque/synagogue/church creating a "sacred environment"—lose
much of their value. Areas physically distant may be perceived as structurally
near. Children in afternoon classes held in a Cairo mosque declared Bosnia-
Herzegovina, the Philippines, and Burma as "lands close to our heart" because of Muslim minorities persecuted there. Other than that they knew
nothing about these countries, not even what their majority religion was.
Haredi school children in Bʿnai Bʿrak easily found Poland and the Soviet
Union on a globe, pinpointing towns in which major Hasidic sects originated. But they were otherwise quite ignorant as to the geography of these
states. Jerry Falwell's moral (or imaginary) space refers above all to the two-
hundred-odd churches whose pastors are graduates of Liberty University—

the saved enclave in pagan America.[101] The Lefebvrists analogue is the network of more than two hundred like-minded communities in France, Germany, Switzerland, Austria, the United Kingdom, the United States, Argentina, and Brazil. The rest of the world gets barely a mention in the movement's press, unless it refers to the Communist bloc, which is outside the pale, the evil kingdom.

Cosmological space is not linear. One may not actually care for "apostate" neighbors, yet feel intense affinity with members of like-minded enclaves. The common model is that of concentric circles in diminishing status of spatial importance. "Egypt for me is this [al-Nur] mosque with its afternoon and evening school, its preschool and outpatient facilities," says a radical shaykh in northern Cairo. "This working-class area [al-Abbasiyya] where most of our members live is our immediate buffer. Beyond, I look at Egypt as a map studded by those mosques engaged in the same sacred work of changing Egyptian society from within. And beyond that? I do care for our long-suffering brethren in Palestine and in the Sudan. And beyond that, well, the whole dar al-Islam [abode of Islam, countries where Islam is the majority religion] at least in as much as it is populated by Muslims enraged by the jahiliyya and resolved to combat it."[102]

What strikes one in this telling interview is that, despite the shaykh's repugnance for the nation-state ideology of Sadat and Mubarak (a "polytheistic idolatry"),[103] Egypt is the outer circle he cares for most. Transforming Egyptian society (not dar al-Islam in general) is the maximum he can hope for. The division of dar al-Islam into territorial states is deplored but accepted as a fait accompli. It certainly helped that the radicals' cherished theologian, Ibn Taymiyya (d. 1328), had attempted to come to terms with the fact that dar al-Islam had been divided since the tenth century into territorial states. Yet even revolutionary Iran, which is not beholden to Ibn Taymiyya and has pan-Islamic aspirations, is suffused with commitment to Iranian patrimony. Defense of the independence and territorial integrity of Iran is a basic tenet of the 1979 constitution (article 9) as well as the program of the governing Islamic Republican Party. This conviction was certainly invigorated by the war with Iraq but was also directed against centrifugal tendencies among minorities (Azeris, Kurds). At a gut level, it is the expression of a powerful politicocultural tradition, rooted in territory and closely entwined, since the sixteenth century, with Shi'ism.[104] Even the Hizbullah, for all their admiration for Iran, have drawn up several scenarios describing their future as bounded by a Lebanese framework, despite the fact that the state is in poor shape. Hizbullah spiritual leader Fadlallah takes great care to point out that even in doctrinal matters the Iranian writ does not run in Lebanon (e.g., with regard to the interpretation of wilayat al-faqih).[105]

American fundamentalists see the United States as the third concentric circle of their "moral landscape," beyond their own independent church and the loose network of churches to which they belong (Baptist Convention, Liberty University graduates, etc.). America is of course endowed with a theological dimension (as the City on the Hill), a dimension usually irrelevant for Muslim movements (except for the Palestinian case; see below). The fourth concentric circle is the Middle East, with the Holy Land as its hub and the war theater of the Apocalypse. The prophetic landscape depicted in the Books of Ezekiel, Daniel, and Revelation saw its veracity confirmed by the strategic role of the Middle East in the international arena over the last quarter century. Cosmology has suddenly been endowed with a down-to-earth significance.[106]

When both theological time and space enter into close interplay, the affective dimension is greatly intensified. For Gush Emunim not only is Eretz Yisrael sacred and the center of creation, but Judea and Samaria are its backbone, with Jerusalem and, in it, the Temple Mount, at its very core. Small wonder that the extreme fringes of the Gush, the terrorist Underground, with its exalted messianism, highlighted the attachment to the core, even at the expense of settlement in the West Bank. Hence their 1984 plot to blow up the al-Aqsa and 'Umar mosques in order to "clear up" the terrain and prepare it for the building of the Third Temple when the Messiah comes, a plot predicated upon a kabbalistic critique of the attitudes of the mainstream Gush, which were said to prefer the "peel" (klippa, external dimension, in kabbalistic lingo), that is, the Western Wall, over the "inner core" (toch), that is, the Temple Mount. The Gush, it was argued, pays homage to the wall as a religionational symbol (accepted also by Zionist doves), while tolerating that the mount is "sullied" by the Islamic presence.[107] Not for the first time in Jewish history, such mystical views had practical consequences.

By a "mimetic desire effect" of the sort Rene Girard speaks about,[108] Gush Emunim cosmology and behavior produced its counterpart among the Palestinians. First came the renewed emphasis on Jerusalem (following the 1967 conquest by Israel) as a third holy city of Islam, a position based on the story of Muhammad's night journey and ascension (isra' wa-mi'raj). By the mid-1970s—in a mode replicating developments during the Counter Crusade of the twelfth to thirteenth century[109]—the city became essentially the focus of the sanctity of the whole of Palestine (the Blessed Land, Land of the Prophets, Land of the Night Journey). Later on, with the Intifada and the rise of the Hamas movement, an innovative concept was hatched out of this medieval framework: Palestine in its entirety is the *waqf* (religious endowment) of the Islamic umma and, in consequence, no part of it can be ceded to non-Muslims. The analogy, willy-nilly, with the idea of Great Israel—without which Judaism is "truncated" (*qetu*ʿ*a*)—is evident.[110]

Finally, what about the human agent operating within the confines of time and space? The Hafetz Haim seems to have said it all for his Christian and Muslim counterparts: "The whole world is topsy-turvy, our religion suffers persecutions, is vilified by infidels, ridiculed by apostates, *let alone that each and every one of us suffers from his own Evil Will*" (my emphasis).[111] Human nature is bad—though perfectible—and subject to constant infiltration of outside impurity. Of course female nature is weaker, enticing males and prone to be ensnared by consumerism—so runs the lament in enclaves in all three religions. The advice to the faithful is clear: always be on your guard, strive hard to bolster defenses against temptations, clean up your act by meditation and strict behavior. Any visitor listening to audiocassettes played by taxi drivers in Cairo and Jerusalem is likely to hear Shaykh ʿAbd al-Hamid Kishk or Rabbi Nissim Yagen dispensing such counsel. The visitor will not fail to detect in these sermons, alternately florid and homespun, the prevalence of terms like *yetzer*, *ta'va* (Hebrew: desire, passion), *hawa'* (Arabic synonym of *ta'va*). Before bracing oneself for the small jihad (*jihad asghar*) against disbelievers (i.e., Israel), the Arabic audiocassette intimates, one should throw oneself into the great jihad, the holy war against evil in one's own heart (*jihad akbar, jihad al-nafs*). Israel cannot be ready for the Messiah, says the Hebrew audiocassette, before the licentious imprint of Zionism is erased from Jewish hearts. All this reminds the listener of hellfire-and-brimstone sermons heard over the car radio in the American northeast and south. The Jim and Tammy Faye Bakker and Jimmy Swaggart cases were used there to illustrate the point.

The underlying assumption is always the same: there is a strong correlation, set and controlled by divine Providence, between the macro- and microspheres, the state of physical nature and human nature, society and morality. Social disorder is but a symptom of the individual's moral transgressions on the inside as well as on the outside (e.g., the decline of the traditional family in the United States, the spread of homosexuality and abortion, higher criminality, AIDS, lower economic performance, and lesser clout in world politics).[112] "Our problems are neither economic nor political, our problems are moral," chanted the Islamic demonstrators in Algeria during the Couscous Riots (fall 1988). Their firebrand preacher, ʿAli Belhadj, claimed later that the consecutive droughts in recent years were the result of sexual permissiveness, mixed education, soccer fever, and the video craze. Belhadj would be surprised to hear that the Gush-affiliated radio, Channel Seven, made that very claim for the Israeli drought in fall and winter 1990. The haredim, for their part, argued that the Intifada was the end product of "promiscuous" norms of secular schools. How different is this from Jim Bakker's groupies a year earlier in Charlotte, North Carolina, depicting Hurricane Hugo hitting their town as the Lord's punishment for the unjustified persecution of their minister?[113]

Yet human nature is capable of improvement. Acting upon this at home, both haredim and independent Baptists point as a guideline to the Proverbs verse, "He who spares the rod spoils the child." By extension, they seek to impose stringent regulations on behavior in schools, streets, swimming beaches, and malls subject to municipalities they control, as did mayors associated with the Algerian Front Islamique du Salut, brought to power in the landslide elections of June 1990. Some harmony between nature and society, society and the individual may be restored, provided the rotten inside is purged, outside influence barred, boundaries reimposed.

AUTHORITY AND EMPOWERMENT

While the enclave can be expected to be quite rigid in defense of its boundaries, I have noted above several cases that exhibit suppleness and room for innovation in legal matters as well as in eschatology. In all such cases it was not enough that this was done for a good cause, the better to ensure the survival (or flourishing) of the group. They always required that initiatives be taken on behalf of the leadership, whose authority was unquestioned.

What is this authority? To what extent is it a throwback to the past or an adjustment to modern challenges?

The enclave, to repeat, is predicated upon voluntary membership and upon the equality of the virtuous insiders (circumscribed by grids of gender and age). Yet these characteristics, combined, produce an unintended consequence: they hamper decision-making and render authority ambiguous. This is all the more acute as formal ranking and differentiated remuneration tend to be shunned (or minimized) for fear of defection. Who is, then, to constrain whom? How will virtue be maintained and strife avoided?

The solution to this quandary lies, in part, in the doctrine of the inerrancy of the authoritative text (and its approved commentaries), which takes pride of place in all the religious enclaves discussed in this essay: the

Scofield Bible; papal encyclicals and conciliar resolutions; the Talmud (and the codes based on it, notably the Shulkhan ʿArukh); the Qurʾan, Hadith (oral tradition), and Shariʿa. So central are these texts even to everyday life that enclave members resort to "bringing out the word," that is, random selection of a page in order to deduce instructions or omens for mundane choices and actions. The term is Protestant, but the custom appears in Jewish and Muslim enclaves as well. Of course, the major use of the texts is to set boundaries between virtue and vice, inside and outside. To function well they require some flesh-and-blood authority, preferably alive, to interpret them. For without interpretation—whether literal, allegorical, or otherwise—how can the text be applied to rapidly changing realities of our time? Still, this has to be done in a manner that will introduce as little institutional hierarchy as possible into the enclave, lest hierarchy disrupt that cherished asset, the intrinsic equality of the insiders.

In no area is the modern nature of the enclave more evident than with regard to authority, fashioned as it is in quite a novel way. Authority is usually vested in a small number of individuals (preferably one, at least for each local community of the enclave). Scholarship and formal training may play a role in the selection of the leader(s), but the crucial factor is charisma: that special heavenly grace (in Arabic *baraka*; in Hebrew *hesed elohi*) that sets one man (virtually never is it a woman) apart from the rest of the enclave members. That man is to combine virtue, decision-making ability, and mastery of the tradition. It is interesting that although Sayyid Qutb, the founder of Sunni radicalism, had considerable renown as a Qurʾanic scholar (the selections from his commentary, *Signposts on the Road,* is still a bestseller in Egypt), memoirs written by his disciples set in relief his personality traits (simplicity, stringency, courage) crowned by martyrdom at the gallows. As models for behavior on matters, large and small, from garb to the treatment of lapsed Muslims, the Sunni movement Tablighi Jamaʿat resorts less to the Qurʾan proper than to *The Garden of Pious Believers,* an anthology of Qurʾanic verses assembled by the nephew of the movement's founder, Muhammad Zakariya, and to hadiths telling about the Prophet Muhammad's life. Khomeini, despite his long career as scholar and teacher in a Qom madrasa, was never considered to possess towering intellectual acumen before he entered the political arena in 1962–63. His most popular book, *Islamic Government,* is based on lectures to theology students and retains a conversational style. His most effective medium, before and after the revolution, was sermons and talks (distributed on audiocassettes, later on television), delivered in a homespun style. These talks were reminiscent of the fables for which Hafetz Haim was famous in that they utilized an old-fashioned,

rural-provincial vocabulary. And while the founder of Comunione e Liberazione, Luigi Giussani, is the author of a number of theological treatises,
the handbook of the movement is his *Conversations* (long interviews with
a journalist). Members explain that his "luminosity" comes across better
there. American Protestantism is, of course, an even more clear-cut case,
given the role of televangelism (followed, at a distant second, by pamphlets
and books, some of which, like Hal Lindsey's bestseller *The Late Great Planet
Earth,* are written in science-fiction style).

The Lefebvre movement is due almost entirely to the initiative of its
founder and the verve of his sermons (taken to be the sole valid interpretation of the inerrant texts), as well as to his leadership style and organizational skills. Following his death (March 1991) supporters and observers
alike were keen to know whether the successor he had groomed for nine
years, Father Franz Schmidberger, would be able to carry his mantle. The
very survival of the movement was seen to depend on it. Similar questions
are raised today in Habad, and with lesser acuity in haredi circles in Israel,
by the demise of the Lubavitcher rebbe and of Rabbi Schach.

Charismatic authority was upgraded to the level of full-fledged (and
new) doctrine in haredi and Shiʿite circles. Faced with the decline of the
authority of the local community's rabbi *(mara de-atra)* throughout the
nineteenth century, the haredim developed, especially during the second
quarter of the twentieth, the concept of daʿas Torah: the authority of the
great Torah scholar *(gadol ba-Torah),* by virtue of his total immersion in the
scriptural-exegetical tradition as well as his model lifestyle and character,
to issue binding rulings, not just on purely Halakhic matters but likewise on
mundane issues of the day, including politics.[114] Each autonomous haredi
grouping *(khug,* i.e., circle) constituted around a major yeshiva or Hasidic
court has such a gadol at its head. The structure of the haredi world, which
leaves sufficient leeway for the various "circles," is, in consequence, a sort
of loose confederation of enclaves—not entirely unlike a network of independent Baptist churches (those grouped around the Southern Baptist Convention, Operation Rescue, Christian Voice, the Religious Round Table; or
churches shepherded by graduates of Liberty University) or Sunni jamaʿat
subscribing more or less to the same ideological variant (e.g., Tanzim al-
Jihad).[115] The major haredi confederation was institutionalized by Agudat
Yisrael in the 1930s with the establishment of the Council of Torah Sages,
comprising half a dozen or so yeshiva heads or Hasidic rabbis set forth by
the principal "circles" (with future changes decided by co-optation).[116] In
1992 there were, in fact, three such coordinating councils, mirroring the
split of the haredim into three large "confederations," each with its own

political party and educational system. Habad, who consider themselves a world apart with claims to superiority over the rest (they dub their rabbi President of the Generation), constitute a fourth such confederal structure, with the ʿEda Haredit, who reject daʿas Torah as a heretical innovation, being a fifth.[117] Within each council there may be one gadol whose daʿas Torah holds sway over the rest (for example, Rabbi E. M. Schach).

Within both the khug (circles) and the "confederation," the rabbi's authority is not just a matter of erudition. What makes his immersion in the Talmud so effective and awesome is the insights he has been endowed with by Providence (helping him evaluate current situations, future events, human nature), insights made all the more credible by his noble personality traits. Hagiography, whether written or oral, referring to dead or living rabbis, is the staple of haredi life, especially in social gatherings and off-the-cuff conversations.

Observers rightly point out that the yeshiva world has undergone a process of admorization (*Admor* is the honorific title of the Hasidic rabbi). And when one looks at the Muslim jamaʿat one notes likewise how closely the members' dependency upon their authority figure, the emir, resembles that of the *muridun* (groupies of a Sufi fraternity) and the *murshid* (mystical leader). Hagiography, again, is a major feature, as are rituals like the kissing of the emir's hand, touching the train of his mantle. All the more so as various jamaʿat have their origins in a Sufi milieu (e.g., the Naqshbandis in Turkey, Syria, and Egypt). Many are the jamaʿat that are indeed called after their emirs (Samawiyya, Shawqiyya, etc.), in the manner of the Sufi fraternity.

To come back to the yeshiva heads: as men who control the core ascetic groups who serve as models for the whole khug, they have transferred into their own hands decision-making powers (on matters political, economic, etc.) that since the Middle Ages had been in the hands of the prominent laity (*baʾale batim*).[118] The charismatic dimension of their power is best encapsulated in the doctrine of *emunat hakhamim*—belief in the sages without daring to question their rulings, or as it is sometimes dubbed, the Fifth Shulkhan ʾArukh (the Shulkhan, the major Halakhic code, has four parts).[119]

This doctrine was crystallized in these far-reaching terms in response to the Holocaust, which raised tough questions as to the perspicacity of the *gedolim* in prewar Eastern Europe who had resisted migration (especially to Palestine), and many of whom had escaped during the war (thanks to affidavits sent by American disciples), leaving their local communities behind.[120] And no wonder. For charismatic leadership finds it arduous to weather the crisis, as a result of which it appears as a manifest failure. Its very grace—the divine insight—is called in question. To bolster such a shaken authority, a sort of "escape route forward" was taken: da'as Torah was elevated to the stature of a fifth pillar of the faith, so to speak.

In actual fact, however, decision-making is heavily influenced by khug or 'asqanim (party organizers) who may not have any formal position but who carry weight either as wealthy laity or as shrewd manipulators and mediators with the outside.[121] Because the gadol depends on the organizer for his information as well as on his uncanny assessment of the "world," the latter's input may be crucial. The gadol is shielded, in part, by the fact that his governing—much like in the Shi'ite case—is not hands-on governing. He tries to intervene selectively and rarely.

Laity carries some weight even in the Lefebvre movement, where priests reign supreme. The archbishop's decision, in May 1988, to renege on the just-signed compromise agreement with the papal delegates—a decision that meant full-blown schism—was due to backlash from the lay associations that could not understand how one could retreat from some ardently defended positions, even in the face of a more conservative pope than the one they had rebelled against. Comunione e Liberazione, on the other hand, had risen in revolt against the collaboration of the Italian Catholic establishment, through the Christian Democrat Party, with the secularized state; therefore, laymen have always been paramount at all levels—laymen who enjoy, much like Giussani, considerable charisma.

In having developed by the mid-nineteenth century a hierarchy, the Shi'ites have the advantage over the haredim and the Sunnis. It was not, however, a Catholic-type hierarchy, for it was constituted of ulama (mullahs) graded by scholarly achievement, not by access to Grace. At the pinnacle of the hierarchy were located the "models of emulation" (Marja' al-taqlid). The maraji' possessed the authority to operate the ijtihad and overrule the lower levels. In principle, but not always in practice, they should be headed by a "supreme model" (marja' a'la); since 1962 this post has been unoccupied.

The authority wielded by this hierarchy, including the higher ranks (from mujtahid to marja'), extended solely to legal affairs. In matters political, they could at most advise and admonish the ruler, which in fact they did quite often as they were less dependent economically than their Sunni counterparts upon the government: they enjoyed a steady income from tithes donated by the believers (as a sort of material acknowledgment of their holiness) and from lands held in mortmain.

Khomeini's revolutionary contribution to Shi'ite thought consisted of the doctrine of wilayat al-faqih. He claimed that in the absence of the

Twelfth Imam governing powers lie in the hands of the mullahs who inherit from this descendent of ʿAli his political and legal—but not spiritual—authority. In a situation in which it is possible to reach some understanding with the ruler, the task of the mullahs is to castigate his aberrations so as to return him to the right path. Yet when the aberrations reach such proportions that accommodation is no longer possible—as was the case, said Khomeini, under the Pahlavi dynasty—the mullahs must take the reins of government into their own hands. This duty falls in particular upon mujtahidun (authorities in matters of jurisprudence) and the marajiʿ. One of the latter, the virtuous jurist (*faqih*) would serve as the apex: in him would be vested not merely religious authority but also political rule (*wilaya, ʿamma*, a concept that originally referred to the authority of the Hidden Imam). The ulama were thus supposed to constitute the nucleus of the revolutionary vanguard to be led by the mujtahidun (ayatollahs), with the virtuous faqih at their head. The faqih mantle devolved upon Khomeini's shoulders almost as a matter of course, although he was just one of six marajiʿ: first, because he conceived the whole doctrine, and, second, because his disciples (mostly mullahs who had been his students in Qom, or later in Najaf, his place of exile) formed a sort of circle or nebula that was to constitute the revolutionary cadre (later, the Islamic Republican Party).[122]

In 1979 Khomeini was elected faqih by the Council of Experts, set up by the new Iranian constitution, and placed above the president of the republic. In actual fact, much like the haredi sages, his was not a hands-on government. He would intervene in matters deemed crucial (certain appointments and demotions, the decree against Rushdie) or in order to break the stalemate within the ayatollah-dominated political elite (on nationalization of land, right to strike, ceasefire with Iraq, etc.). Nevertheless, toward the end of his life (January 1988) he extended the scope of the doctrine, claiming for the faqih the absolute governance of the Prophet (*wilayat al-faqih al-mutlaqa*), that is, the right to overrule or suspend the Shariʿa itself on matters judged vital to the survival of the Islamic Republic, that "liberated portion of dar-al-Islam," whose survival will determine the fate of this religion.[123]

The wilayat al-faqih doctrine is accepted, though not necessarily in its latest version, by most Shiʿite militants in Arab lands as well. The blueprint for a Lebanese Islamic republic drawn up by Hizbullah sees it, for instance, headed by a council of ulama.[124]

Yet there is no mistaking it: Khomeini's death dealt a heavy blow to the charismatic facet of the faqih institution, due to the paler personality of his successor, Ali Khamenei, who can likewise be faulted for his scholarly record (he has not presented the *risala* [book-length thesis] required for the award of great ayatollah, the rank just under marja'). Significantly enough, Khamenei is dubbed commander (*qa'id*) of the revolution, as distinguished from Khomeini, who is still called leader (*za'im*) of the revolution. Khamenei's personal relationship to his predecessor is part of his legitimacy: he is defined as a "brother (or successor) of Ruh Allah [Khomeini]."[125] The latter's rulings (and political testament) are to this day amply discussed in sections headlined the "Method [or Line] of the Imam." Indeed, the popular title vicar of the [Hidden] Imam (na'ib al-imam) was not transferred to Khamenei, and troops on parade swear allegiance both to the present faqih and to the tomb of his predecessor.

This is reminiscent of the late Habad rebbe manifestly sharing his authority with the former one by referring to his rulings and to messages relayed to his tomb.[126] In Gush Emunim, in the absence of any mechanism of succession, the charismatic authority of Rabbi Kook the Younger dissipated after his death. A collective and rather split leadership took his place. Since the crisis of the Underground in 1983–84, the leadership is virtually eclipsed by various settlement bodies and their elected officials.

Without the benefit of a doctrinal innovation, U.S. fundamentalists responded to the authority challenge by raising the status of the pastor at the expense of lay leaders. His is, however, a hands-on government (including finances) assisted by lay appointees. The ingredients of authority are much the same as those referred to above: a shepherd elected by the Lord to lead the flock, virtuous personality traits, biblical scholarship.[127] All three come together in his touted ability to make the right ruling out of a page of Scriptures opened at random. The pastor's unquestioned authority—if and when called in question this would lead (as among the haredim) to strife and splits—is rendered manifest by symbols: the "sacred desk" (pulpit), the nonparticipatory nature of the sermon itself.

Charismatic authority among the Sunnis is cut from a different cloth. Their ulama have never enjoyed any spiritual status except that which their erudition confers upon them; they have had throughout history nothing to match the affiliation of Shi'ite ulama to the Hidden (Twelfth) Imam. The very hadith, "The ulama are the heirs of the prophets," interpreted by the Shi'ites to represent this affiliation, meant in Sunni gloss just the duty of the ulama to provide moral guidance for the community. Furthermore, the ulama have never enjoyed the status accorded their Shi'ite counterparts and have thus been more reluctant to be audacious toward the powers that be. The Sunni sages have actually been instilled with a feeling of subservience with regard to the state, an attitude shaped by the traumatic events of the civil war of early Islam (644–750). The ulama of this formative era concluded that it was incumbent to avoid anarchy at almost any cost. As far as they were concerned, even a bad Muslim ruler (and the latter had always been Sunni, like the ulama) was preferable to chaos.[128]

It is no wonder that Sunni radicalism did not spring from the midst of the ulama and that radicals tend to loath the whole ulama stratum for legitimating the powers that be, even when they trample over religious injunctions; this accusation was of particular salience as the interventionist character of the modern Muslim state was seen as reducing the scope of civil society where Islam had held sway.

Sunni radical leaders tend, in consequence, to be recruited from the ranks of the laity, and even among activists, shaykhs are a rarity.[129] Some of these laypeople were intellectuals of high caliber (for example, the Egyptian Sayyid Qutb, the Indian Maulana Maududi) suffused with modern and traditional culture. It was they who transformed Sunni political theory from an accommodationist to a revolutionary orientation, ready to confront the "apostate" regimes and, if need be, to topple them and seize power. Other lay intellectuals, such as the Moroccan Abd al-Salam Yasin, contributed a reasoned critique of modern ideologies—in the manner of Jewish "returnees to the faith" like Nathan Birnbaum and Moshe Scheinfeld—and helped fight for the hearts and minds of youth lured by Marxism and existentialism.

Inevitably this makes for a much more decentralized organizational framework, for there is no hierarchy of mullahs available, devoted to a particular grand ayatollah or marjaʻ. What one gets is a plethora (or nebula) of jamaʻat. The *amir al-jamaʻa* (lay leader) in Arab lands, Turkey, and Pakistan tends to be an autodidact in matters religious, with no great intellectual acumen. Trained more often than not as engineer, doctor, or agronomist,[130] he may still have a definite advantage over his quite ignorant disciples—usually students in scientific disciplines—who depend on him for those scraps of religious knowledge they have acquired perhaps on top of the little they had imbibed at home. (In the loose and fluid Tabligh movements even this type of intellectual dimension of leadership is irrelevant, for, much like the Pentecostalists, they favor "heart knowledge" over "head knowledge.")

The upshot is leadership that relies heavily on the power of personality and rhetorical skills, thus explaining why Sunni groups are characterized by a Sufi-style murshid/murid relationship. Splits result here more often from a personal challenge to the leadership than from an ideological controversy.

In a way splits are the staple of life within an enclave. Addicted as it is to homogeneity and to equality in purity, a "loyal opposition" has no place there. Any opposition is bound to be accused of treachery and become the object of witch-hunts and ostracism, liable ultimately to be "excised" (the latter term, borrowed from the King James Bible, exists in Protestant usage but has analogues among Sunnis, Shiʿites, and haredim). The sequels of splits, whether recent or long-standing, are the vituperation between "confederations" (disciples of Schach against Lubavitchers, Takfir against other jamaʿat). These consume a lot of energy, generate much heat, and are sometimes more poisonous than invectives directed at secularists. Yet splits are ultimately functional, for they help preserve equality and assure that decision-making can take place. In some situations, however, such as the Algerian civil war of the 1990s, a cycle of splits within splits unfolded virtually ad absurdum, weakening significantly the overall Islamist revolt.

Even without internal squabbles over authority, life inside the enclave is not all sweetness and light, as its denizens would like the outside to believe. Grumbling, bickering, and envious calumny are the price one pays for the ideal of equality in virtue, as they serve too as means for enforcing conformity and for nipping in the bud any formal distinctions.[131] It is not in vain that the Hafetz Haim, fully aware of the claustrophobic, hothouse atmosphere of the enclave and influenced by the late nineteenth-century Mussar (ethics) movement, dedicated a major essay to slanderous gossip (leshon haraʿ), tagged as an insidious vice of the kehillah. That this essay has been and still is a bestseller and provides the topic for many a sermon and adult education class indicates its relevancy.[132] One encounters the same concern in talking to members of jamaʿat, perusing their press, and listening to audiocassettes of preachers such as Kishk, al-Mahalawi, and al-Qattan.

An air of conflict and ambiguity envelops relations of authority within the enclaves. But this is compensated to some extent by the empowerment of its members. Members possess a secret road map with regard to past and future, they know where they are located in space (operational and cosmological), and they hold firm answers on questions related to nature (human and physical). Their behavior is regulated, but in an equitable manner with other enclave members and not just for the benefit of other human beings (as happens, they claim, in other forms of organization). All this is, rather, for a higher entity. Within the face-to-face structures that form the hub of life, members are thus kept virtuous, on a par with other insiders, superior to all outsiders. They have no human master except for one (at most several) gurulike figure, whose unique, virtually out-of-this-world, qualities legitimate his position.

One may hazard a guess that this may account for the particular appeal such movements have for people who find themselves in a social context that is, structurally, the very opposite of an enclave—subordination. Individuals living in such a context are severely constrained, in an inegalitarian manner, as to how they behave, usually in terms of the category (or rank) they are assigned to; yet they do not enjoy the protection and privileges of group membership. They are manipulated, peripheral to all decisions that may determine their destiny, and they have a limited scope for forming alliances. Consequently they are isolated, passive, and conformist. Such people are perhaps not blatantly oppressed or deprived but certainly alienated.[133] Examples abound. American suburbanite commuters feel stuck at midlevel in large corporate organizations. Recent migrants, from small town to urban sprawl in the American South, from villages to the shantytowns of Tehran or Cairo, from the Italian south to Milan or Turin, feel the strain of displacement, as do Holocaust survivors and Moroccan immigrants in Israel, whose old reference groups have been disrupted. Other examples include students in huge, anonymous, congested, and understaffed universities in Italy, Algeria, Iran, and Egypt, who on top of their atomized predicament suffer anxiety as to the likely future awaiting them—as members of the lumpenproletariat of diploma holders. What they also have in common is that they figure prominently among recruits to the enclaves discussed in this essay.

The reason may be that a major strategy for extricating oneself from the manipulated/alienated context is to move into one diametrically opposed: you shed your worst constraint—isolation and subordination to a large and impersonal structure—and you gain what you lacked most, group identity and insertion in a sociability network. Isolates—that is, high grid/low group individuals—have restricted choices. It follows that they have nothing to lose by joining the enclave.

When U.S. fundamentalists fulminate against the bankruptcy of the federally controlled welfare state; or when the members of Comunione e Liberazione decry the inept government bureaucracy captive to political clientelism and big business vested interests; when Islamic jama'at lament the alliance of the all-intrusive state and the economic-opening profiteers linked to multinationals—their message falls on ready ears.[134] Ears are particularly attentive among the multitude of people trapped within the lower ranks of huge, impersonal modern institutions (or dependent upon the benefits thereof). The ideal of comunione, fellowship, khavrusa, or jama'a may mean here not just human warmth, face-to-face interaction, and equality in virtue; it may signify the lessening of outside constraints and a measure of self-determination. Human solidarity, or comunione, becomes, as in the Comunione e Liberazione vision, both the social ideal one hopes to implement one day for society at large as well as a mode of life actually achieved within the group (or countersociety); a mode that satisfies intrinsic needs of the members.[135]

The antistate, anti–big-structures message gains in credibility to the extent that there is a growing consciousness in the society at large that these institutions function badly. Yet the message, couched as it is in lingo and concepts building upon a certain monotheistic tradition, requires that its target population be somewhat familiar with this tradition. This sets no significant limits in Muslim countries where in-depth secularization (and the resulting profanization) is still rather circumscribed. In other traditions this would mean that, among people trapped in the atomized social context, a prime target would be U.S. evangelicals, Catholic traditionalists in France and Germany, the Israeli national religious milieu, recent transplants from the Italian south, and so on. Would it be justified to speak of "black-diaper babies"?

The above is suggested as a sort of speculative coda and would require empirical research. Still, as long as large, impersonal modern institutions endure (with their attendant dysfunctions), that residual category—the isolated and the manipulated—is likely to grow.

May this indeed create a huge pool of potential recruits for enclaves of all kinds, including fundamentalist ones?

IN FLUX

A culture is in process of constant negotiation, *within* its membership and *between* its members and the outside. The enclave should not be viewed as static but rather as a shifting pattern that tends, if successful, toward low grid constraints (category, rank, function) and high group constraints imposed upon members' behavior and perceptions. Shifting and almost never static, both grid and group are in danger of moving each in the opposite direction (high and low, respectively).

The group dimension risks being lowered due to the difficulty of maintaining the boundary in the gray area discussed above. Separating oneself from a blatant secularist, be he atheist or agnostic, is relatively easy. It is more arduous to distinguish oneself from the lukewarm traditionalist, all the more so as many enclave members have relatives, neighbors, and friends among the latter. Behavioral requirements may be useful. Avoiding eating and praying with or visiting lax family members or playing with their children is a protective measure.

A hostile hegemonic society further facilitates separation, yet when that society turns more accommodating, when religion becomes "in" (as happened in Israel from the late sixties), the boundary is harder to maintain. An outside that goes out of its way to establish a dialogue, to be considerate, suffocates the dissenter with kindness. Dependence upon federal and state subsidies made fundamentalist schools in the United States more amenable to pressure and more mindful (and understanding) of the concerns of the authorities. The total refusal of any subsidy, as practiced by Bob Jones University, may be the only way out but one not easily taken. Enduring persecution is a better guarantee of purity (though not of size). Such persecution barely exists in the West, but in the Third World it may be lethal, leading to the physical elimination of the enclave (as happened to the Syrian Muslim Brotherhood in 1982 and to the Iraqi Shi'ite militants in 1980 and again in 1991). A situation of simmering ethnoreligious conflict, however, is a boon for the enclave (as in Israel/Palestine, India, Afghanistan). The Other, at least, is an infidel, hence clearly demarcated; all the more so if he is uniform. He can generate a powerful and lasting hostility.

The nature of the modern, open market society further complicates matters. Unlike premodern groups, such as the Amish, the fundamentalist enclaves are located in urban surroundings or in suburban sprawls and are thus rarely self-sufficient. They establish certain economic niches that facilitate group cohesion, (e.g., the New York diamond trade, electronics retail), but more often than not many members (usually male) work in various sectors and locations. Not only may they be easily "tempted," given human nature as posited by the enclave, but behavioral requirements are harder to keep and less subject to social control. Outside norms (in consumption, entertainment) creep in casually. Vestmental distinguishing marks may help, but just up to a point. Even residential separation can be difficult to maintain. The guards on the "wall of virtue" are lowered, as is the group dimension.

The grid dimension is the hostage of the material success of the enclave. Economic achievements imperil the austerity and genteel poverty upon which the enclave prides itself. Furthermore, material success creates grids or ranks by wealth and position in the society at large, which might eclipse the equality to which the group aspires. Wealthy laypeople may get some sway over the pastor. As contacts with a more benevolent outside environment develop, members of the enclave who are more conversant with outside discourse acquire a special rank as mediators (Egyptian Islamic bankers or members of parliament, for instance). Envy, the deadly sin most typical of an enclave, has thus a fertile ground, fed by flesh-and-blood discrepancies with the egalitarian ideal—discrepancies that have nothing to do with the "legitimate" ranking created by ultrapiety or meritocratic achievement in studying the Scriptures or in fighting the evil outside. Gossip, envy's poisonous weapon, has a field day. Splits and squabbles (inter- and intragroup) become more frequent and more venomous than ever, as material considerations interlock with (or masquerade behind) ideological arguments. Beyond a certain threshold, intragroup splits become dysfunctional.

When a prophecy comes true—when the enclave succeeds—the dangers of instability and decline lurk. When a prophecy fails—the Messiah does not arrive (for Habad in 1992)—a situation almost as potentially deleterious occurs. Or when victory, predicted on the basis of the divine road map, eludes the enclave, decline may threaten to set in. When the electoral triumph of the Islamic Salvation Front (FIS) was canceled by the Algerian army in 1991–92, the enclave was smashed and splintered into mindlessly violent fragments.

Moreover, as the enclaves become richer or more powerful, they tend to rely less on moral suasion and more upon the manipulation of members' dependency through material rewards, such as scholarships for yeshiva students, which the group gets from rich benefactors or from the state. The group thus moves downgrid, that is, toward a loosening of those constraints that govern interaction within a social category. It may slide even farther when membership grows, either due to mass recruitment or to success in retaining members, be it through conviction or dependency (as in the case of haredi students offered draft deferral as long as they are in school and who are not taught any modern subjects or given vocational training). A large membership requires a more differentiated governance body, such as a hierarchy. In the late 1990s and the first years of the new century, voices from within the haredi community suggested that the price of their relative prosperity (for the first time, many of them had their own apartments) was a new class structure, at the top of which are those who are involved in high-tech and other commercial initiatives, the middle level being teachers and religious functionaries. At the bottom of the economic scale are those who are supposed to be elites in terms of status—the yeshiva students, followed by a lumpenproletariat of unskilled workers employed in occasional labor.

Mindful of the need to arrest slippage, enclaves strive to keep hierarchies as small as possible. They even develop new, organizational strategies like the nebula or confederation—that is, a decentralized network of enclaves coordinated by a bureaucracy. The latter may sometimes be headed by a charismatic figure capable of cutting through layers of the bureaucracy and serving as a focal point for the rank and file. This has been the case with certain Islamic jama'at, in haredi circles, and in Falwell's and Robertson's networks (but not in the Southern Baptist Convention). Islamic militants like to describe this structure as resembling "a bunch of grapes."

The nebula is based on a fragile compromise, however, for it introduces the hierarchic mode. Try as they may to trim the bureaucracy down to size, the fundamentalists always run the risk of seeing this body take over the autonomous cells, and thus they also risk dealing a heavy blow to members' motivation. The peril grows in proportion to the expansion of the hierarchy's control over material resources and social rewards. In an insurgency movement such as Hamas, of course, grids and compartmentalization are necessarily tighter.

Depending upon a charismatic authority is a tricky proposition. A leader may die with no successor cut from the same cloth. Kahane's death indeed dealt a heavy blow to Kach; the Lubavitcher rebbe's demise haunts his disciples, as he is childless. A leader may be replaced by a pallid bureaucrat or by one eclipsed by a powerful bureaucracy. Opposition to the successor may bring about splits, which inevitably involve loss of membership and/ or waste of time and energy in fights with other "illegitimate" enclaves and their leaders. This is often the case in Islamic jama'at.

The charismatic figure may likewise be eclipsed by the rise of entrepreneurial, competitive market-type success within the enclave (e.g., rich entrepreneurs gaining power over Agudah-haredi rabbis). Such success might confer upon rising individualists (who are, by definition, low group) a measure of authority. Obviously, this may rarely happen when an enclave is subject to persecution—a situation that encourages austerity, decentralization, and compartmentalization. Adversity has its advantages.

An enclave subject to either or both of these developments—downgroup and upgrid—is likely to lose its religious specificity, become less of an enclave, decline, and even die out. It may introduce outside norms and perceptions accommodating the hegemonic society, as in the case of some haredim becoming a-Zionist rather than anti-Zionist; or Muslim Brothers diluting their opposition to the Jordanian "secularist-minded" state as they are sucked into its political process; or as in the case of corruption and conspicuous consumption spreading through Islamic or haredi banks and enterprises. The enclave may also lose members: they may drift into an outside society as separation landmarks get blurred; or they may defect, as former isolates are disappointed by not finding in the enclave that absence of grid controls and/or solidarity they desired.

The fiery Algerian preacher, 'Ali Belhadj, who remained popular during his imprisonment through audiocassettes of his sermons, never tired of repeating this theme: maintaining the cohesion and purity of the jamaʿa (enclave) is an arduous and everyday task. Before setting upon the "small jihad" against society at large, as he put it, one must engage in the "great jihad" to cleanse one's own heart and group. Jihad, comments Belhadj, means constant struggle. It is a full-time job.[136]

CHAPTER 2

FUNDAMENTALISM: GENUS AND SPECIES

The fundamentalist movements of the enclaves we have just examined emerged from the Abrahamic faiths—Judaism, Christianity, and Islam. We identify these movements as "unmixed" religious movements—movements composed initially of true believers, whose main interest is the protection of a religious way of life. We contrast such movements with ethnoreligious and nationalist movements, which often include a religious element but have "mixed" memberships and goals and seek territorial and political gains on behalf of an ethnic or nationalist bloc. Though Abrahamic fundamentalisms may indeed have ethnonationalist goals (e.g., the Palestinian Islamic Jihad, Hamas, the Jewish Gush Emunim, Sikhs), their primary base is in religion.

Our second category includes Hindu and Buddhist movements that are based at least as much on ethnonationalism as on religion. In such cases racial, ethnic, and religious goals are commingled, and movements called fundamentalist in the media, are actually *syncretic* and often imitative of Abrahamic movements.

Finally, in the analysis that follows we have included a variety of other movements that have been identified as fundamentalist by the media because of their religious trappings, militance, and visibility. These movements do not qualify as fundamentalisms by our definition, however, because they do not originate in reaction to secularization and the marginalization of religion, and they do not strive to create a religious alternative to secular structures and institutions. Such movements include various forms of Pentecostalism in Latin America and the Tablighi Jamaat, the Muslim revivalist movement now spread around the world.

It is also necessary to explain our principles of exclusion. Why are the East Asian religions not included in what follows? Whereas Confucian revivalism in Japan, South Korea, Taiwan, Singapore, and elsewhere in East Asia is concerned with affirming the validity of Confucian concepts of family, community, conduct, authority, and the like, it is more in the nature of a constructive critique of modernity led by intellectuals than a mobilized and militant confrontation.[1] The "new religions" of Japan, while by and large supportive of traditional family values and critical of Westernization, are also not included in our sample for similar reasons.[2]

Nor do religious cults belong in a study of fundamentalisms, which emerge from multigenerational organized religions. Cult members pledge obedience to an individual rather than a religious tradition or organized religious body. Their devotion is often centered on a charismatic figure who claims special (sometimes divine) status and therefore exempts himself from the ordinary constraints of religious law, Scripture, and tradition: Prophecy is fulfilled in him. David Koresh, the leader of the Branch Davidians who died in the 1993 confrontation with federal officers in Waco, Texas, was such a figure. So, too, was Chizuo Matsumoto, the partially blind owner of a chain of yoga schools in Japan. In 1987, after returning from a trip to the Himalayas with a message from God that he had been chosen to "lead God's army," Matsumoto changed his name to Shoko Asahara and founded Aum Shinrikyo (Aum "Supreme Truth" sect), a highly idiosyncratic mixture of Buddhism and Hinduism fused with notions of apocalyptic redemption.

Cult violence tends to follow one of two patterns. Caught up in fervid anticipation of the day of fulfillment, cult members turn inward upon themselves, performing ritual suicides (as in the case of Jonestown, Guyana) or inciting apocalyptic confrontation with the forces of evil (as in Waco). At the other extreme, cult members foment indiscriminate violence against unsuspecting bystanders, as Aum Shinrikyo did by releasing deadly nerve gas in the Tokyo underground subway in March 1995, killing a dozen commuters and injuring nearly four thousand others. Fundamentalist movements and ethnoreligious nationalists, by contrast, are willing to sacrifice their own members, but they do so in pursuit of a concrete political goal (e.g., implementation of religious law, political change favorable to the ethnic group). Neither self-annihilation nor indiscriminate violence (which might incite massive retaliation) is in the best interests of such movements, for survival over the long term is essential to achieving their goals.[3]

Finally, we must specify what we mean by a "case" when we speak, for example, of the Hamas, the Jamaʿat-i-Islami, or the Hizbullah; the U.S. Protestants, the Italian Comunione e Liberazione; the Jewish haredim,

Habad, or Gush Emunim; the Hindu Rashtriya Svayamsevak Sangh (RSS), Sikh Radicals, or Sinhala Buddhists. These are actually plural entities that together make up "movements" consisting variously of congregations, schools, yeshivas, mosques, monasteries, associations, cells of various kinds, and supporting groups and communities. Despite variations in organizational structure, each of these entities contains elements of what we are here calling a movement: a shared ideology; recognized leadership, whether single or multiple; shared resources; and some measure of operational coordination.[4]

The Properties of Fundamentalism

While fundamentalists claim to be upholding orthodoxy (right belief) or orthopraxis (right behavior) and to be defending and conserving religious traditions and traditional ways of life from erosion, they do so by crafting new methods, formulating new ideologies, and adopting the latest processes and organizational structures. Some of these new methods, structures, ideologies, and processes seem to be in direct violation of the actual historical beliefs, interpretive practices, and moral behaviors of earlier generations— or to be, at the least, a significant departure from these precedents, as well as from the praxis of contemporary conservative or orthodox believers. Indeed, fundamentalists often find fault with fellow believers who want to conserve the tradition but are not willing to develop innovative ways of fighting back against the forces of erosion. In other words, fundamentalists argue that to be "merely" a conservative or a traditionalist in these threatening times is not enough.

At the same time, fundamentalists would reject the suggestion that they are doing something radically new; a crucial element of their rhetoric and self-understanding is the assertion that their innovative programs are based on the authority of the sacred past, whether that past be represented in a privileged text or tradition or in the teaching of a charismatic or official leader. Fundamentalists are neither restorationists nor primitivists—that is, they do not wish to return society to the conditions "wherein the greatest excellence and happiness existed at the fount of time," nor are they marked by a special or distinctive longing for "a simpler, less complex world."[5] They are nonetheless careful to demonstrate the continuity between their programs and teachings and the received wisdom of their religious heritage. A pronounced rootedness in Scripture and/or "purified" tradition, coupled with a reluctance to embrace New Age philosophies or Spirit-inspired new revelations, characterizes fundamentalism as a religious mode. Thus Christian fundamentalists, strictly speaking, do not belong to Pentecostal churches or movements, which rely heavily on the immediate leading of the Holy Spirit; similarly, one would not expect Sufi orders to produce Muslim fundamentalists, given the former's emphasis on mystical experience as opposed to religiolegal revelation.

Nonetheless, the twentieth century was characterized by religious syncretism, and that blending of influences affects even conservative movements known for their boundary maintenance. Thus we see new expressions of fundamentalism in which Christian Pentecostals and Bible-believing fundamentalists make common cause for political purposes; or, in which members of Sufi orders may in fact swell the ranks of fundamentalist movements; or, in which Hindu nationalists borrow religious structures and concepts from the Abrahamic religions.

From our study of the enclave cultures we distinguish nine characteristics of fundamentalism—five ideological and four organizational.

IDEOLOGICAL CHARACTERISTICS OF FUNDAMENTALISM

Reactivity to the Marginalization of Religion

Fundamentalism is reactive. Fundamentalist movements form in reaction to, and in defense against, the processes and consequences of secularization and modernization which have penetrated the larger religious community. Protestants, Catholics, Muslims, Jews, Hindus, Sikhs and Buddhists are losing their members to the secular world outright or to relativism (the assumption that any given religion is culture-bound and thus relatively true or false), which leads, fundamentalists believe, to the same end: the erosion and displacement of true religion. Fundamentalism is a militant effort to counteract this trend.

What is being reacted against may include other consequences of secularization and relativism; some movements may be reacting to heightened ethnic or religious pluralism, for example, or to competing ideologies of nation. But to qualify as "pure" fundamentalism in our understanding, a movement must be concerned first with the erosion of religion and its proper role in society. It must, therefore, be protecting some religious content, some set of traditional cosmological beliefs and associated norms of conduct. *This defense of religion is the sine qua non of fundamentalism; without it, a movement may not properly be labeled fundamentalist.*

The four additional ideological and four organizational characteristics discussed below also qualify as defining characteristics of fundamentalism as a social movement, and a movement must manifest a sufficient number of these as well—if not every single one of them in every case—in order to qualify as fundamentalist movement. Reactivity to the marginalization of religion, however, cannot be absent from a fundamentalist movement as its original impulse and a recurring reference. Even in the later stages fundamentalist movements will remain beholden in various ways to that original impulse, even if other pressing concerns challenge it for priority in the later stages of the movement's development.

A movement may seek to gain control of the state in order to resacralize or desecularize that powerful instrumentality. The movement may be ethnoreligiously preemptive—that is, it may seek to limit, suppress, or expel from the national community other ethnoreligious groupings (e.g., the Hindus versus the Muslims in India, or the Sinhala Buddhists versus the Hindu Tamils in Sri Lanka). Or the movement may be defensive—that is, it may seek to survive in the face of majority preemptive ethnoreligious movements (e.g., the Christians of south India versus the Hindus, or the Palestinian Muslims versus the occupying Israelis). In short, the threat to the religious tradition may come from the general processes of modernization and secularization, from other religions and/or ethnic groups, from a secular state (imperial or indigenous) seeking to secularize and delimit the domain of the sacred, or from various combinations of these.

These movements react to secularization both by opposing it *and* by exploiting it for their own purposes. Here we note the fundamentalist adoption and mastery of modern means of communication and recruitment, the fundamentalist readiness to compete in an open marketplace of ideas and a society of fragmented loyalties, and the fundamentalist tendency to appropriate history and tradition selectively for explicit political purposes.

Selectivity

Fundamentalism is selective in three ways. First, it is not merely defensive of the tradition but selects and reshapes particular aspects of the tradition, especially those that clearly distinguish the fundamentalists from the mainstream. For this purpose Protestant fundamentalists of the United States select the apocalyptic prophesies to be found in the Books of Daniel and

Revelation; the Italian Catholic movement Comunione e Liberazione selects Barthian theology, among other ideas; the Shiʿite movements of Iran, Iraq, and Lebanon select and fortify precepts legitimating the political role of learned jurists in times of crisis.

Second, fundamentalisms select some aspects of modernity to affirm and embrace. Much of modern science may be accepted, for example, and modern technology such as radio, television, VCRs, audiocassette tapes, telephone banks, and modern mailing techniques are effectively employed. In reacting to threats and in selecting the parts of the religiocultural tradition to be especially defended, syncretic fundamentalism movements such as the Hindu variety may imitate the theological and organizational structures of threatening religions and cultures. In other words, the syncretic fundamentalist movements, primarily those of the non-Abrahamic traditions, are creative and imitative in a special way, selecting elements from the enemy they oppose as well as from the religious tradition they seek to uphold.

Third, fundamentalisms select certain consequences or processes of modernity and single these out for special attention, usually in the form of focused opposition (as in the cases of the tourist trade in Egypt, abortion on demand in the United States, and "land for peace" in Israel). As with the other two types of selectivity, the precise content of what is selected may change with time. Just as different texts or traditions are selected, just as different positive features of modernity are embraced at different times, so, too, will different particular issues be contested at different times.

More important, these three modes of selectivity are interrelated, so that the retrieved texts match the significant issues, the modern methods chosen convey or support the fundamentalist opposition, and so on. Thus a different text and tactic will be selected if the issue is abortion rather than, say, evolution.

Moral Manichaeanism

A dualistic or Manichaean worldview is one in which reality is considered to be uncompromisingly divided into light, which is identified with the world of the spirit and of the good, and darkness, which is identified with matter and evil. Ultimately, light will triumph over darkness. For fundamentalist movements, as we have noted, the world outside is contaminated, sinful, doomed; the world inside is a pure and redeemed "remnant."

If the movement does not guarantee perfect purity to its members, it does provide certitude and a minimum standard by which members may

be assured at least of protection from contamination. The sinful world outside may be graded in degrees of contamination. For the independent Baptists, the world of evil would first include the mainstream denominational
authorities who have compromised with the secular world and then the
secular world itself. For the Shi'ite Muslims, the sinful world would include
first the secularized Shi'ite Muslims, then the Sunni Muslims, and then the
various infidel Satans great and small.

Absolutism and Inerrancy

The Torah, the Talmud, the Halakah, the Qu'ran, the Shari'a, the Bible, and
the Granth Sahib are of divine (inspired) origin and true and accurate in
all particulars. Here, of course, the degree to which there can be a belief in
"inerrancy" or its analogues (e.g., papal infallibility, a privileged school of
Islamic jurisprudence, etc.) depends on whether there is a sacred code, set
of codes, or canon in the religious tradition. This is true of the Abrahamic
religions, which have a divinely transmitted law and canonical interpretations generally acknowledged within the entire religious community. In
Eastern religions, gurus, monks, or priests may have a freer hand in retrieving sacred texts. In Hinduism, for example, texts are cited, but their normative character is more ambiguous and, in the nature of the case, less authoritative. Nevertheless, in these movements as well there is an affirmation of
the absolute validity of the "fundamentals" of the tradition.

Fundamentalists, then, share a recognizable approach to religious
sources. First, they steadfastly oppose hermeneutical methods developed by
secularized philosophers or critics; these are not appropriately applied to
sacred texts and traditions. This is not to say that fundamentalist interpretation itself is monolithic, only that it does not submit to the canons of critical
rationality as defined by outsiders. Instead of following philological or historical methods, fundamentalists employ their own distinctive strategies of
interpretation, including "hardened" and "updated" traditional approaches,
designed in part to reify and preserve the absolutist character of the sacred
text or tradition.

Millennialism and Messianism

History has a miraculous culmination. The good will triumph over evil,
immortality over mortality; the reign of eternal justice will terminate history.
The end of days, preceded by trials and tribulations, will be ushered in by

the Messiah, the Savior; the Hidden Imam will come out of hiding. Messianism and millennialism promise victory to the believer, millennialism by promising an end to suffering and waiting, messianism by promising an all-powerful redeemer. Abrahamic cosmology offers both; the non-Abrahamic traditions lack such fully elaborated assurances. The promised outcome for the Hindu movements, the radical Sikhs, and the Sinhala Buddhists are nations safeguarded from threatening alien penetrations, though the Kingdom of Ram, Khalistan, and the purely Buddhist "kingdom" of Sri Lanka have millennial overtones.

ORGANIZATIONAL CHARACTERISTICS OF FUNDAMENTALISM

Elect, Chosen Membership

Fundamentalist movements tend to have an "elect," a chosen, divinely called membership, described variously as "the faithful," "the remnant," the "last outpost," the "Covenant keepers," those who "bear witness," who "walk with the Lord," and the like. Some movements divide their adherents into an elect—a fully committed inner group—and a periphery of sympathizers. As indicated in the previous chapter, the notion of an elect inner core is a powerful means of achieving group solidarity and cohesion. The enclave may not be able to offer its members appealing material rewards, but the belief in a divine mandate and a special status for the chosen ones provides a spiritual and psychological boost to the inner core, who devote much of their energy to preserving this sense of distinction and hence to fortifying the boundaries between insider and outsider.

Sharp Boundaries

Indeed, the theme of separation, of boundaries between the saved and the sinful, is general among these movements. The notion of a dividing wall and other spatial metaphors are characteristic markers. This wall may be physical. For example, the ultra-Orthodox (a.k.a. haredi) Jews require their members to live within easy walking distance of the synagogue and require that in each town or community extradomestic life be organized around the sanctified precincts of the Talmud Torah (the school), the synagogue, the kosher slaughterhouse, and the mikva (the ritual bath). Separation may

be implemented through audiovisual boundaries, through a distinctive vocabulary or dress code, and through control over access to the media.

Authoritarian Organization

Membership in fundamentalist movements is voluntary, and orthodox insiders are presumed to be equal. This imparts a certain weakness to the
decision-making process. Bureaucracy in the sense of rational-legal division
of power and competence has no place in this type of community, and its
appearance is usually associated with a decline in mobilization and militance.

The typical form of fundamentalist organization is charismatic, a leader-
follower relationship in which the follower imputes extraordinary qualities,
heavenly grace, special access to the deity, deep and complete understanding
of sacred texts to the great rav, the rebbe, the imam, the virtuous jurist, the
minister. One man is set apart from all others. He may have trusted associates who implement his decisions, but they are not "officials" with clear
divisions of competence and tenure. The distance between charismatic leaders and followers is illustrated in body language and rituals such as kissing
the hand of the emir or touching the prayer garment of the rebbe. This
tension between voluntarism and equality, on the one hand, and charismatic authority, on the other, makes these movements somewhat fragile.
Since there can be no loyal opposition, there is a tendency toward fragmentation.

Behavioral Requirements

Broadly speaking, the member's time, space, and activity are a group resource, not an individual one. Elaborate behavioral requirements create a
powerful affective dimension, an imitative, conforming dimension. This
feature is closely related to the boundary-setting function of the enclave.
There is distinctive music, hymnals, Hasidic chants, Qur'anic psalmodies.
There are rules for dress—the Muslim white galabia and headdress, the
haredi black coat and hat; long beards for the haredim, trimmed beards for
the Muslims; shorts and *lathis* (staves) for members of the Hindu *shakhas*
(small troops), turbans, uncut hair, and knee-length shorts for the Sikhs.
Sinful behavior is proscribed in detail—rules about drinking, sexuality, appropriate speech, and the discipline of children abound. Likewise, there is
censorship of reading material and close supervision of listening and viewing practices. Dating, mate selection, and the like are strictly regulated.

Relations among Properties: Functional Explanations

As we suggest in our diagram, these nine properties are not just a checklist. They are interrelated in important ways, constituting a functional system of interacting properties. Thus, reactivity is the basic impulse behind the other eight properties. Indeed, it constitutes the very essence of fundamentalist movements. They are, by definition, militant, mobilized, defensive reactions to modernity. Millennialism and messianism, on the other hand, may or may not be strongly present. But when they are present they serve as powerful catalysts. The seven remaining properties coalesce in three overlapping clusters—selectivity, boundaries, and election. Selectivity revolves around the need to pare down the tradition to its essentials because of the danger that it faces. Boundaries relate to the challenge of keeping the group's identity in an open and often tempting society, a task rendered all the more arduous as the group cannot adequately reward its members in material or in "normal" status terms. Election is an answer to the challenge of how to maintain efficient decision-making in a group that stresses equality among its members; this very equality is, in turn, an answer to the inadequate material and status resources possessed by the group. Each of these three draws into its cluster other properties that help sustain it.

Reactivity: Fundamentalism and Its Enemies

By reactivity we refer to religious reactivity—a movement mobilizes against secularizing forces in the modern world. The traditional religion is attenuating, adherents are slipping away. Or the community that the fundamentalist movement seeks to defend is threatened with absorption into a pluralistic, areligious milieu. Reactivity draws other properties with it: selectivity, moral dualism, and inerrancy accompany the defense against threat. There are mixed cases in which reactivity is of an ethnonationalist-cultural sort, either of a majority preemptive variety like the Hindu "National Union of Volunteers" (RSS), the Sinhala Buddhists, and the Kach movement of the late Rabbi Kahane, or of the minority defensive sort like the Christians in south India or the Muslims in Soviet Asia. In these cases it is difficult to separate the religious from the cultural and ethnonationalist components. The movements themselves may differentiate the religious component, rework the pantheon a bit, rearrange the sacred texts in order to be more effectively deployed on the cultural battlefield. In such cases it is inaccurate to dismiss the religious motivations or aspects of the movement altogether, but it is important, on the other hand, to note that these religion-cum-ethnonationalist movements behave differently as a category than do movements inspired more exclusively by strictly religious considerations. In table 2.1, we display twenty-two groups in the Christian, Jewish, Islamic, and South Asian religious traditions according to the way in which they perceive and react to threats in their environments.

Six of our cases are Christian movements; eight are Islamic; five are Jewish, and three are South Asian. The table shows that in most cases these movements perceive their own compromising religious establishments as endangering the survival of true religion; they see the interventionist secular state as intrusive in the religious sphere or as failing to provide support to it; and, finally, they judge the civil society to be corrupting and corrosive of religious belief and practice.

The exceptions to a pattern of seeing the religious establishment as the enemy are the Guatemalan Pentecostals, the South Asian Christians, the Hizbullah in Lebanon, the Israeli Gush Emunim and Kach, and the Hindu RSS. In each case special conditions explain why the religious establishment is not viewed as the enemy. The Guatemalan Pentecostals have recently converted to Protestantism from their Catholic or indigenous backgrounds; their former religion thus appears as a competing religion and not their own establishment. The South Asian Christians are very loosely organized, lacking in much of an establishment to hate. The Shi'ite clergy in Lebanon are not sufficiently coherent to threaten the Hizbullah. The concerns of the Gush Emunim and Kach in Israel are nationalist and ethnic as well as religious and some rabbis of the "religious establishment" have lent support to their causes; in any case, the religious establishment is not the primary enemy. In the case of the Hindu RSS, there is no religious establishment as such. Otherwise, regardless of religious tradition, fundamentalist movements are pitted against their mainstream establishments in a struggle to halt the trend toward secularism.

The second most commonly perceived enemy of fundamentalist movements is the secularizing state, with its rationalized bureaucracy, which has penetrated all spheres of life by introducing secular education and/or prohibiting religion and religious practices in the schools and by permitting or encouraging sinful practices such as divorce, extramarital sex, homosexuality, abortion, and the like. Fundamentalists direct their antagonistic efforts toward the state as frequently as they oppose the religious establishment. Again the exceptions are easily explained. The Guatemalan regime (particularly under Ríos Montt) was supportive of the Pentecostals as an alternative to the left-inclined Catholic liberationists. In the case of the Hamas movement in the occupied territories, the Israeli state is viewed as an external imperialist state. In Lebanon there was no powerful state for the Hizbullah to fear or oppose.

Similarly, the civil society is viewed as a threat by the fundamentalists of all of these religious traditions. Among the forces working to alienate the faithful and particularly the young from their religious beliefs and affiliations, fundamentalists blame the corrupting media, including television, cinema, and secular literature; secular voluntary associations and political parties; and the world of secular education.

Fundamentalists, then, can be said to share this family resemblance: across the board they identify three antagonists—the tepid or corrupt religious establishment, the secular state, and secularized civil society—as objects of sustained opposition by true believers.

The last two columns of Table 2.1—ethnonational competition and imperialism and neocolonialism—show how these movements differ in their goals and antagonisms. Thus the Christian movements—with the notable exception of the South Asian groups and the Ulster Protestants—are not involved in ethnonational competition, nor are they engaged in anti-imperialist, neocolonialist antagonisms. The South Asian Christians are defensive against the preemptive pressures of Hindu extremism. All of the Islamic movements are strongly anti-imperialist (Israel being the representative of "imperialism"); and the Lebanese Hizbullah, the Jama'at-i-Islami in Pakistan, and Hamas in the occupied territories are also in competition with ethnoreligious opponents. In the Lebanese case, the conflict is with the Lebanese Christians; in the Pakistani case, the conflict is with the Hindus, Christians, and Ahmadis; in the case of Hamas, conflict occurs with radical Jewish settlers. The Jewish fundamentalist movements (with the exception of some haredi movements) are in ethnonationalist conflict with the surrounding Arab peoples. The Hindus of India and the Sinhala Buddhists of Sri Lanka are involved in efforts to "purify" their societies religiously and ethnically of Muslims and Christians, in the case of the Hindus, and of the Hindu Tamils in the case of the Sri Lankans. The Sikhs are concerned with establishing a Sikh nation cleared of Hindu domination.

Selectivity: Inerrancy, Boundaries, Behavior

The first cluster of functionally associated traits—selectivity—results from the particular state of siege in which the religious tradition finds itself. In such a state of siege, it is possible to defend only so much; one has to highlight the fundamentals. This is more likely to occur in a well-defined religious tradition in which principles are explicit—the more codified and explicit the better. Jews can select from the Shulkhan 'Arukh, where one can emphasize certain rules; Muslims from the Shari'a, where one can pick one of the four schools, such as Hanbalism; Roman Catholics, from certain papal encyclicals, or conciliar doctrines; Protestants, from Christian eschatology, where one can pick either pre- or post-tribulationism. But selectivity is possible even among the Sikhs, whose codified doctrine is rather limited. It is even possible among the Hindu and Buddhist "fundamentalists" who, in their efforts to compete with Western fundamentalists by imitation, may create a canon.

The companion to selectivity is inerrancy. In a doubting and cynical world one needs reliable and sure proof. The doctrines are not only clear-cut, they are of divine origin or inspiration and they are true beyond doubt. Inerrancy promotes unambiguous behavioral rules, enabling a movement to draw clear boundaries between the saved and the sinful in behavior as well as in doctrine. Selectivity may have the strategic purpose of setting the movement clearly apart from its enemies. Often "shocking" (to outsiders) themes are selected—papal infallibility, the completely inerrant Bible, the Hidden Imam, the "sacred spark" in Hasidism and among the Jewish radicals of Gush Emunim.

Boundaries: Behavior, Election, Manichaeanism

The second cluster is related to the maintenance of boundaries, which is fostered by a set of distinctive behaviors, belief in one's election, and the Manichaean division of the world into lightness and darkness. Having sharp boundaries enables a group to maintain the cohesion of a more or less egalitarian elite of the virtuous. This is crucial because the core group, being beleaguered, cannot reward adherents materially or with power but only with status. If group demands on time and conduct are too heavy, gradations may be created—elect, auxiliary, periphery—as among the haredim, Comunione e Liberazione, the Jama'at. The absence of a core may weaken the group, as in the case of the Tablighi Jamaat of Pakistan, in contrast to missionary-type groups such as the Habad and Comunione, which have a strong core and a broad periphery. The sense of being both elect and beleaguered is amplified by moral dualism. However, moral dualism or Manichaeanism is by no means a distinguishing mark of fundamentalism. All of our cases manifest dualism simply as a consequence of being militant. What distinguishes fundamentalist dualism is that it is directed more strongly against drifters from one's own tradition (e.g., sinful Muslims) than against competing religions, atheists, and agnostics. Thus Hamas in Gaza fights "Westoxicated," morally corrupted Muslims first, and infidel Israelis second.

Election: Authority, Charisma, Selectivity

The third cluster sustains confidence in one's election—authority, charisma, and selectivity. To operate effectively, selectivity requires authority. If one is to keep the core of the elect happy while the group is lacking in remunerative and coercive power, however, the membership should be as egalitarian as possible, equal and sharing in virtue. The solution to this dilemma is to have as few leaders as possible, that is, a "small hierarchy" (in Mary Douglas's terms), at the apex of which there is leadership of even higher and undisputed virtue, that is, charisma, touched with divine or supernatural grace. One thinks here of the Hasidic rebbe or the emir of the Muslim jama'a. The development of a bureaucratic hierarchy may signal the transformation and possible decline of a movement, as in the case of the Jewish movement Aguda Haredim. The movement loses much of its "enclave" solidarity and militance, its cohesiveness, once it becomes bureaucratized.

This process of bureaucratization has affected several fundamentalist groups, especially those of longer duration and multiple generations. The Muslim Brotherhood in Egypt is one of several examples. Bureaucratization set in after the assassination of Hasan al-Banna in 1948, and today the original, noncompromising fervor of the mainstream brotherhood has waned as it has participated in "mainstream" politics (even while spawning radical offshoots, which reject the bureaucratizing, compromising tendencies of the main body).

Nevertheless, some groups retain their fundamentalist character over generations. Fundamentalist Baptists in the United States, for example, succeeded in combining the decentralized authority of the local community governed by a charismatic pastor with a measure of control of the denominational bureaucracy in a number of key areas (teaching materials, nomination of pastors from an approved pool of candidates, etc.).

The charismatic leader may be a "cleric"—a minister, priest, rabbi, guru, and so forth—and there has been a decline in the role of the laity in clerically led groups such as the haredim and some Protestant and Catholic movements. But clerical leadership is not an absolute necessity; among Sunnis, for example, the ulama in general were discredited earlier in this century by collaboration with the powers that be, and self-taught charismatic leaders emerged from among the laity.

Charismatic leadership is not always a source of strength, nor is it the only source of strength. Splits may occur when two charismatic leaders clash. Or when the charismatic leader disappears, leaving no real heir, the internal egalitarian core may be weakened, and with it the movement as a whole. This has been the case with Rabbi Kahane and the Kach movement, with Rabbi Kook the Younger and Gush Emunim, and with the Ayatollah Khomeini in Iran. It was also the case with Habad, which split after its nonagenarian leader, Rabbi Isaac Schneerson, passed from the scene (May 1994). The demise of a charismatic leader could even endanger Agudat Yisrael with the death of its leader, Rabbi Schach.

Millennialism and Messianism

Messianism and millennialism are not always strongly present in fundamentalist movements. Movements can flourish when messianism is in a minor key (e.g., Comunione e Liberazione, the Sunnis, the haredim, the radical Sikhs) or even absent. Yet it certainly contributes to morale when millennial beliefs are strong (Habad, Gush Emunim, Protestant Christians). The expectation of the end of normal history, when the rules of the game will be changed, endows a beleaguered movement with the expectation of ultimate victory. Hence risks and costs are bearable. And as this miraculous outcome is to be preceded, more often than not, by an apocalypse, it also confirms, in the short term, the validity of the group's pessimistic vision of historic reality. Yet even groups in which messianism is in a minor key tend toward an apocalyptic interpretation of reality in moments of crisis. Thus weakly millennialist groups in Islam and in Judaism developed apocalyptic visions during the 1991 Gulf War, comparable in power to those of their Protestant counterparts, who are strongly millennialist.

EXAMINING THE CASES

We turn now to the task of sorting out these movements according to this set of ideological and organizational traits in tables 2.2 and 2.3. We group the various Sunni jama'at of the Middle East and North Africa together, and the Shi'ite movements of Iran, Lebanon, and Iraq together, leaving us eighteen movements. This enables us to begin creating a fundamentalist typology. The tables show if the trait is strongly represented (high), if it is simply represented (low), or if it is absent.

Ten of the eighteen movements have the defining characteristics of "pure" fundamentalism. Among the Christian cases, the U.S. Protestants have high ratings in all particulars except charismatic leadership, which, although low, is still present. Similarly, the Italian Catholic movement, Comunione e Liberazione, has all the specified properties and has more highs than lows. Among the Islamic movements the Middle East/North African Sunni jama'at and the Shi'ite cases, Hamas, and the Jama'at-i-Islami of South Asia come out high on these defining characteristics. Among the Jewish cases the haredim, Habad, and Gush Emunim fall in this same category. There is only one case with high ratings among the South Asian religions— the Sikhs. This reflects the fact that our definition of the properties of fundamentalism has been derived from a focus on Christian, Islamic, and Jewish cases, all of which have sacred texts and codified religious laws and share in a millennial-messianic cosmology. Inerrancy is more likely to be asserted where there are well-established sacred texts and codes. Millennialism and messianism are more likely to be present in fundamentalist movements coming out of religious traditions that share an end-of-days cosmology, a viewpoint not present in the South Asian religions. Both millennialism and messianism are present in the Abrahamic movements. Messianism is not present in the South Asian cases, and millennialism only on a limited scale. It is of interest that one South Asian movement, the Sikhs, has a definitive sacred text—the Granth Sahib—and in most other respects that movement fits the category.

ABRAHAMIC FUNDAMENTALISM

Thus similarities in religious tradition attributable to a common heritage explain the association of fundamentalism, as we have defined it, with Christianity, Islam, and Judaism. We speak of movements sharing in these characteristics, in these religious traditions, as Abrahamic fundamentalisms. Fundamentalism was defined from an examination of Abrahamic cases, since it was first observed and studied in these traditions. Militant, restorative-revivalist religious movements in other religious traditions that do not share important features of Abrahamic theology and practice or where some features have been introduced imitatively qualify, in our terminology, as syncretic fundamentalisms. Though not an Abrahamic religion, the Sikh case shares almost all of these specified characteristics. If we include the Sikhs in this category, we can account for ten of the eighteen movements listed in tables 2.2 and 2.3.

As we have suggested, the defining properties of fundamentalism are connected in complicated ways, with one precipitating or requiring the others. And when the movement is in decline, as one property attenuates, so do others. While we have been examining these properties here in synchronic terms as dialectically interdependent we can also examine these movements with a diachronic or genetic logic as they emerged and acquired these characteristics, each creating its own "package." We offer a brief sketch of these ten movements to make this point.

1. Among the Christian groups the U.S. Protestant fundamentalists emerged in the first decades of the present century in reaction to rapid urbanization and industrialization, the spread of secular education and science, the decline of belief in sacred texts and religious tradition, and attenuating religious discipline. The fundamentalist reaction took the form of affirmation of the inerrancy of the Bible by conservative Protestant ministers and scholars, with emphasis on the biblical account of the Creation, and the promise of the return of the Savior. They selected millennial or apocalyptic passages of the Old and New Testaments promising salvation after an end-of-days tribulation. Fundamentalist discourse constituted an elect—a saved "remnant" separated from lapsed Christians and the secular world by sharp boundaries, Manichaean beliefs, and the elect's pious behavior. Bible-believing Christians were governed in individual, autonomous congregations by authoritative ministers, often known for their charismatic preaching, who supervised the community's interpretations of sacred sources and divine purpose.

2. Comunione e Liberazione emerged in Milan in a time of rapid social change and explosive political division. Although in time it responded directly to these challenges, the movement developed as a reaction against secularization. Father Luigi Giussani became well known in the 1950s and 1960s for his classes and study groups in which modern authors from Dostoevsky to Camus were sympathetically read and subjected to a Christian critique. The movement grew in the 1960s and 1970s primarily among university students, attracting many who were disillusioned with revolutionary radicalism and the moral corruption of Italian society. The intellectual attack on secularization was thus joined to a political problem and an organizational solution. Revolutionary protest was bound to fail because there was no one to protest against, but the alienation of modern life could be overcome by the creation of communities based on common belief and shared activities. These communities in turn could conquer and transform society, and Comunione e Liberazione developed programs and publications devoted to a wide range of issues as well as extensive missionary activities.

At the center of all this was Father Giussani's charismatic authority; the *scuole* or communities of Comunione e Liberazione are modeled on the first ones in Milan and privilege a selection of Catholic teachings, largely interpreted by Giussani's writings, which in turn emphasize the role of the laity in renewing "Christendom" through communal living and the personal experience of Jesus Christ. Boundaries are maintained by personal ties (new members adopt a big brother from those who already belong), daily contacts, frequent devotions, and study groups within the community, and by mutual support and elaborate personal networks within secular society, from professors to Christian Democrats.

3. The Islamic *Sunni jama'at* movements of Egypt, Syria, and Tunisia represent reactions to the Arab secular nationalism fostered in the nation-building movements of the immediate post–World War II decades and accompanied by the mass exodus to urban centers. Since the state was the prime instigator of this social revolution, the clergy and Islamic laity selected the part of the Shari'a most suspicious of state authority, the Islamic legal school (Hanbalism), as inerrant doctrine. The primary question raised by the movement, whether the state is Muslim, was answered in the negative. Faith in Islam among the people was said to be undermined by the secular state. The first order of the day for the movement's leadership was to organize the "remnant" against an all-penetrating state and against contamination by lax nominal Muslims. Hence the movement's concern with boundary maintenance and the enforcement of behavioral requirements. Authority was in the hands of the founders, usually charismatic figures (Sayyid Qutb in Egypt, Marwan Hadid in Syria, Rashid al-Ghannushi in Tunisia). Millennialism is a minor element, but dualism is strong when invoked against fellow Muslims, especially Westernized elites.

4. The *Jama'at-i-Islami* of Pakistan was founded by an authoritarian leader, Maulana Maududi, who was not charismatic but who provided a religiopolitical idiom for Islamic fundamentalism. His ideology was dualistic, drawing sharp boundaries between Muslims and infidels. In developing an Islamic politics, he selected Islamic concepts that would be amenable to political constructions.

5. The *Shi'ite* fundamentalist movement of Iran also represents a reaction to state-instigated secularization (under Reza Shah Pahlavi), coupled with industrial development and urbanization. The movement had a strong charismatic figure from the outset in the Ayatollah Khomeini, who enjoyed integral authority over a small hierarchy of leading ulama. Khomeini selected the doctrine of the Guardianship of the Jurist and the hitherto minor activist strand in the Shi'ite tradition. Dualism was very strong, with the

elites (political and otherwise) and, secondarily, the lapsed coming in for condemnation; outside Islam are the various greater and lesser Satans. The behavioral requirements of the movements were heavy and centered on political action. The strategy was to build strong boundaries around an elect, the saved remnant, and then to employ these reliable forces in political action and missionary activity in the society at large. Messianism was present in the form of the expectation of the ultimate return of the Hidden Imam and in the sense that Khomeini was viewed as the "just jurist" and the "vicar" of the Hidden Imam.

6. The founder of Hamas, Shaykh Yassin, was reacting to laxity in belief and practice among fellow Palestinian Muslims; he and his followers were alarmed by the erosion of an outside boundary through Israeli domination of Palestine. Both infidel and modern, the way of life under Israeli occupation contaminates the Muslim community. Hence two sets of stringent behavioral rules emerged, prohibiting "innovations" and any contact other than economic with the Israelis. Hamas selected an activist approach out of the neo-Hanbali tradition, which would lead its members to holy war. The Hanbali text was regarded as inerrant. Hence there developed a very strong dualism. The charismatic authority of the founder, Shaykh Yassin, legitimizes this selection and the rules that follow therefrom. Around the shaykh an elite of the elect was formed with sharp, sometimes clandestine boundaries, dedicated to imposing this rule.

7. The emergence of *haredi* Jewish fundamentalism can be dated to the formation of the Agudat Yisrael in 1912. The Agudat brought together the yeshivot, surviving local Jewish communities, and Hasidic courts of Eastern Europe in reaction to the depopulation of the shtetl at the turn of the century. In the more liberal atmosphere of those decades Jews assimilated in substantial numbers to secular culture and migrated to Eastern European cities, or emigrated to other European countries and in very large numbers to the United States. Secular nationalist aspirations were fostered by Zionism, and atheistic socialist views, by the Bund. The leading figure in this reaction to secularization was the Hafetz Haim, who sought to bring together the "remnant of Israel" as an elect, guided and protected by the Shulkhan 'Arukh as an inerrant text, selected and adapted for vulnerable Jewish life in anonymous urban centers, in the czarist army, and in the United States. Fear and hostility were directed against lapsed Jews rather than against Gentiles. *Frumkeit* (pious behavior) was required—wearing the ritual undervest, use of phylacteries in morning prayer, strict observance of the Sabbath, and the like. The maintenance of boundaries was urged; in cities one should settle in the immediate neighborhood of the synagogue

in order to avoid violation of the Sabbath and the temptations of mixed neighborhoods. One should not socialize with Gentiles after 5:00 P.M., since there might be temptations of various kinds. Messianism was present in a minor key but as a remote prospect about which one could do nothing. It was kept in check by recalling the catastrophe of the false messiah, Shabtai Zvi, in the seventeenth century. Rabbinical authority in the yeshivot was based on learning. The greatest and most inspired scholars such as the Hafetz Haim were endowed with charisma.

8. Under its first four rebbes, Habad (the Lubavitcher Hasidim) was a very traditional movement. In the late nineteenth century, under the fifth rebbe, the movement became mobilized and militant in reaction to the depopulation of the shtetl because of assimilation and emigration. Charismatic authority was present from the very beginning because of the Hasidic mystical tradition. The movement had a missionary orientation toward the larger Jewish community, with an elect surrounding the rebbe and implementing his programs. Thus the boundaries of Habad established an enclave and a periphery. The Halakah and the Tanya (the sayings of the first Lubavitcher rebbe) were selectively plumbed. Charismatic authority was very strong, as was messianism. Behavioral regulations for the enclave were very strict, with dress fixed in the style of the eighteenth century and with ritual garments and the use of phylacteries in morning prayer required.

9. The first nuclei out of which Gush Emunim formed took shape after the 1967 war when what seemed to be the miraculous victories of the Israeli forces were viewed as ushering in the messianic era. The Yom Kippur War in 1973 made these prospects seem problematic, but it was interpreted by Rabbi Kook the Younger as meaning that Jews must play an active role in assuring the triumph of the messianic era. Charisma and messianism thus were built into Gush Emunim from its very formation. The members were an elect, chosen for this last holy role. The one mitzvah (commandment) selected by the Gush as the most important in the age of Redemption was the reestablishment of the Jews in the entire land of biblical Israel. The stringent behavioral requirement was to establish settlements on the West Bank and the Gaza Strip. The boundaries of the Gush were not sharp; members were ready to collaborate with lapsed Jews just as long as they shared their goals. Dualism was expressed in the attitude toward Arabs.

10. Though not in the Abrahamic tradition the Sikh radicals share in these fundamentalist qualities in almost all respects. The Sikh radicals originated out of groups reacting to the growing secularization of their community in postindependence India as well as to the encroachment by the dominant Hindu community upon the Sikhs. They selected the Granth Sahib as

a salient and inerrant text out of the tradition, a text governing behavior (dress, diet, conduct). They declared the whole community to be the elect, there being no sharp internal boundaries. From the very beginning dualism vis-à-vis the Hindus was high. Authority by tradition is in charismatic hands, that is, gurus and sants.

The remaining eight cases are either examples of syncretic fundamentalism or may be viewed as potentially fundamentalist.

Syncretic Fundamentalism

The syncretic movements are those in which ethnocultural or ethnonational features take precedence over religion or are inseparable, as in Hindu fundamentalism. These movements are inspired less by strictly religious considerations than by the actual fundamentalisms profiled above. Whereas fundamentalist movements are most at home in a religiocultural enclave but find themselves drawn into politics as a result of their religious beliefs, syncretic fundamentalist movements tend to reverse the process. That is, to redress social or political grievances they reach for religious justifications, tactics, and organizational patterns in order to mount the most effective opposition possible, based on ethnicity, community, and religion. These movements include the Ulster Protestants, South Indian Christians, Hindu RSS, Sinhala Buddhists, and the Kach movement in Israel. The militance and reactivity of these movements are not directed primarily toward modernization and secularization but tend to be an affirmation of ethnonational identity in the face of threatening ethnonational minorities or preemptive ethnonational majorities.

1. The Ulster Protestants are ethnonationalist and anti-Catholic. In some respects they exhibit strong fundamentalist characteristics. The founder of the Free Presbyterian Church and the Democratic Unionist Party, the Reverend Ian Paisley, is a strong charismatic leader whose personal authority has almost single-handedly forged the movement; a "small hierarchy" of supporting ministers echo his teachings. Likewise, Paisley's rhetoric is reactive and defensive; he traces his movement to the seventeenth century, when the cycle of "oppression" began (at Catholic as well as British hands). Properties of fundamentalism such as inerrancy, millennialism, and absolutism are present. On the other hand, Paisleyism is clearly an ethnonationalist movement: followers rally around the political rather than the strictly religious cause; the religious rhetoric and mobilizing capacity is gen-

erally understood to be at the service of ethnonationalist politics. In the absence of the ethnonationalist component, in other words, it is doubtful that this kind of religious "fundamentalism" would have emerged.

2. The Christian movements of South India similarly are threatened by Hinduizing and syncretic propensities in their own communities and by the preemptive ethnonationalism of the Hindu majority. These movements are secondarily threatened by modernization and secularization, primarily through the activities of the Indian state. In their active competition they have developed fundamentalist traits such as inerrancy, millennialism, and charismatic leadership. In their efforts to compete with the Hindu pantheon with its aggressive and bloodthirsty deities, the Christian movements have turned Jesus and the saints into militant and avenging forces.

3. The Guatemalan neo-Pentecostals are unlike fundamentalists in that they are not retrieving or defending their age-old religious tradition; on the contrary, they have rejected Roman Catholicism for something relatively new, the evangelicalism imported by missionaries over a century ago but given a new legitimacy by the Rios Montt regime in the early 1980s. Yet this new profile includes a fundamentalist-like emphasis on biblical inerrancy, strong moral requirements, millennialism, and support of a political order that seems to favor their growth.

4. The Hindu RSS is a preemptive ethnonationalist-cultural movement mobilized against the dilution of Hindu identity by the penetration of the secular, pluralist Indian state and against the inroads of Islam and Christianity. In reaction to these threats it has created a syncretic fundamentalism, extracting a militant religious component out of Hindu culture, according priority to the god Rama and privileging certain ancient texts.

5. Sinhala Buddhist extremism is not a religious mobilization against modernization and secularization but rather a movement among the Sinhala-Buddhist majority against the threat of the Hindu Tamils emigrating from South India. It is much more a political movement than a religious one, concerned with domination of the Sinhala state and the Sri Lankan territory. The Sinhala Buddhists are seeking to repossess the northern parts of Sri Lanka from the Hindu Tamils. Their readiness to resort to violence on a large scale separates them from their own Buddhist heritage.

6. The Kach movement of Rabbi Kahane is to be understood as a quasi-Fascist movement, drawing on strong antiestablishment sentiment—directed at both the Right and the Left in Israeli politics—and ready to engage in street hooliganism, terrorism, and other forms of extralegal action. It laid claim to the Maccabean and Zealot tradition in Jewish history, advocating the expulsion of the Arabs from biblical Israel, attacking the ruling parties

as having become Hellenized and "Gentilized." Though Rabbi Kahane favored the elimination of all forms of Judaism other than Orthodoxy, specific
religious interests and activities played a small role in the movement.

These syncretic movements are primarily ethnonationalist movements,
mobilized as preemptive majorities against the threat of minorities; or as
minority ethnoreligious movements defending themselves against a majority nativist threat. In these cases religion is not separated from other cultural
practices (e.g., Hindu India) or where it is, as in Northern Ireland, it may
be instrumental to ethnonationalist goals. The affirmation of religious tradition against secularization is a secondary theme.

POTENTIAL AND MARGINAL FUNDAMENTALISMS

Some cases may have superficial resemblances to fundamentalism but properly do not belong in the category. Most prominent among these marginal
cases are those revivalist movements that are not fundamentalist movements, strictly speaking, but that have the potential to become so.

1. Had the Tablighi Jamaat of South Asia been included among the paradigmatic cases, it would strain the definition of the category. In tables 2.2
and 2.3 it was evaluated as low in all nine characteristics. The movement
was formed near Delhi in the 1920s by an Islamic religious scholar, Maulana
Ilyas, who wished to correct the lax and Hinduizing practices of the Islamic
population in northern India. The local population had been converted to
Islam but only partially: most of their rituals were based on Hindu culture.
They could not recite their prayers correctly; there were no religious schools;
they had few contacts with the centers of Islamic culture in India. The new
movement sought to deal with these problems through missionary activity
carried on by volunteers. The missionary activity involved the teaching of
prayers, rituals, and elementary knowledge of Islam by small mobile units
of volunteers sent out to the villages.

The organization of the Tablighi Jamaat is informal. There are no full-
time workers. There is no clear-cut separatism or boundaries. The leadership
of Maulana Ilyas was expressed in saintliness and dedication, a low-key charisma. The aims of the movement were to make better Muslims out of the
half-Hindu peasantry of northern India and, as time went on, to protect
them from the secular influences in the area. The extent of organization
is minimal and communitarian, involving intense personal relationships

among the leaders and the rank and file. Membership takes the form of participation in missionary activity. Moral suasion rather than exercise of arbitrary authority is the mode of decision-making. A single small volume, containing the "Tablighi curriculum" with appropriate material from the Qur'an and the Shari'a, is distributed to villagers. Each member is asked to contribute forty days of missionary work each year, traveling to neighboring areas, delivering simple sermons, and exemplifying proper Islamic behavior. The movement is not activist or political in its aspirations. Its program is focused on the improvement and intensification of Islamic religious practice. Millennialism is relatively low-key but nevertheless present. The movement is very successful. Its international conferences, such as the one near Lahore in 1998, have attracted more than a million Muslims from all over the world.

2. The U.S. Catholic traditionalist case is an example of a strong fundamentalist ideology in search of an organizational structure, resources, and personnel—it is, in short, an ideology in search of a movement. (Contrast the rankings in tables 2.2 and 2.3.) Neither the host religion nor the American religious culture proved useful to the mounting of a fundamentalist movement; these macrostructural elements inhibited traditionalists from exploiting fully the confusion and discontent felt by conservative Catholics in the years immediately following the Second Vatican Council, or Vatican II (1962–65). Resources were abundant in the American Catholicism of the twentieth century, but they did not become available to the postconciliar traditionalist movement for a number of reasons. Catholicism had experienced a revival leading to a newfound prominence and respectability on the American scene in the 1940s and 1950s. The revival was conducted under the ideological canopy of Vatican-sponsored neo-Thomism. Thus, for all of their technical innovation and lay involvement, the new Catholic Action groups actually perpetuated and deepened a cosmology centered on the triumphant true Church of Christ, identical with the Roman church under the headship of the magisterium (the bishops in full communion with the pope). In short, the "cadres" trained in these revival movements were inclined to take their cues from clerical leadership and, ultimately, from Rome; this did not change after the Council. Meanwhile, the G.I. Bill made higher education accessible to a generation of Catholics who moved to the suburbs in great numbers and adapted to middle-class American culture and lifestyle.

To the future members of the traditionalist movement, Vatican II seemed to lift up the more revolutionary elements of the revival, emphasizing an apostolic rather than a medieval paradigm of the church and modifying the traditional emphasis on absolute, exclusivist truth claims. Ideological boundaries between members of "the One True Church" and "heretics" were softened. The worst suspicions of the traditionalists were confirmed by the "triggering event" of Catholic traditionalism, the implementation of the Novus Ordo Mass, the so-called "new Mass"—the central liturgical ritual of the Roman Catholic Church—which is celebrated in the vernacular rather than in Latin. But the movement never really took off, in large part because of organizational problems.

3. Among cases considered elsewhere in the Fundamentalism Project series, the Ecuadorian Puruha do not exhibit selective reaffirmations of tradition in response to the threats of modernization and secularization. Rather than reacting against modernity, affiliation with the new movement is a step toward the modern world in the sense of the adoption of orderly family life and sober work habits.

4. Islamic movements in central Asia since glasnost and in the early post-Soviet era have been marked by the revival of religious practice and belief and ethnonationalist fragmentation, with control being decentralized to the different Islamic regions—Kazakhstan, the North Caucasus, Azerbaijan, and the like. There is a tendency for individual mosques to be taken over by different ethnic groups. Ideologically the revival of Islam rejects the adaptive strategy followed by the Muslim clergy under the old Soviet Union; the new ideological trends in this period were revivalist and traditionalist rather than fundamentalist. In some cases such movements are anti-Russian in the ethnic sense, but (with the exception of Uzbekistan) they are not organized, focused reactive movements possessed of a charismatic leadership, clear lines of authority, and a mythologized or aggrandized enemy against whom they preserve purity and erect boundaries. But given conditions in post-Soviet Russia and in the successor Islamic nations and the possibility of demonstration effect from the mobilized Islamic areas, fundamentalism may take root here in the soil prepared by these revivalist movements.

CONCLUSION

In this chapter we have examined the characteristics of oppositional movements in Christian, Islamic, Jewish, and South Asian religious traditions. We have established that the first three types of oppositional movements, descended from the Abrahamic tradition, share close ideological and organizational family resemblances. We also suggest that these common ideological and organizational characteristics tend to cohere, to require one another, in a functional logic. Among South Asian cases, the Sikhs come closest to fundamentalism.

We describe a second category of movements exhibiting these characteristics as syncretic fundamentalism. In most of these cases, ethnonational considerations dominate religious elements. These cases include Hindu and Buddhist nationalist movements as well as Ulster Protestants. Interestingly, many Islamic cases tend to be borderline between these two categories in the sense that they combine strong religious fundamentalist commitments with strong nationalist, anti-imperialist tendencies. The Sikhs are an interesting deviant case arising at the point of historical contact and synergism between Hindu and Islamic culture. The religious "host" of Sikh radicalism thus had acquired Abrahamic qualities through cultural contact and conflict. Like its Islamic counterparts, it also combines religion with nationalism.

Other movements assigned to the syncretic fundamentalism category, including Guatemalan and South Indian Pentecostals, are activist, but they are religiously closer to evangelical and Pentecostal strains of their respective host religions.

CHAPTER 3

Explaining Fundamentalisms:
Structure, Chance, and Choice

The task of explaining fundamentalism is twofold. We must ascertain why it has emerged in the larger cultural-historical sense—what is the common cause or set of conditions with which fundamentalism is associated? And we must explain the particularities of its emergence—why here and not there, why now and not then, why among these groups and not those, and so on. The goal of this effort at explanation is to consider the future of fundamentalism, a question we address directly in the concluding chapter. By understanding its occurrence, can we forecast its prospects?

The first part of this task is easier to accomplish than the second. The larger historical significance of fundamentalism is implied in its definition as a set of militant, mobilized, antisecularization movements arising in the course of the twentieth century. In the decade-long investigations of the Fundamentalism Project the secularization-fundamentalism dialectic was clear in case after case, always complicated by the specificities of time, space, and social location.

To address the second question—the particular conditions under which fundamentalisms emerge and grow—we begin by asserting that fundamentalist movements are generated and shaped by three sets of causes: (1) long-term contextual or structural conditions; (2) contingent, chance factors; and (3) the particularities of human choice and leadership. Thus, we account for the specifics of fundamentalism in the modern world by a threefold explanatory strategy: structure, chance, and choice. By structural explanation we refer to large and long-term contextual factors such as social class and status—wealth, income distribution, and social rank—the organization and penetration of the state, education and its content and distribution, cultural and subcultural differences. By chance we refer to short-term, contingent variables such as fluctuations in productivity, trade, international and domestic security, demonstration effects, and the like. By choice we refer to the creativity of leaders (or their decline in creativity) and to collective psychic responses of one kind or another.

This relatively open explanatory model is the one presented by such philosophers of science as Karl Popper, Abraham Kaplan, Ernst Mayr, and others. It recognizes the heterogeneity of reality and hence the inappropriateness of the deductive, "nomothetic" model for such disciplines as biology and the social sciences. Ernst Mayr, speaking of biology since Darwin, writes of the obsolescence of the older classical mechanics view of science as determinist, reductionist, mathematical, and experimentalist; and its replacement by probabilism, synergism, and emergence, along with the methodologies of observation and comparison. This transformation has even effected some branches of physics, for example, relativity and quantum theory; and surely is the appropriate model for the social sciences.[1]

In the social sciences increasing rigor and systematization in case study research, comparative historical analysis, and the adaptation of statistical analysis to small numbers reflects the spread of this newer philosophy of science. In common with other themes in the social sciences, in seeking to explain fundamentalism we are in the quandary of trying to generalize about causation from a relatively small number of very complex cases. Arend Lijphart and David Collier would characterize this situation as the "many variable, small n dilemma," a situation in which it is difficult to establish relationships with high confidence.[2] More than thirty years ago Lijphart examined various methodologies for dealing with social movements and other political phenomena. He points out that the two more scientific methodologies—experimental and statistical—are not readily applicable to the study of political movements. We cannot place such movements in laboratories and subject them to controls. And given the possible relations among their many variables, there are not enough cases to enable us to establish statistical significance with confidence.

At the same time, with rare exceptions, individual case studies at best produce hypotheses, not rigorous explanations. David Collier, summarizing progress that has been made in comparative studies, points to improvements in the case study approach associated with the work of Harry Eckstein through the selection of theoretically powerful cases and that of Alexander George through the systematic use of case studies and the employment of focused comparison and rigorous "process tracing."[3] Collier also points to the development of quasi-experimental techniques through the comparative study of the impact of the same public policy on areas having different characteristics. Collier refers to two alternative ways of comparing a small number of cases—the "most similar systems" and the "most different systems" designs. The most-similar-systems approach seeks rigor and control through matching cases on as many dimensions as possible other than the presumed "cause and effect variables." While it is difficult to find in nature or in history what can be made to occur through deliberate control in the laboratory, this kind of controlled small n comparison does produce theory or, at least, very persuasive hypotheses.

In the chapters of *Fundamentalisms Comprehended* the contributors employ controlled comparison as a way of generating explanatory hypotheses. Thus Said Arjomand's chapter, "Unity and Diversity in Islamic Fundamentalism," and T. N. Madan's, "From Orthodoxy to Fundamentalism: A Thousand Years of Islam in South Asia," hold religious tradition constant and examine how other aspects of society, culture, and economy interact with fundamentalism. On the other hand, Daniel Levine's "Protestants and Catholics in Latin America: A Family Portrait" and Harjot Oberoi's "Mapping Indic Fundamentalisms through Nationalism and Modernity" hold the socioeconomic context constant and vary the religious-doctrinal dimension. Both approaches have the virtue of introducing analytic controls—the same religion in differing sociocultural contexts or different religions in the same context.

Adam Przeworski's approach to comparison—the most-different-systems design—requires a set of cases as diverse as possible but all containing a dose of the same phenomenon. The value of this approach is that it forces us "to distill out of that diversity a set of common elements with great explanatory power."[4] Such a design also has the virtue of enabling us to sort out the varieties of the phenomenon and to establish the common properties as well as the properties of the subspecies.

THE CENTRALITY OF RELIGIOUS LEADERSHIP

The structure-chance-choice framework for case-by-case analysis designates "religious leaders" as the key players in founding and shaping fundamentalist movements. The category must be suitably broad and inclusive to capture the array of figures exercising different kinds of authority over the members of a religious community—virtuosi (spiritual exemplars, charismatic figures, sources of moral imitation), intellectuals (a knowledge elite composed of theologians, judges, scriptural scholars, educators, and the like) and religious officials (clerics, patriarchs, bishops, etc., charged with governing institutions and overseeing bureaucracies). Each level of authority has a role to play in the life of a fundamentalist movement; while most charismatic fundamentalist "founders" are virtuosi and/or intellectuals, for example, some movements (e.g., the Catholic Comunione e Liberazione) are the brainchild of a local religious functionary—a priest, minister, or guru.

From their various privileged locations in the community, religious leaders contest certain interpretations of sacred texts and practices and legitimate others. A given religious leader inclined to extremism thereby nurtures the characteristic traits and elements of fundamentalism within the sector(s) of the religious community over which he exercises authority.

While the fundamentalist leader's choice of interpretations and arguments expresses his own preferences and judgments, the latter are determined by a subtle interaction between the leader's experiences, spiritual-moral formation and educational background, and the character and internal dynamics of his religious community, on the one hand (i.e., "the human factor"), and the constraints and opportunities presented by the specific conditions of the society in which he lives (the external environment), on the other. These long-term structural conditions dictate the range of choices available to religious leaders; his range of possible options will be affected by the presence or absence of armed conflict in the region, state policies toward religion and religious or ethnic minorities, religious participation in the political economy, the strength of voluntary associations, the availability and quality of general as well as religious education, social mobility, migration and the status of refugees, and the like. The range of possible choices becomes both focused and narrowed when fate intervenes in the form of an unexpected event ("contingent, chance factors") that may trigger the rise or decline of a fundamentalist movement.

Structural factors may create a niche for fundamentalist movements. Structural unemployment may, for instance, create a pool of potential recruits. Likewise, people who feel relative deprivation because of inconsistency between status and income may express grievances through a fundamentalist movement; persecuted ethnic groups, dislocated people, victims of war, or migrants looking for identity and community may join them.

Chance influences the size and social location of the niche. For example, an area where a riot or a strike has recently galvanized the population or some part of it will be fertile recruiting ground. A new media technology such as the audiocassette introduced in Iran in the mid-1970s enabled Khomeini to smuggle his sermons from Iraq and Paris into Iran where they were easily and cheaply duplicated and spread like brushfire. Defeat in war (Egypt and Syria in 1967) or an evident economic failure (Algeria after the second oil bust of 1984–85) damages the legitimacy of the political system and facilitates recruitment to protest movements, including fundamentalism.

This interaction between external conditions and internal dynamics determines how a theologian, monk, rebbe, or 'alim will "read" or interpret a particular event or situation, define "structural injustice," and make a particular choice.

This is simply a way of saying that a fundamentalist movement, like any movement, exists and changes in space and time. It is "founded," grows, spreads, develops new programs, changes strategy and tactics, wins and loses elections, succeeds or fails in revolutions, declines, disappears. An explanatory theory of fundamentalism, hence, must disaggregate "movement" into its significant aspects, just as we have disaggregated the "independent variables" into specific structural, contingency, and choice components. Thus we expect that leadership would have a special relationship to the founding of movements, their strategy and tactics, and their decline (often associated with the death of leaders); religious structure and theology would have a large impact on fundamentalist organization and ideology; war, economic crises, and population movements may have a close relationship to growth and spread; and so on.

Long-term structural factors such as the organization and theology of the host religion, ethnic and religious heterogeneity, the growth and character of the economy, cultural secularization, and domestic and international politics must be understood as necessary but not sufficient causes of fundamentalism. Without such long-term structural changes and conditions (such as secularization), there would be no fundamentalism. But secularization produced liberalism, radicalism, and romanticism, as well as fundamentalism. It was a strong, necessary cause. But even if we take all the structural causes together, they would only tell us that if a fundamentalist movement arose in this context it would probably have such and such particular characteristics and geographic and social structural distributions. To turn these potentialities into reality we need human choices—the decisions of leaders and the needs and demands of members and supporters. These are the *sufficient* causes in the sense that they convert the "human material" and material resources into actual movements.[5]

Even though we may "explain" a fundamentalist movement by exhaustively investigating the long-run structural causes, the short-term chance developments and the role of leadership, we are far from suggesting that we can predict the rise of fundamentalism, the forms that it takes, or the strategies that it pursues. The impact of structural factors are predictable up to a point. But short-run developments such as the illness or death of leaders, poor crops, and famine, are less predictable or entirely unpredictable; and human factors such as leadership decisions or popular actions are responsive and creative actions and hence unpredictable. In this arena the humanities and the social sciences collaborate to comprehend the depth and complexity of human endeavor.

It might have been possible, for example, to forecast the religious characteristics of Iranian Shi'ite fundamentalism by considering traditional Shi'ite doctrine and organization, to take these particular structural factors. But plotting the vulnerability of Iran to a fundamentalist takeover would require that we be able to forecast the illness of the Shah and the indecisiveness of the regime at a critical moment in the unfolding of the Shi'ite-led revolution; the widespread availability of the audiocassette for propaganda purposes; and changing American policy resulting from the Watergate scandal and the election of Jimmy Carter. Taken together, these two sets of factors might have allowed us to predict some kind of religious-centered revolution in Iran; but we would need to factor in the character and personality of the Ayatollah Khomeini to produce the Iranian fundamentalist phenomenon.

This framework for analysis brings us to the threshold of understanding the complexities of a concrete case. Once we have elaborated the framework, it will be possible to specify the combination of external conditions and internal dynamics necessary to trigger the rise and growth of fundamentalism in particular cases.

We begin with the structural factors, moving from the central theme of secularization to the proximate variables of religion, culture, the media, and education to the more indirect stimuli and constraints based on ethnicity, the economy, the social structure, and the political and international systems. We then turn to contingency and chance, and finally treat human choice and the creativity of leadership.

STRUCTURE

The defining and distinctive structural cause of fundamentalist movements is secularization. As we consider the sweep of fundamentalist movements across nations, cultures, and civilizations, some degree of secularization is present in all of them. Confronted with the threat of secularization, the world of religion responds adaptively or militantly—by assimilating to the values of the secular world or by mobilizing in opposition to this invasion and to the traitors who compromise with the enemy. Protestant, Catholic, and Jewish haredi fundamentalisms fit into this relatively unambiguous cultural category. Perhaps some multigenerational movements, such as Hasidic fundamentalism, ought to be viewed under more than one aspect. In its original formation in the eighteenth century, Hasidism was a reaction against the formalism and intellectualism of shtetl religiosity; in other words, it arose out of religious conflict. In its late-nineteenth-century reformulation it took on its strong antisecular character.

Secularization as a structural cause of fundamentalism is complicated in a variety of other ways as well. Sunni Islamic fundamentalism, for example, while strongly antisecular, has the added complication of a strong nationalist, anti-Western component. That is, it is caused not only by the threat of modern science and technology to religious tradition and values but by the fact that these values are carried by powerful alien and exploitative agents such as the United States, her puppet Israel, and their Islamic "lackeys." Shi'ite fundamentalism adds to these enemies its religious competition and enmity with Sunni Islam. Hindu fundamentalism adds to its antisecular, anti-imperialist-colonialist antagonism, an ethnic, pro-Hindu, nativist component.

Religion

We begin with religion as one of the long-range determining factors. The nature of the host religion out of which fundamentalism arises is perhaps the most important conditioning factor in the explanation of fundamentalism—its theology, its organizational structure, its vitality. Does the host religion have a hierarchical structure as in Catholicism, a semihierarchical structure as in Shi'ism, or a congregational one as in Protestantism and Sunni Islam? Or is it a relatively unspecialized, diffuse set of roles and institutions as in Hinduism, Sikhism, and Buddhism?

Table 3.1 (in the appendix to chapter 3), describing the organization of the host religions of a number of fundamentalist movements, shows most of them to be associated with religions in which authority and legitimacy are concentrated in individual congregations or around individual mosques—in other words, where fundamentalist breakaway is relatively low in cost, where a congregation may simply go fundamentalist, or where new ones may easily be formed. In contrast, there are relatively few cases of effective breakaway among Roman Catholics. Organizationally speaking, since the church is the sole source of salvation, great danger is involved in separation from and opposition to the church establishment. For a fundamentalist movement to arise in Shi'ite Islam with its semihierarchical structure would require the action of an ayatollah having or mobilizing the support of associates and lower clergy. The relatively centralized Shi'ite organization would lend itself more easily to takeover, as the case of Iran suggests. In the cases of Hinduism and Sikhism, clerical organization tends to be diffuse and/or charismatic, consisting of gurus and their followers, temple priests, and administrators. Hindu and Sikh "fundamentalist" organizations are lay associations and not religious organizations properly speaking. Among the Sri Lankan Buddhists, religious organization consists of monasteries of abbots, and monks stratified according to seniority. Buddhist movements in Sri Lanka are lay extremist groups with some participation by monks.

The theology of the host religion is similarly important in influencing fundamentalist movements. Are its beliefs explicit and coherent, codified in texts as in the case of the Abrahamic religions—in Judaism, Christianity, Islam—and in Sikhism? What are its conceptions of deity, of history, of the religious life? Where there are explicit authoritative texts, it is easier for fundamentalist movements to separate themselves from a compromising, secularizing religious establishment. Religions with a millennial, messianic theology are, with some noteworthy exceptions, particularly susceptible to fundamentalism, since the hope of dramatic redemption is attractive to suffering adherents.

Is the religious context a homogeneous one, or are there significant competing religions? Does religion coincide with ethnolinguistic differences? What is the historic pattern of relations among these ethnoreligious groups? A multireligious, conflictual context is more likely to produce ethnonational-religious militance (as in the cases of Northern Ireland, India, and Sri Lanka) rather than simple religious fundamentalism.

Major short-term precipitants in the religious domain include the outbreak of open competition and conflict among ethnoreligious groups, as in India and Sri Lanka; major changes of policy on the part of the host religious establishment, as in the decrees of Vatican II; and individual acts of excommunication, as in the case of Archbishop Lefebvre. But one should not overlook the impact of what are viewed as revelations, epiphanies, and noumenal events of one kind or another—direct interventions of the divine into human affairs. The alleged miraculous vision of the Virgin Mary in a

Coptic church in Egypt in the aftermath of the 1967 war is a case in point. And the vision of the Lord Ram in the Babri Masjid (mosque of Babur) in Ayodhya played a role in its final destruction at the hands of Hindu fundamentalists. The religious Zionists who joined the Gush Emunim in Israel viewed the victory of 1967 and the narrow escape of 1973 as divine signals to shift into messianic gear.

Education

The educational system and the media, like religion and in competition with it, are concerned with the shaping of hearts and minds. The secular schools and universities spread the knowledge and cultivate the analytical skills that challenge and erode religious beliefs. Hence the fundamentalists are in conflict with the educational and scientific establishment, seeking to maintain or establish beachheads, to assert epistemological equality between "creation science" and "secular humanism," to legalize prayer in the schools, and the like.

Changes in government policy toward education may serve as short-term triggers or precipitants for fundamentalist movements. A dramatic example of such a precipitant is the rapid growth of higher education in the United States after the Soviets' successful launching of *Sputnik*, and similar rapid growth in Western Europe and in some parts of the Third World. The sudden increase in the numbers of students and the formation of new secular universities and colleges without traditions contributed to the cultural turmoil of the 1960s, as well as to an imbalance of supply and demand in the job market for university graduates in the Islamic world, in India, and after the 1960s, in the West. The cultural revolution, centered on university campuses, was a threat and shock to religious groups, furnishing ammunition to fundamentalists.

Generally speaking, the most educated strata of populations are least susceptible to fundamentalism; the elite colleges and universities are less susceptible than the marginal ones. This is true in India, Latin America, and the Middle East, as well as in the United States. Having said that, it remains true that many fundamentalists, especially in what might be called the middle management leadership of the movements, have obtained degrees in engineering, in medical technology, or in other technical scientific disciplines. By contrast, one finds few fundamentalists trained in astrophysics or other branches of science that are less empirical and more speculative and theoretical in orientation. Finally, while many fundamentalists were educated in traditional seminaries, madrasas, yeshivot or religious colleges of one kind or another, others attended secular educational institutions, state universities, or vocational colleges.[6]

Communication

Long-run trends of media development—the spread of print, the rise of mass-circulation newspapers and radio, the cultural dominance of cinema and television and, more recently, the world of cyberspace, the Internet, and World Wide Web—have changed the mode and quality of the exchange of information and ideas throughout the world. The exponential growth of communications media is culminating in the phenomenon known as globalization. The term refers not only to the near-complete transgression of erstwhile geographic and cultural borders by instantaneous cable television and cyberspace interventions but also to the ongoing construction of a global culture (increasingly homogenized and standardized, some argue) driven by transnational markets and corporate interests.[7]

Both the communications explosion and the more recent phenomenon of globalization have had several implications for religion and the rise of fundamentalism. On the one hand, these new and powerful media in the hands of the secular world spread the information, knowledge, and moral standards that threaten religious beliefs and practices. But later generations of religious leaders, particularly the fundamentalists among them, discovered that they could put the media to their own uses. Thus the rise of televangelism, the use of data banks for direct mailing, and the use of audiocassettes to proselytize enhanced the New Christian Right's access to potential supporters in the United States (and abroad). Exploiting the Indian cinema, Hindu revivalists turned the legends of the Mahabarata into popular sitcoms. Gush Emunim technophiles were among the first activists to use the cell phone to organize rallies at a moment's notice as unfolding events were broadcast on Israeli television and radio. Dozens of religious activist groups, including the Tamil Tigers, now have a home page on the World Wide Web.

The global world of communication and information increases the speed and significance of "demonstration effect." The impact of suicide bombs on the peace process in the Middle East, the political demands of the surprisingly powerful haredi Jewish parties in Israel's governing coalitions, the electoral success and suppression of Islamic fundamentalism in Algeria, the destruction of the Babri Masjid in India—all of these developments, and many more, were quickly registered around the world. The secularizing impact of the media, on the one hand, and the entrance of fundamentalist movements into the struggle for access to these powerful media, on the other, suggests the quandary of these fundamentalist movements as they modernize themselves in special ways in their efforts to resist the larger modernizing trends.

Civil Society

Civil society refers to the social formations between the state, on the one hand, and family and kinship, on the other—voluntary associations and agencies of one kind or another formed around economic, ethnic, religious, local, and other interests and values. The vitality of such associations and their relations to the state are crucial to the understanding of civil society— which is the realm within which fundamentalism arises. It makes a great deal of difference if a society has strong and independent trade unions, civic associations, communications media, and political parties capable of draining off anxiety and resentment in response to social and economic crises and converting them into secular politics and public policy.

We would fail to understand Islamic movements, for example, if we did not take into account the fact that civil society in Islamic countries has been reduced over the last century by the interventionist state. In this context Islamist movements provide an alternative space for the articulation of discontent and aspiration. The public presence of Roman Catholicism, to take a second example, has been transformed since Vatican II and especially during the pontificate of Pope John Paul II (1978-) by a strategic shift from affiliation with the state, whether in Latin American, European, or Asian nations, to a dynamic and politically independent role in civil society.[8]

Social Structure

Fundamentalist leaders and members are recruited from different parts of the social structure, depending on the structural characteristics of the society, its level of development, degree of urbanization, the pattern of distribution of wealth and income, and differences in patterns of consumption. The social structure creates "fault lines," social "fissures"—anxious and relatively deprived strata that may be drawn to the communitarian, revitalizing, often vindictive appeals of militant religious movements.

In the United States perhaps the most significant religious development in the last several decades has been a decline in the membership of the mainline Protestant denominations (e.g., Episcopalian, Presbyterian, Methodist, Lutheran) and the sharp increase in the size of evangelical and Pentecostal denominations. Thus the Southern Baptists increased from around 10 million in 1960 to 17 million in 2000; Pentecostal denominations increased more than fourfold, from under 2 million in 1960 to almost 12 million in 2000; while the Episcopalians dropped from 3.5 million in 1960 to 2 million in 2000 and the United Methodists dropped from more than 10 million in 1960 to under 8 million in 2000.[9]

Within and as a result of this trend potential political support for the New Christian Right (NCR) grew significantly in the 1980s and 1990s. Social researchers discovered that a number of NCR positions were popular among the mass public. "Large proportions of Americans oppose homosexuality and pornography, favor school prayer and private school vouchers, and support sex education emphasizing abstinence," one team of social scientists concluded. "Smaller, but still substantial groups have serious reservations about abortion. . . . While such a coalition of traditionalists would not constitute a majority of the American people, it could easily exceed 30 percent of the population."[10]

When public support for certain values and standards wanes, fundamentalists may react initially with a vehement reassertion of their position, an insistence that seems calculated to remind people that "traditional," God-given values are not to be trifled with. When it became apparent that the American media and entertainment industry were beginning to exhibit signs of tolerance for homosexuals in the 1990s, for example, the Christian Coalition made the condemnation and restigmatization of homosexuality into something of a cultural crusade between 1996 and 1999.

In her authoritative study of the Southern Baptist clergy and activist laity in the years of struggle for control of the Southern Baptist Convention (a battle won by the fundamentalists), Nancy Ammerman notes that status in the denomination and in society appears to have been related to the positions people were taking in the Southern Baptist Convention controversy. Those who had more comfortable lives—from white collar and professional families, with more income, and a professional at the head of household—were more likely to have occupied positions to the left of center in the denomination and to declare themselves moderate. Pastors of larger urban churches were also moderates. By contrast, "those who came from farming and blue collar backgrounds, who had less money, and whose jobs involved them in a more routine sort of work, were more attracted to fundamentalist ways of thinking." "Status cannot explain all the differences between the Southern Baptist Convention's left and right wings," she concludes, "but it does appear to explain a good deal."[11]

Education levels were also significant in predicting tendencies toward fundamentalism. Many well-educated people were fundamentalists and many moderates had little schooling. "But the differences between the two wings were tangible and real. Almost no pastors on the moderate side had less than a seminary education, while over two-thirds of the pastors on the fundamentalist side had only a college degree or less," Ammerman writes. Less than one-fifth of fundamentalist laity had a bachelor's degree, while over half of the moderate laity had a bachelor's degree or more. "Fundamentalist leaders often had blue ribbon educations and could debate the best-educated moderates on their own terms, but fundamentalist followers were at a considerable educational disadvantage compared to their moderate counterparts." Ammerman concludes that "among the many social sources of Southern Baptist division, then, education must be seen as a leading influence."[12]

Finally, Ammerman's study also demonstrated that urbanization influenced affiliation with the moderate and fundamentalist wings of the Southern Baptist leadership. "People who grew up in suburbs and small cities were the most likely to adopt a moderate theology, while those who grew up on farms were the least likely to locate left of center. There was, in fact, a direct negative relationship between the size of a person's community of origin and the conservatism of his or her beliefs. People who grew up in cities were simply less conservative than people who grew up in the country."[13]

This marginality to the modern and the urban was also characteristic of Hindu fundamentalists, who seem to be predominantly recruited from the "cow belt" Hindu traditionalist country; and of the Sikh Khalistanis, who are primarily recruited from the more backward western districts of Punjab.

Short-run social structural shocks resulting from recession and unemployment, labor conflicts or strikes, the introduction of foreign workers, or ethnic clashes may produce or sharpen grievances in particular sectors of the society, rendering them susceptible to protest movements, including fundamentalism. The Sephardic-Ashkenazic socioeconomic division among Israeli Jews as well as the deterioration of Israeli-Palestinian relations created, with the help of recurrent crises, a ready-made soil fertile to the Kach movement of Rabbi Kahane.

Mobility

Major migrations have had important consequences for the development of fundamentalism. For the Jews the depopulation of the Jewish shtetl in

Eastern Europe at the turn of the nineteenth century was made possible by emancipation and the Jewish enlightenment, resulting in massive emigration to the larger towns and cities and to the United States and other countries. The residual shtetl communities and yeshivot reacted to this depopulation by a drawing of lines and a strengthened orthodoxy. A second major Jewish population movement was the large-scale immigration to Israel, the United States, and elsewhere after the Holocaust and the establishment of the Jewish state. This transplanted Jewish fundamentalist movements from their Eastern European origins principally to Israel and the United States.

The migration of Palestinians after the establishment of the Jewish State sowed the seeds of Islamic fundamentalism, as did the large-scale recruitment of (and subsequent backlash against) Muslim guest workers in Western Europe in the 1960s and 1970s. In Italy the large-scale movement of southern Italians into the prosperous industrial cities of northern Italy formed the backdrop for the rise of Comunione e Liberazione. In the United States the movement of southerners into northern cities and the general movement from countryside to city and from city to suburbs affected recruitment into Christian fundamentalist movements. The mechanism converting the breakup of community into potential fundamentalist affiliation is the need to maintain or reestablish identity.

Mobility may be long- or short-term in its impact. For example, Muslim migration into France has continued since World War I but was precipitated in the boom years of the 1960s and then was terminated after the first oil shock in 1973–74, thus pushing guest workers to become permanent French residents and aggravating their identity problems. More recent migration of refugees from the Algerian civil war spread fear among French citizens that Islamism and the violence and antidemocratic movements associated with it in the popular mind would contaminate French society. These fears were on full display in the controversy over the veiling of Muslim girls in French schools and in the heated debate about the right of permanent residents to vote in municipal elections.

Jewish immigration into Palestine took on significant proportions during the 1930s and then sharply increased after World War II and the formation of the state of Israel. Many of the Haredi communities date from the immigration of Eastern European Holocaust survivors to the United States, Israel, France, and Great Britain, where they have transplanted their Hasidic communities and yeshivot, recreating them in new forms adapted to the various local situations. In the Protestant Christian case, as we have noted, the rise of fundamentalism was triggered in part by the migration of industrial laborers and their families into the urban Northeast.

Ethnic-Regional Factors

The ethnic-linguistic-regional composition of a society—its ethnolinguistic homogeneity or heterogeneity, the distinctiveness of regional divisions, the historical background of relations among ethnic and regional groups—may have important implications for the development of fundamentalism. The subordination and exploitation of one ethnic or regional group by another as well as historic ethnic tensions may create grievances in the long term. Violent clashes in the short term may convert these grievances into collective awareness and action. Militant religious movements in a heterogeneous country such as India carry distinct ethnic imprints. In Northern Ireland the Ulster Protestants and the Irish Catholics have been locked for decades in an intractable struggle. Chapter 5 provides an extended discussion of ethnicity and fundamentalism.

Economic Development

The economic circumstances of a society—including its level of development and GNP, its natural resources, its rate of growth, and the unevenness of the geographic spread of growth—relate to the emergence and life of fundamentalism in a variety of ways. This is true whether a society is "First World" or Third; whether it contains a growing tertiary sector, as well as an industrial one; and whether it is primarily agricultural or extractive. We do not have to subscribe to the Marxist or "dependencista" view that tends to reduce all religious categories to economic ones in order to recognize these interactions between economy and religion. We have observed that rank-and-file fundamentalists tend to be recruited from the less-developed, less "modern" parts of societies, from the rural population, from the poorer parts of cities, from the less well educated, from social strata relatively deprived in economic and social development and improvement, and the like.

In the short run, recessions, depressions, inflation, strikes, unemployment, and famine may create attitudes and grievances among particular groups in the population, inclining them favorably to fundamentalist arguments, themes, and practices. Contrariwise, the availability of abundant natural resources such as oil may make it possible for some countries to offer opportunities and services to their people that may obviate or blunt the impact of such economic shocks, thereby lessening the attraction of fundamentalist movements. In Tunisia, for instance, Islamism declined in the 1990s, it is argued, thanks to the success of export-driven economic growth spurred by the government, which enabled the middle class to expand, home ownership to increase, and the auto industry to enjoy boom times. The level of economic productivity and prosperity, in short, is one among several factors to be considered in explaining the emergence and growth of fundamentalist movements.

When fundamentalist movements have, in fact, assumed power in a state, as they did in Turkey (for a short period), in Iran, and in the Sudan, poor or disappointing economic performance led to disenchantment with the fundamentalist government. Even fundamentalists, in short, must provide effective economic solutions to the crisis that had a hand in bringing them to power in the first place. Most fundamentalist movements have not been put to the test in this manner, and there is no evidence that they would pass the economic test.

Political Characteristics

The authority structure of a state, the legitimacy of its institutions and leadership, the extent to which the state penetrates the society, the level of popular participation, the degree of partisan polarization—all may shape the nature of movements arising in that society. Different kinds of political and constitutional arrangements may be associated with differences in the goals and tactics of fundamentalist movements. Thus in secularized democracies such as the United States, Italy, and India fundamentalist movements operate openly in political and partisan competition. In contemporary India the governing Bharatiya Janata Party (BJP), dominated by militant Hindu ethnoreligious movements, has been accused of seeking to eliminate secular pluralism. Earlier, right-wing Hindu movements were suppressed in the crises following the assassinations of Mohandas, Indira, and Rajiv Gandhi, and the destruction of the Babri Masjid in Ayodhya.

Israel is a semisecular democratic state in which the Orthodox rabbinate and the Halakhah have privileged positions. Jewish fundamentalist movements, given Israel's electoral system, have the electoral support, and an ideological location in political space, that enables them to bargain for the extension of Orthodox Jewish regulations into the public law. Algeria and Egypt are secular authoritarian regimes following repressive policies vis-à-vis their fundamentalist oppositions. Iraq and Syria are strong authoritarian, anticlerical regimes in which fundamentalist opposition has to operate largely underground. Pakistan has a partially clericalized regime that limits the autonomy of secular movements; and Iran is the outstanding example of an authoritarian clerical regime in full control of the state and following repressive policies against secular movements.

In the short term, revolution, civil war, changes of government, changes in policy, or important judicial decisions may serve as triggers to the formation of movements or to their subsequent development. The Islamist current in Algeria swelled after the opening up of the Algerian political system to free elections in 1988; skillful fundamentalist leaders captured a majority of the voters who were alienated by the failure of the Algerian oil economy. In Israel the rise to power of the Likud in 1977 created a political atmosphere supportive of the Greater Israel aspirations of the Gush Emunim. The U.S. Supreme Court's 1973 *Roe v. Wade* decision legalizing abortion nationwide increased the appeal of fundamentalism among conservative Protestants. Chapter 5 provides an extended discussion of politics and fundamentalism.

International Environment

We cannot overestimate the importance of Western imperialism in the explanation of fundamentalism in the Third World—in the Middle East, Africa, and South Asia. Commerce and the secular culture of science, technology, and modern industry appeared in the Third World under the auspices of exploitative, colonialist Western powers. The independent governments established in these formerly colonial countries continue to bear these neocolonialist stigmata long after the departure of the imperial authorities. Thus Third World fundamentalist movements tend to have nationalist and anti-imperialist tendencies in addition to their religious ones.[14] They tend to be parochial and isolationist in their relations to the outside world. The lively exchange of goods and ideas implied in open diplomacy, trade, and communication threatens the integrity of their traditions and opens their members to competing religions, debilitating materialism, and moral corruption.

As these movements come closer to power, they are constrained to adopt more open policies vis-à-vis their internal and external political and cultural worlds. A fundamentalist movement is under pressure to hedge its isolated approach in order to engage in the coalition-making essential to effective politics. The attempt of the Islamist Refah party to form a coalition government after its pluralist victory in the 1995 Turkish parliamentary election failed despite its efforts to compromise and win the confidence of possible coalition partners. Throughout the 1990s media reported intermittent overtures between the leaders of the Islamist underground and the Algerian military and government establishment. Once in power, similar pressures might constrain a fundamentalist movement to relate to secular domestic groups or to external societies, cultures, and value systems.

Inevitable ambivalence exists in the external and foreign affairs of fundamentalist movements. There are difficulties, perhaps inherent limits, in accumulating power internally and in spreading internationally. Once in power, there are difficulties in the long run in avoiding the compromises and pluralism required by effective coalition making and conduct of foreign policy.

In the short term, the appeals of fundamentalism are influenced by international events that create grievances—wars and their aftermath; terms of trade and global economic fluctuations harming Third World economies; "demonstration effects" such as the Khomeini revolution in Iran that arouse hopes. The 1967 war and the capture of Jerusalem by Israel was an exhilarating moment for Jews as well as for fundamentalist Baptists; it was a deep shock and a mobilizing force among Muslims everywhere.

CONTINGENCY AND CHANCE

In normal social situations there are lines of cleavage of an economic, social, ethnic, religious, or political sort. Typically it takes some precipitant, shock, or trigger to turn these inert potentialities into "live" ones. It might be a depression; a famine; deteriorating economic situations among particular groups; riots over migrant labor; sudden population movements; ethnic clashes; sharp changes in government policy; wars and other signal international events; governmental interventions in education, culture, religion; church decisions, noumenal events, and the like. These shock and trigger factors are contingencies, matters of chance. The Green Revolution accentuated economic inequalities in Punjab. The development of the cassette extended the range of the ayatollah's voice. The 1967 war deepened the feeling of humiliation among the Arabs. A judicial decision in India, the celebrated Shah Bano case, gave special status to Islamic marriage law and thereby provoked mass anti-Islamic reactions among the Hindus.

There are two types of "chance" events that may trigger the rise or transformation of fundamentalist movements. Neither can be predicted, but events such as a bread riot or a controversial legal ruling may be anticipated as an expression of structural weaknesses or cleavages. Though its timing, force, and impact are impossible to predict, a bread riot, for example, is hardly unimaginable or unpredictable in a society known to suffer economic instability and chronic food shortages as a result of state distribution policies, agricultural and trade practices, etc. It is, nonetheless, a "chance" occurrence that may provide an opening for fundamentalist recruiters and mobilizers.

A second type of contingent event is the truly unexpected occurrence: the shah of Iran is crippled by terminal cancer just as a coalition of revolutionaries riot in the streets of Tehran; a massive earthquake in Turkey opens the way for Muslim relief agencies who bolster the fortunes of the national Islamist party; reported appearances of the Virgin Mary in Conyers (GA), Medjugorje, and other sites create an opportunity for traditionalist Catholic recruiting. In this sense the triggering event comes from out of the blue, the result of unpredictable human action or natural event. Such events cannot be predicted in any sense; they are matter of luck, fate, or destiny, but they, too, can create opportunities for fundamentalist movements. Of course, the triggering event may be a combination of both types of chance occurrences, with latent trends surfaced and transformed by the inspired free act of a leader. In this regard one thinks of the election of an aging and obscure Angelo Roncalli who, as Pope John XXIII, convened an ecumenical council (Vatican II) that transformed the face of modern Roman Catholicism by legitimating a reform movement that had been growing within the church for several decades.

Chance events, in short, have the effect of mobilizing people along the structural lines of cleavage. Fundamentalists, as shrewd observers and diagnosticians of their societies, are poised to take advantage of the polarization of society. They are particularly effective in exploiting longer term structural weaknesses; their treatises, tracts, sermons, and educational programs are devoted to identifying and denouncing such weaknesses.

Chance and contingent events may be necessary aspects of explanation; without them there might not be a fundamentalist movement. But they are not the sufficient explanation. For this we must turn to choice—the choices of threatened, aggrieved, and anxious people looking for safety and security; and the choices of their religious leaders offering fundamentalist solutions—ideas, organization, and programs to meet these needs.

CHOICE AND LEADERSHIP

A movement requires leaders and followers. For the formation and maintenance of a fundamentalist movement, followers must be "prone," susceptible to fundamentalist appeals and tactics. Leadership converts these susceptibilities into commitments, mobilizes these members around particular goals and programs, and makes the decisions regarding interaction with the outside world.

There are different kinds of fundamentalist leaders in terms of their skills and specialization. They may be seen as ideologues, organizers, coalition builders or some combination of the three. There are *ideological catalyzers* such as the Hafetz Haim (the haredim), Rabbi Kook the Elder (the Gush Emunim), C. I. Scofield and J. Gresham Machen (the American Protestants), Sayyid Qutb (the Sunni Muslims), the Ayatollah Khomeini (the Shi'ite Muslims), V. D. Savarkar (the Hindu "revivalists"), Jarnail Singh Bhindranwale (the radical Sikh guru), Archbishop Lefebvre (the Catholic restorationist), and others.

There are *organizers and coalition makers* such as Rabbis Ovadia Joseph and Eliezer Schach (the haredim), Father Luigi Giussani (Comunione e Liberazione), the Reverends Frank Norris and Bob Jones (the fundamentalist Baptists), K. B. Hedgewar, and M. S. Golwarkar (the Hindu RSS). In fundamentalist movements, as in any movement, leadership constitutes a very large part of the sufficient causation, effectively inventing and presenting ideas, converting them into action programs, seeking and accumulating resources, devising formulas and negotiating the formation of coalitions.

Yet leadership does not operate in a vacuum; there must be a mobilizable mass of potential followers. Often, as noted above, the movement really gets off the ground only when a cataclysmic, transformative event occurs either within the movement itself or, more likely, in the local, national, or international environment external to the movement. The trigger creates a new set of circumstances that provides an opening for a fundamentalist movement to expand and assert itself under the guidance of a charismatic authoritarian leader.[15]

Explaining Fundamentalism:
The Case of Militant Hindu Nationalism

Suppose we illustrate our explanatory model by exploring actual cases in some detail. "Hindu fundamentalism" is a good place to start since it would seem improbable that fundamentalism would rise in the Indian setting.

Without the Moghul and British invasions and occupations, Hinduism never would have acquired a mobilized ideological identity or even a militant collective consciousness.[16] The term *Hindu* is derived from the Indus River; the Hindus lived beyond it. That is what being Hindu meant all the way back to the Achaemenids and the Greeks. The Hindus had no orthodoxy, no "book." Organized in a multitude of castes and sects, they were not conscious enough of an "other" to be conscious of a "self." It was the construction of an antagonist "other" by the Moghuls and the British during the course of the nineteenth century that created the tension leading to Hindu nationalism. The Hindus responded to the stigmatization, particularly by the British missionaries, of their "idolatrous" religion and caste system by the elaboration of a counter-stigmatization of Western materialism and the invention of a distant indigenous "golden age" cleansed of all the criticized features. For India to have acquired a fundamentalism (even though syncretic) comparable to that of Christianity, Judaism, and Islam, however, challenges explanation.

The synthesis of a Hindu style of "fundamentalism" was accomplished through a set of interrelated strategies, the first of which involved the formation of an ideological identity. The organization in 1915 of the Hindu Mahasabha (Hindu Great Council) and the publication of *Hindutva* by V. D. Savarkar were key moments. Affirming the sacred right of the Hindu nation to the whole of prepartition India and laying claim to a history beginning in a golden age, *Hindutva* ("Hinduness") established the doctrinal foundation for a Hindu nationalism. As adopted by the various organizations of Hindu nationalism, the doctrine of *Hindutva* provided the missing millennial-messianic and inerrant features normally associated with Abrahamic fundamentalism.

The Hindu nationalist organizational strategy was syncretic; it borrowed in part from Western political party innovations of the early twentieth century. Founded in 1925, the Rashtriya Svayamsevak Sangh (RSS; National Union of Volunteers) is a brotherhood of believers trained in the martial arts and subject to discipline. It was originally to serve Lenin's transmission belt function, forming "front" and instrumental organizations in the various regions, among the various social groupings, and in the numerous Indian diaspora.

The RSS was a direct reaction and response to the threat to Hindu ideas and practices mounted in the course of the late nineteenth and early twentieth centuries by two powerful secularizing agencies, the British imperial presence and the Indian Civil Service, and the growing Congress movement. From the perspective of the traditional Hindu elites the Congress Party continued the destruction and displacement of Hindu culture begun by the British and the Muslims. The Hindu response—the invention of Hindutva and the formation of the RSS—reproduced the typical fundamentalist pattern of militant reactivity, selectivity, moral absolutism, inerrancy, and an elect membership with sharp boundaries, authoritarian organization, required behaviors, costume, psalmody, and the like.

In 1964, RSS leaders founded the Vishwa Hindu Parishad (VHP; World Hindu Society), a cultural organization that stages huge religious processions designed to arouse popular fervor for "Hindu causes" and to intimidate Muslims and other "outsiders." The VHP promotes Hindu revival in the remote corners of India and among the Hindu diaspora. Organized at two levels, with a "religious assembly" at the center directed by advisory committees made up of leaders from participating religious communities in the regions, the VHP boasted three hundred district units and some three thousand branches throughout India in 1994. It reported more than 100,000 members, with three hundred full-time workers, each dedicated to reaffirming "Hindu values." The movement remains strong in 2002. Outside India it claims to have several thousand branches in twenty-five countries.

By sketching a broad and somewhat vague definition of "Hindu values" the VHP seeks to transcend internal differences among Hindus, to bring secularized Indians back to the fold, and to reclaim the Untouchables to Hinduism. The VHP strategy is to propagate a coherent modern version of Hinduism as the national religion of India. Thus it downplays local differences in Hindu religious doctrine and represents Hinduism, ahistorically, as a single all-embracing ethnonational religious community including Jains, Buddhists, and Sikhs.

The third and final piece of the Hindu nationalist puzzle is the Bharatiya Janata Party (BJP; Indian People's Party). The BJP emerged in 1980 out of the Janata coalition that displaced the Indira Gandhi regime in 1977. Most of the BJP leaders were formed in the RSS, but as a political party contesting nationwide elections, the BJP has attempted to appeal broadly to all Indians, including Sikhs and Muslims. In the 1996 national elections, the BJP won the largest bloc of seats (160) in the Lok Sabha (the lower house of Parliament), thereby helping to topple the Congress Party from power for only the second time in the forty-nine years of Indian statehood. Atal Bihari Vajpayee, then head of the BJP, served as prime minister of India during the two weeks in May 1996 in which the party attempted unsuccessfully to form a minority government to rule the nation's 930 million people. In March 1998 he became prime minister a second time after the BJP successfully contested the February 1998 elections, winning 178 of the 543 elected seats in the Lok Sabha. Again, Vajpayee was forced to form a coalition government that included regional parties long opposed to the religious nationalists' doctrine of Hindu supremacy.[17]

Explaining the Political Success of Hindu Nationalism

For most of its seven decades the Hinduism-based complex of nationalist movements occupied the extremes of the political spectrum, a marginal player winning only very small representation in the Lok Sabha but with greater strength at the state and local level.

How, then, can we explain the stunning political success of Hindu nationalism in the late 1980s and 1990s, when with the decay of the Congress Party, the BJP finally became the plurality party in the Lok Sabha and was able to form a majority coalition?

The greater political potential of the BJP became evident as the Congress Party fell on bad times. Its composition and structure are such that in its more secular and bargaining mode it has sufficient strength to be a parliamentary coalition maker; and in its ideological mode it is capable of high levels of mobilization.

The vitality and survival of the larger movement that formed the core of the BJP's electoral success depended on the concentration of "Hindu culture" in a number of north Indian states, the so-called "Cowbelt"—primarily Maharashtra, Gujarat, and Uttar Pradesh. The headquarters of the RSS and other Hindu organizations were located in these traditionalist ethnocultural regions, and this is where their committed cadres were recruited. In its weaker moments the movement drew strength from these more tradition-bound regions.

To become the plurality party, however, Hindu nationalism needed to move in a populist-secular direction while drawing on the traditionalist elements among the electoral support of the Congress Party.

Indian parliamentarism and federalism are political structures that contributed significantly to the rise of Indian "fundamentalist" Hinduism. Given the ethnoregional concentration of traditional Hinduism in India, a federal polity with substantial power at the state level makes it possible for such an extremist movement to survive.

The significance of other structural variables for the development of Hindu nationalism are treated in greater detail in chapter 4. They include the character of Indian education, the role of the media, and state and national economic growth and fluctuations. A careful exposition of these patterns describes the fault lines of Indian politics—the lines of language, religion, level of economic development, status, class, education, media, and the like. As we will demonstrate in the next chapter, these structural variables created the context in which Hindu fundamentalism emerged, but it was the political structure of Indian federalism that provided the sufficient cause.

In addition to structural conditions, the impact of chance events is dramatically illustrated in the history of Hindu nationalism. The two world wars dramatically weakened the legitimacy of Western imperialism and created conditions that fostered a process of Indian emancipation. The two wars created the political arena in which militant Hindu nationalism could carry on its struggle with the Indian Congress Party's version of secularization. India had no place in the causation of the wars. Their impact on Indian politics was contingent, a transformation of the basic structure of power in which India was an object.

The assassinations of the three Gandhis similarly included important elements of chance that dramatically affected the fate of Hindu nationalism. The assassination of Mohandas Gandhi in 1947 at the hands of a militant member of the Hindu Mahasabha resulted in the arrests of tens of thousands of Swayamsevaks and the suppression of the Mahasabha. The assassination of Indira Gandhi at the hands of her Sikh bodyguards in 1979 demoralized the Congress Party, as did the assassination of her son, Rajiv, a decade later. The Hindu nationalist BJP is the heir of votes of the right wing of the Congress Party, as that party lost its cohesion and momentum in the late eighties and early nineties.

The importance of leadership and choice in the rise of the Hindu fundamentalist movement is unambiguous. The great events of Hindu identity formation and institution shaping were stimulated by dynamic ideological and organizational leadership. This was apparent in the creation of the Mahasabha and the writing of *Hindutva* by V. D. Savarkar; the formation of the RSS by K. B. Hedgewar and M. S. Golwarkar; and in the successful merger of the ideological and organizing skills of these leaders with the populistic and bargaining skills of the BJP leaders, L. K. Advani and A. B. Vajpayee. These half-dozen leaders represent in substantial measure the essential elements of effective power. These include the invention and dissemination of powerful ideas (Savarkar), the recruitment and effective organization of human effort (Hedgewar, Golwarkar), the accumulation of resources (Deoras), and the formation of effective coalitions (Advani, Vajpayee).

Vajpayee, for example, a high-caste Brahmin, former Marxist and member of the RSS, was perceived as a moderate who had led his party's turn to more inclusive policies and language. His public discourse usually employed the ambiguous rhetoric of a veteran politician but occasionally projected an aggressive religious nationalism that appealed to his militant Hindu followers. On the one hand, he condemned Gandhi's assassination by a Hindu nationalist as a "terrible crime" and criticized the December 1992 destruction of the Babri mosque, the oldest Muslim shrine in India, by a Hindu mob as a "blunder of Himalayan proportions." At political rallies he made it clear that discrimination on the basis of religion "is not our way in India . . . not in our blood, or in our soil." On the other hand, he often described India as essentially a Hindu nation that should enshrine "Hindu culture" at its core. In March 1998 he named Lal Krishna Advani as home minister, thereby giving police powers to a vociferous nationalist still under indictment on charges that he incited the Hindu mob to raze the Babri mosque.

JEWISH ZIONIST FUNDAMENTALISM: WHAT TRIGGERED THE FORMATION OF GUSH EMUNIM?

This question has several possible answers, each of which generates intense and useful debate. In this regard, the case of the Jewish radicals who settled the territories occupied by Israel in the wake of the Six-Day War in 1967 is not dissimilar to other cases of fundamentalist emergence: seldom is a monocausal theory capable of explaining the emergence and growth of a fundamentalist movement. Thus Gideon Aran, the acknowledged expert on the early years of Gush Emunim (the Bloc of the Faithful), identifies not one but at least three triggering events that led to the solidification of the movement in its formative years (1974–77).[18]

The earliest triggering event, according to members of the movement itself, began with a sermon delivered in May 1967 at Jerusalem's MerKaz Harav Yeshiva (Talmudic Academy) by Rabbi Zvi Yehuda Kook (a.k.a. Rabbi Kook the Younger). In the sermon Kook elaborated elements of the messianic mystical system contained in the writings of his father, Rabbi (Avraham) Kook the Elder; this theological-political system, known as "Kookism," would become the ideological base of a new movement whose nucleus was the small but zealous group of Mizrachi (religious Zionist) youth discipled to Kook. On this day, weeks before the surprise attack on Israel by her Arab neighbors, Kook told his listeners that the time of redemption, at least in its national-political dimensions, was at hand. The current state of Israel embodies the fulfillments of the messianic ideal, Kook proclaimed; therefore, true believers should hasten to support the Israeli army.

The sudden attack, the "miraculous" swiftness of Israel's military victory, the Zionist state's success in bringing the historical heart of biblical Palestine (i.e., Judea and Samaria) under Israeli control, and the subsequent wave of national euphoria—all this was irrefutable evidence for Kook's disciples of the rabbi's mystical and prophetic powers. Indeed, the war changed the fortunes of Kook's disciples, including the religious Zionism's activist youth movement, Bnei Akiva, which served as a sort of ready-made cadre. The group of young leaders that coalesced around Kook the Younger saw the settlement of Judea and Samaria as a way of securing the divine gift and hence advancing the Redemption. This was a religious gloss on the old secularist Zionist belief that tilling the Land of Israel is the only way toward true return to Zion.

Thus the 1967 war—a chance event, if not a random one, explicable in part in terms of certain structural conditions such as the geopolitical dynamics of the Middle East after 1948—was an unexpected trigger for the rise of what Aran refers to as Jewish Zionist fundamentalism. He points to a second, more immediate triggering event, in spring 1968, when Rabbi Moshe Levinger and ten Torah scholars and their families celebrated the Passover seder at the Arab-owned Park Hotel in the heart of Hebron and remained in the area as squatters—the spearhead of post-1967 settlements in the territories.[19]

Yet the 1967 war barely gave the movement visibility; it was not enough to give it scope and prominence. Thus Aran identifies a third trigger, Israel's near escape from defeat in the 1973 war, which goaded the Bloc of the Faithful into intensive settlement activity. The true believers responded with alacrity to defeatism among Israeli elites, who had lost their sense of invincibility and seemed ready for territorial compromise. In February 1974, at kibbutz Kfar Etzion in the territories, the name Gush Emunim was coined and perpetuated by the media, and the composition of the movement expanded beyond the circle of religious Zionist youth to include secularist allies (e.g., the Ein Vered circle of the Labor movement). A full-scale ideological assault on secular Zionism commenced. Until 1977, settlements had to be created against the government's will, and that made them all the more attractive for the young Bnei Akiva activists, as a ritual acting out of the struggle between the true-blue Zionism and tired, washed-out defeatists. Still, without the coalition-building abilities of some Gush leaders, the recruitment of these secularist allies would not have come about. It solidified during the struggle against the evacuation of Sinai in the early 1980s.

In this case we have the blending of structural conditions, triggering events, and leadership choices that help explain the rise and prominence of fundamentalist movements. Among the structural conditions, one must take into account the aforementioned geopolitical dynamics of the region (the structural category we call "international setting"); the ideological prehistory of Gush Emunim in the phenomenon known as Gahelet (literally, "the embers")—the Pioneer Torah Scholars' Group that sought to infuse

Zionism with Jewish messianic elements (the long-term structure, "host religion"); and the role played in Israeli society by the various political, religious, cultural, and ethnic factions ("social composition"). The triggers include structure-related but unpredictable events such as the outbreak of the Six-Day War and purely chance events such as the coincidence of Rabbi's Kook's "prophetic" sermon and Israel's stunning victory. The role of dynamic religious leadership, from Kook's command to support the Zionist army to Rabbi Levinger's decision to spearhead the settling of the territories, was the sine qua non of Gush Emunim's emergence.

CONCLUSION

The three coauthors, appropriately seated in a suite in the Mishkenot Shananim within direct view of the Jerusalem Wall, tallied the frequency with which they viewed structure, chance, and choice factors as decisive in the development of fundamentalist movements in the Christian, Jewish, Islamic, and South Asian religious traditions. These tabulations, appearing as tables 3.2 and 3.3 in the appendix, provide the answers to the questions posed in chart 3.1, that of demonstrating how structural, chance, and choice variables explain the origins, ideology, organization, strategy and tactics, growth and spread, and decline of fundamentalist movements.

The most striking conclusion of this exercise was the importance imputed to leadership. Leadership was viewed as significant for all aspects of fundamentalist movements—origins, ideology, organization, strategy, growth, and decline—in almost all of the cases we reviewed. Leadership plays the quintessential creative role in the formation, transformation, and maintenance of fundamentalist movements. Its significance may be elaborated in ideological, organizational, and resource terms, as in the capacity to transform preferences and attitudes through creative ideas, to create and modify organization, to discover and mobilize new resources, and to broker combinations and coalitions, both within the movement and with powers external to it. Leadership is, of course, constrained or stimulated by the long-term trends we have described. A leader may wish to resist and transcend certain latitudinarian trends of his religious denomination in order to ensure the survival of the tradition. But he must still use the language and concepts of the tradition and reinterpret it in an innovative yet orthodox manner. Such skills as a sense of timing and the ability to use the "right dosage" in response to opportunities that become available due to short-term crises are important capacities in the leadership of militant movements.

These leadership talents and skills, as well as other qualities that we associate with personality, may be explained, of course, by family background, parental and sibling relations—that is, in terms of individual life history. These background characteristics and experiences help explain why a leader does what he does and is able or constrained to do so. But the explanation of these personality characteristics is quite separate from the explanatory logic of the movement as a whole. Two systems of causation intersect in the recruitment and performance of the fundamentalist leadership, as is true in any movement. The strength, uniqueness, and success of Khomeini consisted in the combination of his scholarly stature, his boldly innovative political theory, his charisma, his down-to-earth provincial homeliness, his mastery of conversational homiletic style, his shrewd understanding of the way the political game was played within Iran, and his capacity to broker broad but ever-shifting coalitions. His physical decline in his later years, his ignorance of the larger world, his tendency to nourish grievances and harbor personal hatred (illustrated by his animosity toward Saddam Hussein, which needlessly extended the Iraq-Iran war), were qualities that constricted the movement he had created. We do not intend to undertake explanations of these personal characteristics of leaders, but we call attention to them as they enter into the explanation of the fate of the movements that they lead.

In our comparison of cases we concluded that the host religion was centrally important for determining the original ideology and organizational structure of fundamentalist movements, whereas the politics, public policy and economic trends of the state or local government, as well as social factors such as ethnic composition, migration, and the like, increased in importance (both as stimulants to growth or causes of decline) once the movements became established as fundamentalist (i.e., as aggressive, interactive, religiously based movements).

If religious leadership is decisive, it is important to note that the external conditions most significant for influencing the disposition of religious actors are those that affect the autonomy of religious leaders and institutions in a society—their independence from state control or excessive regulation, their status vis-à-vis other religious bodies, their ability to recruit members, raise funds, and amass resources, and most decisive, their ability to educate and train their adherents in the precepts, principles, and practices of the religious tradition. The quality and kind of spiritual-moral formation provided by the host religion is particularly significant in determining whether religious communities become fundamentalist. How, where, by whom, and for whom formation is provided—and to what ends—determines the religious identity of the community, which is always a construction of the sacred past from among a myriad of possibilities. The content and quality of instruction in the home and in formal religious institutions, from parochial or mosque schools to seminaries, yeshivot, monasteries, and madrasas, shapes the religious community's attitudes toward the other and informs its response to social and religious crises.

Earlier we noted the debates surrounding the origins of Gush Emunim. We would be pleased if the explanatory scheme outlined in this chapter and further complexified and illustrated in the next two chapters proved useful in generating such debates. The facts do not speak for themselves; they must be accumulated, weighed, and interpreted. Here we have drawn selectively on the facts of two cases in order to illustrate how our explanatory model works in practice. Any single case deserves more thorough scrutiny. In the next chapter we further complicate the model and consider different dimensions of our cases.

WRESTLING WITH THE WORLD:
FUNDAMENTALIST MOVEMENTS
AS EMERGENT SYSTEMS

Once we have taken structure and chance into account in explaining the causes of fundamentalist movements, we must recognize that, as the movements emerge and define themselves by their actions, fundamentalists still have a choice as to how to respond by adopting a basic orientation to the world. In this chapter we identify and describe four basic fundamentalist orientations to the world.

When we look at fundamentalism in its particular historical manifestations, we see that fundamentalist movements are quite complex phenomena. They are founded and organized; they develop programs and devise tactics that are more or less successful in acquiring members and resources and achieving their goals. However one may posit generic "fundamentalism," actual fundamentalist and "fundamentalist-like" movements come in a confounding variety of shapes, sizes, and types; they are found in different settings.

Yet these disparate movements share not only a set of identifiable traits but a certain "logic" in their unfolding. They follow certain patterns of relating to the world. Furthermore, the pattern followed by a given movement at a given time is determined by a set of factors that we classify under the rubrics of structure, chance, and choice. In this chapter, we will describe the patterns themselves, and we will explain the ways that structure, chance, and choice combine to determine the patterns. Finally, we will illustrate this "logic" of fundamentalism by reference to specific cases.

Patterns of Relating to the World

All fundamentalists, by our definition, intentionally interact with the outside world in some way. Different fundamentalist movements—or the same
movement at different times in its life—relate to the world according to
various patterns or modes of behavior. Some spread throughout the society
gradually; others attempt to overthrow their enemies in a dramatic, concerted campaign; still others may withdraw to the periphery, decline, or even
cease to exist.

An objection may be raised at this point. Are separatist fundamentalists
really acting in relation to the outside world? Indeed, they are. The separatism of the enclave is an important mode of fundamentalism, and it is also
a form of fundamentalist interaction with the outside world. This is true
in two ways. First, fundamentalists are religious sectarians who build their
enclaves with one eye trained on the threatening enemy. Fundamentalist
parents raise their children with the goal of strengthening them to resist
the enemy's lures. Fundamentalist movements recruit their members on the
basis of a sophisticated critique of the outside world. Hence, fundamentalists calculate the height and strength and constitution of their walls according to their evaluation of the enemy's invasive power. In this sense, the
enemy helps to determine the strategies of the fundamentalist.

Second, fundamentalists look to the future, not to the past. Unlike sectarian separatists such as the Amish, fundamentalists expect the sinful world
outside the enclave to be transformed sooner or later. The transformation
may come directly at the hands of the true believers, or it may be solely
God's doing. Yet even separatist fundamentalists, who would renounce the
world and wait upon God, are actors in the world—even if their interaction
takes the form of a running commentary on the "signs of the times," that
is, on where the world currently stands in its headlong cascade toward obliv-
ion and final redemption. The fundamentalist renunciation of the world is,
therefore, tactical and incomplete.

We have identified four patterns of fundamentalist interaction with the
world. They are the world conqueror, the world transformer, the world creator, and the world renouncer. Before discussing these patterns in detail,
however, we must establish two interpretive principles.

First, over the course of its lifetime a movement is likely to exhibit two,
three, or even all four of these patterns. A movement may go into a kind
of hibernation, later to reemerge, reconstituted and fortified for battle. In
addition, a movement may simultaneously exhibit more than one pattern

of relating to the world; we often see two patterns linked together in the complex behavior of fundamentalisms. The world-creating impulse, for example, often accompanies the world-renouncing pattern: a movement simultaneously rejects the external world and turns inward, creating its own world as an alternative to the threatening outside. Times of social or political crisis present the fundamentalist movement with an opportunity or a danger. If the crisis is seen as an opportunity, the movement may abandon its world-transforming orientation in favor of the more aggressive program of the world conqueror. If the crisis is seen primarily as a danger to the life of the movement, the world transformer (or the world conqueror) may retreat to the enclave of the world creator or world renouncer. Usually, however, at any particular point in its development a dominant impulse can be attributed to the movement.

Second, the "world" of fundamentalism varies in definition and scope according to how particular fundamentalists understand the concepts of space and time. In terms of space, the world may be a village or nation-state rather than the entire globe, the whole of human civilization. In other words, the world is the immediately significant environment of the movement in question. To the followers of Khomeini in Tehran in 1978, for example, the world was the nation-state known as Iran. This was the primary environment with which the Iranian Shi'ite radicals were interacting at the time. And their particular form of interaction at that time was militant-hegemonic—what we are calling the world-conqueror model. That is, Khomeini's followers focused their fervor on a defined world and set out to conquer that world (rather than transform it gradually, create their own alternative world in competition with that world, or withdraw from that world as much as possible).

Of course, other "worlds," such as that of the "Great Satan"—the United States—were also invoked in the Iranian Shi'ite ideology of that time. But these were secondary; in terms of their actual program, the operative target, so to speak, was Iran, not the United States. The immediate purpose for the taking of U.S. hostages in 1979 was not a desire to conquer or otherwise influence the United States, notwithstanding the harsh anti-American rhetoric of the captors; rather, the purpose of the episode was to consolidate the revolution in Iran, the primary world of immediate significance for Khomeini's followers. We will be classifying movements according to their actual behavior rather than their professed intent.

As the goals and status of a movement change, of course, the "world" changes, and vice versa. After the Shi'ite movement in Iran came to power, the world of immediate significance expanded to include not only Iran but also other nation-states (especially Iraq), the larger Shi'ite world, and indeed, the whole of the Islamic world, over which Iran sought a transformative influence. In terms of its world of origin, Iran, Khomeini's movement now focused its efforts on transforming the conquered world. The movement changed its strategies to adapt to its changed environment.

In terms of time, the external world no less than the movement itself may be seen in historic time or in messianic time. This makes an enormous difference in how the fundamentalist movement chooses to relate to the world. Historic time is open-ended, plentiful, amenable to a gradualist, transformationist approach to the reconstruction of society. Messianic time is trickier: the end is fast approaching, the enemies are about to be conquered—but who is going to do the conquering? Depending on their answer to this question, fundamentalists acting in messianic expectation may become world renouncers (i.e., leave the outside world alone—God will do the conquering), world transformers (God expects the true believers to pave His way), or world conquerors (God establishes His kingdom through the agency of the true believers). In any case, the fundamentalist is also always a world creator (whatever the condition of the outside world, God is present in the enclave or "world" of the true believer).

Apocalyptic sects of Judaism, Christianity, or Islam may normally despair of seizing immediate control of society outside the enclave—unless and until the messianic figure arrives, causing an eruption in or cessation of historic time. At that point, they may enter a world-conquering phase, as did Gush Emunim at its inception as a radical settler movement. In other cases, however, the expectation of an eschatological deliverance seems to intensify in proportion to the distance fundamentalists are from seizing real power in historic time. Haredi Jews do not seek to dominate Palestinian Arabs in the Holy Land. Why try to conquer the world, they reason, if the Messiah is about to arrive to do the work for you?

In sum, the fundamentalists' stance toward the world will depend, first, on their assessment of the outside world, and, second, on the role they think they are supposed to be playing in the divine plan. But whether they operate in historic time or in messianic time, whether the threatening "world" is the village across the river or the powerful nation-state rival, all fundamentalists expect the enemy to be abolished one way or another, sooner or later. God's world is pure, not pluralist.

There are four ways of abolishing the enemy. First, one may eliminate the enemy altogether. This is the goal of the fundamentalist pattern of behavior we are calling the world conqueror. The primary strategy of the world conqueror is to assume control of the structures of society that have given life to the enemy. Once in control of the means of coercion and the resources in a society, the world conqueror is in a position to define and dominate outsiders, eliminating them or placing them in cultural, political, or geographic exile or converting them forcibly to the cause. World conquering is usually undertaken by those fundamentalist movements in a position, they feel, to meet these ambitious objectives. Radical, revolutionary fundamentalisms adopt world-conquering ideologies and corresponding organizational structures and programs of action. Ideologically, as we saw in chapter 2, they place heavy emphasis on dualism and reactive selectivity; organizationally, they feature authoritarian leadership in control of disciplined cadres or militant cells. Theologically, world conquerors make a claim that redemptive action is scheduled to occur at least in part in historic time, not solely in eschatological time. If the Messiah is to come, the fundamentalists must first prepare the threshing floor.

It is tempting to say that all fundamentalists aspire to be world conquerors. By this way of thinking, fundamentalism is defined as essentially reactive, militant, and antipluralist; in its complete expression it must therefore seek to suppress alternative visions and movements within a given society or world. As we have just noted, however, the world-conquering tendency can be modified even in messianic fundamentalisms in which the ultimate victory over evil is to come at the hands of the longed-for Messiah or Mahdi. The world-conquering impulse of fundamentalism may be modified for purely pragmatic reasons as well as for theological ones. Even messianic movements acknowledge that they must operate in historic time. And even those fundamentalists who do intend to conquer their world in historic time often find themselves forced to adopt other strategies in order to survive the vicissitudes of history.

Thus a second means of abolishing the enemy is to reinterpret and influence the structures, institutions, laws, and practices of a society so that opposing fundamentalism may become more difficult and so that conditions become more favorable for the conversion or marginalization of the enemy. The world transformer adopts this strategic approach to the fundamentalist problem of pluralism. It shares with the conqueror the ultimate aim of reforming the society in its image but adopts a variety of accommodating strategies over a longer period of time, to achieve this end. Ideologically, the movement may selectively relax its boundaries to include some shades of gray and adjust organizational requirements to this strategy. Legal advocacy, political lobbying, cultural warfare, and missionary work may be emphasized as heavily as militant activism. Civil society rather than the battlefield is the primary arena for fundamentalist interaction with the enemy. (The arena may shift, of course, if transformational strategies are frustrated and abandoned for the sword or the bomb.)

The world creator and world renouncer also displace the world-conquering mode. Both devote considerable energies to the building up of the enclave, the demarcation of boundaries, the securing of the niche. The movement's ultimate aims may or may not be clearly envisioned or even attainable within history. In both patterns, God is the agent of justice and power; world conquering will be left to the deity. In the meantime, militance, reactivity, and antipluralism will be the preserve of the remnant, the anxious ones awaiting the day of redemption.

The world creator, however, is intentionally in direct competition with the outside world; fundamentalists acting in this mode seek to enlarge and replenish their own world to attract others as a clear alternative to the fallen world. The world-creator strategy, therefore, is to create alternative and encompassing societal structures and institutions. Missionary work is important, not to transform the structures of the world outside but to increase the numbers of the enclave. In a certain sense, as we have noted, all fundamentalisms are world creators: Unlike mere traditionalists, they begin by creating enclaves set apart from the world. They may move quickly into world-conquering or world-transforming modes, but they will never entirely abandon their world-creating activity. In other words, a world creator need not be a world conqueror—but a world conqueror will always also be a world creator.

The world renouncer, a relatively rare mode of fundamentalism, seeks purity and self-preservation more than hegemony over fallen outsiders. Ideologically, the world renouncer may be as doctrinaire and rigid as the world conqueror but the energy is directed inward to the self-construction of the fundamentalist world in contrast to the threatening outside. Not intent on building a world parallel to the outside world, fundamentalists operating in this mode concentrate usually on education, domestic life, and religious ritual. Strategically, the world renouncer relates to the outside world in a complex pattern of dependence and rejection.

Of course, all fundamentalists, whatever their pattern of relation to the world, seek purity, draw sharp ideological boundaries, value mission work, and want to avoid the evils of the fallen world even as they seek to redeem it. But in different times and circumstances, certain ingredients of the fundamentalist recipe are present in greater doses than others.

WORLD CONQUEROR

In the world-conqueror pattern we see the most virulent type of fundamentalist movement in terms of the disruption of a previous order. Here
everything, or almost everything, is clicking for the emergence of a durable
movement: abundant intellectual and theological resources from the host
religious tradition; social and economic displacement creating human need
that has gone unmet; and, most of all, the leader who combines these elements in an innovative package often tied to his personal authority and
status. These movements are hegemonic and tend to seek to export the revolution, renew the faith and orthodoxy of the tepid believer (or eliminate
him or her), and convert the unbeliever. Their ideologies exhibit strong nationalist or theocratic elements. The world, a realm of Satan and darkness,
must be overcome if not brought back into the fold. Its institutions, structures, and values must be brought under the control of the true believers.
Depending on the specific political objectives of the movement, the world
may ultimately be conceptualized as the *umma*, or merely, for example,
Northern Ireland. In either case, it is a "kingdom" or "sacred realm," the
borders of which are to be reclaimed and, in some millennial visions, expanded.

The Al Qaeda organization represented world-conquering fundamentalism in a sensational and unprecedented form, given the global reach of its
terrorist network. Its leader, Osama bin Laden, however, while targeting the
World Trade Center, the Pentagon (and perhaps the Capitol and the White
House) on September 11, 2001, clearly had in mind the umma, or transnational Islamic community, as the "world" to be conquered. By dealing a
crippling blow to the United States, he sought (in vain) to create a crisis that
would force Islamists to join an all-out war against the West, and middle-of-
the-road Muslims to declare their loyalty to Islamism (bin Laden style).
Other cases of world-conquering fundamentalisms include:

1. *Revolutionary Shi'ism in Iran: Origin and emergence, 1960s and 1970s.*
The fundamentalist movement itself, as opposed to its precursors in nine-
teenth- and twentieth-century Iran, emerged in the 1960s and 1970s in the
coalescing of two long-term trends: a secularization process (built upon the
expansion of education and the media) and the strains of rapid and unequal
socioeconomic development, entailing mass migration (rural to urban) as
a result of demographic growth. The state served as the locomotive of the
two processes, vigorously intervening everywhere and further sapping an
already enfeebled civil society. In revitalizing civil society, in order to re-

spond to the challenges of secularization and economic development, the Islamic movement had to take on the state, that is, to get into politics. The ideology that established a cosmological framework for this endeavor was developed when the regime seemed successful and impregnable (in the early 1960s) and gained wide currency when strains and failures accumulated (in the 1970s).

One could already in the 1960s speak of a radical Islamic movement due to the hierarchical and autonomous nature of the Shi'ite clergy (especially in Iran), which enabled part of the clergy to serve as a ready-made cadre for such a movement. These mullahs were helped in this endeavor by the very existence of a hierarchy, by its self-sufficient economic basis, and by a tradition of circumscribed collaboration with the powers that be (i.e., a long-standing ideological heritage, typically Shi'ite, that privileged the "right of resistance"). None of these three factors exists among Sunnis.

An overpowering leader, Khomeini brought all of this together, while interpreting the heritage creatively. The movement did not have to develop a cadre of laymen (as in the Sunni world, where ulama had been tarred by servile collaboration with the powers-that-be), and the ideological challenge of justifying insurgency was less daunting than the one facing Sunnis.

Iran was oil-rich. The socioeconomic strains thus had less to do with a stalling development (though on the eve of the 1979 revolution oil prices declined) than with the unequal (in terms of sectors) and inegalitarian nature of this development. Furthermore, it was molded by an exponential rise in expectations, fueled by the shah's megalomaniacal discourse as the country became awash with money in 1973–74. The size of the native "profiteering" elites was much larger than in Egypt, for example, and their conspicuous consumption, more salient. All this led to a severe syndrome of relative deprivation. Actual perspectives of decline (in status and income) were relevant merely for the old merchant classes (*bazaari*). In fact, even the "disinherited" lower classes, in whose name Khomeini spoke, had known some material improvement.

If 1973–74 was thus a powerful trigger, so was the onset of the shah's terminal illness sometime later—an illness that made his wielding of power more erratic and less resolute. This, in an autocracy, sent signs of flagging strength throughout the political community. The enfeebled state, harassed by its American patron to observe human rights, watched helplessly as the Islamic movement expanded, drawing the dissatisfied lower-middle class and part of the professional urban classes (the countryside was apathetic or mute).

Yet the movement could not have maintained that momentum, despite the availability of a cadre of clergy, without Khomeini's hands-on charismatic leadership as developer of an innovative ideology, buttressed by the aura of his scholarly authority; as a master communicator of this ideology and its application to specific, tangible cases, combining an attractive, homespun provincial (i.e., populist) style with adaptability to technological innovations (e.g., audiocassettes); and, not least, as coalition builder (with rival Shi'ite top clergy and reformist Shi'ite liberals, with the secular democratic opposition, and even, momentarily, with Marxists). Personal leadership, operating through the Shi'ite hierarchy, was the linchpin of the whole endeavor.

2. *Sunni radical movements in Egypt: Origins and emergence, late 1960s.* The Egyptian case is paradigmatic of Muslim Brotherhood evolution elsewhere in the Middle East and North Africa. Founded in 1928 by schoolteacher Hasan al-Banna, the movement emerged in a world-transformer mode through a network of Islam-inculcating schools, youth clubs, trade unions, and syndicates. It was radicalized into a world-conqueror mode by confrontations with secular Egyptian governments unsympathetic to its Islamization project. (Other elements of the larger movement, like the Samawiyya sect, turned inward, in a world-renouncing mode.) Both orientations continue to exist side by side, although the political activists, journalists, and syndicalists of the "mainstream" Islamic current, no less than the terrorist cells, see and seek an ultimate victory for (their construction of) Islam.

The radicalization, its seeds present in Banna's insistence on involvement in politics, took definitive ideological form only well after his death and after the movement had suffered as a result of its forays into power politics. (The Brotherhood was bitterly disappointed when the victorious Free Officers under Nasser outlawed it and later imprisoned its leaders.) Interestingly, the radical ideology, developed in the prison writings of Sayyid Qutb, anticipated the actual emergence of the radical movement.

Qutb, influenced by the writings of Pakistani thinker and Jama'at-i-Islami founder Abul Ala Maududi, justified the shift to world conquering by diagnosing a case of *jahiliyya* (pre-Islamic barbarism) infecting Egypt. Organizational shifts following his execution in 1966 mirrored the ideology: *takfir wal hijra* cells (identify and flee the enemy in order to retaliate against him) sprang up, led by Qutb-inspired charismatic preachers. These charismatic leaders differed on strategy and targets (was all of Egyptian society the enemy, or just the state, or primarily the head of state?) but agreed that the infidels should be vanquished, by violent means if necessary. Qutb's ideology, which justified radicalization and world conquering, was an innovative response, given the absence of strong eschatological or religious-polity justifications in the host religion (Sunni Islam being neither as messiah-friendly nor as hierarchical/semitheocratic as Shi'ism).

3. *Hamas: Growth and radicalization, mid-1980s to mid-1990s.* The movement of Islamic resistance of Palestine, an offshoot of the Muslim Brotherhood in Gaza, also began as an Islamization project. Under the guiding genius of its founder (the crippled Shaykh Ahmed Yassin), however, and goaded by the daring acts of the tiny Islamic Jihad sect, Hamas in the mid-1980s moved from its world-transforming mode to a world-conquering one. In so doing, it assimilated nationalist elements by imitating and competing with the PLO for control of the resistance to Israeli occupation. The first Intifada was a trigger for Hamas's rise to prominence in this new mode—a trigger shaped and exploited by the movement's leadership. The Oslo Accords of 1993 left Hamas as the best-organized and most influential obstructionist force in the territories. In its world-conqueror mode Hamas seeks the domination of Israel and hence is reluctant to shift ideologically and organizationally in response to peace initiatives.

4. *Ulster Protestants: Emergence and growth (the Ian Paisley era).* The Ulster Protestants are an interesting contrast to the North American Protestants in their world-transformer mode, who share the basic religious doctrines and symbolic resources with the Paisleyites. In Ulster, however, the political and social context, determined by the entrenched ethnic conflict between Scot- and English-derived Protestants and Irish Catholics, has dictated strikingly different patterns of mobilization and organization. The Ulster case suggests comparisons, instead, with other ethnonationalist movements that display a completely different religious portfolio (e.g., Sikhs, Sinhala Buddhists, perhaps even Hindutva militants). In each of these cases, the "fundamentalist" movement adopts religious symbolism and discourse and strives for dominance of an ethnic opponent who is also constructed in religious terms (i.e., Ulster Protestants versus Irish Catholics, pure Sikhs versus false Sikhs and militant Hindus, Sinhala Buddhists versus Tamil Hindus, and Hindu nationalists versus upwardly mobile Indian Muslims).

In the early nineteenth century the politicization of the Irish and a Catholic church–sponsored nationalist movement mobilized the conservative Presbyterian minority (its origins in Ulster dating back to 1630) to forge an alliance with Anglo-Episcopalians and Scottish Presbyterians, upon whom they subsequently depended for economic and political resources. Steve Bruce points out that Protestantism and Catholicism were not just different religiopolitical traditions in Ulster: each defined itself in opposition to the other, with strict prohibitions on intermarriage, economic cooperation, and other alliances that would transgress strong boundaries and weaken ethnoreligious bonds. In the early twentieth century, however, the religious element of this affiliation was affected by secularizing trends brought on by industrialization; this was especially true of the Presbyterian presence.

This long-term structural factor provides an important set of structural conditions for the rise of fundamentalism, but the sufficient cause for its emergence in the twentieth century was the charismatic leadership of the Reverend Ian Paisley. Here we see a dynamic that social scientists can determine with high levels of accuracy—predictable patterns of social, economic, and political competition between ethnic groups—flavored and to a significant degree shaped by the unpredictable variable of personal choice. Paisley's brilliance has been to make a narrow premillennial sectarian religious discourse serve as a political idiom and rallying cry for Protestant Unionists, people who would not normally be recruits to a fundamentalist movement. (Many of Paisley's followers are not active church participants or born-again Christians.) He has done this by stoking the embers of the centuries-old conflict while creating ex nihilo two very modern vehicles, one religious (the Free Presbyterian Church, founded in 1951, now with ten thousand members in forty-eight Ulster congregations) and one political (the Democratic Unionist Party, established in 1972). Despite secular trends, Paisley perceived that religion remains a vital part of the Scottish and Anglo-Irish heritages, and he appropriated conservative Protestant ideologies and symbols to make sense of their apparently beleaguered position in the north of Ireland and to give purpose to their political agenda, which is dominated by a desire to remain part of the United Kingdom.

From 1921 to 1972, Northern Ireland was governed by a directly elected parliament at Stormont. Protestants enjoyed considerable material and cultural advantages over Catholics, but many were uneasy when Catholics were allowed their own institutions. Catholics could migrate to the republic and teach in southern schools. They had a monopoly in Catholic schools and a legal claim on jobs in state schools. In 1971 Paisley charged the Unionist government with cowardice for not opposing resurgent Irish nationalism and a compromising British government. Since then, his Democratic Unionist Party has come to be accepted by other Unionist parties as an equal partner in various campaigns against British government policy. For a time Paisley was the most popular Unionist politician; in the 1984 elections to the European Community parliament, nearly a quarter of a million people—a sixth of the whole electorate—voted for him.

   5. *U.S. Protestant Christians: Second public emergence, late 1970s to the*

present. There was a subtle but decisive theological shift in Protestant fundamentalism in its second emergence as a public force in the United States. The shift, from a strict premillennialist orientation to an operative postmillennialist orientation, had profound ideological and organizational implications; in short, it prepared the way for and justified the movement's turn to a new pattern of relating to the world. Premillennialism, the doctrine that the world would sink deeper and deeper into sin until Jesus returned to establish the millennial kingdom of the righteous, had provided the theoretical framework for the previous world-relational patterns of fundamentalism. After 1925, for example, the movement had retreated from the fallen world and established alternative institutions—independent churches, schools, radio stations, clinics, and the like—in the expectation of Christ's imminent return. "I am a fundamentalist," proclaimed the Reverend Jerry Falwell in the 1950s, "and that means that I am a soul-winner and a separatist." The task of the premillennialist was to renounce the fallen world of sin, create an alternative world of grace in which to win souls, and await the rapture and Jesus' triumphant arrival. Politics was off-limits.

The shift to an operative postmillennialism—the belief that Jesus would come only after Bible-believing Christians had prepared the way by inaugurating the era of righteousness on earth—was triggered by the moral and social crises of the 1960s. In establishing the Moral Majority in the late 1970s, Falwell explained that the forces of secular humanism had become so invasive in the 1960s and early 1970s—taking the form of the drug culture, the "new morality," the U.S. Supreme Court decisions (against prayer in public schools and in favor of abortion), and legislation "enacting secular humanism"—that Bible-believers could no longer wait passively for Jesus but must protect the next generation of Christians by concerted political efforts to "repeal" or "roll back" secular humanism. Although he avoided explicit postmillennial rhetoric on most occasions for fear of scandalizing the old guard,[1] Falwell and his associates in the Religious Roundtable and other Christian Right lobbying groups pushed Protestant fundamentalism toward a new, world-conquering pattern of political activism in reaction to the threatening pluralism of belief and lifestyle that appeared to be overtaking "Judeo-Christian" America.

The first wave of this new political activism, designed to "take back" the courts, schools, and Congress from the secular humanists (and, presumably, to vanquish them or at least diminish their role in public life), was active during the Reagan presidency and followed a strategy of applying pressure at a national level. A second wave, inaugurated by the Reverend Pat Robertson's Christian Coalition in the late 1980s and 1990s, profited from the lessons of the Moral Majority era and focused its impressive and far more successful political activism on local politics—state assemblies, school boards, state political parties. The goal, however, remained basically the same, and the Christian Right made a significant impact on national politics in the 1994 and 1996 national elections. Decline set in, however, toward the end of the decade due to financial mismanagement and, ironically, as a result of success at the polls. In 2001, Robertson stepped down from the leadership of the Christian Coalition, placing its immediate future in jeopardy.

Two aspects of this version of Christian evangelical world-conquering fundamentalism must be noted. First, the activists of the Christian Right prefer the language of restoration over the language of revolution or transformation. The political structures and founding principles of the United States need not be overturned but merely returned to their philosophical-theological basis in "the Judeo-Christian tradition." This may seem like a revolution, the Christian activists say, given how far we Americans have strayed from our divine origins. Second, the theological precision of separatist, Bible-believing fundamentalism in its early stages of origins and growth has given way, ironically, to an internal theological pluralism tied together by political coalitions (the Christian Right) rather than by historic theological and religious distinctions (fundamentalist, Pentecostal, etc.). Robertson, the leader of the Christian Coalition in the 1990s, is a Pentecostal rather than a fundamentalist; he affiliates not only with fundamentalists like Falwell but also with the "Reconstructionist" Christians led by Gary North and the ideologue Rousas John Rushdoony, who preaches the concept of "theonomy" and would base U.S. law on the Mosaic codes of the Hebrew Bible.

In the world-conquering phase of fundamentalism, ideology and political considerations tend to muffle potentially divisive religious and theological elements.

6. *Sikh militants: Bhindranwale and after, 1980s to present.* Sikhism is a religion of fourteen million adherents, concentrated in the Punjab in the north of India but also found in several thriving diasporic communities in the United States, England, Canada, and elsewhere. The religion originated in the late fifteenth century under the leadership of the Guru Nanak, a member of the Kshatriya (warrior) caste. All ten of the Sikh gurus came from this caste. The Adi Granth, the Sikh holy book, contains sacred documents and hymns composed by the first five gurus and the Bakhta saints; it was revised by the last guru, Gobind, in 1704.[2] The sixth guru, Hargobind, affirmed the inseparability of state and religion and legitimized reliance on the sword in the defense of Sikh interests.

Gobind, after persecutions by the Mughals and the execution of the two preceding gurus, founded the Khalsa (the pure), a fraternity of holy warriors all assuming the common name of Singh (lion). The Khalsa is a "chosen" corps of soldier-saints committed to a rigorous code of abstinence, prayer, and virtue. The number five has a mystical significance in Punjab; the first members of the Khalsa were the five Sikhs whom Gobind baptized and named Singh. The members of the Khalsa commit themselves to the five Ks—*kesa* (unshorn hair), *kangha* (comb), *kacch* (military shorts), *kirpan* (saber), *kara* (bracelet of steel). Unlike Hindus, the Sikhs are monotheists and are opposed to image worship. There are some two hundred Sikh temples (*gurdwaras*) governed by temple priests, custodians, and congregational committees. Yet the Guru role persists in the form of sants, with disciples and followers. Since every Sikh has the right to read Scripture, they recognize no priestly caste. There is a general governing body, the Shiromani Gurdwara Prabandhak Committee (SGPC), in Amritsar, the Sikh holy city.

In the power vacuum created by Persian penetration into Punjab in the mid-eighteenth century, the Sikhs were able to establish their own kingdom, which had an autonomous existence until the mid-nineteenth century when the British took the area under their protection. After several Sikh-British wars in the 1840s, the area was assimilated into British India. The Sikhs sided with the British in the Indian mutiny and were thereafter favored in recruitment into the British army, in government service, and through investment in the development of agriculture in Punjab.

In the partitioning of India in 1947 almost three million Sikhs were forced to leave Pakistan and resettle south of the new border, in less desirable areas vacated by the Muslims. The new government of free India reduced the various privileges that the British had granted to the Sikhs, including special access to the military and civil services. A second aspect of chance was the introduction from the West of the Green Revolution (new, high-yield seeds and agricultural practices) into Punjabi agriculture during the 1960s and 1970s. This enriched many Punjabis, but accentuated Punjab polarization, leaving the western rural regions relatively backward and impoverished. After the partition a strong separatist mood developed among the Sikhs. Their religious party, Shiromani Akali Dal, led the agitation that culminated in the mid-1960s in the division of Punjab into three states, one of which had a Sikh majority. But the division of water rights among the three states left the Sikh Punjab with a major grievance.

The Akali Dal shared political power with the Congress Party in Punjab and controlled the Sikh temples through the SGPC. Sikh agitation, however, led to the formation of a smaller Punjab with a Sikh majority.

The Sikh leader of the time, Sant Fateh Singh, used fasts and threats of self-immolation on the roof of the Golden Temple to bring pressure to bear on the Congress authorities.

Indira Gandhi's efforts to play secular bargaining politics with the Sikh leadership ended in tragic failure and catastrophe. In order to offset the extremism of the Akali Dal under the leadership of Sant Harchand Singh Longowal, she supported a new organization, the Khalsa Dal (group of the pure) formed by Jarnail Singh Bhindranwale in the early 1980s. Far from becoming a moderate alternative to the Akali Dal, the Khalsa Dal under Bhindranwale led an increasingly violent tendency toward assassinations. Bhindranwale found support among impoverished and displaced elements among the Jat farmers and from the All India Sikh Student Federation, mobilized by his second in command, Amrit Singh. Bhindranwale's sermons defined the Sikh enemies as the secularism of the Indian state, the moral decay of urban life, and the threat of Hindu religious nationalism. He advocated the formation of an independent Sikh state (Khalistan) in which state and religion would be combined (miri-piri). In this sense he was a world creator; in order to create the world he envisioned, however, the Sikhs must conquer the alien in Punjab and control the land entirely.

Bhindranwale's followers thus engaged in violence and terrorism. The emergence of the radicalized movement was triggered in 1983 when Bhindranwale and his followers headquartered themselves in the Golden Temple in Amritsar and accumulated weapons. Longowal also occupied the Golden Temple, and violent skirmishes between the two groups ensued. After months of futile negotiations with both groups, Prime Minister Indira Gandhi sent in the Indian army. After a bloody battle in which the Golden Temple was profaned and damaged, Bhindranwale was killed, and more than a thousand lives were lost, the occupation and rebellion were terminated. In revenge, two of Gandhi's bodyguards who were Sikhs assassinated her. Longowal also was assassinated by Bhindranwale's followers.[3]

The radical Sikh groups—those associated with Bhindranwale and militants among the Akali Dal favoring Khalistan—clearly fulfill the criteria of fundamentalism, more so than other South Asian varieties. At the same time they share with them, as well as with Islamic fundamentalism, a strong ethnonationalist component.

Ideologically, Sikh fundamentalism is reactive, first, to the Sikh apostates—those who fail to adhere to the five Ks—and second, to the secular Indian state and the menacing Hindu nationalists, whom, in the eyes of the Sikhs, the state seems to support. It is selective of the tradition, emphasizing the sixth guru, Hargobind, who justified the sword, and the tenth guru, Gobind Singh, who originated the Khalsa. It stresses moral dualism, outlawing, even condemning to death, "heretics" such as the Niranjiri, or compromisers such as Longowal of the Akali Dal. It attributes absolute and exclusive validity and inerrancy to its Scripture, the Granth Sahib. The aspiration to Khalistan—the ultimate Sikh theocracy—has utopian and millennial overtones. Thus there is a strong nation building as well as religious component in Sikh fundamentalism. Ideologically the miri-piri doctrine of the unity of religion and the state continues to be the central principle of a separate Khalistan.

The form of organization is charismatic-authoritarian in its sant-disciple version, with the ideas of the Khalsa as a group of baptized holy warriors and of the ultimate domination of the Sikh community by such an elect body. Organizationally, the diffuseness and totalism of the sant-disciple relationship makes for great difficulty and instability in forming organizations and coalitions and may be the principle reason for the breakdown of communication and resort to violence. Almost all of the Sikh militants come from 10 percent of the Sikh villages in western Punjab, where the Green Revolution has had the least effect. The uneven impact of the rapid agricultural development in Punjab polarized Sikh society. The Sikh militants are subsistence-farmer Jats, marginal small farmers, and depeasantized farm laborers. Support for Sikh extremism also comes from that part of the population forced to leave productive farms in what was to become Pakistan and to occupy inferior properties vacated by the Muslims. The Sikh militants are thus recruited from the least educated, least literate strata of the population. Bhindranwale completed only the first five primary school grades. The Sikh sants have been educated in Sikh seminaries such as the Damdami Taksal.

If we take regional backwardness, economic marginality and downward mobility, minimal and predominantly religious education, low media exposure, and relative absence of civil society, we have a picture of Sikh militancy as drawing on the social sectors and strata least affected by economic benefits, educational opportunity, and civic vitality.

7. *Gush Emunim: Origins and emergence, 1970s.* Starting out as a world-conquering movement, the Gush Emunim also appears in the world-transforming category because its tactics and ideology change after its initial messianic fervor and it recognizes itself to be involved in a longer struggle for control of "the whole Land of Israel." In its origins the Gush was guided by the authoritative teaching of the Rabbis Kook. The rise of the movement itself is due, however, to an unexpected trigger, the 1967 war. In its miraculous swiftness and in bringing under Israeli control the historical heart of biblical Palestine (i.e., Judea and Samaria), the war ignited a wave of na-

tional euphoria and changed the fortunes of a tiny group of Mizrachi youth (religious Zionists). This hitherto insignificant group, formed in the ideology of Rabbi Kook the Elder and led by his son, considered that the redemptive era had already begun with the return of the Jews to Palestine in the 1880s and had been significantly advanced by the establishment of the state of Israel as a sacralized tool of the messianic endeavor.

This is somewhat similar to the Egyptian case, where ideology was developed long before the movement emerged. The ideology developed in both cases in different (and inauspicious) circumstances and was given its chance when its prognostications suddenly came true. The marginal group of Merkaz Harav yeshiva, headed by Rabbi Kook the Younger, saw its gospel becoming attractive to the sector of religious Zionism and especially to its activist youth movement, Bnei Akiva, which served as a sort of ready-made cadre. The group of young leaders that coalesced around Rabbi Kook the Younger saw the settlement of Judea and Samaria as a way of keeping the divine gift, locking it in, so to speak, and hence setting forward the Redemption. This was a religious gloss on the old (secularist) Zionist belief that tilling the Land of Israel is the only way toward true return to Zion.

Yet the 1967 war barely gave the movement visibility; it was not enough to give it scope and prominence. A second trigger, the 1973 semidefeat, soon endowed it with the latter. The 1973 war goaded the movement into intensive settlement activity, cognizant of the fact that the Redemption was not on "automatic pilot," as could be construed in the six preceding years; setbacks were coming to block, nay, even subvert, it; defeatism among Israeli elites (ready for territorial compromise) was liable to magnify the scope of these setbacks. Until 1977, settlements had to be created against the government's will, and that made them all the more attractive for the young Bnei Akiva activists as a ritual acting out of the struggle between the true-blue Zionism and tired, washed-out defeatists. Still, without the coalition-building abilities of some Gush leaders, the recruitment of these secularist allies (e.g., the Ein Vered circle of the Labor movement) would not have come about. It solidified during the struggle against the evacuation of Sinai in the early 1980s.

8. *Kach: Meir Kahane.* This is the story of a double emergence. The first incarnation of Kach, then (late 1960s) called the Jewish Defense League (JDL), represented the response of lower-middle-class Jews in large metropolitan areas, mostly New York, to the rise of Black militancy, claims for affirmative action, the surge of insecurity, and the minority drive for empowerment over local education and welfare agencies in the United States. In the same breath it capitalized upon the feelings of marginality and resent-

ment that these Jews, many of them Orthodox and/or newcomers (post-Holocaust), harbored toward the liberal (Conservative and Reform) establishment, which seemed to disregard the interests and sensibilities of their less fortunate brethren.

By stressing a bleak view of all Gentiles and a confrontational activist stance toward them, the JDL preached—and practiced—Jewish inclusiveness, empowerment of Jewish have-nots, and a sharp divide between the beleaguered Jewish community and those outside the fold. By JDL one means Meir Kahane, for the movement was the brainchild of this charismatic rabbi, and he served as its major communicator, strategist, and organizer. (To the above-mentioned themes he would soon add the cause of Soviet Jews.)

When Kahane moved to Israel in 1971, he tried to transplant this brand of ideology cum practice and incorporate it into the context of the Arab-Israeli conflict, endowing the conflict with ethnoreligious (virtually racist) overtones. The transplantation to Israeli soil took more time to accomplish, for Kahane was alien to the indigenous discourse. The movement continued to be a one-man show even in Israel. Kahane hit his stride only in the late 1970s when he developed a lingo appealing to the Sephardic residents of the poorer quarters of big cities and of the new "development towns." These populations found in him a leader who articulated their tribalistic notions of Jewish ethnicity as well as their age-old suspicions of the Arabs from whose lands they had been chased in the 1950s. Because their ethnic notions differed from those of the Ashkenazic liberal establishment (for which Jewish identity was based upon individual choice), Kahane also expressed their resentment as a marginal sector with a growing sense of relative deprivation (hence his appeal in big cities where poor neighborhoods border on middle-class, liberal ones). The competition between poor Jews and Arabs in the job market (due to the employment of West Bank and Gaza residents) created ethnic friction in the unskilled and semiskilled categories. This situation lent particular virulence to Kahane's call for exclusion of the Arab—first, exclusion from Jewish neighborhoods and businesses, and later, from the Land of Israel altogether.

Exclusion (a.k.a. transfer) was presented as a panacea to the Arab-Israeli conflict as well as to daily economic competition. The militant tactics that Kahane inculcated in his young, uneducated groupies, incarnated a "by force alone" and "it is a jungle out there" vision of the Middle East, a vision typical of Jews with origins in Arab countries. All this was couched in religious terms (Kahane was a yeshiva graduate) that rendered it custom-made for the traditionalist bent of Sephardic Jews, a bent quite distinguished from that of the Ashkenazic haves. In this overarching context, the Intifada was a useful, if rather late, trigger, following the trigger of the economic crisis of the early 1980s (the inflation that hit the have-nots hardest).

9. *Sri Lankan Buddhist extremism: Origins and emergence, 1956.* Theravada Buddhist doctrine was codified in the first century in a canon consisting of three texts, one pertaining to monastic discipline, a second containing the discourses of the Buddha, and the third concerned with higher doctrine. Organization consists of a monastic order (the Sangha) grouped into monasteries and around Buddhist shrines, and educational institutions. The monk (*bhikku*) commits himself for life to an ascetic, mendicant, and chaste existence, engaged in meditation intended to attain tranquility and insight.

Yet the withdrawal from worldliness was historically balanced in two ways. The monks and the Buddhist schools inculcated a morality drawn from the lives of great Buddhist heroes such as Prince Vessantara and Emperor Asoka—a moral code emphasizing generosity, righteousness, compassion, nonviolence, and similar virtues. In addition, over the centuries individual monasteries acquired substantial landholdings and other properties granted by kings and noblemen; thus they developed "interests" that led to political and policy involvements. And as Buddhism encountered the rituals, beliefs, and practices of other religions such as Hinduism, Islam, and Christianity, it picked up assorted gods, saints, rituals, and liturgies, which were worshipped and practiced alongside the normative disciplines of suffering, renunciation, and deliverance.[4]

For more than four centuries Western imperialism—Portuguese, Dutch, and British—influenced Sri Lankan culture and society. By the mid-nineteenth century the Protestant and Catholic missions had established a near monopoly of the educational system. Christian converts were favored in appointments to government service, and Buddhists were handicapped in other respects. Western religious, cultural, and political ideas and practices threatened the survival of Buddhist culture and institutions. Yet a Buddhist revival began in the late nineteenth century, supported by the American Theosophical Society, an organization that challenged the supremacy of Christianity, claiming that there were superior metaphysical and ethical qualities in Asian religions. Henry Steele Olcott, its president, helped to establish the Buddhist Philosophical Society and encouraged the successful campaigns by Sri Lankan monks and laymen to establish Buddhist schools, to return controls of temples and temple lands to the Buddhist clergy, and to reinstitute Buddhist holidays.

Shortly thereafter, Anagārika Dharmapāla sought to create a "Protestant Buddhism." He legitimated religious nationalism by his interpretation of the *Mahavaṃsa*, a Sinhala Buddhist chronicle, and of stories about King Duṭṭhagamaṇi, who defeated the Tamils in the second century B.C.E. and reestablished Buddhist rule. Dharmapāla formed the Mahabodhi Society of Colombo in 1891 and started a journal that fostered a revivalist, moralistic, and nationalist Buddhism appealing to the educated and urban Sinhala elite.[5]

Dharmapāla died in 1933; four years later, S. W. R. D. Bandaranaike, a member of the Anglicized elite reconverted to Buddhism by the revivalist movements, founded the Sinhala Maha Sabha, a revivalist party that initially played coalition politics. By the 1956 elections, however, Bandaranaike was exploiting an economic downturn and conducting a successful pro-Buddhist, pro-Sinhala campaign. A significant event in the 1956 election was the controversy surrounding *The Betrayal of Buddhism*, a report of the Buddhist Commission of Inquiry, which had been appointed by the All-Ceylon Buddhist Congress of 1953 to investigate what had happened to Buddhism under the British. The report presented in detail the long record of British suppression and discriminatory practices. Celebrations in 1956–57 of the 2,500th birthday of the Buddha kept alive these denunciations of British suppression and created widespread millennial expectations of the revival of Buddhist glory in terms of the *Mahavaṃsa* and the triumphs of King Duṭṭhagāmaṇi.

The government of the victorious Bandaranaike immediately enacted pro-Buddhist legislation. It established a Ministry of Cultural Affairs, which took charge of Buddhist shrines and institutions, prepared a new translation of the Buddhist Canon, published a Buddhist Encyclopedia, and upgraded Buddhist colleges. A movement to make Sinhalese the state language ran into the vigorous resistance of the Tamils and culminated in the language riots of 1957. These bloody clashes inaugurated the tragic confrontation of Buddhist and Tamil extremists which has dominated Sri Lankan politics ever since. Bandaranaike was assassinated soon thereafter by elements in the United Monks' Front.

Sri Lankan development in the twentieth century has been marked by increasing urban and industrial growth and economic inequality. Much of village community life has broken down as a consequence of the resettlement of population into new towns and the larger cities. Class antagonism, social mobility, and intensely conflictual language and ethnic politics led to extreme political polarization, the acceptance of violence and intimidation as normal instruments of political action, and increasingly authoritarian and coercive government. The two leading Sri Lankan political parties are the United National Party (UNP) and the pro-Buddhist Sri Lanka Freedom Party (SLFP). The UNP has been in the majority for much of the post–World War II period, and under the pressure of Buddhist-Tamil polarization and violence has become increasingly authoritarian and repressive. The Tamils have been represented by the Tamil United Liberation Front (TULF), favoring a separate Tamil state in the north, but through negotiation and compromise. Yet extremist groups on both sides—the Janata Vimukti Peramuna (JVP, or National Liberation Front) and the Liberation Tigers of the Tamil Eelam (LTTE)—incited much violence and bloodshed during the 1970s and 1980s. A substantial part of the bloodshed was caused by the security forces of the government.

Only in small part can Sri Lankan Buddhist fundamentalism be described as reacting to the characteristics of the host religion. Yet Dharmapāla's authoritarian leadership demanded that Theravada Buddhism rid itself of syncretic accretions—Hindu gods, magic, sorcery, and the like, and return to the Theravada simplicities. As part of his scheme of domination, Dharmapāla focused his attack on the British colonial suppression of Buddhist culture and institutions and on the Hindu and Islamic threat to Buddhism resulting from the Tamil occupation of the north. His stress on sober worldly conduct imitated the Victorian English rather than the world-renouncer ideals of Buddhism. And the emphasis he placed on nationalism, despite his effort to legitimate it by his interpretation of the Māhavasa, could not be unambiguously derived from Buddhist doctrine.

Sri Lankan Buddhist fundamentalism thus rests on a basic ideological ambivalence. On the one hand, Theravada Buddhism stresses withdrawal from worldly values, including politics. The Four Noble Truths and the Eightfold Path do not include the cultivation of intimidation and violence. Hence, it is difficult to characterize the radical ethnoreligious nationalism of Sri Lankan Buddhist extremism as "selected" from the Buddhist canon; there is nothing in the canon to legitimate the fierce violence in which the bhikkus themselves have participated. While the Mahavasa celebrates military prowess in the defeat of the Tamils and accords legitimacy to the Buddhist claim to Sri Lanka, it was reinterpreted by Dharmapāla and later Buddhist leaders to legitimate a much more unequivocal and aggressive nationalism. From this point of view the ideological reactivity and selectivity of Buddhist nationalism shares with Hindu and Islamic fundamentalisms the elements of anti-imperialism and ethnonational preemptiveness.

Other ideological properties of fundamentalism such as Manichaeanism, inerrancy, and millennialism are in some measure applicable to the Buddhist extremists. They view the Tamils, as well as the moderates in their own Buddhist camp, as evil in contrast with their own virtue. The favorite text of the extremists, the Māhavạsa, is a chronicle, not a doctrine or set of disciplinary rules. The realized Sri Lankan Buddhist millennium would be a Sri Lanka rid of Hindus, Muslims, and Christians, its people living in a Buddhist "kingdom."

None of the organizational examples—Dharmapāla's Mahabodhi Society, the Sinhala Maha Sabha, the SLFP, or the partly underground terrorist JVP—exhibit in an unambiguous way the typical organizational patterns of fundamentalist movements. The notion that the JVP is an elect group and that it has a tendency to draw sharp boundaries can as easily be attributed to guerrilla and terrorist activities as to their religious beliefs. Rigorous codes of behavior are characteristic of the Buddhist monks in their capacities as members of monasteries and not as members of these organizations. Strong, charismatic leadership is not a characteristic of Sri Lankan Buddhist social and political movements. Leadership, organization, and membership in Sri Lankan Buddhism is more fluid, more populistic, and more easily fragmented than other world-conquering movements we have analyzed.

The historic encounter of Sri Lankan Buddhism with Christianity and Hinduism has been of greater significance in the rise of Buddhist fundamentalist extremism. The Hindu Tamil minority in the north, backed by the seventy million Tamils across the twenty-five mile Palk Strait, imparts a degree of paranoia to Buddhist defensiveness. In recent years the emergence of aggressive Hindu nationalism has added fuel to the fire of these fears.

Economic growth in Sri Lanka in the last forty years has resulted in a substantial movement of population at the cost of agricultural and village life. Increasing income inequality has impaired the sense of community, and unemployment, particularly among young men, has created potential recruits for guerrilla and terrorist action. Practically all of the civil disturbances in Sri Lanka—the election and the racial and religious riots—have occurred in settlements in colonization schemes, in the traditionless new market towns, and in Colombo.

James Manor attributes Buddhist extremism to the breakdown of traditional village organization and the rise of modern trading towns and "mass society" urban areas. But Manor also accounts for Sri Lankan violence by noting a thoroughgoing lack of capacity for organization and discipline throughout the whole of Sri Lankan government—central and local—the party system, and individual political parties, as well as the Sri Lankan clergy. Prime ministers cannot control their ministers, and cabinets cannot be counted on to act in concert in the sense of collective responsibility. Ministers cannot count on their officials, and local government, largely ignored by the central government, has little revenue with which to implement policies. Political parties have minimal organizational substance; they are little more than leaders with diffuse followings. Buddhist religious organization is similarly fragmented. Individual monasteries move in their own directions, and individual monks have considerable autonomy to engage in whatever religious and political activities they prefer. In a culture such as this, leadership has little capacity to pursue policies effectively, producing rhetoric rather than careful strategy and tactics. And social and political action deteriorates into reactive movements—demonstrations, mobs, and riots.[6]

Thus the international and religious contexts, Sri Lankan economic development, population displacement, and organizational propensities extending throughout Sri Lankan culture are the necessary causes of its Buddhist extremism. But chance and contingency have had significant triggering impacts. The intervention of Olcott and the American Theosophical Society gave Dharmapāla the authority and visibility he needed to gain an audience and begin the reversal of British Westernizing and Christianizing policy. The crucial election of 1956 was greatly influenced by the economic distress caused by the decline in world commodity prices and in Sri Lankan exports. This election of a government on a Sinhala Buddhist platform, followed by provocative legislative measures favoring the establishment of the Sri Lankan language and the Buddhist religion, set that polity on its course of polarization and violence from which it has not yet recovered.[7]

The high incidence of mob violence—the extent to which outcomes in Sri Lankan politics have been shaped by these traumatizing, unpredictable, uncontrollable events—is extraordinary. Sri Lankan Buddhist extremism is a limiting case of weak leadership and strong and chaotic mass action. The leaders who have entered Sri Lankan religious movements and politics since the beginnings of Buddhist revivalism have not been effective ideologists, skilled organizers, or coalition makers. The leaders of the major Sri Lankan political parties have outdone each other in demagogy and in Tamil bashing. Leaders are reluctant to form organizations with explicit divisions of labor, since this deprives them of discretion. Each major party when in opposition challenges the governing party for failing to go far enough in asserting Buddhist predominance. The many Buddhist monks who participate in these extremist movements and activities add another irrational component. Monks are objects of worship in Sri Lankan Buddhism; despite their inexperience and naiveté, their political interventions, which occur on a substantial scale, are not disputed.

Thus we conclude our discussion of the world-conquering pattern with an anomalous case in which political choices and decisions have been frustrated and distorted by anomic violence rather than calculated by strong charismatic/authoritarian leadership. The kind of process described by those who know Sri Lankan politics is a vicious circle of violence feeding on violence, with governments, opposition parties, terrorist movements, and Tamil separatist movements locked together in a tight, irrational embrace.

WORLD TRANSFORMER

Movements in the world-transformer mode occupy a niche in society, but they are constrained from hegemonic activity and forced to negotiate their circumstances and transform the environment over time. Leadership may be diffuse, shared by a number of authoritative leaders mobilizing followers on particular issues; the teachings or fate of any one leader is less important than in the world-conqueror pattern. The community is drawn at times into public confrontation with outsiders; the dominant considerations for the analyst are the character of the host society, the resistance it mounts to fundamentalist movements, and the strategies these movements adopt to increase their influence over society. The organizational structure may be described as an expanding and contracting enclave: it may consist of diffuse organizational networks that may be coordinated in times of mobilization. Movements in this mode exhibit an approach-avoidance pattern of withdrawal from and engagement with the surrounding society. Such a movement may be a religious or ethnic minority with aspirations of achieving a consolidated and multigenerational status. Cases include:

1. *U.S. Protestant Fundamentalism: First emergence, 1875–1925.* Given the synergy between certain unique features of American political culture and the ideological and organizational configurations of nineteenth-century evangelical Protestantism, it would have been rather surprising if fundamentalism, or something very much like it, had not emerged on cue when the new threats posed by liberal religion, secular philosophy, and science triggered a rift between these two powerful modes of public discourse—religion and politics—in the early twentieth century.

By fortifying the wall of separation between church and state while ensuring freedom of religion, the U.S. government had created a cultural environment marked by religious and ethnic pluralism and religious voluntarism in which competition between sects was encouraged and social spaces, or niches, for a variety of religious expressions were secured. Evangelical Protestantism further encouraged the splintering and diversification of religious movements and institutions and thereby created a vast network of social sources for old-time religion (e.g., revivalist preachers, Bible institutes, seminaries, strong local congregations, the Princeton School of Theology, etc.). Fundamentalism emerged ready-made from this mix, exploiting the resources at hand while fortifying itself as a unique movement by organizing rapidly around its central ideological principle—separatism—backed by the recently crafted theological doctrines of premillennialism and inerrancy. Early recruits came from disaffected ranks of the preexisting evangelical network. If the invasion of secularism, especially in the form of liberal religionists who embraced Darwinism and the Higher Criticism of the Bible, initially prompted the fundamentalist reaction, the relative heterogeneity of religion in America made the movement's growth possible.

Over the decades the niches filled by fundamentalism changed and grew. In its first incarnation the movement appeared in Baptist and Presbyterian churches of the Northeast; it appealed to newly urbanized middle- and lower-middle-class professionals and laborers, primarily of British and Scottish ancestry, seeking cultural stability and certitude in a time of social and economic dislocation brought on by rapid industrialization. With its specialized lingo, behavioral requirements, exclusivity, and stress on doctrinal uniformity and moral rigor, fundamentalism was for its recruits the functional equivalent of the immigrant enclave. Local pastors and preachers self-consciously created "cultural capital" with which to build a distinct subculture.

In weighing the importance of the social sources of fundamentalism, however, most commentators emphasize the central and seemingly independent role of ideology: more than many other protest movements, this one was about religious doctrines, values, and norms, and the motivations of its adherents cannot be understood apart from this integrity of belief (the particulars of which were frozen around the turn of the century). (It may even be argued that the belief system itself outweighs the importance of the individual charismatic preacher who brings it alive on the local level, but this is perhaps a chicken-and-egg argument.) By comparison, social, economic, and educational factors pale in importance. Rural-urban tensions are overplayed in many analyses of the movement's emergence, for even the first generation had adapted to the basic conditions of urban life.

It should be emphasized that the fundamentalist spirit of independence, if not defiance, was in keeping with classic Protestant (especially Baptist) emphases. The come-outers came out of churches that had been on the right course before the infiltration of secularizing agents. The basic organizational structure of fundamentalism is therefore in continuity with the evangelical heritage, but the noncompromising approach proved effective in attracting people beset by fears of assimilation. And as subsequent generations proved, this approach remained appealing in another region, the South, in a time of greater social and economic mobility and prosperity.

2. *Comunione e Liberazione.* Comunione e Liberazione (CL) has an altogether different story from most Catholic reactive movements. Still in its first generation, it is defined by its attempt to formulate a conservative Catholic ideology and strategy of power politics. Unlike Catholic traditionalist movements, CL in its initial emergence offered a blueprint for the future to the young, upscale Italians it sought to recruit. The movement is expert at articulating its ideological principles, social programs, and concrete goals; its organizational structure is a fundamentalist-type blend of political cadre, religious association, and social club. Yet it wavers between attempts to transform society gradually through the growing prominence of its religious culture, on the one hand, and significant involvement in local and national politics, on the other hand, where it hopes to further its ends more directly.

The movement emerged in Milan as a brilliantly idiosyncratic answer—Father Luigi Giussani's—to the religious declension and political upheaval of postwar Italy. Giussani blended disparate modern ideologies and philosophies. He drew, for example, upon the early-twentieth-century Protestant neo-orthodox theologian Karl Barth to infuse Italian Catholicism with a prophetic realism; and he cited an unlikely existentialist source, Camus, on the priority of grace (and, by Giussani's extension, Catholic sacramentalism) over Protestant scrupulosity to justify moral rigor and severity.

Giussani was a charismatic university and high school teacher in the 1950s and 1960s. He formulated a Christian critique of modern culture, coupled with a political philosophy of "the new Christendom," which Pope John Paul II later endorsed as a way to revive moribund Italian (and general European) Catholicism. Giussani's movement grew in the 1960s and 1970s, primarily among university students and young professionals, attracting many who, facing poor employment prospects, were disillusioned with revolutionary radicalism and the moral corruption of Italian society. In CL, the intellectual attack on secularization was joined to a political program and an organizational solution. CL developed programs, implemented through its *scuole* (local chapters of students), and publications devoted to a wide range of social issues, as well as extensive missionary activities. The movement organization also included the Momento Popolare, an inner core of devoted adherents, and the Compagnia delle Opere, a nonprofit organization founded in 1986 to promote cooperation among Italian companies and institutions for the sake of employing young Catholics. Boundaries are maintained by personal ties (new members adopt a big brother from among those who already belong), daily contacts, frequent devotions, and study groups within the community and by mutual support and elaborate personal networks within secular society, from professors to Christian Democrats.

Although the new Christendom rhetoric suggests theocratic elements, the real transformation CL seeks is cultural, and the political connections are seen as short-term means to a long-term end. This movement now faces the question of whether it can develop second-generation leadership.

3. *Pentecostalism in Guatemala.* Among the causes for the emergence of the Guatemalan neo-Pentecostals were: (1) the influence of North American missionaries and televangelists such as Bill Bright (Campus Crusade for Christ) and Pat Robertson (CBN), who contributed millions of dollars for media blitzes and short-term, intensive evangelizing; (2) covert political operations and funding designed to strengthen both the budding evangelical movement (seen as a source of "foot soldiers in the advancement of U.S. foreign policy") and right-wing governments; and (3) the decline of the status, fortunes, and influence of the Roman Catholic Church over both the people and powers that be of Guatemala—a decline that backpedaling hierarchs like Archbishop Penados blamed, somewhat disingenuously, on the first and second factors (i.e., the "invasion of the sects" as an imperialist economic and political strategy).

The causes of Catholic decline also lay in the foreign character of the clergy, the unsuitability of its European ideology and religiosity, and the historic and increasingly unpopular Catholic identification with the landed aristocracy and its failed economic policies, which had resulted in undernourishment, slavery, illiteracy, forced migration, crowding, a highly stratified social order, and the exploitation and repression of the masses.

The necessary cause of the rise and growth of the neo-Pentecostal movement was the rapid attempt to transform the structure of the Guatemalan political economy. Within this attempted economic transformation, the short-term trigger for the explosion of the movement in the 1980s was the rise of a born-again retired general, Efraín Ríos Montt, to the presidency of the country.

In these developments the Pentecostal communities played, at most, a passive supporting role. They were not concerned with domination or world conquest as much as with transforming their religious, social, and economic situation from the Catholic, hierarchical model, which seemed to keep them in poverty, to an evangelical, egalitarian, localized, and indigenous form of religious ideology and organization that inspired cultural transformation and the domestication of husbands, the renewing of the nuclear family, and the emergence of small-scale entrepreneurial businesses. Retained in this transformation was a passive approach to political involvement, though it should be noted that Guatemalan evangelicals by and large supported Ríos Montt and, in any case, did not resist him, and turned their backs on the Catholic liberationists who risked their lives to do so.

4. *Hindu Nationalism: Origins and growth in staggered emergences of RSS, VHP, and BJP, 1915 to present.* In chapter 3, we examined the three related fundamentalist-like organizations of national significance in India—the Rashtriya Svayamsevak Sangh (RSS, or National Union of Volunteers), the Vishwa Hindu Parishad (VHP, or World Hindu Society), and the Bharatiya Janata Party (BJP, or Indian People's Party).

These Hindu movements differ from the Abrahamic ones in a number of significant respects. First, while they are reactive to the growth of the secular, pluralist Indian state, they are also reactive to the competition of Islam and Christianity. There is also an ethnonationalist component—an Aryan, "blood and soil," nativist, preemptive ideology.

Second, the RSS and the VHP differ in the way in which they select from Hindu tradition. The RSS emphasizes the Kshatriya military tradition (in its Maharashtrian version). Its central headquarters are still in Nagpur, its capital. The VHP, with its revivalism and inclusive missionary activity, downplays distinct doctrines and reaches out to Untouchables, Tribals, Sikhs, Buddhists, and Jains, excluding only the Muslims and the Christians. In their concern over the possible appeal of Islamic and Christian egalitarianism to the Untouchables, they have attacked caste hierarchy as socially divisive, blocking the kind of social solidarity its leaders believe is necessary for a strong India.

Third, these Hindu movements are not enclaves as is the case with Abrahamic fundamentalisms, but rather tend to be revivalist and missionary networks. They view Sikhs, Jains, Buddhists, Tribals, and Untouchables as belonging within the Hindu "community" and argue that most Muslims and Christians are "Hindu by blood," that is, converts to alien religions, though this is explicitly denied by Muslim and Christian leaders.

A fourth, and related, mark of distinction lies in the fact that textual inerrancy is difficult to sustain in view of the large and complex corpus of Sanskritic and traditional Hindu literature of hymns, ritual prescriptions, sagas, philosophical writings, and the like.

Fifth, there is nothing comparable to the "end of days" and the final afterlife as found in Jewish, Christian, and Islamic theology. Modern Hindutva, however, has borrowed from the Abrahamic traditions an eschatology of ultimate destiny, with Hindutva being realized as the Kingdom of Ram (Ram Rajiya or Ram Rashtriya). Ram is represented as both man and god—imitative of Christianity. This is a synthetic cosmology, an effort to validate a claim to a Hindu version of fundamentalism.

The notion of the elect is present in the ethnoreligious notion of the Aryan race and in the self-selection of the celibate and highly disciplined staff organizers, trainers, and workers of the RSS and VHP, many of whom are Brahmans or from the other two "twice-born" castes—Kshatriya and Vaishya. There are full-time workers from other lower castes and groups. But this is not the enclave idea of a "returning and loyal remnant."

Finally, only the RSS requires specific behaviors and disciplines of its members, the wearing of uniforms, the carrying of the lathi, participation in drill, and the like. Discipline is especially required of the training cadres, some of whom live celibate lives and devote themselves full-time to RSS work. But these propensities pervade the related movements as well.

Hindu "fundamentalism" thus appears to be as much a militant nation- and state-building (or rebuilding) movement as a traditional religion-affirming movement. *Hindutva* defines the geographic, racial, and religious boundaries of Hinduism. It rejects the secular, separated, pluralist state and would replace it with a Hinduized state fully occupying the land within sacred boundaries and peopled homogeneously by believing and practicing Hindus, however this is defined. The threefold organization of Hindu fundamentalism, with its paramilitary, recruitment, and propagandistic groups and its political party, is intended to pursue these various goals. The Hindu movements are "more" than simple militant religious movements struggling against a secularizing state and society, but they are "less" than Abrahamic fundamentalisms in their lack of clear-cut doctrinal content. (The Hindu fundamentalist "doctrine" is in part synthetic and may not go very deep in belief and practice.)

Structural features that contribute to the explanation of Hindu fundamentalism are social aspects such as ethnicity, region, caste, and class. All three Hindu organizations are concentrated in the cities and towns of the tradition-bound "cow belt" of India—the northern states of Maharashtra, Gujarat, and Uttar Pradesh—and to a somewhat lesser extent in Bihar and Madhya Pradesh. Despite the criticism of the caste hierarchy by the VHP, in particular, the leadership and supporters of these movements are recruited primarily from the Brahman, Kshatriya, and Vaishya castes threatened by the anticaste propensities of the secular Indian state. Here there is a tension, if not an internal contradiction, within the Hindutva movements. Their favorite deity, Lord Rama, is very pro-caste. The leadership and membership of these Hindu fundamentalist movements are drawn primarily from the upwardly mobile middle class and lower-middle-class professionals, merchants, and cash-crop farmers, with little penetration among the industrial workers, artisans, subsistence peasants, and agricultural workers.

The educational characteristics of the elite and rank and file of these movements are related to the above-mentioned social-structural features. The full-time professionals of the RSS are at most secondary school graduates. The rank-and-file *svayamsevaks* in large part are illiterate or have some primary school education. The VHP elite include graduates primarily from provincial colleges or religious educational institutions. The BJP elite of parliamentarians and state legislators also are college and university graduates but not from the elite universities such as New Delhi and Bombay. One of the BJP leaders, M. M. Joshi, was a professor of physics at the University of Allahabad. The lower leadership of the party is primarily secondary school–educated. From a social-structural point of view, then, the leadership and support of these movements comes from groups fearing marginalization by the modern economy and secular society. Thus their interests lie in the preservation of "traditional Hinduism," the putative ideological opponent of the secular Indian state.

The political structure of India can explain aspects of the organization, ideology, strategy, and tactics of these movements. Under the British brand of imperialism—indirect rule—the Hindu intellectual elites were encouraged to codify and render coherent their complex and variegated Hindu cultural heritage and to view it as a world religion on the same level with Christianity, Islam, Buddhism, and Confucianism. Temples, other cultural centers, and monuments were made subject to the protection of the state, and temple officials and priests acquired a quasi-bureaucratic status.

Thus, the international context laid the ground for the emergence of Hindu fundamentalism by encouraging the development of a relatively coherent Hinduism. Under the pluralist and secular British Raj, Hinduism was one of several religions, the existence and autonomy of which were protected by the state. Independent India continued as a secular, pluralist state, seeking to accord equal protection to all religions and to remove or at least mitigate the inequalities of caste. The secular pluralism of the Indian state was a threat to the higher castes in traditional India, producing the fundamentalist movements with their antipluralist, antisecular programs.

Furthermore, the British Raj and the successor Indian state have been governed by the rule of law and freedoms of press, assembly, and organization. This political structure permitted the formation of organizations, recruitment of members, and legal participation in the struggle for power. These arrangements make possible the dual strategy followed by Hindu fundamentalism—the legal contest for control of the national and state governments, attended by considerable success at both levels; and a more threatening revolutionary strategy implied in its preemptive ethnoreligious, nationalist ideology and in the paramilitary structure and tactics of the RSS.

Taken together, these religious, social structural, civil society, political, and international conditions are the necessary causes of Hindu nationalism. They would explain the form nationalist movements would take in the Indian context, assuming that such movements developed. But there was much here that would have to be explained not by necessity but by contingency or chance. The perturbations of international politics (e.g., the impact of the two world wars on Indian internal political development) are contingencies from external arenas. Similarly, the assassinations of Mahatma Gandhi, Indira Gandhi, and Rajiv Gandhi explain the changing leadership chemistry in Indian politics, which, in turn, helps account for the ups and downs in the growth, spread, and effectiveness of Hindu fundamentalisms.

Structure and contingency create propensities and provide triggers for development and transformations, but they do not determine the specific form that ideas, programs, and institutions take. For these "sufficient" causes of fundamentalist movements we need to factor in the creativity of leaders—the plans, choices, and decisions of individuals, which turn these possibilities into realities.

We distinguish three types of leadership creativity in the Hindu movements—ideological, organizational, and coalitional. The ideological leaders included the Swami Dayananda Sarasvati, founder of the Arya Samaj, who played a major role in giving coherence to modern Hinduism. Savarkar wrote the ideological bible of Hindu nationalism *(Hindutva)* while imprisoned by the British for sedition. The key concept of Hindutva was its blending of nationalist and religious sensibilities: "A Hindu regards his land as his fatherland as well as his holyland." K. B. Hedgewar, the founder of the RSS, was an organizational leader who created institutions intended to shape Hindu cultural unity. A Maharashtrian Brahman and medical school graduate, Hedgewar chose a celibate career of nation-building. Hindu leadership, according to Hedgewar, was not fascist, but rather guru-like, with the leader as a spiritual guide, planning, implementing, and determining policy, and bringing comrades around to his point of view on the basis of his moral authority. The RSS supplied the leadership of the VHP and the

BJP. M. S. Golwarkar, who followed Hedgewar as leader of the RSS in 1940, was long-haired and ascetic. Under his more than three decades of rule, the RSS grew rapidly and proliferated chain-link organizations such as student, labor, and women's groups. He formulated the "five unities" of Hinduism—geography, race, religion, culture, and language (Sanskrit as the "language of the gods"). Golwarkar was both organizer and ideologue.

The contemporary leaders of the Hindu nationalists are coalition-builders. Balasaheb Deoras, leader of the RSS, has placed special emphasis on efforts to overcome caste division and to open the movement to the Untouchables, Tribals, Sikhs, Jains, and Buddhists. The VHP was formed during his tenure out of fear that Hinduism might lose the Untouchables to Islam. In the 1990s, L. K. Advani and A. B. Vajpayee, the president and vice-president, respectively, of the BJP, effectively appealed to a far larger political base that includes Sikhs. The Sikhs were given support by the BJP at the time of the disorders attendant on the Golden Temple riots. The strength of the BJP in the Lok Sabha and the state legislatures could not have been achieved without this cross-religious mobilization and dilution of caste norms.

Strong arguments could be made for placing the Hindu variant of funda-mentalism in the world-conqueror category, but its circumstances of emer-gence dictated a transformer pattern. Hindu fundamentalism clearly seeks to "conquer" India and to replace the secularist constitution by a still vaguely defined order based on Hindutva, but it must contend with a secularist gov-ernment with a considerable military presence and some legitimacy (the degree of which is constantly debated). It must also operate in a setting of cultural and religious pluralism not easily bent to autocratic visions. Thus the Hindu nationalist strategy is diverse, operative on many levels, and long-term in its goals and consequences.

5. *Sikh militants, immediately prior to the rise of Bhindranwale and the Golden Temple massacre.* The basic background of the Sikh saga is provided above in the world-conqueror section. It is important here, however, to underscore that the Sikh activists were not committed to a radical course prior to the implementation of certain Indian governmental policies. Not least among these was Indira Gandhi's support for what turned out to be the radical elements in a Sikh movement that was moving in a transformationist rather than a revolutionary mode.

But it should be remembered that other government policies—the re-moval of special privileges accorded to the Sikhs under the British Raj, and the social and economic displacement of farmers in the western region as a result of the Green Revolution—contributed mightily to the polarization in the Sikh community itself. The Sikh religious party, Akali Dal, was pursuing a world-transformer pattern of interaction with the Indian government, hoping to influence its policies by sharing political power with the Congress Party in the Punjab and by controlling the Sikh temples through the SGPC. But Sikhism as a religion did not exhibit the capacity to move readily from its own religious world to a mode of constant political interaction and compromise, which is required of the world transformer. Thus its world-transforming stage was relatively brief; it ended when Sant Harch and Singh Longowal, the leader of the Akali Dal in the 1970s, made demands for Sikh autonomy in Punjab. To head off extremism, an attempt that ultimately backfired, Indira Gandhi abandoned the Akali Dal for Bhindranwale and the Khalsa Dal—a case of jumping from the frying pan into the fire.

6. *Sri Lankan Buddhist extremism: Growth, 1940s.* In 1937, Bandaranaike founded the Sinhala Maha Sabha, which brought together a number of Buddhist groups including the supporters of Dharmapāla. Bandaranaike sought to influence and transform Sri Lankan politics rather than to seize control of it. In 1946, the Sinhala Maha Sabha joined the independence coalition of the UNP. In the mood of national unity after the attainment of Sri Lankan independence, Dharmapāla's version of Buddhist nationalism remained latent while the UNP followed a policy of compromise, Western-style pluralism, and parliamentarianism.

As in the Sikh case, however, the Buddhists did not linger long in the transformer mode. By the mid-1950s, a series of economic crises resulting from declining world market prices that affected Sri Lankan exports created substantial dissatisfaction and unrest. The SLFP of Bandaranaike withdrew from the UNP coalition in 1951 and ran a spirited and successful pro-Buddhist, pro-Sinhala campaign in the 1956 election. Bandaranaike's victory was not only associated with the economic downturn of the 1950s but also resulted from a significant rise in world-conquering Sinhala Buddhist nationalism and a remarkable politicization of the Buddhist religious establishment.

7. *Sunni movements in Egypt: Origins and first emergence, late 1920s–1940s.* Hasan al-Banna, the founder of the Muslim Brotherhood, described his mission as a *"salafiyya* [traditional or, literally, ancestral] mission." He described his society as a "Qur'anic, Muhammadan, Islamic society, which follows the way of the Noble Qur'an, takes the path of the Great Prophet, does not deviate from what has come down to us in God's Book, his Messenger's Sunna, and the conduct of the venerable fore-fathers."[8]

According to the Egyptian historian Abdel Azim Ramadan, the name *fundamentalist* appeared in the Egyptian press only upon the rise of militant

Islamic groups in the time of Sadat; it was used to distinguish them from
the Muslim Brotherhood. "Because they adopted the concepts of *jahiliyya*
(pre-Islamic idolatrous society), *al-hakimiyya* (God's sovereignty), and *al-
takfir* (branding with infidelity), these groups were considered radical, and
thus a part of the modern radical Islamic trend," Ramadan writes, "while
the Muslim Brotherhood was largely considered a part of the traditionalist
Islamic trend." Banna, a teacher at an elementary school in Ismailia in 1928,
challenged religious leaders to defend Islam from the encroachments of the
imported, secular, Western colonial culture. The initial goal, Ramadan says,
"was merely to hold fast to the basic principles of Islam in the face of ob-
scenity and apostasy." The first steps included the formation of Islamic societies, the publishing of Islamic newspapers, preaching, and providing guidance to the people. "The Muslim Brotherhood was thus a purely religious
society, a reformist Islamic movement. Its goal was to bring up youth in
accordance with proper Islamic ethics, and to disseminate the merits and
purposes of Muhammadan prophecy, including the moral virtues of truth-
fulness, chastity, and good social relations."[9]

The Brotherhood in its origins thus sought to transform the Egyptian
world of Islam by calling its members to reform. Missionary work was paramount; branches of the Brotherhood extended into several cities such as
Port Said, Suez, Abu Suwair, and Al-Bahr al-Saghir. Its headquarters was
moved to Cairo in October 1932.

The transit to a world-conquering mode was visible even in Banna's original ideology, however, which emphasized the oneness of religion and state
and the need for pan-Islamism in the face of Egyptian nationalism. (The
Brotherhood spread quickly outside Egypt, particularly into the Sudan,
Syria, and the Maghreb.) Banna came to consider noninvolvement in politics an "Islamic crime." The Brotherhood was the first Islamic association
to shift its activities from the traditional Islamic centers such as Al-Azhar,
the Sufi orders, and the uneducated popular classes to the secular universities and the educated classes influenced by Western culture. The Brotherhood shifted the responsibility for establishing Islamic government from
the religiously educated class to the Westernized class, from the shaykhs to
the lawyers, doctors, engineers, pharmacists, and army and police officers.
Its political activism soon led to clashes with the Egyptian state and to a
radicalization of the movement.

In 1948 Egyptian prime minister Nuqrashi dissolved the organization
and detained its most important leaders. Neither he nor Hasan al-Banna
survived this initial clash between Islamic fundamentalism and the Egyptian
government. The Brotherhood supported the military officers of the July

Revolution, but the victorious officers ordered the Brotherhood dissolved on 14 January 1954. In retaliation, the Brotherhood attempted to assassinate Nasser in Alexandria. Its leaders, including Sayyid Qutb, were jailed for terms of five to ten years, and the world-conquering ideology and organizational structure of the Brotherhood jelled in Qutb's jail cell.

8. *Hamas: Origins and trigger events.* Hamas followed a similar pattern in its origin. It began as an offshoot of the Muslim Brotherhood in Gaza, dedicated to the Islamization of society. After Nasser's repression, the remnants of the movement saw its destiny changed, twice, by external triggers: the Israeli occupation (1967) and the first Intifada (1987).

The world-transforming mode lasted beyond the period of Egyptian rule and for the first twenty years of Israeli occupation, as Hamas established clinics, schools, and other social service institutions in the territories. Under the leadership of Shaykh Yassin, however, Hamas later developed a world-conquering mode in competition with the PLO. This development was triggered by events in the early 1980s, including the rise of the Islamic Jihad and the example set by Hizbullah in opposing Israel's invasion of Lebanon. On this terrain it had a rival in the form of Islamic Jihad, but that nascent movement was decimated by efficacious Israeli repression. In both the Gaza Strip and parts of the West Bank, Hamas, while focusing on a militant core of young males (mostly lower-class and lower-middle-class), succeeded in gaining a cross-class support periphery due to an all-out ethnoreligious opposition to the occupier.

WORLD CREATOR

As in the world-conqueror mode, leadership in the world-creator mode is charismatic, authoritarian, and centralized. But the appeal is to a narrower band of elements within a society; hence, social and cultural resources are not vast but very particular. Diverse disaffected segments of society are not immediately attracted to the specialized message and terminology of the movement. The ideology calls for preserving the religious tradition by building it up and/or returning to a state of purity. This pattern of fundamentalism emphasizes the puritanical strand in the religious tradition, the need to avoid corruption from intermingling with outsiders.

Accordingly, the stance is defensive rather than offensive or proactive; dualism is high in the origins of the movement. Further, the movement rejects or suppresses nationalist and theocratic elements in the religious tradition; it retrieves those teachings of the tradition that support the inward turn, and it may borrow selectively from the outside. The organization is that of a typical enclave: charismatic leader, small hierarchy, egalitarian core. The public impact is middle level, somewhere between the disruptions of the world conqueror and the negligible impact of the world renouncer. In relating to the outside world, a fundamentalist movement may seek political or legal concessions to enable world-creating activities—missionary outreach, religious exemptions—or to safeguard privileges and inhibit encroachment of worlds against which it is competing.

The world creator, for all his defensiveness, may one day find himself strong enough to become a world conqueror or world transformer. Cases include:

1. *Lubavitcher Hasidim*. Habad was the only Hasidic sect in the early nineteenth century with a relatively small local power basis (in Byelorussia) and a universalistic, pan-Jewish bent in ideology and (to a lesser extent) in organization. It was thus positioned to adapt itself to the new circumstances created by the mass migration of the late nineteenth century and especially to the disruption created by the Bolshevik Revolution and its aftermath. The revolution cut it from its original power base, exiling the Lubavitcher rebbe to Poland and then (with the advent of World War II) to the United States.

Habad could thus create a centralized worldwide structure, headed by the rebbe and his bureaucracy, which makes ample use of media techniques, controls far-flung local groups, puts them in direct touch with the rebbe (i.e., via satellite), supplies them with indoctrination and information material, and appoints and moves around emissaries and organizers. Western economic prosperity and the welfare state were also put to good use.

Yet underlying it all was the twofold ideological innovation introduced by the fifth and sixth rebbes: emphasis upon the oncoming messianic redemption as an explanation for the Holocaust and other historical disruptions and as a goal for intensive action; and missionary (outreach) action among that majority of the Jewish people won over by the secularist way of life. This missionary activity serves to reaffirm the identity of those who perform it regardless of how many souls it actually saves. In this work it was helped by the growing good will among Jews toward the haredim in the wake of the decline of the melting-pot ideal and the rise of particularistic identity. Haredim came to be seen as a remnant of a by now idealized shtetl or (in Israel) as carriers of a messianic gospel not unlike the one that erupted in Israel following the 1967 victory.

Discontent with modernity, whether due to the cultural critique of the 1960s or to economic crisis in the 1970s, enlarged the pool of susceptible recruits. Habad's emphasis on the special, innate essence of Jewish identity, inextricably combined with messianism, enjoyed a powerful appeal among Jews in the United States due to deteriorating relations with the Black community and even more so among an Israeli public that had become infused with "tribalized" concepts of Jewish ethnicity and was increasingly preoccupied (due to the Arab-Israeli conflict) with the Jewish-Gentile divide. The late rebbe, it should be noted, was a devotee of Greater Israel, an idea much in vogue since the 1967 war. That war is an important trigger for Habad but not for the rest of the haredim.

2. *Christians in South India.* Certain similarities between the south Indian and Guatemalan cases are striking; one may even be tempted to place the Guatemalan case in the world-creator category, were it not for the Pentecostals' support of the regime—the world already in place. In both cases, however, the rise of assertive "fundamentalist-like" forces is very recent and triggered by increased competition for religious loyalties and for social and economic resources, the competition occurring, moreover, among groups that have heretofore been marginalized socially, politically, and economically. In both cases a niche has been created for neo-Pentecostal activists and proselytizers as a result of larger social-religious-economic upheavals, in south India. These upheavals, in turn, were aggravated by large-scale campaigns of assertive Hindu nation building by the RSS and the VHP, which claim to represent the interests of the expanding Hindu middle class (newly prosperous entrepreneurs, substantial cash-crop farmers, and urban professional people); and by Islamizing campaigns in the southern states of Tamil Nadu and Kerala, which contain a disproportionately large number of India's fifteen million professing Christians.

In both cases the new Christian forces are so diverse—so eclectic in worship style, ideological particulars, and organizational profiles—that one cannot speak of a unified movement. In south India, in Kerala alone, they include liberation-theology-style Roman Catholic communities led by social justice priests, and hundreds of Pentecostal or "Holy Spirit" churches with some affiliation to the North American denomination, the Assemblies of God. In both Guatemala and south India, however, the new Christian activists have adopted a fundamentalist-like awareness that organized fundamentalisms have power as bearers of political and economic resources in times of social upheaval. Each movement thus is groping toward creating a distinctive Christian world—an identifiable subculture and enclave, with borders, existing within a hostile environment. These nascent movements have been influenced by outsiders and by the example of fundamentalisms elsewhere (including, for the south Indian Christians, not only Christian fundamentalism in North America but Islamic and Hindu radicalism on the subcontinent), but they are nonetheless independent, indigenous movements that are not controlled or funded or inspired in their particulars by foreign missionary organizations.

The important differences between the two cases can be traced to the different long-term structural environments. In India, religious diversity and cultural pluralism are hardly new realities; religious groups of bewildering diversity have shared pilgrimage sites, shrines, and temples with little apparent regard for confessional boundaries. Yet the presence and pace of religious competition has accelerated sharply, and various strategies, religious communalism being the most significant, seem to have been refined, developed, and fortified in a relatively short time. In the last fifteen to twenty years there has been a growing nationwide sense that everything is up for grabs in the race for communal development resources. (Even the caste system itself, which helped bring order and a certain stability to the pluralism, is challenged by the new Hindutva devotees.)

In Guatemala, the fortunes of the rising Christian movement were largely dictated by the patronage of the state and its ruler; in India, the secular state has been opposed to religious communalism (fundamentalism). However, because the Indian state has been a relatively weak guardian of the values and principles of the secular constitution—undermining its chances by falling prey to corruption, mismanagement, and ill-advised policies—it has played into the communalists' hands. In this regard the short-term trigger for the emergence of the new religious activism was the twenty-one-month state of emergency imposed by Indira Gandhi, which suspended the constitution and in effect made the state merely another (albeit dominant) player in the civil strife. When the ban was lifted in 1977, there was a sense that, as the state had been discredited in its role as the guarantor of national coherence and order, every community must now look out for its own interests. Something like "fundamentalism" was the blueprint of choice for many of the communities as they reinvented themselves and harnessed the resources of civil society to their ends.

Within the strained demographics of south India, the competition has an economic as well as a spiritual edge. Oil prices rose in the late 1970s, bringing about double-digit inflation just as large hinterland and coastal tracts in the states of Tamil Nadu, Karnataka, and Andhra Pradesh experienced drought and crop failures. This led to waves of short- and long-term migration by displaced cultivators to the packed slum colonies of Madras and other large cities. Such shifts in regional political geography paved the way for violent clashes initiated by self-styled "sons of the soil"—Hindu militants who had organized themselves to resist threats to employment and control of regional political institutions at the hands of "aliens." In Kerala state, to take another example, Christian and Muslim migrant workers returning from the Persian Gulf or from other Arab countries after the collapse of the oil boom in the mid-1980s experienced lengthy unemployment and restricted opportunities, making them prime candidates to join political activist groups organized along religious lines.

Susan Bayly notes that Hindu "fundamentalist" rhetoric, unleashed with a new intensity after 1977, turns on a strategy of portraying the Christian and Muslim "opponents" as both more foreign and more cohesive and monolithic in organization than in fact they are. This has proved, however, to be something of a self-fulfilling prophecy, as various Christian groups have responded to the Hindu-majoritarian rhetoric by taking on their own fundamentalist characteristics: they interpret local disputes as part of a larger pan-regional and pan-Indian conflict; they embrace the literal and political interpretation of Scripture and/or the supernatural charismatic authority of individual leaders and spiritual adepts; and they emphasize corporate identity, promote symbols of "true" Christianity, and repudiate emblems and forms of worship that express common ground with Hindus and Muslims in the same densely populated sacred landscape. "In this shift towards exclusiveness and a strengthening of previously loose and fluid communal boundaries, the fact of interaction, of being spurred to assertive behaviour by the example of others, has been a crucial element in the rise of organized fundamentalism in the southern states."[10]

In accounting for the rise of Christian fundamentalisms, therefore, we may speak of many triggers of the same general type: militant responses to the challenge of other communalists who are claiming sacred sites, as well as economic resources, for their own.

3. *Sikhs, under the leadership of Sant Fateh Singh, mid-1960s.* Sikhism, as we have seen, moved rapidly from a world-creator orientation to a world-conqueror one, pausing only briefly in an ill-begotten attempt to transform Punjabi and Indian politics through political power brokering. The Sikh religion was a "world" unto itself, unaccustomed to the negotiations of identity necessary for political compromise. The Sikh leader of the world-creating stage, Sant Fateh Singh, used fasts and threats of self-immolation on the roof of the Golden Temple to bring pressure to bear on the Congress Party authorities. He wanted the world outside to conform to the requirements of the Sikh world.

Sikh political organization and leadership have distinctive characteristics. The inseparable mix of politics and religion makes bargaining and coalition making highly risky. Hence political leadership as such is confined to authoritative ideologizing; political decisions are sacred acts made by persons with sacred powers. Pragmatic "cost-benefit bargaining" and coalition-making have no legitimate place in the religiopolitical process. Typical means used to attain goals are self-destruction through dramatic fasts or suicides or destruction of property or persons. And the predominance of the sant-devotee form of political relationship rules out lower-cost bargaining and compromising as legitimate modes of political action. Moderate politicians are short-lived and constantly in physical danger. World creating, if it gives way in Sikh fundamentalism, yields to the revolutionary radicalism of the Sikh world conqueror.

4. *Sri Lankan Buddhist extremism: Origins, 1890s–1930s.* The world creator, like the world renouncer, may withdraw from the outside world for a time, but the withdrawal is tactical rather than permanent or principled. The case of Angarika Dharmapāla's alliance with the theosophists is exemplary. He withdrew from the alliance when affiliation meant giving up specifically Sri Lankan rituals and holy places. Dharmapāla sought to recreate the world of Sri Lankan Buddhism by ridding it of its syncretic features, inculcating the basics of the Four Noble Truths and the Eightfold Path. In this effort, however, he was influenced by and imitative of the outside world, specifically, the world of the Victorian Protestant missionaries. Thus the world he sought to create was a "Protestant Buddhism," a moralistic and ascetic as well as intensely nationalistic "updating" of traditional Buddhism. Note that the world he was creating was tailored ultimately to fundamentalist-hegemonic ends; he was a creator of Buddhist nationalism as much as a renewer of Buddhist religion.

5. *Arya Samaj: Pre-RSS.* In 1875, Swami Dayananda founded the Arya Samaj, a Hindu religiocultural organization that with the Hindu Mahasabha was the predecessor of the contemporary Hindu movements, especially the RSS. The Arya Samaj and the Mahasabha were religion-building movements reacting to the competition with codified and organized Islamic and Christian religions. At the same time, as fundamentalist world creators they were nation-state–building movements reacting against the secular state instituted by the British Raj and then against the indigenous secular-pluralist state of independent India. The explanation of the mixed character of Hindu fundamentalism hence is in substantial part a consequence of the interaction of particular kinds of religious structure in a particular international context. Today the Arya Samaj numbers more than a million members in India and in foreign countries. It supports, primarily in northern India, a

network of colleges and schools with Sanskrit-Vedic-Hindu as well as secular curricula. It is especially powerful abroad.

WORLD RENOUNCER

Movements in the world-renouncer mode often emerge from an existing, long-standing tradition that is modernized abruptly. The leadership is charismatic, authoritarian, renegade, and prophetic—often defining itself and the movement in contrast to tepid, compromising, liberalizing religious leadership that has jeopardized the integrity of the religious tradition. Leaders point to widespread apostasy and marshal resources for apocalyptic battle (or drawn-out conflict, when that hope is disappointed). The ideology is counter-acculturative, with elaborate warnings against selecting from either tradition, which is presented whole (at least rhetorically), or especially from modernity, which is insidious. The true enclave with high walls is the only hope. These movements tend to rank low on the scale of fundamentalist elements precisely because they are so resistant to adaptation and are niggardly in their sharing with modern processes. Such movements exercise some public impact, for the outside world has to accommodate them; but they are not seeking to transform or conquer outsiders, who are anyway condemned. The world renouncer is a separatist par excellence. Examples include:

1. *The French Catholic Lefebvrists.* The Lefebvrists, whose leader's authority was derived not from personal charisma but from his ecclesial office, are an example of a Catholic traditionalist movement rather than, strictly speaking, a fundamentalist movement. Granted, it did exhibit some of the marks of fundamentalism, such as a strong moral and cosmological dualism, authoritarian leadership, and an inner core of disciplined, elect adherents ("remnants"). Yet its primary appeal was (and is) to a certain type of restorationist Catholic who is nostalgic for the social stability and ethnic privileges of the ancien régime (in Lefebvrist rhetoric, a hallowed time prior to the "unholy trinity" of liberty, equality, and fraternity introduced by the French Revolution and against which Lefebvre constantly railed). This kind of Catholic also longs to return to the time before Holy Mother Church had succumbed to the numbing, differentiating influences of modernism (church differentiated from state, liturgy from social activism, moral reasoning from institutional authority).

Like other forms of nostalgia, the Lefebvrist lament is not accompanied
by strategies for change. The "movement" looks to the past. When a future
is envisioned, it assumes apocalyptic proportions: the vengeance of God is
imminent. In terms of their impact upon existing structures, the Lefebvrists
began in the 1970s as "bureaucratic insurgents" who sought to restore their
place of privilege in church and state. Even when they broke away from the
church that had nurtured them, they retained many of its customs, organizational and ideological assumptions, and habits of mind. That they were
more bureaucratic than charismatic, more hierarchical than egalitarian,
more routinized than ideologically and organizationally dynamic, is indicated not only by their limited influence on young people and even middle-
aged French Catholics but also by the slight upsurge in their ranks after their
founder died and was replaced by a German bureaucrat.

Nationalism is not a strong binding force in this case; it provides no
basis for a vital fundamentalist movement, despite the nativist Jean Marie
Le Pen's modestly successful attempts to draw upon a traditionalist Catholic
base.

Archbishop Lefebvre was ultimately after loftier goals than ridding the
world of the Jews and Masons who had corrupted mundane politics; he
sought nothing less than the restoration of the one, true church. But his
movement withdrew from both church and world and has not been notably
successful in reforming either, preferring instead to concentrate its energies
on denunciations and some measure of world building. But the world creation is not a fundamentalist-style competition with the world as much as
it is intended to provide a spiritual haven in a fallen world.

2. *Haredi Jews.* The haredim's is a story of a double emergence. Leadership was crucial for the movement's takeoffs early in the century and again
in midcentury. Leadership set forth an ideology that transcended past internal division (between Hasidim and Misnagdim) and responded to the challenges of victorious Zionism and of the American way of life. Ideologists
(such as the Hafetz Haim and the Hazon Ish) were greatly helped by institution builders and coalition makers (such as Rabbi Kahaneman of the
Ponovezh yeshiva or Agudat Yisrael politicians, e.g., J. Rosenheim and I. M.
Levin). The genius of the latter (especially the Agudat, established in Poland
in 1912 and later moving to the United States and Israel) consisted in maintaining a decentralized structure of "affinity groups" (to borrow a term
coined by anthropologist Steve Rayner). Such groups were locally led but
shared ideology, religious practice, major educational institutions, and political affiliation.

The haredim are distinguished from most other fundamentalist movements (except for American Protestants) in being multigenerational. They rely less on new recruits than on old-timers. Their large families "produce" and shape recruits, for the fourth generation, channeling them through *heder*, small yeshiva, great yeshiva, and *kollel* (or *ulpana* for girls). The totalistic atmosphere of the haredi world, predicated upon clustered residence, facilitates in-group marriage and provides employment (beyond years in yeshiva for males; before and throughout marriage for girls). Deferral from Israeli military service provides yet another incentive (this time negative) for remaining in the fold, and indeed attrition has been brought to a minimum in later generations through the impact of socialization, scholarship, employment, marriage, and army deferral.

While the haredim began as world renouncers, they always were world creators as well; and it may even be said that they emphasized this mode above all others when they accepted public monies and privileges from the Israeli government and shifted in the late 1980s from anti-Zionist to a-Zionist ideology.

Pure world renouncers are rare among fundamentalisms; the Neturei Karta, a sect within the haredim, qualify, as do Islamic sects like the Samawiya of Egypt. Fundamentalism, however, includes a dynamic engagement with the outside world. Even if that engagement takes the form of a renunciation of the outside world, fundamentalists find that they depend increasingly on that world's resources in order to construct their alternative.

CONCLUSION

Tables 4.1 and 4.2 (in the appendix to chapter 4) convey our conclusions in schematic form with two X marks indicating the dominant pattern at a given time. In table 4.2, we show how structural, chance, and choice variables explain the transition to these four world-relational patterns. Beginning with structural variables, the world-creator phase of the Jewish haredim—the formation of the Agudat Israel and the coalition of ultra-Orthodox movements—was a response to the depopulation of the shtetl through emigration to the larger cities and to the United States in the nineteenth and twentieth centuries. The rise of fundamentalist churches and institutions among the American Protestants in the period between the 1870s and the 1920s exemplifies fundamentalism in its world-transformer manifestation, which can be explained in part by the threat of cultural secularization in a pluralist and fragmented religious organizational context. The Gush Emunim's world-conquering phase was a response to the 1967 and

1973 Arab-Israeli wars. The impact of structural variables (the theology of the host religion) in a world-renouncing case is exemplified by the Neturei-Kartei in their withdrawal from allegiance to the Zionist state on the basis of a literal biblical interpretation of premessianic Judaism.

The impact of chance on the emergence of fundamentalism in its world-creator manifestation is exemplified by the influence of the American Theosophical Society on Sri Lanka Buddhist revivalism. Chance causation in the world-transformer form of fundamentalism is exemplified by the impact of the Holocaust on the formation of haredi communities and yeshivot in Israel and the United States. Chance events ushering in the world-conquering phase of fundamentalism is exemplified in the coincidence of the shah's illness and the presidency of Jimmy Carter, which made possible Khomeini's seizure of power in Iran.

There are, of course, many examples of leadership "explaining" the various manifestations of fundamentalism. Swami Dayananda, for example, was a world creator of Hindu fundamentalism in founding the Arya Samaj in 1875, as was Savarkar in writing *Hindutva* in 1925. Father Giussani was a world transformer in establishing the scuole of Comunione e Liberazione. Among leaders who triggered the shift to the world-conquering phase, the Egyptian Sunni ideologue, Sayyid Qutb, is a striking example. The classic Shi'ite case, of course, is Ayatollah Khomeini. Finally, a good example of the importance of leadership in a world-renouncing case is the French Archbishop Marcel Lefebvre, who led his small flock out of the Roman Catholic church after the "heresies" of Vatican II.

Table 4.2 is merely suggestive of the complexities of any one fundamentalism's movement from pattern to pattern. Consider the haredim, who emphasized separatism and world creation during the interwar years in Europe, with world-transforming tendencies also evident via Agudat Israel as a political party. Against the threat of "infidel" Zionism, the extreme wing split from Agudat Israel in the late 1930s to form the Eda Haredit, an offshoot that combined world-renouncer and world-creator traits. Its nucleus is the Satmar Hasidim, who persist to this day, though the world-creator traits became more prominent in the 1990s due to economic interaction with the Israeli environment. In the United States, Satmar separatists accept federal money and even go to court for it (e.g., the Supreme Court case involving the Kiryas Joel school district and special school established for disabled Hasidic children in New York state), but in Israel they do not take money from the Israeli state.

In the wake of the Holocaust, most Hasidic groups in Europe, Israel, and the United States passed through a period of world creation in order to reconstitute their identity and network. However, they tended to combine their world-creating efforts with a measure of separatism (i.e., world renouncing). But due to economic prosperity beginning in the late 1950s, they tended especially in Israel to renounce their rigid separatism and manifest world-transformer strategies, hoping against hope to change Israeli society. From anti-Zionism they turned to a-Zionism, participating in Israeli government coalitions and recruiting separatist Israelis from high-status groups as proof that they are able to transform Israeli society over the long haul through *teshuva* (conversion). Whenever their fortunes ebb, however, they return to their separatist tendencies.

In Islam, the Tablighi Jamaat is like Habad in that it exhibits both world-creating and world-renouncing tendencies simultaneously. The Muslim Brotherhood, by contrast, began as world creators and moved quickly into the role of world transformers. Extremist groups among them in the 1940s and 1950s tried their hand at world-conquering but were obliterated by Nasser. When the Brotherhood turned again to world-conquering in the mid-1960s, they experienced failure and decided to concentrate on world transformation.

On the margins of the phenomenon are tiny sects like the Samawiya, heavily impregnated with Sufism, which conclude that society is completely lost and that the only way out is to renounce the world. Such sects, built around powerful charismatic leaders, exist in Upper Egypt in caves and barely accessible deserts and hilly areas and sometimes also in small town environments. They live completely self-enclosed, recruit sparingly, and limit interaction, including marriage, to group members.

Other movements may pass through a world-renouncer phase. Thus Takfir wa-Hijra in Egypt, having created their own world in the late 1960s and early 1970s, concluded that the external environment was so vile and menacing that the only acceptable response was to emigrate, like the Prophet, to caves, hills, and apartments, where they lived as a sort of self-enclosed commune (even assigning female members to marry male members), attempted to be self-sufficient economically, and shared resources. They deemed the larger environment to be infidel/apostate *(takfir)*.

By contrast, the jama'at that proliferated during the 1970s are not world renouncers; they vacillate, according to circumstances, between world-transformer and world-conqueror tendencies. The Qutb ideology is subtle enough to permit such a gamut of interaction. By the mid-1970s, however, some leaders such as Shukri Mustafa thought that they were strong enough to conquer society by force (there was no point of transforming it, for it was too steeped in apostasy). But the 1977 coup failed, and its leaders were executed. The group then split, with many continuing in an armed underground existence, biding their time. A minority moved back into world-renouncing existence in tiny sects.

We respect the complexity of these movements' changes over time by focusing more narrowly, in chapter 5, on political and ethnic aspects of fundamentalism.

Testing the Model: Politics, Ethnicity, and Fundamentalist Strategies

In this chapter we apply our analytical grid of structure, chance, and choice and our four fundamentalist orientations to an examination of the strategies pursued by fundamentalist movements in differing political and ethnic macrostructures.

What determines the behavior of fundamentalist movements? As we explained in chapter 3 and described in detail in chapter 4, structure, chance, and choice, taken together, determine the direction a fundamentalist movement will take in its relation to the world. Now let us approach the question in a slightly different way in an attempt further to clarify our analytical model. Of structure, chance, and choice, policy analysts can be most confident in their understandings of the structural setting in which a movement exists. We can know whether a host society is democratic or nondemocratic, religiously and ethnically heterogeneous or homogeneous, economically advanced or impeded, and so on. Analyzing or "predicting" contingent events like a war, the illness of a leader, or the eruption of a riot, is a far riskier proposition. This is the case even when the event seems less like a chance occurrence (e.g., the election of a pope who surprises everyone by convening Vatican II) and more like a recognizable, if not entirely predictable, outcome of long-term structural tensions (e.g., bread riots, while unpredictable, are hardly a surprise, given long-standing economic mismanagement). Finally, basing an interpretive model in any degree on the choices of fundamentalist leaders, with all the vagaries involved therein, requires more boldness than we are able to muster.

Thus we are left with structures, and while they do not tell us everything, they do tell us quite a bit about the possibilities open to fundamentalist movements. Among the major conditions influencing the strategy, growth, and decline of fundamentalist movements are the nature of the political regime under which they compete for influence and power, and the ethnic heterogeneity or homogeneity of the society in which they emerge. The regime—whether it is authoritarian or democratic—sets the operating rules of political competition, thereby determining whether the struggle is to be overt or covert, the methods peaceful or violent, and the approach gradualist or integralist. The ethnic character of the society may determine whether a purely religious form of fundamentalism emerges or whether it is subordinated and intermingled with ethnic and nationalist purposes.

In the preceding chapters we introduced these themes of politics and ethnicity, along with others, in broad theoretical terms. Here we adopt a narrower and sharper focus on political regime and ethnocultural context. We are not setting aside our threefold explanatory logic of structure, chance, and choice. But we argue that the other structural variables are filtered through the political-governmental structure and process. Similarly, the cultural identities distributed among the population determine the options available to fundamentalist leaders. If ethnicity and religion are intermingled in the population of a society, what emerges may be a threat not only to the form of government and the content of public policy but also to the continued allegiance of minority groups to the national community. The very integrity of the state may hang in the balance.

In what follows, we elaborate these assertions by examining the strategies, growth, and decline of fundamentalist movements in three structural settings: democratic societies, societies that are nondemocratic, and societies riven by ethnoreligious conflict.

STRATEGIES

By strategies we refer to the programmatic means fundamentalists adopt for achieving their goals. The strategies of fundamentalist movements will vary according to their different modes of relating to the world (see chapters 3 and 4) and according to the possibilities available to them in their structural settings.

Nondemocratic Structures

By nondemocratic we mean strong, repressive, centralized governments. Especially in the Islamic world such governments have been expanding pervasively at the expense of civil society—since the end of World War II in most Islamic countries, but since the mid-nineteenth century in Egypt, Algeria, and Muslim India. The media and education are under government control, and the economy, another structural factor, is dominated by the public sector.

This set of circumstances has tended to militate against the rise of opposition movements, yet some changes in the structure have provided opportunities, notably the development of the private sector in the 1970s. This development was due to a modified international environment: the open-door policy initiated in Egypt after the 1973 war led to a measure of political liberation, and the availability of Saudi money after the oil bonanza led to the funding of various Islamic movements. The decline in the "systemic legitimacy" of the regimes, due to defeat in war (Egypt, 1967) and grave socioeconomic crisis due to a steep decline in oil prices (Algeria, 1988), likewise prepared the terrain.[1]

Two strategies have been devised by trial and error to deal with this set of circumstances. They may be followed alternately by the same movement or simultaneously (but with no coordination) by different branches of the movement.

The first option is a combination of world-creator and world-transformer patterns of relations. The building-up of enclaves comes first in the process, followed by their expansion in a civil society, which needs to be reconstructed after ravages by government. The build-up may be facilitated by an opening up of democratic process (a change in government structure), which creates room for maneuver and the possibility of gaining assets in civil society. This path has been followed by the Muslim Brotherhood in Egypt under Sadat and, more recently, under Mubarak. During periods of the relaxation of the laws on associations and the press, as well as the availability of elections, the Brotherhood garnered a base of support. In Iran, similarly, the Islamic movement used opportunities provided by the shah from the late 1960s to the mid-1970s, before turning to the second strategy.

The second strategy option in a nondemocratic structure, adopted when the movement shifts to a world-conqueror mode, consists of seizing power by violent means: destabilization by mass demonstrations (Iran, 1978; Tunisia, 1984; Algeria, 1988), assassination (the Egyptian Jamaʿat murdering Sadat, 1981; their attempts against higher officials and tourists in the 1990s), and open revolt (Syrian radicals in Hama, 1982; Shiʿites in southern Iraq, 1991). Alternatively, the movement may create an alliance with (or infiltrate) a military group that then takes control; this was the case in Sudan in 1989 and in Pakistan under Zia ul-Haq. This process unfolds according

to the world-conqueror ideology and organization and is followed whenever the democratic process is either unavailable or seen (in its present
guise) as a trap. Government structure, public policy, and control of media
and education are the crucial factors in forcing fundamentalist opposition
movements in this radical direction.

If the revolutionary movement does not succeed but the movement sur-
vives, the transformer pattern tends to be chosen again as soon as state
control and repression of the movement wanes.

This should by no means be considered an exclusively Islamic pattern.
It does not cover Islamic cases of ethnic domination (see the world-creator
pattern), but it does include movements such as the Pentecostals in Guatemala during the 1970s and 1980s. The contingency that gave Guatemalan
Pentecostals the opportunity to grow in number (from disaffected Catholic
ranks) consisted in the rapid attempt of the government to transform the
structure of the political economy in much the same pattern as occurred in
Iran (1962–78) and Egypt (post-1973). The difference was that the Guatemalan evangelicals had available to them a short-term trigger or chance
factor, namely, the rise of a born-again retired general, Ríos Montt, to the
presidency. Fueled in part by major investments by North American (and
Korean) businessmen, the large-scale agricultural and industrial development opened up avenues of opportunity and upward mobility for the lower
classes and rural peasants—without, however, providing the necessary educational support and training for the displaced farmers and small-scale entrepreneurs who would make up the bulk of the workforce (and the new
recruits for neo-Pentecostal churches). In the 1980s, Ríos Montt promoted
evangelicalism as an ideology and a cultural force with the potential to provide significant political and social support for the transformation of the
economy from small-scale agricultural and entrepreneurial activity to large-
scale industrial production.

The evangelical movement, planted by missionaries in the nineteenth
century, had developed its own indigenous forms of worship, which combined North American Baptism and Pentecostalism. Yet the boom in the
1980s was the result of Ríos Montt's policies. He surrounded himself with
leading Latin American evangelists, supported the burgeoning evangelical
media and educational initiatives, and vigorously discredited the Catholic
church as standing in the way of moral regeneration and economic development. Membership in Pentecostal churches swelled, reaching about one-
third of the population by the end of the decade—the highest such share
in Latin America. Thus the Guatemalan evangelicals expanded from congregational enclaves to a world-transformer pattern.[2]

Democratic Structures

In other settings the government structure is democratic (whether centralized or decentralized), civil society is well developed, the media is free, and
education is public-democratic but with some private space. In such cases,
fundamentalists can raise money in the developed local economy (as is the
case with the Protestant and Jewish fundamentalists in the United States,
with Italian Catholics of Comunione e Liberazione [CL], and others) or
venture abroad to other developed countries (as with Israeli Haredim col-
lecting money in the United States).

In democratic structures the fundamentalist strategy is predicated upon
enclave building and expansion, designed first in order to create a "defensive
perimeter" and later as a mode of enlarging the hold over civil society, with
the hope of achieving hegemony there. Using the terminology of our four
patterns of fundamentalist world relation, we may say that fundamentalists
operating in democratic structures pursue a simultaneous (or consecutive)
strategy of world creation and world transformation. They exploit the freedoms of a liberal society, that is, in two ways. Relatively unhindered by the
government, they carve out social space and amass cultural resources in
order to create alternative, oppositional structures and institutions. From
this base they attempt to transform the world of the secularized opponent
by transferring the values and procedures of their own strongly competitive
institutions to the weakened institutions of the larger culture. (When the
second phase of this strategy comes to dominate the efforts of the fundamentalist movement, we may speak of the movement as a world conqueror,
as in the case of second-emergence Protestant Christian fundamentalism,
the political expression of which became so well developed that it emerged
as an entity unto itself, known as "the Christian Right.")

The organizational basis for this world-creator/world-transformer strategic mode—that is, the initial manpower resources—consists of traditionalists in the host religion. Action is limited to the hard core in the world-
creating enclave phase (from the second to the sixth decade of the twentieth
century among U.S. Baptists and Jewish Haredim) and even when the movement expands. It seeks lukewarm (or "fallen") believers. This was true of
CL as well, targeting as it did nominally Catholic high school and university
students in northern Italy. Returnees to the faith (ba'ale teshuva, as the
Haredim call them)—that is, former secularists—have media value in the
struggle for hegemony (in the United States, Italy, Israel), but their numerical weight is small. And this is true even for the Lubavitcher Hasidim, who
have better results among secularists.

It should be stressed that not all movements transcend the enclave phase. The French Lefebvrists, for example, could not cross this threshold due to the marginality to which they relegated themselves in their schism from the Church, which is still seen as the vehicle of salvation for most traditionalists.[3] They further complicated their position by pitting themselves against a protraditionalist and popular pope. Finally, in 2001, they began to negotiate their return to the fold.

In the case of the Neturei Karta (Satmar) extremist Haredim in the United States and Israel, staying within the enclave is voluntary: they deem the modern world too dangerous to venture into and expect expansion and hegemony only when normal history ends and the age of Redemption dawns.

The consolidation of the enclave and its expansion are greatly facilitated by economic trends in democratic societies. Paradoxically, the modern economy that endangered the faith (e.g., the boom in the postwar United States, post–Marshall Plan Italy, post-1967 Israel) also created opportunities to finance the fundamentalist movements: niches for believers in the service economy (e.g., retail electronics, computer programmers) and jobs in the expanding public educational system (e.g., Haredi teachers in the National Religious Party school in Israel). Public policies stimulate the growth of the movement's own educational (and social) institutions, which are the linchpin of its activity. Such help is given either because of conviction, as under President Reagan, or because of government coalition calculations, as in Israel where the ultra-Orthodox parties (Agudat Yisrael, Shas, Degel ha-Torah) could swing the balance in favor of either of the two big political blocs. A mix of both motivations operated in favor of CL as long as the Christian Democrats were in power in Italy (until 1994).

It is around such economic and political institutions that fundamentalist community building is pursued in democratic societies. The process is facilitated by media technology (audiocassettes, videotapes, radio, television, satellites, cellular phones, and the like), which enables people to keep in touch in far-flung places. Negative propaganda directed against the secular world is therefore possible, with outlets (such as the CBN-TV network) in the global village of media markets wooing eventual recruits outside the social networks of churches and synagogues. Nonetheless, the religious communities themselves serve as the launching pad in the fight for additional social space; they utilize the social mobility of their members, their economic clout, and their access to media.

When the movement enters politics, this is done mostly for defensive reasons, so as to establish a *cordon sanitaire* for the enclave at either the local or the state level. Later, it may be greatly helped when the general attitude toward religion improves, as was the case in Israel following the euphoria of the 1967 war. Impetus may likewise be provided when the possibility arises of becoming a power broker (the Moral Majority within the U.S. Republican Party in the 1980s; the Christian Coalition in the 1990s).

The role of chance, as opposed to structure, is not substantial with regard to this pattern (except for an exogenous chance such as the Six-Day War modifying the religious context in Israel). Choice, however, plays a vital role, especially at the leadership level, where the cocktail of tactics and strategy is devised and community institution building is initiated. For example, Father Luigi Giussani of Milan, the leader of CL, provided charismatic leadership and concocted an ideology blending neo-Thomist theology and existentialist thought in order to justify mobilization and his critique of modern culture. He also concocted, with the help of efficient deputies, a mix of social programs and a plethora of organizational forms (notably the scuole, the cooperatives, and publishing houses), which in the 1960s and 1970s attracted students disillusioned with revolutionary radicalism and with the moral corruption of Italian society. These structures evolved from enclaves into missionary tentacles, extending from social action into politics, through the Movimento Popolare.[4]

In a different context ultra-Orthodox rabbis such as Shlomo Kahaneman in Israel or Aharon Kottler in the United States established a network of modern yeshivot around which the Haredi enclave was reconstituted after the mortal blow it received during the Holocaust. The network branched out, in the Israeli case, from the traditional confines of Ashkenazis into the milieu of Oriental Jews. This "world of learners"—comprising long-term (ten to fifteen years' curriculum) yeshiva students, together with their wives (employed in the community) and high birthrate—became a self-regenerating enclave with a broad basis of peripheral support among lay-people (ba'alei batim), many of whom are former yeshiva students now gainfully employed. The parallel political organizations that existed prior to the Holocaust in the Agudat form were greatly expanded and variegated.[5]

Members do count, not only in the Jewish and Italian cases but also in that of U.S. Protestants. Due to the decentralized, egalitarian nature of the enclave, as well as to the emphasis on action in civil society, the role of the rank and file (their degree of participation, commitment, and initiative) is of import.

The initial impulse in virtually all of these movements is that of dissent and separation. The missionary bent was paramount from the beginning in only a few cases. Even among the Lubavitchers, who are distinguished today by their missionary zeal, this dimension was introduced by the fifth dynastic rebbe in the 1920s. The sole case of missionary zeal from the beginning is that of the Islamic Tablighi Jama'at.

The Tablighi Jama'at, founded in British India in the 1920s, reacted to the predicament of a particular sector of Islamic society, namely, borderline Muslims who retained many Hindu rituals and customs and were now the object of proselytizing efforts by Hindu groups in northern India. To counter these efforts the Tablighi Jama'at launched a "purification" campaign. It had a populist, cross-class appeal thanks to its emphasis upon learning by doing, its suspicion of learned Islam, and its simple doctrinal principles and minimal and repetitious behavioral requirements. The Tablighi Jama'at's acceptance of modern secular education accounted for its continued appeal in the modernized sectors of postpartition India and Pakistan. Imported to Western Europe in the 1970s, the movement did not change its modus operandi, but its ideology was transmuted by the new context. The basic rituals that the Tablighi Jama'at asked its converts to perform took on a powerful new meaning when acted out in public on the infidel soil of Europe—they became a binding declaratory rite of one's identity as Muslim. It determined the way the European environment treated the Muslim person in question, usually a "guest worker." It thus reaffirmed his identity, which may have been not all too deep at the moment the act was first performed.

The Tablighi Jama'at has no enclave, just a loose core of activists who are expected to participate in short-term, intense "missionary tours" and then relapse into the low-intensity daily rhythm of the "purified" convert. In this modus operandi as well as in ideology, it is a glaring exception. All other movements that fit the world-transformer pattern began as a fight for mere survival against heavy odds, including persecution. Even once survival is guaranteed, they must insure themselves against recurrence of such dangers; hence the importance of the enclave as a basis for peripheral activity and as ultimate refuge.[6]

Ethnoreligious Confrontation

In many settings of ethnoreligious confrontation, a strong nationalist element is evident: the ethnic and/or religious groups or communities identify their particular heritage in an exclusive way with the national identity. Conflict in these cases is not inhibited by the checks and balances of democratic societies. (U.S. Protestant fundamentalists, with their own nativist, nationalist rhetoric claiming special privilege in the "Judeo-Christian" nation, find the rhetoric undermined by a competing discourse of pluralism and by laws and customs proscribing religious exclusivism.)

In cases of ethnic or religious minorities fighting back, the group resents being dominated or marginalized (e.g., Muslims in Afghanistan after the Soviet invasion; Palestinians in Gaza and the West Bank, post-1967; Sikhs in India in competition with Hindu nationalism against the background of the decline of the pluralistic Indian state). In other cases, however, a majority group is anxious about the imminent loss of its hegemony. Thus we find Hindutva supporters fearing competition with Islam and Christianity facilitated by the Nehru-established liberal state; Gush Emunim activists perceiving that the defeatism of the secular Israeli government may lead to the loss of the "redeemed" territories in the name of the "false slogan" of "refraining from dominating an alien [Palestinian] people"; Ulster Protestants uneasy about the "cowardly" Unionist government, which does not oppose resurgent Irish nationalism and a compromising British attitude.

The common denominator for all the above (as well as for, among others, the Kach movement and Sri Lankan Buddhist extremism) is that the ethnic group identity comprises powerful religious components so much so that it is quite difficult to disentangle the nation-building component from the fundamentalist one. In two cases, however, one can clearly state that the latter element has precedence over the former: Hamas, which began as an offshoot of the Muslim Brotherhood in Gaza dedicated to the Islamization of society and only in the mid-1980s became a national resistance movement; and the Gush Emunim, which had its origins in the mystical-messianic thought of Rabbi Kook the Elder, transmuted into the creed of the yeshiva nucleus (Merkaz Harav) of a religious youth movement (Bnei Akiva), and then became the standard-bearer of the hard Israeli Right after the 1967 war.

The strategy pursued by the majority in cases of ethnic confrontation is three-pronged. First, fundamentalists tend to insist upon sharp external boundaries. As could be expected from an ethnonationalist movement seeking to consolidate a state, emphasis is put on a demarcated territory, one that has a hallowed character in terms of the host religion. Savarkar, the father of the Hindutva concept, asserted that Hindus had sole legitimate claim to all the lands watered by the sacred Ganges, Brahmaputra, and Indus rivers and to all the lands stretching from the Himalayas to the confluence of the southern seas at Cape Comorin. The claim is based on many thousand years of continuity in identification, by blood and culture, with the "holy land" and its "holy waters." Gush Emunim is likewise wedded to the notion of the Whole Land of Israel, promised to the Jews by Divine Providence in the Bible and destined to become the theater of Redemption, an age that dawned with the establishment of the state of Israel. (Although the divine boundaries cover lands east of the River Jordan as well, the Gush cut down its aspirations to lands west of the river, controlled in their entirety by the Israeli army after the 1967 war.) The same notion of divine promise and hallowed land were taken over, partly in imitation, by Hamas, for whom the sanctity of the land flows from Al-Quds, the holy city of Jerusalem. In Hamas's charter the claim is pushed even further: Palestine is a *waqf*, a religious endowment, and as such cannot be appropriated, even in part, by non-Muslims.

The second element of this strategy attempts to bolster the sharp external boundaries by a notion of supremacy, electivity, and internal unity of the group the movement wishes to defend. Hindutva disciples affirm the racial, cultural, and religious superiority of the Hindus and the inferiority of all who cannot legitimately make such claims. Internal differences between Hindus are to be transcended, and even the Untouchables are to be reclaimed and fully integrated into a society governed by "Hindu values." (This was, of course, the "Hindu" response to the possibility that two of its competitors, Islam and Christianity, would win points for affirming the equality of believers. By the same token it also rejects the secular pluralist state created by Nehru and endeavors to replace it with a Hinduized state, fully occupying the land within sacred boundaries and peopled homogeneously by believing and practicing Hindus.)

The Sikhs likewise stress their inherent difference with the Hindus. Thus, the Sikh ideology notes that the Hindu pagans worship various deities as well as the sun, rivers, trees, and so forth, while the superior Sikhs worship one God and hold in sole reverence their holy book, the Adi Granth (a Scripture the Hindus do not possess). And because the sixth guru, Hargobind, posits the inseparability of state and religion, Sikh separatism must find a distinct political expression.[7] The chosen political expression legitimizes reliance on the sword in defense of Sikh interests. Ian Paisley and his Free Presbyterian Church (as well as its political offshoot, the Democratic Unionist Party) resort to Calvinist-derived discourse about the predestination of an elect people whose chosen status was confirmed in their right religion and their industrious self-sacrificing character.[8] All this serves as an irreducible, sacred basis for nationalist exclusivism.

Jewish exclusivism of a different nature was the battle cry of Rabbi Kahane and Kach: the Jews are a chosen people that dwells alone, virtually a race by dint of endogamy (the fight against mixed marriage was a core issue for Kach). In order to maintain the sharp divide between the beleaguered Jewish community and those outside the fold, Kahane preached and practiced Jewish inclusiveness and empowerment of Jewish have-nots (lower-middle class in the United States, Orientals in Israel)—ultimately by the exclusion of competing Arabs from Jewish neighborhoods and businesses and eventually from the Land of Israel altogether.[9]

The third strategic element follows inexorably: dramatic, at times spectacular, confrontational tactics. We have noted, in the description of Kach, the interplay of Jewish pride, the "it's a jungle out there" view of the Middle East, and tactics designed to heighten ethnic friction. The belief in the legitimacy of violence undertaken in communal self-defense led the Sikhs under Bhindranwale and his Khalsa Dal party to engage in violence and terrorism. The resulting Operation Blue Star and its "theater of cruelty" set off large-scale violence that undermined the moderate Sikh party, Akali Dal, which played the political game according to the rules of the pluralist, secular Indian democracy.

In terms of our four world-relational patterns, we see a combination of the world conqueror and the world creator in the three-pronged strategy of the ethnoreligious fundamentalist. The ethnoreligious minority, no less than the aggrieved, relatively deprived majority, must sustain and fortify its niche in society to defend itself from alien, penetrating forces; but it also strikes out violently at the enemy in the absence or weakness or inattention (or calculated policy) of the otherwise restraining state.

In long-term conflicts the gradualist rhythms of the world transformer may eventually appear. The modern media of communication (print, radio, television, cinema) and the institutions of civil society (interest groups, voluntary associations, and informal groups of one kind or another) are the bearers of modernization and secularization, and hence are threats to fundamentalist movements. The tactics followed by ethnoreligious minorities or aggrieved majorities is to protect their membership from secular civil society or from the alien interloper by forming their own network of interest groups and to penetrate and use the media for their own purposes.

Civil society and modern media in India, for example, are concentrated in the modern metropolitan and urban areas. In the nonmodern sectors where civil society has not had a significant development, the RSS, VHP, and BJP are carrying out a campaign to penetrate or preempt civil society through the formation of their own trade unions, professional associations, sports organizations, pilgrimage centers, and the like, as well as through the proliferation of their own media. Hindu revivalism and fundamentalism have effectively penetrated the cinema. The broadcast of the Ramayana in the form of a serial, starting in late January 1987, made a standardized version of the Hindu epic known and popular among the Indian middle class. It enhanced the knowledge of Ayodhya as Ram's birthplace and therefore as one of the most important places of pilgrimage in Uttar Pradesh.

The VHP shock troops of Hindutva organized aggressive, "in-your-face" campaigns that resembled the mode of the world conqueror, however, rather than that of the world transformer. Led by caravans of trucks (simulating chariots of epic imagination), one such procession marched on Ayodhya in Uttar Pradesh, first to protest and then to destroy the Babri Masjid. The destruction of the mosque, begun as an act of collective nationalist vindication, was transformed by the ecstatically participating Hindutva believers into a high point of religious awakening, directed against the age-old enemy, Islam.[10]

It is amply evident that the crucial factor in ethnoreligious confrontation, fundamentalist style, is leadership. Leaders conceive ideology and concoct tactics all within the confines of the religious context and the nature of the host religion. The role of chance (the 1967 war, the assassination of Indira Gandhi) is of secondary importance.

GROWTH

In the cases covered by democratic and nondemocratic settings, a combination of structural factors may be exploited in such a way as to lead to the growth of a fundamentalist movement. The coming together of these factors is greatly facilitated by contingency and chance. It could be an endogenous chance (riots that lay bare an economic crisis due to faulty development policy) or an exogenous chance (defeat in war). In either case the legitimacy of the present order is deeply shaken—either just the "performance legitimacy" or, in graver situations, the "systemic legitimacy."

In the case of ethnoreligious conflict, the international environment (e.g., the Arab-Israeli conflict, the Soviet invasion of Afghanistan) and government policy (the crisis of the Indian pluralist, secular regime) are the predominant structures that influence growth. Chance occurrences operate here also as a trigger. Consider the road accident in which an Israeli army vehicle killed bystanders in Gaza, leading to the first mass demonstrations of the first Intifada; or the appearance of shoulder-held anti-helicopter missiles, which gave the Afghan resistance a fighting chance.

Nondemocratic Structures

To see the interplay of structure, contingency, and chance, we look first at two nondemocratic cases, Egypt and Algeria. While a real fundamentalist movement surfaced only in the early 1970s, the nuclei had been formed a decade earlier, when hard-core remnants of the embattled Muslim Brotherhood were alarmed by the success of the secularization drive carried on by the victorious Nasserist regime. Thanks to Sayyid Qutb, the nuclei developed a new ideology in response to the danger that pan-Arab populism constituted to Islam—backed as this populism was by an aggressively interventionist state. Yet the impact of the nuclei was small, whereas the Nasserist regime enjoyed both "systemic legitimacy" and "performance legitimacy."

The 1967 defeat was a short-term trigger that shook both legitimacies and rendered prescient and credible Qutb's critique of the nefarious effects of Nasserism. Moreover, it heightened religious sensitivity among the masses (such as the miraculous appearance of the Virgin Mary in a Coptic church, leading to a huge flow of Muslim pilgrims to this site).

Islamic radicals could now broaden their critique to embrace the long-term social effects of the regime's policies, effects that, though present because of Nasser's policies, became more evident and aggravated under Sadat. These social strains were due to an ever-accelerating demographic explosion (the result of high fertility and a decline in infant mortality caused by preventive medicine) and an exodus from countryside to town and from town to metropolis. Such strains were rendered particularly acute by the expansion of secondary and higher education (from the late 1950s on), which created hordes of diploma-holders with high expectations bred of their presumed proficiencies, facing limited employment opportunities in the (still limited) modern sectors of the economy. Most of these graduates had to make do with poorly remunerated government jobs. Expectations grew even higher following the oil bonanza in the Gulf states in 1973–74, which the Egyptians assumed (wrongly) would have a spillover effect on them; they were further catalyzed by Sadat's "open-door policy" (consisting of privatization, foreign investment, and imports), which created a class of nouveaux riches. The combined effect was to render more acute the relative deprivation felt by the modern lower-middle class. As Nasserism's socioeconomic promise fizzled out, so did its concomitant trait—"progressive"-minded secularism in a pan-Arab garb. And whereas liberalism had been tainted by collaboration with the corrupt monarchy, a return to old-time religion was virtually inevitable—by default.

Prompted by triggers such as the "bread riots" of 1977, the nuclei expanded into a full-fledged movement, with no real modification of Qutb's
ideology. The nuclei spawned a plethora of autonomous associations (jama'at), mostly of students (usually of migrant origin) and young professionals employed in the impoverished public sector. All this occurred in a
context in which civil society was showing greater vitality.[11]

The Algerian case is similar to the Egyptian one (including the ideology,
which is Sunni and inspired by Sayyid Qutb) but differs in two crucial aspects. First, the extent of the socioeconomic crisis is far more acute, not just
a matter of stalled growth as in Egypt. Second, the movement developed
first as one of pure social protest, with no religious agenda, and was later
hijacked by Muslim radicals who transformed it into the Front Islamique
du Salut (FIS).

The long-term economic crisis took place in the context of an oil-rich
yet densely populated country. It was the end product of an erroneous strategy of development, pursued since 1962, that gambled on the buildup of
capital-intensive, know-how-intensive, and labor-extensive industries while
neglecting agriculture and import-substitution (i.e., labor-intensive, light
and medium) industries. The resultant unemployment (in a country where
the natural growth rate exceeds 4 percent) was "absorbed" by make-work
public sector jobs and by subsidies for major staples. This policy could be
pursued as long as oil prices were high, for the heavy industries had proven
themselves in the course of the 1970s to be uncompetitive; not only did
they not bring in foreign currency, they incurred a spiraling cost in service
of the debt.

The crisis was brought to a head by the second decline in oil prices in
1985–86, which halved the state's foreign currency revenues; of the revenues, three-quarters had to be set aside for servicing the debt. Lavish subsidies (for employment, staples, housing) were no longer tenable well before
the International Monetary Fund (IMF) set its stringent conditions for re-
scheduling the debt. The state was, hence, crippled in its "performance legitimacy" as benefactor, and that at a time when it had barely any "systemic
legitimacy" left due to the disappearance (in 1978) of a charismatic president (Boumedienne) and to the erosion of the Front de Liberation National
(FLN) governing party's heroic image as leader of the war of liberation
(1954–62), due to its long, self-serving, and increasingly corrupt monopoly
on power.

Triggered by the "couscous riots" of 1988 (following the abolition of
subsidies), a huge, yet amorphous, social protest movement spread like

brushfire across classes and regions but was particularly strong in the lower and lower-middle classes in the overcrowded towns. Its spearhead was young unemployed males (of all education levels). Devoid of positive ideological vision and powerful leaders, this movement would be overtaken in the span of less than a year by an ad hoc coalition of Muslim radicals. The latter had shown themselves to be consummate organizers (at the grassroots level as well as the national level), coalition builders (drawing on various Islamic tendencies), and adept at playing the new electoral game, which had been opened up by concessions granted by the beleaguered regime. Yet perhaps their greatest contribution consisted in endowing the movement with a coherent vision, both positive and negative, an interpretive prism that helped adherents make sense of Algeria's failures during three decades of independence. On the other hand, this interpretive scheme drew up the picture of an alternative moral and political order. The FIS promptly built up its power basis and proceeded to win municipal elections (1990) and then the first round of general elections (1991).[12]

The broad gamut of structural factors operating in the two cases is an urbanization/migration/modernization process catalyzed by the international environment (e.g., an oil-price hike, economic slump, etc.). The dysfunctions of the process provide fundamentalism with opportunities for growth. It should be noted, however, that fundamentalism does not find itself capable of availing itself of such opportunities in each country thus hit, Syria and Iraq being two notable examples.

The jama'at movement is urban, that is, the product of economic migration (from rural or small towns to city), a phenomenon that also encompasses vertical mobility and educational attainment relative to the host culture. As we shall see, this generalization holds for the democratic setting as well. It is true even for ethnoreligious conflicts, although there the weight of the urbanization/modernization phenomenon is smaller. Only in the Sikh case do we have a movement that is rural and comes from the regions least touched by modernization of the countryside (i.e., by the Green Revolution) and whose members feel relative deprivation because of this very backwardness.

Contingency is present in both the Algerian and Egyptian cases as the culmination of a cumulative process, namely, misguided development policy plus a demographic explosion left unchecked by the government. In Egypt, however, the chance trigger not only is a direct result of inherent structural problems, it is also present in another guise, "coming out of left field," as it were. That is, the triggers were the 1967 and 1973 wars, which were not "inevitable" in the same way that economic and demographic problems were inevitable. (And of course, those wars had a different impact on Jewish fundamentalism.)

The basic point is this: short-term catalysts, or triggers, inject urgency into a situation and provide openings for various destabilizing movements, fundamentalisms primary among them in these cases. Among these catalysts in Egypt and Algeria over the past decades were oil-price hikes and sudden drops; Boumedienne's death and the selection of Chadli as successor; the French restrictions on immigration from the mid-1970s on; Nasser's death and Sadat's departure from pan-Arabism and etatism.

Structural factors are necessary conditions for the growth of fundamentalisms in their various aspects. The sufficient condition was in each case provided by leadership. In the jama'at case this was mostly midlevel leaders who transformed the moralistic critique of a victorious regime (Nasser's) into a moral-cum-socioeconomic critique of a faltering regime (Nasser's in the late 1960s, then Sadat's and Mubarak's). The leadership also knew how to identify resources (e.g., their use of disaffected members of the armed forces; their exploitation of the freedom of expression and association granted by Sadat and of new media such as audiocassettes) and build coalitions (with the populist Labor Party). Government aggression, though less ferocious than under Nasser, was both a constraint (nipping in the bud many an initiative, deterring potential recruits) and an opportunity used by the fundamentalist leadership in order to point out the true nature of the secularized regime as unjust, morally corrupt, and ultimately relying upon brute force.

The leadership of FIS designed the interpretive scheme offered to a restless public during the crisis year 1988–89—an innovative adaptation of Sayyid Qutb's ideas to the particular Algerian case. The scheme was presented by eloquent media manipulators who appealed to a symbolic capital deeply embedded in Algerian Islam; they likewise drew upon a populist strain, originally generated by the FLN during the struggle against the French, namely, the myth of an inherently united people overcoming all divisions introduced by special interests and various dwarfs, or *sanafir*, who serve as their spokesmen. The myth was given a religious gloss yet retained its antidemocratic punch.

Institution builders and organizers among the cadres created supple alliances between the myriad of Islamic groups that existed before the crisis or emerged during it. The organizers also integrated the private mosque networks into this alliance.

Democratic Structures

A similar combination of structure, contingency, and leadership is obtained when fundamentalist movements in democratic settings seek to expand their niche. However, here the openings for fundamentalist growth provided by urbanization and migration are greatly enhanced, not only by new media technology (also available in nondemocratic settings) but also by the public policies of the welfare state, which provides a minimum of economic support to would-be social movements in measures such as aid to parochial schools. The interplay may be illustrated by two cases of post–World War II growth of movements that had flourished in the interwar years and then declined, either because of internal factors (in the United States) or because of an unexpected contingency (the Holocaust, liquidating ultra-Orthodox Jewry in Eastern Europe).

After 1925, Protestant fundamentalism in the United States withdrew to its own "enclave" existence. It was, at the same time, an enclave that, as the putative heirs of the Puritans, claimed "insider" status. Resurgent in the 1970s and 1980s, the movement used the Puritan theme as a principle of continuity in order to claim a role in the establishment of the national heritage. The new activism, like the old, saw the state as encroaching upon civil society, but after the 1960s there could be no more ambiguity about the secular (-humanist) character of the state itself, nor about its hegemonic intentions. Thus the Protestant movement entered its own world-conqueror phase.

Despite the theological and religious fragmentation they have experienced as a result of their politicization, American Protestant fundamentalists exhibit a large degree of social cohesion; even as they participated in secular politics, they continued to renew their social base through their schools, publishing houses, and seminaries, with relatively little resistance from the government and the larger American society.[13]

In terms of growth and endurance over time, the multigenerational American Protestant movement is similar to the multigenerational Haredi movement. The Haredi Jews had to deal in their first wave with the migration that disrupted the world of the Jewish shtetl of Eastern Europe in the last third of the nineteenth century: migration to large urban centers driven both by push (persecutions, pogroms) and pull (opportunities in urban economy, the lure of secular secondary and higher education). Age-old communities were disrupted, with all their heavily traditionalist and localized cultural and social networks. Hence the migrants were receptive to new ideologies such as socialism and Zionism. Unlike these new rivals for Jewish loyalty, the Haredi movement offered a new ideology with generational continuities. Rather than replace and demolish the Jewish tradition and worldview, Haredi Judaism intended to preserve as much of its essence as possible while adapting it to new circumstances (e.g., by developing a new, universal modus operandi in the practice of *mitzvot* [precepts] instead of the plethora of local customs). The Haredim appealed in particular to those migrants who, shocked by cultural discontinuities produced by changes of occupation, residence, and culture, wanted to cling to the anchor of that old-time religion.

The Holocaust wiped out these achievements and made Israel and the United States the two major centers of the Jewish people—two countries where the impact of tradition was less; modernity, more advanced; and social mobility, easier. In Israel the country also presented a grave theological dilemma. The already converted tradition had to be further transformed in the wake of these twin triggers, the Holocaust and the establishment of the state of Israel. The rebuilding of tradition was carried out on the basis of nuclei existing in both countries and, above all, with the help of Holocaust survivors who migrated there. Many of the latter, as in the first wave, found adaptation arduous and disappointments galore. The anchor of reconstructed tradition offered reassurance.

What helped the spread of new-fangled ultra-Orthodoxy were the prosperous economies of the West from the 1950s on, where Haredim could find a niche (or rather niches) in the urban market (e.g., the 47th Street Photo chain of electronics shops or the diamond business). They were thus able to sustain a middle-class way of life based on a work environment that is controlled by the ultra-Orthodox community. The welfare state, which was expanding in this period, contributed in turn by sustaining parochial schools (in the name of pluralism) and through direct aid to needy individuals and families—especially heads of family involved in study. Support also came from the numerous Haredim who grew rich in the postwar years. In Israel direct aid to individuals, families, and institutions was expanded due to the Haredi role as a swing party in government coalitions. And for this reason young Haredi males were offered there an additional incentive: long military deferrals for those who studied from ages eighteen to twenty-nine.

Leadership made all these factors work in unison. It concocted, on solid bases laid down by Agudat Yisrael in the interwar years, an ideology that transcended past internal divisions (between Hasidim and Misnagdim) and developed a coherent answer to the challenge presented by the state of Israel (and, to a lesser degree, to the Holocaust). In the post–World War II era great thinkers (like the Hazon Ish) were rare, however. The major contribution of leadership was rather in institution building (the yeshiva network) and coalition making between sects and political movements. There developed a centralized structure of locally led groups that share ideology, religious practice, major educational institutions, and political affiliation.[14]

In the haredi Jewish as well as in the U.S. Protestant case, the needs of the rank and file—urban isolates from a traditional background—were a necessary condition for movement growth, but leadership response was the sufficient condition for growth.

Ethnoreligious Confrontation

Movements in a setting of ethnoreligious conflict grow when they find a social niche. Kach started to expand in Israel only when Rabbi Kahane tailored his message to the resentment of the Oriental lower classes in big towns, to their feelings of deprivation vis-à-vis middle-class Ashkenazis of secular outlook, and their economic competition with Arabs for semiskilled jobs. The common denominator for both resentments was the demand for Arab exclusion in the name of a tribalistic notion of Jewish ethnicity and prejudices against Gentiles—symbolized by the Arabs (from whose lands the Orientals had been chased).

In India the Hindu nationalists of the RSS, VHP, and BJP attracted members by portraying local Muslims and Christians as an alien and cohesive presence—one that is economically competitive with Hindus. Hindu nationalism thereby found a constituency among the new (and traditional) Hindu middle class and lower-middle class in the "cow belt." These upwardly mobile professionals, merchants, and cash-crop farmers were deeply envious of the Brahman secularized upper class. Despite their own recent achievements, they felt endangered by inflation as well as by Muslim (and Christian) economic rivalry.

The same holds for the crisis of the Kemalist state in the 1960s and 1970s, which was triggered by the corruption of government and the alienation of rural Anatolians flocking into western Turkish cities; the secularist ideology had never meant anything to them. This crisis gave birth to the rise, in 1971, of Erbakan's National Order movement, the first Islamic party ever given permission to function by the omnipotent, secular-oriented military. The party would be rebaptized the National Salvation Party (1973–80), the Welfare Party in 1983, and the Virtue Party in 1998. The ideological fatigue of Kemalist secularism accounts for the rise of the Welfare Party.

From 1995 to 1996 the Welfare Party, after winning a slight plurality, headed a coalition government. Their achievements while in power were quite limited, with better results on social issues than religious ones. As to the latter, they introduced government aid to Islamic schools, outlawed many secularist entertainment activities, and recruited Islamists into government positions, though not into the army. Even these results were short-lived, however. When the army stepped in and forced the resignation of Erbakan in 1996, most of the proreligious initiatives were rolled back, and the military declared the Welfare Party itself unconstitutional.[15]

In these cases socioeconomic aids to growth were dwarfed by the worsening ethnic conflict, which was a product of the international environment in the case of Israel (the 1967, 1973, and 1982 wars) and of public policy in the Indian case. India has seen the crisis of the secularized secular state founded by Nehru, the inheritor of the British Raj. Hinduism was just one of several religions, the existence and autonomy of which were protected by the state, which guaranteed the rule of law and freedom of press, assembly, and association. The state of emergency decreed by Indira Gandhi was the trigger that brought this crisis to a head and gave the followers of Hindutva a huge push.

The Arab-Israeli conflict has a differentiated impact upon the growth of three movements, each with its specific social base. The Kach breakthrough into poor neighborhoods was greatly facilitated by the spread of locally initiated terrorism in the occupied territories from the late seventies on and its spillover into Israel proper, which created a climate of fear among the civilian population. Certain car-bomb and knifing incidents in Jerusalem were deftly used by Kahane to mobilize the underclass and lower class against the Arab one-fourth of that city's population. This clientele continued to remain in the Kach orbit following the assassination of Rabbi Kahane by a Muslim activist in New York, and it remains intact after the assassination of his son and successor in 2000.

In Gush Emunim the post-1967 euphoria gave the marginal group of the Merkaz Harav yeshiva its first opportunity: following the "liberation of Judea and Samaria," its gospel of Redemption became attractive to the whole sector of religious Zionism and especially to its youth movement, Bnei Akiva, which served as a sort of ready-made cadre. Bnei Akiva also had distinct social characteristics: Ashkenazic, middle-class, educated yet feeling deprived vis-à-vis the secularized Labor-affiliated middle class (also Ashkenazic), which enjoyed hegemony in society, politics, and culture. But 1967 was just a moment of emergence; most former Bnei Akiva members contented themselves with sympathy for the Merkaz Harav group, for nothing more seemed to be required: after all, God was directing the victorious rise of Redemption. What goaded them into activism was not the 1967 triumph but the 1973 semidefeat: it became apparent that Redemption was not on "automatic pilot." Setbacks were about to block, perhaps even subvert, it, and defeatism among Israel's secular elites was liable to magnify the scope of these setbacks. The intense settlement activity—launched in 1974 and sustained until 1977 against the Labor government's will—galvanized the Bnei Akiva sector, in a sort of ritual acting out of the struggle for hegemony. In the atmosphere of soul-searching engendered in Israeli opinion by the 1973 war, the essentially optimistic, combative mood of the Gush, untainted by links to the establishment, was appealing to quite a few secularized Israelis. Movements of an activist bent saw in the new type of settlement effort the answer to the predicament of secular Zionism, which was perceived as being at the end of its rope.[16]

Hamas is also the product of two distinct phases of the Arab-Israeli conflict. It originated in the ranks of the Muslim Brotherhood in Gaza, persecuted and decimated under Egyptian occupation for its opposition to Nasser. The Israeli occupation in 1967 endowed the brotherhood with greater freedom for association and expression than under Nasser as long as its members limited themselves to educational and cultural activities. The q, now dubbed Mujamma', was determined to avail itself of these opportunities and was not prone to expand into the political sphere, given the terrible price it had paid for political agitation under Nasser. A vigorous, well-organized movement took shape, especially among high school and college students, elbowing out its leftist rivals. Saudi and Kuwaiti money was helpful for organizational buildup. The nationalist issue was relegated to a lower plane; the movement limited itself to protest against the occupation, hoping to "deal with it" at a later date, when society would be Islamized. Yet this was by no means a moderate movement—as evidenced by the vigilante terror tactics of the Mujamma' designed to punish (or deter) transgressors of religious precepts.

A second shock hit the movement when the first Intifada was launched by the radical militants of Islamic Jihad (1987). Taken by surprise, the Mujamma' was torn by internal debates for several months, until it decided to join the Intifada and attempt to take it over. Ideology was completely modified, making the liberation of the Holy Land of Palestine from infidel occupation the most urgent task, the justification being that the occupier also brings in a contaminating and seductive culture and, hence, no authentic

Islamization is possible as long as the occupation endures. The language became national-Islamic rather than universal-Islamic. Organization was likewise overhauled, and strict compartmentalization introduced. Recruitment was greatly aided by the "demonstration effect" of heroic acts by members (and by Hizbullah in Lebanon), as well as by the dwindling of employment opportunities in the Gulf for the excess manpower of the Gaza Strip as a result of the decline in oil prices from 1985 on. These two factors help explain the spread of the movement to the West Bank, especially to the southern and more traditionalist part, which was sensitive to the religious idiom with which Hamas couched the strategy of militant resistance.

While the movement had a cross-class support periphery going back to its Mujamma' days, its hard core came to be constituted by lower-class young males, unemployed or underemployed, especially in situations created by the oil-price slump as well as by the economic crisis in Israel, where 100,000 of them were employed. Employment in Israel entailed not only the combination of national and economic domination but also exposure to harassment by military police, a reality that made Palestinians working there a particularly resentful group.[17]

Still, without choice—the choices made by leadership—the opportunities for fundamentalist growth would not have been exploited. Kach was always a one-man show. In the Gush, Rabbi Kook the Younger worked out the adaptation of the ideology to the 1973 crisis and incorporated in it a critique of secular Israeli society. A group of young disciples (including, notably, Hanan Porat, Zvi Katzover, and Daniella Weiss) set itself up as a collective leadership innovating the modus operandi of settlement as the great endeavor of the movement, building bridges to nonreligious nationalists, and organizing the National Religious Party periphery as a support network. In the BJP of India the entry of Hindutva into confrontational politics—including the 1993 Ayodhya campaign—was engineered by L. K. Advani, from a strategy devised earlier in the RSS by Balasaheb Deoras and from an ideological critique of Indian secularism laid out by M. S. Golwarkar. In Hamas the move from Islamization to Islamic-Palestinian nationalism was spearheaded and endowed with theological justification by Shaykh Ahmed Yassin; its implementation in organizational and military terms was left to his younger lieutenants. Yassin continued in this role during the second Intifada, suffering house arrest during the escalation of Israeli-Palestinian violence in the final months of 2001.

The role of chance, as short-term, was important at particular junctions yet by no means crucial. If the December 1987 road accident had not taken place, some other clash between Israelis and Palestinians would have sparked the Intifada in the tension-laden atmosphere then prevalent in Gaza.

Decline

Movements that rise may decline for a short or long while and may or may not rise again. We shall examine the gamut of possibilities in the three settings we have identified.

Nondemocratic Structures

Public policy is the most prominent danger to fundamentalist movements in nondemocratic societies. By that we mean, above all, policies of repression. President Assad dealt a mortal blow to the Syrian Muslim Brotherhood in the massacre of Hama. Saddam Hussein did the same to the Shi'ite Da'wa first when he executed its cadres in 1980 and then when he ruthlessly put down its revolt in the wake of the Gulf War (1991). More selective but still ferocious repression cut down the wings of the Tunisian Nahda movements (1987–90). Pakistan, compelled by pressure from the United States following the terrorist attacks of September 11 and the subsequent war on the Taliban and Al Qaeda, cracked down on Islamist movements operating within its borders.

Other regimes use a different but also efficacious dosage: repression against the more extremist elements combined with a buy-out of the rest (in the form of government jobs and/or some parliamentary representation following "managed" elections). This is the case in Egypt, Jordan, and Morocco. Repression may be terribly demoralizing for the surviving members, for it creates an atmosphere of "failed prophecy": history does not go the way the enclave believed it should go; the road map it put its trust in appears to be wrong. Compromise with the powers that be after a period of flamboyant speeches (and even acts) may cripple the leaders' credibility. Note the generous-devious (in the sense of co-optation) gesture of King Hussein of Jordan, who granted amnesty to two Muslim Brotherhood leaders who were found guilty of a plot to topple him.

Dynamics internal to the movement also may contribute to its decline. By its very nature an enclave cannot tolerate internal opposition (which contradicts this ideal of unity cum equality); hence enclaves have trouble negotiating any ideological dispute or competition between powerful leading figures. What may further weaken loyalty to the enclave is the emergence of an evolving hierarchy of leadership due to the growth of the movement

or in response to demands for specialization brought to bear by the technological requirements of the armed struggle. To put it in Albert O. Hirsch-
man's terms, when loyalty to established leaders or to a distant hierarchy
is weakened for lack of voice, exit becomes a more likely possibility. This
goes against what cognitive dissonance theory would have led us to expect,
namely, that hard core membership would stick it out. Such time- and
energy-consuming splits and squabbles, which push activists out of the
movement altogether, are the bane of the Egyptian jamaʿat.

As for the periphery of the fundamentalist movement, it is particularly
sensitive to changes in the economic environment (and public policies in
this domain). A substantial economic improvement, as occurred in Tunisia
in the late 1980s and early 1990s, resulted in sympathizers dropping out
in droves. The very reason for their protest, through the movement, had
been greatly attenuated.[18]

Factors of chance may catalyze such peripeties. Bad chemistry between
leaders who cannot get along (e.g., Mourou and Ghannushi in Tunisia,
Fadlallah and Nasrallah in Lebanon, Chebouti and Layada in Algeria) may
produce debilitating splits. Or a key leader may die (or be executed), leaving
no worthy successor (Marwan Hadid in Syria, Muhammad Baqir al-Sadr in
Iraq, and, of course, Khomeini). The very dependence of the enclave upon
charismatic figures makes it terribly vulnerable in such cases. Moral failures
in leaders that are exploited (or provoked) by government agents (as was
the case in Tunisia in the early nineties with the sting operations against
Islamist leaders) may likewise topple linchpin personalities and undermine
the movement's cohesion.

Last but not least, the international environment may create chance occasions for the leaders to make bad tactical decisions, as during the Gulf
crisis of 1990–91, when the Jamaʿat, the FIS, and Hamas backed Saddam
Hussein, thus forfeiting vital Saudi financial aid. The Taliban of Afghanistan
made a similarly fateful choice when it opted to support Osama bin Laden,
thereby winning for itself the wrath of the United States and its B-1 bombers.

Obviously, as in such examples, bad choices by leaders also precipitates
the decline of fundamentalist movements. Leaders may decide upon a strategy of confrontation, underestimating the government's ability and readiness to engage in efficacious repression (Syria in 1982, Iraq in 1991, Pakistan in 2001–2). When a movement is involved in terrorism, it may likewise
opt for methods that make it lose public sympathy and aid, as when the
terrorist attacks engineered by Osama bin Laden and Al Qaeda led to the
murder of more than 2,800 innocent civilians from dozens of countries
(who were in the World Trade Center towers on September 11, 2001); when

the Egyptian jama'at started to kill tourists (striking at a very key economic sector) in the nineties; or when the Islamic extremists in Algeria started "executing" nonveiled women in 1994.

Democratic Structures

Decline may lurk in too much success too soon, or problems of digestion, one might say. In a democracy it is quite likely that the majority society will co-opt the dissenting minority and even smother it with kindness: financial aid, access to the media and to the educational system. This is not necessarily a Machiavellian ploy but rather the upshot of cultural change in the form of greater acceptance of religion in general. Such an evolution, if bolstered by economic trends, may constitute an even more formidable challenge to the fundamentalist movement: rising levels of affluence in a society may enable fundamentalists to carve out a lucrative niche in the expanding economy. Moreover, the media, so ably manipulated by fundamentalist groups, may be turned against them; an opportunity becomes a threat. The electronic media may infiltrate every nook and cranny in the enclave.

In the exact moment when the dissenting minority seems to be moving toward ascendancy, rot sets in. The outside boundary weakens and gets fuzzy; greater inequity evolves inside. In Mary Douglas's terms the movement becomes "lower group" and "higher grid"; that is, it begins to lose the tight, clearly bounded, united, and egalitarian structure of yore. The upshot is growing bureaucracy, greater distance between leaders and the led, disaffection in the ranks. The rank and file may all the more easily venture out of the movement, for society at large is seductive in its economic possibilities (for individualists) and thus makes dependency on group solidarity less crucial. Paradoxically, because society is no longer starkly opposed to religion as such, it may seem now both culturally less menacing and materially more appealing. High turnover rate is in such situations the harbinger of slow decline.

Alternatively, decline may stem from the host religion, that is, from the tendency of dissenting minorities (here as well as in nondemocratic settings) to split over doctrinal issues, a tendency exacerbated by enclave dynamics (intolerance of opposition, clashes between charismatic personalities). Whatever the reason, splits may enfeeble enclaves and make them waste energy on infighting rather than directing their fire against outsiders.

As in nondemocratic settings, some decline may be precipitated "when prophecy fails." Demoralization may creep in when the majority society shows resilience and does not crumble and fundamentalist dreams of hegemony are thwarted.

The role of chance in decline appears in the untimely disappearance of leaders like Archbishop Lefebvre and Rabbi Kook the Younger, whose special mix of qualities could not be replaced. Such a loss is all the more sensitive given the charismatic leader's role in the movement's origins and growth. This is true even when a successor has been preselected and trained, as was the case with Lefebvre's successor. It is certainly truer when no successor was designated or when a successor was nominated but in violation of set norms. (The recently deceased Lubavitcher rebbe, for example, designated in his will his secretary, who not only is not a member of the Schneerson family but who also lacks charisma.)

Ethnoreligious Confrontation

The movements that come under this heading are young, so one can only speculate about eventual decline. Because economic dysfunctions catalyzed growth, economic growth may lead to a decline in the appeal of fundamentalist movements. More threatening to their well-being may be a political solution (achieved or in process) for the ethnoreligious conflict, which was grist for the fundamentalist mill; once such a solution is found, the hardcore fundamentalists may remain, but the periphery and some rank and file may drop out (as happened to the Gush Emunim in the immediate wake of the Oslo Accords). As in nondemocratic settings, recourse to terrorism may isolate the movement and/or create splits inside its core (e.g., in Gush Emunim with the discovery of the Jewish Underground in the mid-1980s).

Leadership is a sore point in all enclaves. The assassination of Rabbi Kahane led to the fragmentation of his movement, which was tarnished by mudslinging between the two factions into which Kach split. In the Gush the demise of Rabbi Kook the Elder did not deal a mortal blow, for he was promptly replaced by a collective leadership, respected but not charismatic. This was sufficient to run affairs whenever events were on a steady course according to the messianic road map. But whenever prophecy seemed to run awry (as in the Israeli evacuation of Sinai, the outbreak of the Intifada, and the Oslo Accords), uncertainty and dissension appeared at the top, hampering the fortunes of the group. Even after 1995 and Oslo, one could not yet speak definitively of a decline in Gush Emunim, for the international environment once again smiled upon the Gush as the Palestinian autonomy agreement ran aground in 2001.

CONCLUSION

In this chapter we have applied the explanatory scheme presented in chapter 3 to fundamentalist movements in different political and ethnic contexts. As we have shown, the political regime and the ethnic context condition the strategies and influence the growth and decline of fundamentalist movements in more direct and important ways than do other structural variables, however important they may be. Other structural variables such as the international environment and the economy influence fundamentalism indirectly through governmental policies. The ethnic composition of a society divides it into basic identities, and these are even more sharply divided if they combine with religion. Interrelating in complex ways, these structural variables are "turned on and off" by chance events and converted into options by the decisions of leaders.

We suggest a number of conclusions as to how fundamentalism is basically conditioned by the nature of the political regime and the ethnonational composition of the society. In authoritarian regimes such as the Islamic ones, the form that the fundamentalist movements take varies with the coerciveness of the regime. The emergence of fundamentalism in its world creator/enclave mode is possible in most types of Islamic regimes. In traditional authoritarian regimes such as Saudi Arabia and the Gulf states, fundamentalist movements engaged in anti-Israeli activities have relied on financial and logistical support. But in these regimes world-conqueror fundamentalists, and most world transformers as well, encounter suppression. In secular and coercive authoritarian regimes such as Syria and Iraq, efforts on the part of fundamentalist movements to penetrate and transform society encountered extreme coercion, forcing these movements to operate underground to the extent that they continued to operate at all. But it seems impossible to root out these movements in their entirety. Any relaxation finds them rising once again to the surface.

The historical experience of modernizing Islamic regimes suggests a dialectic relationship between government policies and shifting fundamentalist strategies. In the past thirty-five years there has been a continuous power struggle in which the relaxation of coercive authority leads to rapid changes in fundamentalist patterns of behavior (primarily a move from an enclave-based world-creating separatism to world-conqueror–style bids for power). It does not appear possible to maintain a stable equilibrium in these authoritarian regimes, as the experiences of Iraq, Syria, Saudi Arabia, Egypt, and Algeria attest. If an authoritarian regime relaxes its authority and vigilance, fundamentalists tend to "up the ante" until the regime calculates the cost of suppression as being less than the cost of toleration.

In democratic regimes the emergence of fundamentalist movements from their enclaves is relatively unhindered by the political setting. They have access to and can seek to transform the world of politics, civil society, and the media. Even when they take on world-conquering strategies, fundamentalists are constrained by the criminal, civil, and constitutional law, implemented by an independent judiciary. In their transformative and conquering efforts fundamentalists encounter ideological and cultural resistances in a pluralist, secularized society. Furthermore, there is an inherently parochial aspect of fundamentalism, which limits its appeal even across religious lines, to say nothing of the resistance found among members of an informed and largely secularized society. In democratic regimes, when fundamentalist movements make their bids for power by bargaining and making coalitions with infidels, fundamentalists' beliefs attenuate and their boundaries become relaxed and diffuse. Thus the dialectic that operates under democratic regimes is different from that of authoritarian regimes. As fundamentalist movements leave their enclaves and seek power and hegemony in a democratic society, they may be penetrated and immobilized by the surrounding culture, which is full of temptations and challenges. In order to avoid this cultural co-optation, fundamentalists periodically withdraw to their enclaves and seek a limited and local influence, until another historic opportunity presents itself.

Where religious fundamentalism is able to tap the power of strong ethnic and/or nationalist commitments, it may produce nativist, preemptive ideologies and movements of a very violent sort, provoking responsive violence on the part of the threatened ethnoreligious minorities. Recent South Asian history provides vivid evidence of the virulence of this combination.

Religious fundamentalist movements are distinct from other religious movements in that they are inherently interactive, reactive, and oppositional—that is, they are inexorably drawn to some form of antagonistic engagement with the world outside the enclave. In other words, fundamentalisms are inevitably political. This judgment can be made perhaps only after the end of the twentieth century, as we look back on long-term developments in movements that, for a time, seemed to be purely separatist (e.g., U.S. Protestants, Haredi Jews). But because they look to the future rather than to the past and because they are essentially active in preparation for the future, fundamentalisms cannot resist being caught up in modern bureaucratic and institutional dynamics—the dynamics of change.

While they are political in nature, fundamentalist movements are also genuinely religious, which puts them in an analytical category distinct from other social protest movements or political opposition parties. We will fail to understand these movements if we neglect their irreducible religious dimension. The religious dimension manifests itself, among many other ways, in the person of the charismatic leader, whose authoritative interpretation of the religious tradition legitimates his religiopolitical diagnoses and prescriptions and guides his associates and assistants in setting and implementing policy. Militance, coalition building, "diplomacy"—all of the "ordinary" pursuits of minority political movements—take on unique rhythms and patterns in fundamentalisms due to their religious character.

While all fundamentalisms tend to be hegemonic, their world-conquering impulse is modified in practice in a variety of ways. As political entities, fundamentalist movements are often at the mercy of long-term economic, political, and social-structural trends in their host societies. As religious entities they are constrained by the boundaries of the host religion and by their own antitraditional character—that is, by their willingness to manipulate the religious tradition and introduce innovation for political rather than strictly spiritual purposes—a propensity that delegitimates the so-called true believers in the eyes of many other believers. Our analysis of the various patterns of world relation and of the diverse factors affecting fundamentalist strategies, growth, and decline demonstrates the complexity of the situation in which fundamentalisms find themselves: authoritarian absolutists in a pluralist world.

THE PROSPECTS OF FUNDAMENTALISM

Perhaps it is too much to ask that the universe be understandable; we
may have to be content with the fact that it is describable.

Anon.

In this concluding chapter we ask how fundamentalist movements around
the world are likely to fare in the next decades. Will the environment be
favorable or unfavorable to their growth and influence? What strategies are
they likely to employ? In particular, is the resort to violence and terrorism
by fundamentalist movements likely to increase or abate? Our conclusion is
organized around three historic trends that have influenced fundamentalist
movements and are likely to influence them in the future—cultural secularization, democratization, and the spread of the market economy.

Cultural Secularization and the Impact of Science

We begin with the theme of secularization, since it was this threat to sacred
institutions, along with the undermining of religious beliefs and practices in
the nineteenth and twentieth centuries, that produced the militant religious
movements that came to be called fundamentalism. The sociologists Daniel
Bell and José Casanova have called attention to the fact that secularization
is not a unitary process.[1] Casanova suggests a threefold breakdown of the
concept into structural differentiation, decline of religious belief and practice, and privatization. Bell considers a twofold breakdown as sufficient,

implying that differentiation and privatization are really the same phenomenon. Bell's structural differentiation refers to the historical process of institutional disaggregation in the West in the last several centuries—the casting off of sacred bonds by the state, the economy, the educational system, the world of the arts and literature, recreational life, and the like. His second secular trend is the subjective one of religious belief and practice.

These two trends, though interrelated, vary independently. Thus, in the United States, religious belief and practice continue at levels higher than in European countries, while the separation of church, state, and other institutions has gone much farther than in Europe. A country such as France, noted for its "de-Christianization" in the sense of decline in religious belief and church attendance, subsidizes the parochial primary and secondary schools of the Catholic Church. Despite waning religiosity in the German people, the German government provides the financial support for religious institutions through a church tax that it collects and distributes. In addition, church officials are regularly appointed to planning and supervisory committees dealing with education, social services, and family affairs. Churches are also represented on the supervisory boards of radio and television networks.[2]

At the center of the struggle between science and religion is the battle over cosmologies, explanations of the origin and destiny of the universe, and the meaning of human existence. We can identify three stages in the confrontation of scientific and religious cosmologies. The first stage was dominated by the portrait of an orderly, lawful universe implied in Newtonian physics and reconcilable with a belief in the existence of a "providence." Thus Darwin's teachers at Cambridge in the 1820s and 1830s accepted the creationism of the Bible. But their lawful, "deistic," providential cosmos began to give way to a second stage in the confrontation of science and religion with the publication of their prize student's *Origin of Species* in 1859. Darwin's views of the origins of life and of humankind were in direct conflict with the creationism, the anthropocentrism, and the teleology that then dominated Western thinking. His theory of the origin of species presented a picture of an evolving world of great age in which all living forms stemmed from a single origin, which became differentiated into species as a consequence of natural selection. Species were viewed as populations in the statistical sense and not as *essentially* distinct classes. Natural selection is an ongoing process in which accident and probability explain much of the biological past and will continue to make the biological future uncertain.

As Darwinism challenged the substance of certain fundamental religious beliefs in the latter part of the nineteenth century and the first decades of the twentieth, the religious establishment was further undermined on its own ground by the success of biblical scholarship in deciphering the creative and editorial history of sacred Scripture, leading to the questioning of divine authorship and inspiration. It was this twofold challenge—to the creationism affirmed in the Bible, and to the authorship and provenance of the Bible itself—that occasioned the rise of fundamentalism among American Protestants in the first decades of the twentieth century.

But Darwinism was only the first step. The Darwinian notion of evolution required enormously greater lengths of time and assumed a biology and a geology radically different from that of Genesis, but it had not deciphered the mechanics and chemistry of hereditary transmission of biological characteristics and of variation and speciation. The revolution in our understanding of the origins of life and the evolution of its various forms was advanced in the work of later biologists, culminating in the discoveries of DNA and the "double helix" of Crick and Watson in the early 1960s. As we move into the twenty-first century, the new genetic sciences and technologies are making enormous advances in knowledge and medical therapy, including organ replacement and cloning.

From the side of physics, the ordered Newtonian cosmos of space and time was replaced over the last seven or eight decades by an account of an incredibly ancient and unstable cosmos whose properties are bewildering and elusive. Its origin, at least its "most recent" origin, was the "big bang," said to have occurred approximately fifteen billion years ago. The universe has been "exploding," expanding, and differentiating ever since. The basic forces governing these processes at both the particle and the astrophysical levels are gravity, electromagnetism, and the nuclear "strong" and "weak" forces. How these forces relate to each other is one of the great puzzles of science, solvable, if at all, only at prohibitive levels of energy expenditure. Hence, in the words of the cosmologist Steven Weinberg, speaking at the millennium celebration of the American Philosophical Society, "[T]here are irreducible mysteries in the explanation of nature."[3]

Scientists are in agreement that the present structure of the universe—the galaxies, the stars, the solar system—and the biota of the earth—the species and the various ecosystems—can only be understood as evolving with a large component of chance and accident. Even though there is polemic as to how large a role chance played in the unfolding of our physical and biological world, the probability of the present outcome from the known origins was quite low indeed.[4] With chance operative at every stage and in every context, these processes would not come out the same way again "by a long shot." The physicist Murray Gell-Mann, the discoverer of the quark, speaks of the universe as consisting of "frozen accidents—galaxies, stars, planets, stones, trees—complex structures that serve as the foundation for the emergence of still more complex structures."[5] The paleontologist Stephen Jay Gould, commenting on the uniqueness of human life, argued that "we have been shaped by a contingent series of evolutionary events so rich in their number, and so unrepeatable in their intricacy, that the same sequence could never occur again in the same way—not even on this planet if we could start all over again from the first single-celled living form. Humanoids, in other words, are not predictable consequences of nature's laws, but fortuitous results of history's contingency on this particular planet."[6]

Thus, in the secular-scientific worldview, chance in the physical world combines with chance in the biological world to make any imputation of orderliness and planning to the universe far-fetched. Indeed, we seem to be entering a third stage of scientific development in which scientists share a somewhat deflated mood, best exemplified in recent observations by Weinberg, who concludes his little book, *The First Three Minutes*,[7] on a note of existential bemusement. "The more the universe seems comprehensible, the more it also seems pointless." In his *Dreams of a Final Theory*,[8] Weinberg expresses this disillusion once again: "As we have discovered more and more fundamental physical principles they seem to have less and less to do with us."

Five years after Weinberg offered these reflections, John Horgan, a career editor of *Scientific American*, forecast a declining rate of growth in the scientific enterprise, a kind of "end" of science in the sense that the great discoveries have now been made. John Maddox, an editor of the British journal *Nature*, hastened to respond by laying out the major physical, chemical, and biological secrets still to be discovered.[9] In so doing he provided "an agenda for several decades, even centuries, of constructive discovery that will undoubtedly change our view of our place in the world as radically as it has been changed since the time of Copernicus."[10]

Although Maddox speaks with authority, there can be no doubt of a change in the mood of science and in its public esteem at the dawn of a new millennium. The bloom of the scientific revolution has somewhat faded. Nature and the cosmos turn out to be irreducibly mysterious, prohibitively costly to investigate at the levels that are now required; the technologies that these new scientific insights have enabled have troubling side effects. What we are finding in the cosmos is not as unambiguously thrilling as was the case when the great telescopes, powerful atom smashers, and electronic microscopes first began to bring nature and the universe under close observation.

Not unrelated to the decline of enthusiasm for what science has discovered or might discover is growing concern and protest over the sheer, massive financial cost of techno-scientific research and development. High-energy physics, manned exploration of space, charting the genome, and the like, have ever more forbidding price tags. Most damaging to science's status, however, are the unintended problematic consequences of the technologies based on scientific discoveries—the degradation of the physical environment, the threat of large-scale disease and death from nuclear and biological weaponry, the erosion of community as a consequence of industrialization and urbanization, and so on. These side effects have contributed to a mood of public doubt and hesitation about science, perhaps to an even greater extent than the bewildering substance of scientific cosmology itself. Like everything that has grown "big," science has known sin.

This "third stage" in the development of science might free up metaphysical space previously occupied by the aggressive, unquestioning science of the nuclear and molecular biology decades. The leap of faith may have become less daunting. If nature is in some sense ultimately mysterious, it becomes less naive to believe in something beyond nature.

This opening of metaphysical space may come at some cost to religious fundamentalisms. The changing mood of science and of the public attitude toward science stands to benefit adaptive and accommodationist religions and spiritualities, as well as traditional and establishment religions, all of which are willing to coexist peacefully in the free marketplace of ideas theological and cosmological. Mainstream religions offer their ritual and liturgical portfolios, their often magnificent physical plant, their hagiographies and demonologies, their art and music. A tiny indicator of a possible turn in the strategy of the mainstream religious elite was the recent decision of the Reform Jewish rabbinate in America to return to the Hebrew liturgies as well as to other religious practices.

New Age religious movements, displaying their technical mastery of showmanship and special effects, are spectacularly consumer-friendly. Fundamentalisms, by contrast, may long for the renewal of the secular-scientific menace, their response to which has kept them in business and prominent in the public eye.

The rate and course of secularization changes dramatically before our eyes. We do not propose to predict its trajectory into the new century. But if fundamentalism has been a reaction against aggressive secularization, the less triumphal contemporary demeanor of science may take some of the wind out of fundamentalist sails.

FUNDAMENTALISM AND DEMOCRATIZATION

From the point of view of the leader attempting to build or sustain a fundamentalist movement, the religious and spiritual legacy of late twentieth-century modernity is mixed. In addition to the loss of scientific momentum and the decline in the rate of secularization, in recent decades there has been a rapid spread of democratic ideas and institutions around the world as well as the diffusion of a market economy—trends accompanied by a kind of radical individualism. These political, economic, and religious trends promise to exert a profound influence on extremist religious movements in the new century.

In nondemocratic regimes, the long-term transformation of attitudes through education and politically quiescent religious observance and training is a feeble option, unlikely to appease the young and zealous, who seek more immediate results. Cultural change modified by strong religion is more likely in open societies, where communications, schools, political parties, and state assemblies are accessible to fundamentalist participation and shaping.

Yet even in open societies, fundamentalisms are unlikely to expand much beyond their role as dissenting minorities who hope to nudge the culture in their sociomoral direction. What is loosely called "globalization" today is actually corrosive of fundamentalisms to the extent that the growth and extension of markets, escorted by the global media and its seductive display of consumer-friendly cultural styles, can be said to force societies to become ever more open and accommodating to diversity.[11] Diversity and plurality, however, are the bête noire of fundamentalisms. So, too, in a way, is materialism—the chance for greater material prosperity offered by the market economy, which suffocates other competitors in the arena of meaning and value. The expansion of the middle class in developing societies makes the beneficiaries less tolerant of high-risk social reform movements and more amenable, for the sake of preserving stability, to governments and regimes that resist genuine liberalization and turn a deaf ear to religious and moral critiques.

Globalization does not ensure genuine democratization, then, and it may strengthen the so-called illiberal democracies—states that allow limited democratic reforms while denying the full range of basic human and civil rights to its citizens. (In this regard, it is often noted, the weakness or absence of human rights regimes and full-fledged democracies in the Arab Middle East and parts of Africa has less to do with the traditions or teachings of Islam than with the restrictive and authoritarian political soil in which Islam has taken root.) Repression of fundamentalists, ironically, may be easier in the new "open" societies fostered by the victory of multinational corporations, NGOs, and the World Wide Web.

In democratic states, fundamentalist movements have repeatedly come under pressure to make compromises, to bargain and form coalitions with other political movements, and to give way even on matters of principle in order to gain and maintain power. Democratic regimes confronted by fundamentalist tactics can use a combination of firm but fair-minded application of law and order and adherence to basic democratic procedures to resist, contain, and perhaps moderate fundamentalist influence. Thus in Israel during the late nineties, the ultra-Orthodox parties became members of the Likud coalition of Netanyahu and the Labor coalition of Barak, and pressured their coalition partners to support them in efforts to extend prohibitions on worldly activities on the Sabbath, to defend their monopolies on marriage and divorce, to enforce dietary restrictions in public institutions, and the like. Whenever they were frustrated on such issues, they raised their demands for, among other things, financial subsidies for their educational institutions and exemption from military service. In other words, despite religious doctrine, there is pressure on political movements to treat all issues as fungible in a political power currency—votes in elections and seats in legislative bodies.

The Bharatiya Janata Party (BJP), heir to the Hinduization tendency in Indian politics, after winning a plurality in the May 1996 election, failed in its first efforts to form a governing coalition, in part because it could not convince its opponents of the sincerity of its expressed intent to pursue moderation and religious tolerance. BJP leader and Prime Minister designate Vajpayee, who included in his proposed cabinet a Muslim, a Sikh, a lower-caste Hindu, and a member of one of the tribal groups, played down Hindutva prescriptions for the Hinduization of Indian society. But this was not enough to win him coalition partners sufficient to form a government at that time. Further concessions allowed the BJP to assemble a governing coalition in 1998, but it lasted for less than a year. Although its own parliamentary delegation remained the same (178 seats) from the 1998 to the 1999 elections, Prime Minister Vajpayee was able to put together a coalition of the BJP with more than twenty other (mostly statewide) parties in support of a government designed to ensure relatively stable rule. But this hope depended on a continued moderate course and on the lowering of Hindutva rhetoric and mobilization.

The story in Turkey differs from the Indian case, primarily because of the secularism of the military. The Islamic party in Turkey, having similarly won a plurality of the votes in the 1996 parliamentary election, was successful in forming a majority coalition. But with the military unwilling to tolerate an Islamic movement in power, the Islamist-led government lasted only until 1997. In the spring 1999 elections, the Islamic Virtue Party lost substantially to the center and to the secular, nationalist right. The intervention of the military seems to have inhibited what might otherwise have been a movement toward successful bargaining and political dealmaking on the part of the Islamists.

In the bargaining over party platforms in the U.S. presidential campaign of 1996, the "religious right" was divided into more and less principled wings. At that time, more than 20 percent of the registered members of the Republican Party regarded themselves as members of the New Christian Right. Nevertheless, this faction was divided on tactics. A more worldly, pragmatic, compromising element, led by Ralph Reed, ran afoul of Gary Bauer, Bay Buchanan, and other "purists" who refused to soft-pedal their virulent opposition to abortion. "Any leader of a social reform movement who is on the cutting edge of tactical and strategic shifts by that movement," Reed explained, "is going to experience opposition from others in that movement."[12] The choice of words is telling: a hard-shell movement of conservative evangelicals and fundamentalists—the original core of the Christian Right—had become simply "a social reform movement" in which coalition-building from diverse social groups is a sine qua non of electoral success. The putative leader of the Religious Right, Gary Bauer, was an active candidate in the run-up to the Republican presidential primaries of 2000 but dropped out of the race for lack of support.

The Southern Baptist Convention also attempted to soften its image as the major institutional bastion of fundamentalism in the United States by issuing a statement apologizing for its racist attitudes and policies of the past. As with fundamentalists elsewhere, the enclave's projection into the cultural realm as a permanent player evokes such acts of cultural accommodation—often following a bitter internal tug of war—that are accompanied by a reassertion of traditional values in other realms. Hence the Southern Baptists followed their plea for forgiveness for the sins of racism—a gesture whose sincerity is not in doubt—with a proclamation reasserting the subordination of the wife to the husband in marriage and the dependent role of women in general.[13]

In short, it is clear that fundamentalist movements today must compete in pluralistic and politically competitive situations or, where this is not the case, in a larger international context in which liberal and/or democratic ideas and practices are accorded legitimacy.

The Spread of a Market Economy

In addition, fundamentalist leaders have to adapt their policy orientations and recruitment activities to a world in which there are strong pressures to introduce liberal, free market measures, to reduce taxes, government expenditures and regulation of the economy, to encourage foreign trade, and to avoid inflation. It is argued that more rapid economic growth is associated with these trends toward economic liberalization.[14] But it also appears that liberal economic growth is associated with an increased income and wealth gap between the more developed and the less developed countries and, within countries, between the rich and the poor.

One may argue that the spread and consolidation of democracy would have a solvent effect on the extremism of fundamentalist movements. As they move closer to power they move farther from absolutism and rigidity. The effect of the spread of the market economy on fundamentalism is more ambiguous. On the one hand, economic growth, insofar as it improves the material lives of people, may reduce frustration; but insofar as it increases inequality, targeted prosperity may increase resentment. Thus, while the New Christian Right made its home in the Republican party in the 1990s, one part of it favored economic liberalism, and another (the Buchanan wing) followed a populist, protectionist course appealing to working-class "hard hats." This ambivalence partly explained Buchanan's withdrawal from the Republican party in 1999 and his bid for the presidential nomination of the Reform party.

Islamic fundamentalism in Turkey has tended to be antiliberal and prowelfare in policy inclination. Iran under President Khatami has been a fascinating study in the struggle to achieve a postfundamentalist state, with hardliners bitterly contesting reforms in economic policy, free market orientations, international relations and, especially, social policies. Khatami's supporters, largely the new generation of Iranians with little or no memory of the Ayatollah Khomeini and the Shi'ite revolution, clamor for an open society with freedoms of press, speech, and dissent assured.

While fundamentalist movements are necessarily socially and culturally conservative, in short, there is variety in their economic orientations. In situations of growing inequality and the weakening of traditional safety nets, fundamentalist movements may adopt corporatist and populist policies. As internationalization and globalization make inroads into popular consciousness, it becomes increasingly difficult for fundamentalists to contain the momentum toward economic reform; and successful economic reform, in turn, may weaken the plausibility structures for what is now seen as repressive social policy.[15]

The new internationalism, that is, impedes the momentum of radical fundamentalisms and shapes their future prospects in undeniable ways. Just as participation in electoral politics has transformed the leadership and organizational structure of fundamentalist movements from within, diluting the strong religious ideology that once undergirded them, globalization threatens to have a similar effect.

What hard-core fundamentalists would view as an insidious pluralism is the most powerful cognitive by-product of exposure to global markets and media. The technologically driven assault upon the confines of time, space, and custom erodes traditional orthodoxies and liberates people from social roles and behaviors once considered obligatory. Much of what traditional societies upheld as "given," as inscribed in nature and therefore immutable, is revealed to be ephemeral and alterable. With the explosion of new sects, cults, protest movements, and religions, modern societies have experienced the proliferation of religious forms and options at a rate far more rapid than obtained in premodern societies. Furthermore, by shrinking time and space through communications and transportation technologies, modernity has made it much more likely that Sikhs, Buddhists, Christians, Jews, Hindus, Muslims, and nonbelievers are in close proximity to one another, especially in large urban areas around the world.

In this globalized milieu strong religion, preoccupied historically with defending the boundaries and walls of the enclave, is suddenly vulnerable to penetration by the invisible enemy. Images beamed across continents subtly transform attitudes. Islamic attitudes toward the United States were famously affected by Hollywood products such as *Dallas*, the televised serial that glamorized the opulence and licentious lifestyles of affluent Americans, sharpening the true believers' sense of relative deprivation and their feelings of envy, desire, repugnance, and resentment. Less well known is a more recent trend—the powerful impact of law-and-order dramas (e.g., *Law and Order*, *N.Y.P.D. Blue*) in which the accused are read their rights and accorded "due process" under the law. Televised proceedings of democratic legislative bodies in deliberation—e.g., the Knesset or the U.S. Congress—also register an impact. They project a model of public decision-making in which disagreements can be rather vitriolic and severe, for high stakes, but ultimately nonviolent and managed according to civil procedures.

THE VARIETY OF RELIGIOUS RESPONSES: FUNDAMENTALISM'S COMPETITORS

Trends within organized religion during this latest phase of secularization, democratization, and globalization reflected two countervailing tendencies: the atomization of society and the quest for community. Fundamentalism is but one response to these countervailing tendencies. In parts of the Middle East, Africa, and South Asia, fundamentalism remains a powerful stimulus for religious mobilization. In Europe, the Americas and in other parts of the world where religious pluralism, cultural diversity, and/or vibrant civil society precludes or diminishes the chance of any one "strong religion" dominating a society, fundamentalism finds itself to be no more than one of many options, and it is not competitive in every setting.

In the United States, for example, fundamentalism has been transformed by the social and cultural context. During its second public emergence in the 1970s, Christian fundamentalism made gains by opposing radical individualism, a trend made possible by unprecedented levels of prosperity and mobility and fueled by what Philip Slater in 1970 described as *The Pursuit of Loneliness*.[16] Fundamentalists led a wide-ranging cultural reaction in the eighties, helping to trigger the crisis over the decline of "family values."[17]

Yet the crisis spawned religious reactions that were unanticipated and unwelcomed by the fundamentalists. "Do-it-yourself" religion was a by-product of the consumer- and individualist-oriented society. Traditional beliefs and practices were "disembedded" from their original setting in the enclave and recombined with other disembedded bits to craft new, lightweight, consumer-friendly "spiritual" products—from the ready-made kosher kitchen (just visit the convenient specialty store) to the mixed-marriage rent-a-minister/priest/rabbi—all the more subversive for its seeming triviality and ubiquity.

Ministers to the baby boomer generation experienced the difficulties of sustaining an orthodox religious community whose members were becoming accustomed to living individualized lives in a culture of affluence and heightened personal choice.[18] The attempt to bind together modern Americans through religious or other communal ties becomes increasingly problematic in such a society driven by prerogatives of the autonomous individual. As the upwardly mobile boomers came of age, the 1970s saw the rise of the "culture of narcissism" and the "me generation"; the '80s were "the decade of greed," punctuated by Robert Bellah and associates' warning that unbridled individualism was eroding the communitarian *Habits of the Heart.*

In such an environment the intentional and deliberate familial and communal process of building character gave way in some instances to the "mere anarchy" of individual self-creation. Sheila Larson, a nurse interviewed by Bellah, memorably described her faith ("my own little voice") as "Sheila-ism"—a sui generis blending of scattered bits of her own personal experiences: growing up in a Protestant Christian home, experimenting with Eastern mystical traditions, incorporating secular self-help philosophies, adding a dash of New Age spirituality. Larson's personal journey captured vividly what sociologists described as a broad shift in American culture away from "collective-expressive" religious life toward "individual-expressive" forms. This trend deepened in the 1980s and continued unabated in the 1990s. "Americans are deeply committed to the principle of religious choice," reported two American sociologists in 1995. In separate pollings, large majorities (81 percent and 78 percent) believed that "one should arrive at his or her religious beliefs independent of a church or synagogue" and that "one can be a good Christian or Jew without attending a church or synagogue."

By these and other measures, it became clear that the majority of the U.S. population—whether or not they belonged to churches—considered religion a private matter best left to the autonomous individual. Several studies showed that traditional family structures, while still in the numerical majority, were increasingly seen as but one viable arrangement among many acceptable options.[19] In 1996, Bellah reported that he had actually underestimated the pervasiveness of individualism and its corrosive effects on American institutions.[20]

Fundamentalism was the road not taken for this so-called "generation of seekers."[21]

THE FUNDAMENTALIST RESPONSE

"Strong religion" has been increasingly hard-pressed to offer a powerful and popular corrective to these "disembedding" trends. At risk is the viability of religion itself—its fundamental capacity to bind a people together in common creed, code, cult, and community organization.

There has been a threefold fundamentalist response to the "third stage" in the development of modern science and to the virtual explosion of religious and cultural diversity within societies being transformed by transna-tional markets, cyber-space, and other agents of globalization. First, funda-mentalisms have turned increasingly to legalism as a means of ensuring the required certainty, as well as precision of practice. Second, and closely re-lated, fundamentalist movements have exalted the authority of the religious leader, extending it into realms once thought to be far beyond the leader's competence. Third, fundamentalisms have developed new ways of compet-ing with science in the realm of meaning.

Fundamentalism's formal concern with securing certainty for their worldview and religious beliefs is often reduced to punctilious observance of the law or technical efficiency in the performance of religious practice—late modern "virtues," indeed. Legalism and a minimal sense of certainty—I have followed the law precisely—must suffice, because the faith tradition is no longer imbedded in the daily warp and woof of life in a "naive" religious culture; the fragmentation and differentiation of the premodern religious community into an enclave is the insidious victory of the rational-scientific mentality. Haym Soloveitchik, analyzing the new role of texts in haredi soci-ety, demonstrates that ultra-Orthodox or "fundamentalist" Judaism offers its adherents a sense of divine providence and cosmic order but not in the manner of traditional Judaism, where God was involved in the personal lives and fates of His people. The God of the fundamentalist Jews is more remote from personal lives, evoking less a sense of fear and dread, Soloveit-chik argues, than duty and obligation. If no less in command of the cosmos, His governance is impersonal—one might say, rational, efficient, technically to be admired. The god of science has been transposed to the God of "strong"—reliable, constant, comprehensible—religion. The enclave, in its bid for strength, jeopardizes the very treasure it was meant to guard—a per-sonal relationship with an intimate deity whose Spirit binds together family and kin in ways beyond measure.

This quest for certainty disrupts the traditional balance between institu-tional and domestic or popular religion, because a deep mistrust of the latter undergirds fundamentalist attitudes—a loss of confidence in the ability of the people to observe and practice the faith "correctly." Hence the authority of the religious leader—in Soloveitchik's case, the rabbi—expands to en-compass realms of personal and home observance previously left to the discretion of the parents or extended family.

In democratic and pluralist societies such as the United States, even au-thoritarian measures, recognized as the last-ditch maneuver of a desperate leadership, yield to the kind of customer-satisfaction mentality on display in megachurches and in the electronic media of once-defiant fundamentalists.

Some fundamentalists have depended upon the freeing up of some meta-physical space previously occupied by an aggressive, unquestioning science. Pat Robertson's media empire, for example, is attempting to create an opening for strong religion to provide remedies and meaning, as their religious predecessors did in previous eras of scientific encroachment. In this case, they hope to counter the "Weinberg effect"—estrangement from the universe that prompts an existential mood of cosmic loneliness.

To the second conundrum posed by the success of modern science—the severe human costs entailed—science answers: The only solution is more and better science. Only science and improved technologies can lead us from the path of self-destruction (the erosion of resources, the damage to physical and psychological health, the threat of nuclear or biological holocaust). This argument of science is more plausible and compelling than anything else the scientific community has offered by way of public philosophy. Not even the most severe critic of technoscientific modernity can gainsay its amazing transformative powers. Unless and until the scientific community makes good on this boast and promise, however, a hermeneutics of suspicion will continue to accompany the "advances" of science—and their high price tags. "Strong religion" and other metaphysical alternatives, contesting secular science's elitism and hegemony over knowledge, continue to find sizeable niches, not only in popular culture but in schools, hospitals, politics, and government (e.g., public debates over "life issues" or military funding) and other domains over which scientists feel they should have full sway.

The current dilemmas of secular science add up, in other words, to a combination of lower satisfaction, higher cost, and a situation in which consumers begin looking around for different ways of filling their meta-physical shopping carts. Meaning-systems unburdened by ambiguity might profit from science's loss. Certainty, or assurance of one's importance in the larger scheme of things, is already at a premium. We have noted that the "leap of faith" that religion asks of believers could become somewhat less daunting. While scientists may stop short of positing a "something else" in cosmic causation, the laity confronted by a choice between this estranging cosmology of science and the disciplines and comforts of religion may choose the latter in larger numbers. Traditional or "orthodox" religions might benefit from such a trend; in their houses of worship, belief in an underlying cosmic order and divine intentionality is reinforced in ritual and ethic. But fundamentalists may benefit as well, for they are most likely to exploit the weaknesses of secular meaning-systems.

The globalization of culture and religion, however—to the extent that we can speak meaningfully of such a phenomenon—complicates the picture considerably. In the first place, fundamentalisms, as we have seen, find themselves faced with a growing number of competitors in the religious arena. Second, and more insidious from the point of view of those who equate strong religion with purity, absolute truth and strict adherence to the religious authority of the enclave, fundamentalisms tend to adopt the sensibilities of the milieu in which they exist. This means that they are fated to concede the epistemological battle and contest modern secularity on its own terms, in an adaptive, innovative—that is, nontraditional—manner.

While various fundamentalists or their spiritual kin in the world of militant religion have adopted these various strategies—competing with science in the realm of meaning, relying ever more insistently on conformity to the authority of the religious leader, substituting legalism for the genuine experience of community and tradition—others, keenly aware both of the threat facing them and the ground they are losing, have responded with ever more desperate measures.

THE LOGIC OF FUNDAMENTALIST VIOLENCE

As fundamentalist extremists have struggled to expand or secure their niche in a world in which borders are daily under assault and in which religious as well as secular enemies proliferate, they have turned increasingly to violence as a means of advancing their religious-cum-political objectives: hostage-taking, assassination, terrorist bombing, and the like. The attacks by Islamist extremists on the World Trade Center and the Pentagon were the most sensational and consequential acts of fundamentalist-related terrorism, but they were hardly unprecedented.

On occasion, dramatic and consequential acts of violence are conducted by loners or by tiny bands of radicals operating independently of a movement or its command structure. One thinks of the Jewish extremist Yigal Amir, who relied only on two confederates in plotting and carrying out the assassination of Israel's prime minister, Yitzhak Rabin; or John Salvaterra, the Catholic antiabortionist who went on a killing spree in a Boston abortion clinic. In such cases, the actors are inspired by a farrago of radical ideas and religious precepts, including those provided by fundamentalist movements such as Gush Emunim or Kach (in the case of Amir) and Operation Rescue (in the case of Salvaterra). Aggrieved and fanatical assassins tend to concoct their own ideological cocktails of vengeance, however; strong, aggressive religion, while a tried and true ingredient, can be borrowed and transformed by (self-)possessed individuals who hold no membership card in any organization that exists outside their own imaginings. Their acts of violence, strictly speaking, are not those of an organized fundamentalist movement.

Nor are the acts accompanying a very different type of violence often associated with fundamentalisms—collective or mob violence, whose contagion often spreads from its initial site in a religious or ethnic protest or celebration to expanding circles of dispossessed and discontented individuals and groups. Fundamentalists sometimes help instigate communal violence of this kind, primarily found in South Asia (e.g., the communal riots following the razing of the Babri mosque in Ayodyha, and anti-Christian riots in Kerala). More often they exploit the situation by turning social chaos—and the crisis of legitimacy it represents—to their own advantage. But this type of violence is nonetheless diffuse and eclectic in purpose and consequence. As a form of popular protest against oppressive regimes or ethnic rivals, riots and mob action would likely continue apace in the absence of fundamentalist manipulators. It is equally certain that fundamentalists will continue to seek opportunities to gain advantage from communal violence.

Fundamentalist violence, per se, is a response to government oppression and/or to the growth or empowerment of social groups deemed threatening to fundamentalist interests. Here we refer primarily to operational or strategic violence—the well-planned and coordinated, timed, large-scale acts of terrorism or warfare, usually involving hundreds of conspirators, which are designed to destabilize the regime and/or eliminate roadblocks to fundamentalist takeover of sectors of a society or the state apparatus itself. Examples include the 1997 Islamist attack on tourists at Luxor, a transparent attempt to destabilize the state economy by crushing Egypt's tourist industry; the 1983 Hizbullah suicide attacks on the Marine barracks in Lebanon; the Jewish Underground's plot to destroy the Islamic shrines on Temple Mount in Jerusalem; Hamas car bombs on the eve of the 1996 Israeli elections; the Hindu nationalist mobilization of young kar sevaks in the 1992 assault upon the Babri mosque in Ayodyha; and large-scale military operations such as the incursion of the Taliban into northern and northwestern Afghanistan. The most prominent of these large-scale operations, of course, was the Shi'ite revolution that brought Khomeini to power in Iran.

Secondarily, we refer to expressive violence—the slitting of throats of unveiled Algerian women, the self-martyrdom of the Hamas youth at an Israeli checkpoint, the stoning of Sabbath-breakers in Israel—as a response by which fundamentalist groups project their anger, resentment, strength (or frustration and impotence) and, above all, their zeal and dedication to God's cause.

There are signs that fundamentalists, who never fail to learn from their experiences and who adapt rapidly to new facts in the field, are questioning the utility of large-scale operational violence. In the Islamist world at least, the fate of Osama bin Laden and his goals will certainly be influential if not decisive in this deliberation. In democratic societies, violence of this kind is customarily put down by the rule of law backed by popular consent—a formidable combination that requires most radical elements, including extremist fundamentalists, to channel their reform energies into shaping the institutions of civil society. If and when democracy works in securing public order and enabling economic growth, fundamentalists may accommodate themselves to the new reality by showing a willingness to compromise and participate in the give-and-take of politics in a pluralistic society in which civil rights are protected by law and solemn assemblies are politically consequential. Their religious structures and worldview, however, will likely remain highly nonegalitarian, authoritarian, and absolutist. This "compartmentalized mind" may not be able to sustain itself over the long haul.

In nondemocratic societies it has become clear that the modern state can be a ruthless and efficient opponent. What complicates matters is that the ruling elite is not magnanimous in victory; it considers the vanquished party no longer a threat only when it is virtually eliminated from the scene or reduced to impotence, as is the case in Tunisia, Syria, Iraq, Algeria, and Egypt. (At this writing it remains unclear whether Pakistan under General Musharraf, compelled by the United States and by India, will muster the will to eliminate or even substantially weaken the virulent Islamist movements operating within its borders, including the terrorist cells and networks that provided support to the Taliban, to Al Qaeda, and to the groups that attacked the Indian parliament in December 2001.) The cycle of mutual demonization means that the secular nationalist party in power will not consider appeasing the opposition in any way, much less incorporate it into democratic or quasi-democratic structures. (Indeed, it was oppressive or dictatorial regimes in the Middle East whose insincere flirtation with democracy—under Nasser and Boumedienne—turned Islamists decisively against democracy.)

Fundamentalists have also learned that the devotion of significant resources and energies to operational violence often ends in transforming the character of the fundamentalist movement itself. What began in earnest religiosity ends in mere hooliganism. The movement leadership becomes peopled with mercenaries and young ruffians, religious in their way but less patient with the refined religiolegal guidance and judgments of the spiritual guides and virtuosi who once restrained the violence by limiting it to the requirements of the religious law. The charismatic religious leader was never meant to be an operational, hands-on supervisor. But when the middle managers far outnumber and outweigh the charismatic leaders, how is one to speak of fundamentalism as a religious movement? Shaykh Yassin of Hamas, for example, continues to exercise powerful influence over the Islamist movement in Palestine, but only rarely does he make his presence felt in the substantive operations of this now-complex, three-tiered organization (military command and control inside the territories, political leadership in the territories, and political and financial infrastructure abroad). Sri Lankan Buddhist monks, engrossed in crushing their Tamil Hindu rivals, study martial arts rather than the ancient wisdom; is this not, ultimately, a self-defeating turn?

Fundamentalist violence has gained certain concessions along the way—alcohol is prohibited in the military, tourist, and other sectors, for example—but these are relatively minor among its positive accomplishments. More significant is the ripple effect on social practices; for example, the impact of abortion clinic bombings on women's actual and psychological access to abortion. But perhaps the most significant impact of fundamentalist violence is its limiting effect on the regime's room for maneuver. The knowledge that fundamentalists are poised to lead riots and demonstrations, for example, might cause the state to hesitate before abrogating subsidies to the poor demanded by the IMF; or to limit women's access to the non-nurturant professions or to positions of authority. Demonstration-effect violence—operations that garner headlines, cause anxiety, and effectively proclaim, "See what strong religion can do"—is also useful in recruiting young belligerents, although this is a double-edged sword, as we have noted.

THE IMPACT OF SEPTEMBER 11

The questions that we introduced at the outset of this volume nonetheless loom large in many quarters: Has the way of operational violence been sufficiently tested and found lacking? Or will fundamentalism turn increasingly toward terrorist violence and on a global scale?

This set of questions brings us back to the tragedy of September 11 and the subsequent "war on terrorism." Why and how did Islamic fundamentalism within the Sunni orbit "go global" in the September 11 attacks?

During the eighty-year "period of humiliation" (following the defeat of the Ottoman empire and the abolishment of the caliphate), to which bin Laden repeatedly referred during his period of worldwide notoriety following the attacks, Islamic fundamentalism increasingly took root in popular circles within the Sunni Arab world as ordinary Muslims recognized the elements of truth in the fundamentalist critique. In the wake of the Ottoman defeat and the secularization of Turkey, the colonizing Western powers established both a visible military and commercial presence in the Middle East, accompanied by a far more insidious moral and cultural presence via the export and marketing of American goods and (self-indulgent, promiscuous, and godless) ways of life. The heart of the Islamist critique, however, has to do not with colonialism or American hegemony but with the corrupt and godless behavior of the postcolonial, indigenous leaders who betrayed Islam and accepted Western "bribes."

Meanwhile, U.S. policy toward the Middle East and the broader Islamic world has been seen as serving the narrow interests of an affluent and comfortable American public, which consumes a grossly disproportionate percentage of natural resources (oil-based products in particular) while the mass of humanity in the countries being exploited for their oil live below the poverty level. Muslim lives and livelihoods, in this view, are routinely sacrificed to support luxurious American lifestyles. The United States is a great hypocrite, espousing democracy and freedom in its rhetoric while providing critical financial and military support to antidemocratic and repressive regimes like those of Egypt and Saudi Arabia, where the voice of the Muslim people is silenced.

A staple of the discourse of Islamic fundamentalists is the claim that the traditional religious leaders of the Islamic world such as the shaykhs of Cairo's al-Azhar seminary and university—the center of the Sunni educational and religious establishment—have been co-opted by dictatorial rulers such as Egyptian president Hosni Mubarak, the FLN of Algeria, or the monarchy of Saudi Arabia. These putatively Islamic regimes make a habit of compromising Islamic principles for the sake of their alliances with Europe and the United States. Traditional Muslim religious leaders, as a result of their towing the state line, have been marginalized and delegitimated in many circles of the Islamic world, leaving the field open to the religiously unschooled but disgruntled "laymen," many of whom come from educational backgrounds in engineering, applied science, or business.

In the late nineties Osama bin Laden, exploiting the weakness of the clerical leadership, began to refer to himself as "Shaykh" Osama bin-Muhammad bin-Laden, as he did in the "fatwa" he issued on 23 February 1998 announcing his legal "ruling" that every Muslim now has the individual duty to "kill the Americans and their allies—civilians and military."[22] Bin Laden was not original in his view of the conflict as a global war; he merely repeated what both Sunni and Shi'ite radicals had long been teaching their cadres, namely, that the war against Islam, against the true believers in particular, was being waged by traitorous forces within the geographical borders of the Islamic world—by apostates such as Mubarak and the Saudi monarchy, who pretended to be orthodox but were in fact betraying the Dar-al-Islam—but also by external agents of cultural and economic colonization such as Israel, Great Britain, France, and the United States.

But bin Laden was uniquely successful in driving the message home—literally—and thus operationalizing it. His well-funded and expertly trained networks and camps transformed the Mujahidin from disparate and undisciplined bands of Muslim fighters, drawn from across the Arab world—above all, they were refugees of defeated Islamist groups, as well as Muslim expatriates and immigrants—into tightly organized terrorist cells dedicated to a radical program of action.

In attempting to launch a global jihad against the West, bin Laden sought to rally Muslims to his tendentious reading of the Qur'an and the Shari'a. In so doing he recognized implicitly that Islam—like Christianity, Judaism, Hinduism, and Buddhism—is a living tradition, the meaning of its sacred texts and moral laws ever awaiting a new and compelling *ijtihad* (that is, "the right of a qualified scholar to go back to the primary sources and work out from them what he thought were the Islamic principles involved"[23]).

The expertise of bin Laden (who enjoys no scholarly authority) has not gone uncontested in the Islamic world, however. Religious leaders as well as heads of state within the Sunni Muslim world have denounced the "kill all Americans" fatwa, the attacks of September 11, and indeed, the violent approach to redressing Islamic grievances. Strikingly, even Islamist movements, such as the Jama'a Islamiyya of Egypt, rejected the bin Laden modus operandi and saw it as a strange phenomenon of the Muslim diaspora. Mohammad Khatami, the Shi'ite president of Iran, joined his Sunni colleagues in condemning what he calls "a new form of active nihilism [that] assumes various names, [some of which] bear a semblance of religiosity and some proclaim spirituality." Khatami denigrated religious extremists as "superficial literalists clinging to simplistic ideas," and he called for the development of a cross-religious language that would allow religious communities

"to be understood and [provided with] a capacity to listen and understand."
President Khatami also proposed an alliance of religiously rooted moderates, from across faith lines, who could offer a vision for their respective
societies that uses "neither materialistic secularism nor religious fundamentalism as a starting point."[24]

The current conflict between fundamentalist and moderate orientations
to religion, politics, and society is something less than a "clash of civilizations." More accurately, it is a contestation *within* societies regarding not
only the priority of culture but, more fundamentally, its content. Most vex-
ing to the fundamentalists are millions of their coreligionists—the vast majority of their fellow Jews or Christians or Muslims—who share the same
"fundamental" religious beliefs and practices but who reject the fundamentalists' resort to various forms of militancy, including lethal violence, in the
name of the religion. Indeed, the mainstream believers consider themselves
to be quite sufficiently orthodox, and they judge the fundamentalist call to
arms, whether metaphorical or literal, to be a distortion of the faith and an
egregious misreading of its Scriptures and doctrines.

Underlying the internal debate over first-order religious discourse—over
the proper interpretation of sacred texts and doctrines—are oppositions
that, if anything, are more "fundamental" to social identity. These include
tensions over the roles of women in patriarchal societies; the continued
viability of patriarchal societies themselves; the status of human rights discourse and practice, including minority rights, within the religious and political communities; the role of violence in protecting and extending the
faith and the various ethnic groups seen to be upholding or embodying it;
the public presence and accountability of religious leaders within a pluralist
society; and, indeed, the inevitability of pluralism within late modern societies.

In this respect, as we have shown, the fundamentalists behave not as
traditional or conservative believers, who are bound to and by the religious
tradition as a complex but coherent whole. Rather, they are innovative manipulators of the religious tradition who retrieve its minor, normally muted,
"only in case of emergency" teachings that legitimate retaliatory violence.
The fundamentalists justify their extremist interpretations of these selected
texts and teachings by pointing to the terrible assaults on the faith by both
outsiders and, above all and far worse, by misguided or corrupted believers.

Yet the complexity of Islamic radicalism itself also undermined the possibility of a "global jihad" against the West. Reports surfaced that in the
nineties bin Laden had approached the Shi'ite fundamentalists among Iran's
ruling elites for the purpose of forging an anti-Western alliance—to no

avail. Nor was there evidence that other powerful Sunni groups, such as the Algerian Armed Islamic Group [GIA], had joined forces with Al Qaeda, bin Laden's terrorist network. Indeed, the various Islamist movements have different targets, which are limited to their own respective countries.

Long after bin Laden and Al Qaeda are removed from the scene, however, the problems in the governance of the Arab and Muslim worlds that gave them legitimacy—the fact that such governments are widely perceived as self-serving, inefficient, corrupt, and beholden to non-Muslim powers and causes—will continue to nurture fundamentalist movements of this type. The strongest counter to the "strong religion" of the fundamentalists would be economic reforms that promote economic growth and greater equality of income distribution, as well as political reform that extends the process of self-determination well beyond its current narrow circle of governing elites.

If reforms in the direction of greater levels of political self-determination do not occur, one might expect wave after wave of tactical violence, including the possibility of biological and chemical warfare. But evidence from Egypt, Algeria, Tunisia, Iran, India, and perhaps even Israel/Palestine suggests that it is more likely that fundamentalists—especially those living in heavily militarized states whose rulers have a strong grip on power—have begun to abandon hope that the balance of power can be shifted via insurrection or wars of attrition. Given the opportunity to integrate into the polity, the disillusioned Islamists might opt for peaceful activism.

THE FUTURE OF STRONG RELIGION

Throughout this book we have emphasized the innovative and shrewdly adaptive character of fundamentalisms. How fundamentalisms choose to adapt to these emergent trends—of abating secularization and the proliferation of religious experimentation, marketization, globalization, and democratization—will most certainly decide their fate in the twenty-first century. While we have engaged in informed speculation about the prospects of fundamentalisms, the analytical tools we have applied to these movements—our structure, chance, and choice analysis through which we can comprehend changes over time in an extremist movement's ideology and organizational structure—help us to understand the past rather than predict the future. Choices and decisions, especially those taken by charismatic and authoritarian religious leaders, will continue to shape these movements in ways that no analytical scheme can fully anticipate.

Moreover, fundamentalism qua fundamentalism (i.e., as an aggressive, enclave-based movement with absolutist, reactive, and inerrantist tendencies), the recent global pretensions of bin Laden and Al Qaeda notwithstanding, is quintessentially a local phenomenon, a struggle for cultural and political influence over the "tribe," whether conceived along narrow or expansive geographical lines. This remains true today despite the various efforts to internationalize the financial and logistical structures of movements such as Hamas, the Tamil Tigers, and the Jewish radicals' resistance to the peace process. International developments and affiliations will continue to influence fundamentalisms, but they will remain confined ideologically within the boundaries set by fundamentalists' selectively traditional and selectively modern, inerrantist, and Manichaean worldviews.

In sum, the phenomenon of fundamentalism will subsist well into the twenty-first century. Chances are, it will thrive mostly in opposition as a dissenting minority, although in some settings it may assume power directly or by infiltration. In this respect it is important to underscore the heightened possibility, due to technology, that a small group can change the structures of power by a series of violent acts or have an impact on international relations. In this new technological environment, it is relatively easy for a movement to shift strategies quickly, to adopt a new mode of orientation to the world; this makes analysis of movements all the trickier. Nonetheless, the move from disrupting the social/political order to taking actual power remains a quantum leap.

We note, further, the ambivalence of fundamentalisms—they want to rule the world but they are intrinsically parochial or particularistic, which reduces the probability of menacing international combinations. At the same time, the erosion of fundamentalist goals is likely to occur in power-sharing situations that inevitably require compromise and coalition building.

Can such politically self-limiting religious worldviews survive in an increasingly borderless world of markets and democratic polities, and in states where the limits of effective insurrectionist, retaliatory, and tactical violence have been reached? Can fundamentalisms realistically expect to thrive in the twenty-first century, when other religious and spiritual alternatives find their appeal enhanced by a growing cultural pluralism and by a diminished scientific/cosmological project?

History teaches us not to rush to answers to these questions. If the prospects for the growth of politically effective fundamentalisms seem dim, their persistence is telling. The undeniable impact of fundamentalists on church, state, family, and secular society has compelled virtually every religious

community to confront the issue of adaptation and survival and to formulate for itself a viable answer to the question posed by the fundamentalist
phenomenon: What constitutes "strong religion" in a post-traditional, secularized society? What combination of moral imperatives, doctrinal developments, ritual practices, ideological commitments, recruiting strategies, and
organizational structures are most likely to ensure the vitality and viability
of recognizably religious forms in the future?

For religious movements that have equated strength with political
power, economic status, or military might, will the price of survival be moderation? Will militant religious leaders seek compromise with secular elites
rather than dilute their strength in a potentially debilitating round of confrontations? Is nonviolent resistance, motivated by the rejection of extremism on pragmatic if not principled grounds, the path most likely to garner
the support of the masses who often share the fundamentalist critique of
corruption and drift while shrinking from the lethal violence that threatens
home and loved ones? How might such models of resistance, as they become more pervasive and publicized, shape fundamentalist goals and remake attitudes toward civil society and the rule of law?

Nonfundamentalist religious communities that choose to ignore these
and other questions raised by fundamentalisms will do so at their own risk.
And, as should be abundantly clear by this point in society's encounter with
this brand of strong religion, the same is true for politicians, diplomats,
educators, and scientists, including those who continue to wonder ruefully
how militant religion inherited a new lease on life in our supposedly post-
religious age.

APPENDIX

Diagram 2.1 A Functional Theory of Fundamentalism: Reactivity to Secularization

Selectivity	Boundaries	Election
Inerrancy	Behavior	Authority
Boundaries	Election	Charisma
Behavior	Manichaeanism	Selectivity

Table 2.1 The Perceived Enemies of Fundamentalism

Religious Movement	Religious Establishment	Secular State	Civil Society	Religious Competition	Ethnonational Competition	Imperialism and Neocolonialism
Christian:						
U.S. Protestant I	xx	x	x	x		
U.S. Protestant II	x	x	xx			
Guatemalan Pentecostal			x	xx		
U.S. Catholic	xx	x	xx			
Italian CeL	x	x	x			
South Indian		x	x		x	
Islamic:						
Egyptian jama'at	x	xx	x	x		x
Algerian FIS	x	xx	x	x		x
Hamas	x		x	x	x	xx
Iranian Khomeini	x	xx	x	x		x
Iraqi Shi'ite	x	xx	x	x		
Lebanese Hizbullah			x	x	x	xx
Pakistani Jama'at-i-Islami	x	x	xx	x	x	x
Indian Tablighi Jamaat		x	xx	x		
Jewish:						
Haredi I	xx	x	x	x		
Haredi II	x	x	xx	x		
Habad	x	x	x	x		
Gush Emunim		x	x		x	
Kach		xx	x		xx	
South Asian:						
Hindu RSS		x	x	xx	xx	x
Sikh radical	x	xx	x	xx	x	
Sinhala Buddhist	x		x	xx		

Table 2.2 Ideological Ratings of Fundamentalist Movements

Religious Tradition	Reactivity	Selectivity	Dualism	Inerrancy	Millennialism
Christian:					
U.S. Protestant	High	High	High	High	High
Catholic traditionalist	High	High	High	High	Low
Comunione e Liberazione	High	High	High	High	Low
Guatemalan Pentecostal	Absent	Low	High	High	Low
Ulster Protestant	High	High	High	Low	Low
South Indian	High	High	High	High	Low
Islamic:					
Sunni jama'at	High	High	High	High	Low
Shi'ite	High	High	High	High	High
Jama'at-i-Islami	High	High	High	High	Low
Tablighi Jamaat	Low	Low	Low	Low	Low
Hamas	High	High	High	High	Low
Jewish:					
Haredi	High	High	High	High	High
Habad	Low	High	High	High	High
Gush Emunim	High	High	High	High	High
Kach	High	Low	High	High	Absent
South Asian:					
Hindu RSS	Low	Low	High	Absent	Low
Sikh radical	High	High	High	High	Low
Sinhala Buddhist	Low	Low	High	Absent	Low

Table 2.3 Organizational Ratings of Religious Movements

Religious Tradition	Elect-Chosen	Boundaries	Charismatic Leadership	Authority/ Behavior
Christian:				
U.S. Protestant	High	High	Low	High
Roman Catholic	Low	Low	Low	Low
Comunione e Liberazione	High	High	High	Low
Guatemalan Pentecostal	Low	High	High	Low
Ulster Protestant	Low	Low	High	Low
South Indian	Low	Low	High	Low
Islamic:				
Sunni jamaʿat	High	High	High	High
Shiʿite	High	High	High	High
Jamaʿat-i-Islami	Low	High	Low	High
Tablighi Jamaat	Low	Low	Absent	Low
Hamas	High	High	High	High
Jewish:				
Haredi	High	High	High	High
Habad	High	High	High	High
Gush Emunim	High	Low	High	High
Kach	Low	Low	Low	Low
South Asian:				
Hindu RSS	Low	Low	High	High
Sikh radical	Low	Low	High	High
Sinhala Buddhist	Absent	Low	Absent	Low

APPENDIX

APPENDIX TO CHAPTER 3

Chart 3.1 Explaining Aspects of Fundamentalist Movements

		Origins and founding
Structural variables	$\longrightarrow$	Ideology
Contingency variables	$\longrightarrow$	Organization
Choice variables	$\longrightarrow$	Strategy and tactics
		Growth and spread
		Decline

A fundamentalist movement is shaped by its religious setting—the theological and organizational characteristics of the host religion and competing religions and the ways in which its own religious establishment adapts to the secularizing policies of the state and to secularizing trends in the civil society. Table 3.1 indicates the organizational structure of selected movements.

Table 3.1 Organization of Host Religion

	Diffuse Charismatic	Congregational	Semihierarchical	Hierarchical
Christian:				
U.S. Protestant		x		
Catholic traditionalist				x
Guatemalan Pentecostal		x		
Comunione e Liberazione				x
Islamic:				
Egyptian jama'at		x		
Algerian FIS		x		
Gaza Hamas		x		
Iranian Khomeini			x	
Lebanese Shi'ite			x	
Jewish:				
Haredi		x		
Habad		x		
Gush Emunim		x		
South Asian:				
Hindu RSS	x			
Sikh radicals	x			
Sinhala Buddhist	x			

To explain fundamentalist movements means to show how structure, chance, and choice combine to determine their formation, growth, and fate—and their shifting patterns of relation to the world. We tallied the frequency with which structure, chance, and choice factors were important in the development of fundamentalist movements in Christian, Jewish, Islamic, and South Asian religious traditions. We specified how these factors influenced the emergence, growth, and decline of movements, their ideological and organizational characteristics, and their strategies. Each of us was required to make these judgments about the historical experience of those movements with which he was most familiar.

The conclusion of this exercise appear in tables 3.2 and 3.3. Table 3.2 sums up the frequency with which these factors were cited for all of our fundamentalist and fundamentalistlike cases grouped together. For example, if the host religion had been scored as influential for the origins and founding, the ideology, the organization, the strategy, growth, and decline of all sixteen of our cases, then the category "host religion" would have received a perfect score of 96 (6 × 16). In fact it received roughly half of that number. This was the highest score among the structural variables, with religious context, public policy, and civil society next in order of significance. However, leadership looms by far as the most significant factor, receiving a tally of 77 out of a possible score of 96. The rightmost column of table 3.2 gives the weighted frequency for our three sets of variables. Each factor for each fundamentalist movement was given a score from one to three, ranging from "some importance" (1) to "important" (2) to "very important" (3). Thus, if host religion had received "very imporant" ratings for all sixteen cases, in all six aspects (3 × 16 × 6), it would have a score of 288. It actually had a score of 88, roughly one third of a perfect score, while leadership had a weighted total score of 189, roughly two thirds of a perfect score. Again religious context, civil society, and public policy had high weighted scores as well.

Table 3.2 Impact of Explanatory Factors in Sixteen Fundamentalist Movements by Number and Weighting of Importance

	Frequency	Weighted Frequency
Structure:		
Host religion	47	88
Religious context	38	75
Civil society	37	81
Migration	27	54
Government structure	27	49
Public policy	41	88
Economic trends	31	59
International environment	31	62
Chance:		
Endogenous	19	39
Exogenous	18	42
Choice:		
Leadership	77	189
Rank and file	26	57
Total possible score:	96	288

Considering the impact of these variables on the different aspects of the fundamentalist phenomenon (see table 3.2), we have the striking finding that leadership was rated as significant for all aspects—origins, ideology, organization, strategy, growth, and decline—in almost all of our cases. Among the structural variables, host religion was important in the origins, ideology, and organization of these movements; public policy, in the origins, strategy, and growth; religious context, in the origins and ideology; economic trends, in origins and growth. International environment was of signficance in the origins and ideologies of these movements. Migration was very significant in the origins and growth of these movements.

Table 3.3 Factors Affecting Aspects of Fundamentalism by Frequency

	Origins	Ideology	Organization	Strategy	Growth	Decline
Structure:						
Host religion	10	16	12	4	1	4
Religious context	12	10	3	7	5	1
Civil society	8	4	6	7	5	1
Migration	13	3	1	3	6	1
Government structure	9	5	5	5	2	1
Public policy	9	1	6	8	10	7
Economic trends	9	1	2	5	10	4
International environment	9	9	3	3	4	3
Chance:						
Endogenous	8	1	1	2	4	3
Exogenous	8	1	1	1	4	3
Choice:						
Leadership	16	14	12	13	10	12
Rank and file	3	1	3	9	7	3

APPENDIX

Table 4.1 Fundamentalist Patterns of Relation to the "World" over Time

	World Conqueror	World Transformer	World Creator	World Renouncer
U.S. Protestant:				
Origins (1875–1925)	x	xx	x	
Growth (1925–75)			xx	x
Resurgence (1975–)	xx	x	x	
Catholic Traditionalist			x	xx
Guatemalan Pentecostal		xx	x	x
Comunione e Liberazione		xx	x	
Islamic Jama'at:				
Origins	x	xx	x	
Radicalization	xx	x	x	x
Haredi:				
Origins			x	xx
Growth			xx	x
Habad		x	xx	x
Gush Emunim:				
Origins	xx		x	
Radicalization	xx	x		
Decline		x		xx
Arya Sama			xx	
Hindu RSS, VHP, BJP:				
Origins (1915–25)			xx	
Kingdom of Ram	x	xx	x	
Ayodhya crisis (1992)		x	xx	

	World Conqueror	World Transformer	World Creator	World Renouncer
Sikh radical:				
Fateh Singh (1960s)			xx	
Longowal (1970s)		xx		
Bhindranwale (1980s)	xx			
Sinhala Buddhist:				
Origins (1890s–1930s)			xx	
Growth (1940s)		xx		
Radicalization (post–1956)	xx			

Table 4.2 Explaining Fundamentalist Transitions

	World Creator	World Transformer	World Conqueror	World Renouncer
Structure	Pre–World War II: Jewish migration from shtetl function of Aguda and ultra-Orthodox coalition	1875–1925: American Protestant impact of pluralism and congregationalism on development of fundamentalist institutions	1970s: Jewish Gush Emunim—in response to 1967 and 1973 wars	1947: Jewish Neturei Karta rejection of Israeli state on literal biblical grounds
Chance	1890s: Sri Lankan Buddhism—impact of American Theosophical Society on Dharmapāla	Post–World War II: Jewish impact of World War II and Holocaust on haredi response in the U.S. and Israel	1970s: Iran Shi'ites coincidence of shah's illness and Carter presidency	
Choice	1875: Hindu founding of Arya Samaj by Swami Dayananda	1950s–1960s: Italian Catholic Father Giussani and formation of *scuole* of Comunione e Liberazione	1960s: Egyptian Sunnis, Sayyid Qutb advocacy of radical political course for Muslim Brotherhood	1970s: French Catholic archbishop Lefebvre withdraws from church

Introduction

1. Ignatius of Antioch, "To the Romans," in Cyril C. Richardson, *Early Christian Fathers* (New York, 1975), pp. 104–5. "I am corresponding with all the churches and bidding them all realize that I am voluntarily dying for God—if, that is, you do not interfere. I plead with you, do not do me an unreasonable kindness. Let me be fodder for wild beasts—that is how I can get to God. I am God's wheat and I am being ground by the teeth of the wild beasts to make a pure loaf for Christ," writes Ignatius. "Come fire, cross, battling with wild beasts, wrenching of bones, mangling of limbs, crushing of my whole body—only let me get to Jesus Christ!"

2. Jay. P. Dolan, *The American Catholic Experience* (Notre Dame, Ind., 1985), p. 422.

3. Jansen, *The Dual Nature of Islamic Fundamentalism*, p. 11.

4. *Columbia Encyclopedia*, 6th ed., s.v. "denial."

5. Mary Douglas, *Natural Symbols: Explorations in Cosmology* (London, 1970), p. viii.

6. James Moore, "The Creationist Cosmos of Protestant Fundamentalism," in Martin E. Marty and R. Scott Appleby, eds., *Fundamentalisms and Society: Reclaiming the Sciences, the Family and Education* (Chicago, 1993), pp. 46–60.

7. Bassam Tibi, "The Worldview of Sunni Arab Fundamentalists: Attitudes toward Modern Science and Technology," in Marty and Appleby, *Fundamentalisms and Society*, pp. 73–102.

8. Everett Mendelsohn, "Religious Fundamentalism and the Sciences," in Marty and Appleby, *Fundamentalisms and Society*, p. 38.

9. See Shahla Haeri, "Obedience versus Autonomy: Women and Fundamentalism in Iran and Pakistan," pp. 181–213; Helen Hardacre, "The New Religions, Family, and Society in Japan," pp. 294–311; and Andrea B. Rugh, "Reshaping Personal Relations in Egypt," pp. 151–80, in Marty and Appleby, *Fundamentalisms and Society*.

10. Michael Rosenak, "Jewish Fundamentalism in Israeli Education," pp. 374–414; Susan Rose and Quentin Schultze, "The Evangelical Awakening in Guatemala: Fundamentalist Impact on Education and Media," pp. 415–51; Susan Rose, "Christian Fundamentalism and Education in the United States," pp. 452–89; Quentin Schultze, "The Two Faces of Fundamentalist Higher Education," pp. 490–535; Krishna Kumar, "Hindu Revivalism and Education in North Central India," pp. 536–557, in Marty and Appleby, *Fundamentalisms and Society*. On the role of women in Christian education and formation, see Susan D. Rose, *Keeping Them Out of the Hands of Satan: Evangelical Schooling in America* (New York, 1988).

11. Elaine Sciolino, "Iran's Problems Raising Doubts of Peril to U.S.," *New York Times*, 5 July 1994, A1, A5.

12. Cf. R. Scott Appleby, *The Ambivalence of the Sacred: Religion, Violence and Reconciliation* (Lanham, Md., 2000), pp. 79–83.

13. Hamid Algar, introduction to Murtazá Mutahhari, *Fundamentals of Islamic Thought: God, Man, and the Universe*, trans. R. Campbell (Berkeley, 1985), p. 20.

14. Mutahhari, *Fundamentals of Islamic Thought*, p. 59.

15. Jerry Falwell, *Listen, America!* (Toronto and New York, 1980), p. 219.

16. Abd al-Rahman Abu al-Khayr, quoted in Johannes J. G. Jansen, *The Dual Nature of Islamic Fundamentalism* (Ithaca, N.Y., 1997), p. 80.

17. Haym Soloveitchik, "Migration, Acculturation, and Accommodation: The New Role of Texts in the Haredi World," in Martin E. Marty and R. Scott Appleby, eds., *Accounting for Fundamentalisms: The Dynamic Character of Movements* (Chicago, 1994), p. 198. Custom was "a correlative datum of the Halakic system"; frequently, the written word was reread in light of traditional behavior. Haym Soloveitchik, "Religious Law and Change: The Medieval Ashkenazic Example," *AJS Review* 12 (1987): 205–13.

18. Soloveitchik, "Migration, Acculturation, and Accommodation," p. 199.

Chapter 1

1. Nathan Birnbaum, *Gottesvolk* (Vienna, 1919); Hebrew trans., ʿAm ha-Shem (Bʾnai Bʾrak, 1977), pp. 62–63, 117–22; idem, *Ktavim Nivharim* (Tel Aviv, 1943), pp. 17–25. Cf. Hazon Ish (Rabbi Abraham Karlitz), *Igrot* (Bʾnai Bʾrak, 1955), 1: 102–3.

2. Hafetz Haim, *Yalqut Meshalim* (Tel Aviv, 1952), p. 31; Moshe Yoshor, *Ha-Hafetz Hayyim* (Tel Aviv, 1959), 2: 525 and cf. 1: 202, 260, 438; Elhanan Wasserman, quoted in *Be-ʾEin Hazon* (Haifa, 1976), p. 93, and see pp. 12–13, 94. Cf. memoirs of Shlomo Lorincz in *Diglenu*, November 1990.

3. Arieh Surasky, *Marbitzei Torah u-Musar* (Bʾnai Bʾrak, 1973), 3: 68, and see p. 158. Cf. Moshe Scheinfeld, "In Exile among Brothers," *Diglenu*, October 1951, and his articles in *Diglenu*, October 1948 and April 1966.

4. E.g., *Yated Neʾeman*, 8 October 1990. Cf. Yaʿacob Kanievsky, *Qarayna deigreta* (Jerusalem, 1990), 3: 40, 191; Moshe Scherer, *Bi-Shtei ʿEinayim* (New York, 1988), p. 275.

5. Rashid Rida, *Tafsir al-Manar* (Cairo, 1906–34), to Qurʾan V, 44–48.

6. Maulana Maududi, *Islam and Jahiliyya* (Lahore, 1939); Sayyid Qutb, *Maʿalim*

fi-l-Tariq (Cairo, 1964); Muhammad Mahdi Shams al-Din, *Bayna-l-Jahiliyya wa-l-Islam* (Beirut, 1975).

7. 'Ali Belhadj, *Ghurbat al-Islam al-Haditha*, audiocassette no. 11; Ra'id Salah, mayor of Umm al-Fahm, Israel, *Fada'il al-Quds*, audiocassette; 'Ali Khamenei, Friday sermon in Keyhan (Tehran), 3 November 1982; Shaykh Yazdi, sermon in *Ettela'at*, 10 January 1981.

8. Luigi Giussani, *Le mouvement communion et libération* (Paris, 1988), pp. 15 ff., 82; Luigi Amicone, *In nome del niente* (Milan, 1982), p. 21. Sadr articles, in *Al-Adwa'* (Iraq, 1958–59). Cf. also Abd al-Salam Yasin, *La révolution à l'heure de l'Islam* (Paris, 1981); Wa'il 'Uthman, *Hizb Allah fi Muwajahat Hizb al-Shaytan* (Cairo, 1976).

9. E.g., Muhammad Husayn Fadlallah, *Al-Islam wa-Mantiq al-Quwwa* (Beirut, 1976); and *Qadiyat al-'Izz wa-l-Dhull fi-l-Islam* (Beirut, 1979).

10. Selection of speeches and articles from this period in Marcel Lefebvre, *Un évêque parle* (Jarze, 1974),vol. 1; and *La Fraternité St. Pie X: Une oeuvre d'église* (Martigny, 1982).

11. Frances Fitzgerald, "A Disciplined, Charging Army," *New Yorker*, 18 May 1972, esp. p. 64; Tim LaHaye, *The Battle for the Mind* (Old Tappan, N.J., 1980); Steve Bruce, *The Rise and Fall of the New Christian Right* (Oxford, 1988), p. 77; Hal Lindsey, *The Late Great Planet Earth* (New York, 1973), pp. 38, 91, 171; Gary North, *Unconditional Surrender* (Tyler, Tex., 1988), pp. 182, 213, 228–29.

12. Fitzgerald, "Disciplined, Changing Army," pp. 70, 73, 108, 110; H. Rodeheaver and B. P. Ackley, eds., *Great Revival Hymns* (New York, 1911), hymn by E. T. Cassel; Mary Beth McGuire, *Pentecostal Catholics* (Philadelphia, 1982), pp. 190, 56–58, 89, 91; North, *Unconditional Surrender*, pp. 103, 112, 122. For Catholic theologians: Henri de Lubac, *Le mystére du surnaturel* (Paris, 1965); Hans Urs von Balthasar, *Cordula ou l'épreuve décisive* (Paris, 1968); Luigi Giussani, *Il senso religioso* (Milan, 1968).

13. Shmuel Cohen, ed., *Pe'er ha-Dor* (B'nai B'rak, 1973), 2: 291; interview with a yeshiva student in *'Emda* (June 1987); *Ha-Modi'a*, 17 January 1990.

14. Yisrael Eichler in *Ha-Mahane ha-Haredi*, 10 January 1990.

15. Hazon Ish, *Igrot*, 1: 111, 125; Eliezer Menachem Schach, *Mikhtavim u-Ma'marim* (B'nai B'rak, 1986), 2: 4, 12, 41–42, 84; Elhanan Wasserman, *Iqveta di-Meshiha*, 2d ed. (B'nai B'rak, 1969), pp. 40, 145, 150; Yoel Teitelbaum, *Divrei Yoel* (New York, 1980), p. 91; M. al-Hakim, *Thawrat al-Husayn* (Tehran, 1982); Raghib Harb, *Al-Minbar al-Muqawim* (Beirut, 1986).

16. Birnbaum, *'Am ha-Shem*, p. 127; Jalal Al-e Ahmad, *Gharbzadagi* (Tehran, 1962); Moshe Feinstein, *Bastion of the Faith* (New York, 1973), p. 250; George M. Marsden, *Fundamentalism and American Culture* (New York, 1980), p. 219; LaHaye, *Battle for the Mind*, p. 64 ff.; Marcel Lefebvre, *Ils l'ont découronné* (Escurolles, 1987), p. 235.

17. *Be-'Ein Hazon*, pp. 93, 65. Cf. Natan Wolpin, ed., *Seasons of the Soul* (New York, 1983).

18. Kol Yisrael (Aguda, Jerusalem), 17 July 1930; Agudat Yisrael, *The Struggle and the Splendour* (New York, 1982), chap. 1; Moshe Scherer in *Jewish Week*, 28 July 1970; Hazon Ish, *Igrot*, 1: 31, 43, 111; Moshe Scheinfeld in *Diglenu*, August 1974.

19. Marsden, *Reforming Fundamentalism*, p. 162; LaHaye, *Battle for the Mind*.

20. Nancy T. Ammerman, *Bible Believers* (New Brunswick, N.J., 1987), p. 62. On *idtirab* (confusion), see Bassam Jarrar (Hamas), *Al-Sakina*, audiocassette; Shaykh Kishk, *Sermons*, audiocassettes nos. 206, 419; ʿAli Sorush, *Danesh va Arzesh* (Tehran, 1979).

21. Birnbaum, ʿ*Am ha-Shem*, p. 131. Cf. Scheinfeld in *Diglenu*, October 1958.

22. Mary Douglas, *Cultural Bias* (London, 1978); idem, ed., *Essays in the Sociology of Perception* (London, 1982); Mary Douglas and Aron Wildavsky, *Risk and Culture* (Berkeley, 1982); Mary Douglas, *How Institutions Think* (Syracuse, N.Y., 1986); Michael Schwarz and Michael Thompson, *Divided We Stand* (London, 1990); Michael Thompson, Aron Wildavsky, and Richard Ellis, *Cultural Theory* (Boulder, Colo., 1990); Mary Douglas, *In the Wilderness* (Sheffield, 1993).

23. In the jargon of cultural theory, the enclave is low grid/high group.

24. For example, Marsden, *Reforming Fundamentalism*, p. 241; Lindsey, *Late Great Planet Earth*, pp. 163, 174; North, *Unconditional Surrender*, pp. 287, 329.

25. For example, Reuven Grusovsky, *Baʿyot ha-Zeman* (B'nai B'rak, 1960), pp. 10, 17, 20–21, 41; Kanievsky, *Qarayna de-Igreta*; Scherer, *Bi-Shei 'Einayim*, pp. 109, 246; Schach, *Mikhtavin u-Maʿmarim*; *Milhamta shel Torah* (B'nai B'rak, 1977); *Kovetz mikhtavim . . . meʾt Rabotenu* (B'nai B'rak, 1975).

26. Or *yereʾim* (those afraid of God). Other significant synonyms: *shomrei Torah, sridei helqa tovah*.

27. Synonyms (mostly Qurʾanic): *mutakhadhilun, mutdahadun, mahrumun, mazlumun*. These terms were given a Fanon-inspired, Third World twist by ʿAli Shariʿati (d. 1977). See the concept *mardon e-khofteh* (oppressed people), as in a sermon reproduced in *Ettelaʿat* (Tehran), 10 January 1981; ʿAli Belhadj, audiocassettes nos. 10, 2, 7. For examples of usage by Sunnis, see Yasin, *La révolution à l'heure de l'Islam*. Cf. Said Amir Arjomand, *The Turban for the Crown* (New York: Oxford University Press, 1988), p. 136.

28. In Islamic Republican Party organ *Jomhuri-e Eslami*.

29. Ammerman, *Bible Believers*. For the less common terms, see King, "Bob Jones University," p. 54; North, *Unconditional Surrender*, pp. 315, 336.

30. Hazon Ish, *Igrot*, 1: 109, 111, 2: 80.

31. In the Islamic case: *murtaddun* (apostates), *zandaqa, mushrikun* (polytheists), *taghut* (false god), *firʾawn* (pharaoh), *yazid* (Shiʿite term for oppressor); the Sunni equivalent, *nimrud*. In the Jewish case: *Qaraʾim* (Qaraʾites), *Shabtaʾim* (Shabbateans), *Knaʾanim* (Canaanites), *soneʾi Yisrael* (enemies of the Jews), *rodfim* (persecutors).

32. For the same reason, tradition-specific vituperative terms, such as the Christian "religion of the beast" and "allies of Antichrist," are best consigned to a footnote. This is usually a Christian metaphor (King, "Bob Jones University," p. 56). Muslims prefer *muʾamara* or *taʾamuriyya*, and the Jews, *horshei mezimot*.

33. Lefebvre, *Ils l'ont déc.ouronné*, p. 217; cf. Muhammad ʿAta, *Sifat al-Nifaq* (Beirut, 1985).

34. We do not deal here with the few cases where the enemy is an infidel affiliated with another, long-established tradition (e.g., in Gaza and the West Bank, in Afghanistan). On the conspiratorial vision in Iran, see Ervand Abrahamian, *Khomeinism* (Berkeley, 1993), chap. 5; cf. ʿAli Belhadj, audiocassettes, nos. 40, 41.

35. Ahmad Fardid seems to be the thinker who coined *khod-bonyadi;* cf. Birnbaum, *'Am ha-Shem,* p. 242 ff.; LaHaye, *Battle for the Mind,* p. 117 ff.; Ammerman, *Bible Believers,* p. 135; *Ettela'at* (Tehran), 11 October 1980; 28 February 1981; 21 October 1981 (on hypocrites).

36. Toshihiko Isutsu, *Ethico-Religious Concepts in the Koran* (Montreal, 1966); North, *Unconditional Surrender,* pp. 131, 255, 287; Lindsey, *Late Great Planet Earth,* pp. 170–72; *Kovetz mikhtavim,* introduction; Wasserman, *Iqveta di-Meshiha;* Birnbaum, *'Am ha-Shem;* Yoshor, *Hafetz Hayyim,* p. 11; 'Ali Belhadj, audiocassette no. 5; N. Yagen, *Ason ha-Me'a,* audiocassette.

37. A competing (but not dominant) infidel community, such as the Copts in Egypt, may also help set up the boundary; so do old-type heresies from within the tradition (e.g., the Ahmadiyya in India and Pakistan, the Baha'is in Iran).

38. Only among Protestant Reconstructionists does the term *white* also have a racial connotation, i.e., Caucasian.

39. Hazon Ish *Igrot,* 1: 43, 113. *Neliza,* a geometric term, is borrowed from Maimonides and given a theological twist.

40. In the United States, outreach activity is called by the ultra-Orthodox "klal work."

41. Yoshor, *Hafetz Hayyim,* p. 591; King, "Bob Jones University," p. 52; George M. Marsden, "Unity and Diversity in the Evangelical Resurgence," in David W. Lotz, ed., *Altered Landscapes: Christianity in America, 1935–1985* (Grand Rapids, Mich., 1989), pp. 66–69.

42. Kanievsky, *Qarayna de-Igreta,* 1: 125–26; Cohen, *Pe'er ha-Dor,* 1: 128, 2: 246 ff.; *Be-'Ein Hazon,* pp. 65, 93–94; Hazon Ish, *Igrot,* 1: 36, 102, 108.

43. Cohen, *Pe'er ha-Dor,* 4: 245–47; Grusovsky, *Ba'yot ha-Zeman,* pp. 26–36; Moshe Scheinfeld, *Beyn Medinat Yisrael ve-'Am Yisrael* (B'nai B'rak, 1975), esp. articles from 1951, 1952, 1964. The most militant haredim, the Toldot Aharon yeshiva, have this slogan: "May the State of Israel perish but so that no Jew is harmed."

44. The best expression is Rabbi E. M. Schach's televised sermon of 26 March 1990. But see already in Hazon Ish, *Yoreh De'ah* (Jerusalem, 1951), chaps. 2, 5, 16, 25; and Yequtiel Yehuda Halbestamm in *Diglenu* (March 1960). The greater the integration of the haredim into Israeli politics, the stronger this trend. See also the jocular cassettes of Rabbi Shabtai Yudelevitch (on tape) poking fun at secularist "bestiality."

45. Cf. Gideon Aran, "Jewish Zionist Fundamentalism: The Bloc of the Faithful in Israel (Gush Emunim)," in Martin E. Marty and R. Scott Appleby, eds., *Fundamentalisms Observed* (Chicago, 1991), pp. 265–344; Teitelbaum, *Divrei Yoel.*

46. Salman Rushdie, *In Good Faith* (London, 1990).

47. Sati' al-Husri, *Ara' wa-Ahadith fi-l Wataniyya wa-l-Qawmiyya* (Beirut, 1944); Sayyid Qutb in *Al-Risala,* 5 January 1953, p. 16; idem, *Ma'alim fi-l-Tariq,* pp. 30–31, 194–97; Muhammad al-Ghazali, *Haqiqat al-Qawmiyya* (Beirut, 1961); Salah Jawhar, *Al-Mawta Yatakalamun* (Cairo, 1977), pp. 33–38, 86–87, 129, 135. Cf. Yann Richard, "Du nationalisme à l'islamisme," in *Le fait ethnique en Iran et en Afghanistan* (Paris, 1988), p. 267 ff.

48. Scheinfeld, *Beyn Medinat Yisrael;* Grusovsky, *Ba'yot ha-Zeman,* pp. 7–11, 46–47.

49. Muhammad al-Sawwaf, *Al-Mukhattat al-Istiʿmariyya* (Beirut, 1979); Fathi Yakan, *Mushkilat al-Daʿwa wa-l-Daʿiya* (Beirut, 1967); Anwar al-Jundi, *Sukut al-ʿIl-maniyya* (Beirut, 1973); ʿAli Jarisha, *Shariʿat Allah Hadima* (Cairo, 1973); Muhammad al-Bahi, *Mustaqbal al-Islam* (Cairo, 1978); Yusuf al-Qardawi, *Al-Hall al-Islami* (Cairo, 1974); Muhammad Mahdi Shams al-Din, *Al-Ilmaniyya* (Beirut, 1980); Muhammad Dandawi, *Kubra a-Haraqat al-Islamiyya* (Tunis, 1978); Rashid Ghannushi, *Maqalat* (Paris, 1984).

50. Qutb, *Maʾalim fi-l-Tariq*; Saʿid Hawwa, *Durus fi-l-Amal-Islami* (Amman, 1981); idem, *Min Ajl Khutwa ila-l-Amam* (Beirut, 1979); ʿAli Uways, *Al-Muslimun fi-Maʿrakat al-Baqa* (Cairo, 1979). For the neo-Hanbali doctrine, see Ibn Taymiyya, *Fatawa* (Cairo, 1909), 4: 198, 280–81.

51. Muhammad ʿImara, ed., *Al-Farida al-Ghaʾiba* (Cairo, 1982); Abdallah Abu-l-Khayr, *Dhikriyati maʿa Jamaʿat al-Muslimin* (Kuwait, 1980); Hassan Hassan, *Muwaja-hat al-Fikr al-Mutatrif* (Cairo, 1978); *Bayan al-Thawra al- Islamiyya fi Suriya* (Damascus, 1980). Note that radical Jewish fundamentalists do not envisage the use of violence against lapsed coreligionists, perhaps due to a Diasporic tradition where Jews did not control tools of violence. The lapsed are to be excommunicated.

52. Cf. Michael Cook, "Ibn Hanbal and al-Amr bi-l-Maʾruf," paper presented to the fifth colloquium, "From Jahiliʾyya to Islam," Jerusalem, July 1990. In revolutionary Iran this precept would be given an institutional embodiment in Bonyad-e Monkarat, a sort of morality militia.

53. Cf. Mumtaz Ahmad, "Islamic Fundamentalism in South Asia: The Jamaʿat-i-Islami and the Tablighi Jamaat of South Asia," in Marty and Appleby, *Fundamentalisms Observed*, pp. 457–530.

54. This is based, in Judaism, upon the adage "mitoch she-lo li-shma baʾli-shma."

55. In the words of the Satmar rabbi (Yoel Teitelbaum) in *Der Yid* (New York), 5 Av 5681/1981.

56. The second scenario is envisaged, only by Islamic radicals; their Jewish counterparts do not expect to have political power before the advent of the Messiah.

57. Editorials in *Yated Neʾeman, Ha-Modiʿa, Ha-Mahane ha-Haredi*; Schach, *Mikhtavim u-Maʾmarim*.

58. Jerry Falwell, *Listen America!* (Garden City, N.Y., 1980), pp. 6, 18–19, 205; Pat Robertson, *America's Dates with Destiny* (Nashville, 1986), p. 191 ff.; Frances Fitzgerald, *The Battle for the Public Schools* (Old Tappan, N.J., 1980), p. 72 ff.; Lindsey, *Late Great Planet Earth*, pp. 150, 171, 173; Marsden, *Reforming Fundamentalism*, pp. 96–98, 125–27, 173.

59. Luigi Giussani, *Communion et Libération* (Paris, 1988). But perhaps not Communists; see Lefebvre, *Ils l'ont découronné*, p. 235.

60. Fitzgerald, "Disciplined, Changing Army," pp. 78, 107; Falwell, *Listen America!*; Ammerman, *Bible Believers*, p. 199 ff.

61. Cf. the title "Soldiers of the House of David" for Lubavitcher militants.

62. This cluster of ideas, which hark back to the church fathers, was developed in a full-fledged manner in the early nineteenth century by E. Irving in Scotland, then by John Nelson Darby in Ireland.

63. Could this defeatism be the case, implicitly, with separatists of the Bob

Jones hue? It is certainly not the case for the reconstructionists (see North, *Unconditional Surrender*, pp. 120, 370, 374).

64. A. C. Gabelein, "The Present Day Apostasy," *The Coming and the Kingdom of Christ* (Chicago, 1914), p. 154. Cf. Lindsey, *Late Great Planet Earth*, pp. 119, 171.

65. Orah hayyim is also the name of one of the four parts of the Shulkhan 'Arukh, the authoritative halakhic compendium (dating from the sixteenth century).

66. See Haym Soloveitchik, "The New Role of Texts in the Haredi World," in Martin E. Marty and R. Scott Appleby, eds., *Accounting for Fundamentalisms* (Chicago, 1993); and P. Connerton, *How Societies Remember* (Cambridge, University Press, 1990).

67. For the haredim the major text is the Babylonian Talmud (500 c.e.) and its commentaries. For the Muslims it is the Qur'an (and to a lesser extent, the hadith, or oral tradition; shar'i treatises are more rarely used).

68. Or rock's local equivalent, such as the *rai* in Algeria, a hodge-podge of rock and Maghrebi folk chants; town councils taken over by the Front Islamique du Salut in the June 1990 elections in effect hastened to ban rai. An exception is Communione e Liberazione, which has ample recourse to gospel and jazz music (but not to rock).

69. Cf. Yusuf al-Qardawi, *Fatawa Mu'asira* (Qatar, 1984); 'Abdallah 'Ulwan, *Hukm al-Islam fi Wasa'il al-I'lam* (Hama, 1978); 'Ali Jarisha, '*Indama Yahkumu al-Islam* (Cairo, 1975); Ahmad 'Abduh, *Wad' al-Riba* (Cairo, 1977); Muhammad 'A. Khamis, *Al-Mar'a bi-l-Taswwur al-Islami* (Cairo, 1975).

70. Shlomo Min ha-Har, *Shi'urei ha-Torah* (Jerusalem, 1966); Hazon Ish, *Igrot*, 1: 115, 2: 47; Kanievsky, *Qarayna de-Igreta*, 1: 129–31, 182, 2: 10, 95; Shlomo Elberg, "Bnai Brakism," *Ha-Pardes* 38 no.3 (December 1963); M. Schöenfeld, ed., *Yalqut Da'at Torah* (Tel Aviv, 1962); editorial in *Jewish Observer*, October 1990.

71. 'Abdallah Abu-l-Khayr, *Dhikriyati ma'a Jama'at al-Muslimin* (Kuwait, 1982); Hassan, *Muwajahat al-Fikr al-Mutatarif*.

72. Hazon Ish, *Igrot*, 2: 82–83. The letter was written in Lithuania, but he did not change his prescription when he moved to Palestine three years later.

73. See my "Islamic Resurgence: Civil Society Strikes Back," *Journal of Contemporary History* 25 (June 1990): 353–364; "The Islamic Republic of Egypt," *Orbis* 31 (spring 1987): 43–53.

74. Ammerman, *Bible Believers*; King, "Bob Jones University"; Fitzgerald, "Disciplined, Charging Army."

75. 'Ali Jarisha, *Din wa-Dawla* (Cairo, 1979); Qardawi, *Fatawa Mu'asira*; *Al-Liwa al Islami* (Cairo), 17 June 1982; *Mayo* (Cairo), 24 December 1982; *Al-Siyasa* (Kuwait), 27 October 1979.

76. Muhammad Husayn Fadlallah, *Mafahim Islamiyya* (Beirut, 1982), 2: 54–56, 74–75, 77.

77. E.g., Moshe Feinstein, *Igrot Moshe: Yoreh De'ah*, 2 vols. (New York, 1973).

78. Ammerman, *Bible Believers*, p. 132.

79. Ammerman, *Bible Believers*, p. 135; North, *Unconditional Surrender*, p. 193.

80. Yoshor, *Hafetz Hayyim*, pp. 426–27; Cohen, *Pe'er ha-Dor*, 2: 113 (Hazon Ish: "The yeshivas are the deserts and caves of our times"); Kanievsky, *Qarayna de-Igreta*, 1: 37, 67, 2: 12–13. Dietary law also creates a market relationship, consolidating that of residence, marriage, and social control (by gossip, street posters).

81. McGuire, *Pentecostal Catholics*, chap. 8.

82. For such a model in other social contexts, see Gerald Mars, "Hidden Hierarchies in Israeli Kibbutzim," in James Flanagan and Steve Rayner, eds., *Rules, Decisions, and Inequality in Egalitarian Societies* (Aldershot, 1988), p. 98 ff.; and Rayner's own essay in the same volume.

83. Cohen, *Pe'er ha-Dor*, 4: 240 n. 15; Hazon Ish, *Igrot*, 1: 109–11; Baruch Hirsch in *Yated Ne'eman*, 15 July 1990; Moshe Gifter, *Pirkei Emuna* (Jerusalem, 1969). For the Muslim formula, see sermons of Shaykh Kishk, audiocassettes nos. 206, 386, 418, 425; ʿAli Belhadj, audiocassettes nos. 2, 35, 43.

84. Marcel Lefebvre, *J'accuse le concile* (Martigues, 1976).

85. Lindsey and North are typical of this approach.

86. Tractate Sota.

87. Typical of this approach are Tim LaHaye, Luigi Giussani, Ahmad Fardid, Abd al-Salam Yasin, Shmuel Rafael Hirsch, and Yaʿakov Rosenheim. The major organ of this persuasion in Catholicism is *L'ANTI-89*, published by pro-Lefebvrists.

88. Ammerman, *Bible Believers*, chap. 8; Jeffrey K. Hadden and Anson Shupe, *Televangelism: Power and Politics in God's Frontier* (New York, 1988), pp. 99–105; Razelle Frankl, *Televangelism* (Carbondale, Ill., 1987), pp. 99, 114.

89. Yaʿakov Katz, *Halakha ve-Kabbalah* (Jerusalem, 1986), pp. 226–29.

90. North, *Unconditional Surrender*, pp. 307, 325, 354, 367, 385.

91. Cf. Wasserman, *Iqveta di-Meshiha*.

92. See the sermon appended to *Be-'Ein Hazon*, pp. 97–104. Cf. Schach, *Mikhtavim u-Ma'amarim*, 1: 41, 86.

93. See Hussein Ahmad Amin's article on radical scenarios for the future, *Al-Musawwar*, 26 September 1986.

94. Peter Von Sivers, "The Realm of Justice," *Humaniora Islamica* 1 (1973).

95. Muhammad Amin al-Alim, *Dirasat fi-l-Islam* (Beirut, 1981). Some messianic rhetoric can be detected among Hamas in Gaza and in the Front Islamique du Salut in Algeria as evidenced by audiocassettes (Shaykh Asʿad al-Tamimi, Bassam Jarrar, ʿAli Belhadj). The same was true of the Abu Kurus messianic Sufi order active in Nimeiri's Sudan (1983).

96. Ethan Kohlberg, "From Imamiya to Ithna-Ashariyya," *Bulletin of the School of Oriental and African Studies* (1975): 521 ff.; Abdulaziz A. Sachedina, *Islamic Messianism* (Albany, 1981). An eschatological format is, for instance, absent from Shiʿite writings in Baghdad at the time of the fall of the Abbasid caliphate (1258 C.E.), where one would have expected it to surface (Muhammad Kashif al-Ghita', *Asl al-Shiʿa wa-Usuliha*, 10th ed. [Beirut, 1958], p. 128). A good summary of the Sunni position is Shaykh Kishk's audiocassette *Al-Mahdi al Muntazar*.

97. Lindsey, *Late Great Planet Earth*, pp. 52–57; cf. Cohen, *Pe'er ha-Dor*, 2: 121–22.

98. Schach, *Mikhtavin u-Ma'marim*, 1: 13–15, 33.

99. Interview with yeshiva student in *ʿEmda*, June 1987; polemic against such views in Scheinfeld, *Beyn Medinat Yisrael*, p. 22 ff. The Gulf War (1991) saw a surge of messianism not only among Sunnis but also among haredim; see Rabbi Moshe Hayyim Sofer, audiocassette on the lessons of this war.

100. Susan Harding, "Imagining the Last Days: The Politics of Apocalyptic Lan-

guage," in Marty and Appleby, eds., *Accounting for Fundamentalisms*, pp. 57–78. Cf. S. Abruzzesse, *Communione e Liberazione* (Paris, 1990).

101. This space is not too imaginary. These churches constitute a loose network bound by doctrine, information exchange, and educational material dispatched from Falwell's headquarters. The network also influences the selection of pastors by providing an approved list of candidates.

102. Shaykh Salomeh, in interview with the author (Cairo, June 1987).

103. *Al-Mukhtar al-Islami* (Cairo), September–October 1985, pp. 37–38; *Al-I'tisam* (Cairo), April–May 1986, pp. 10–12. So is Egypt for preachers (on tape) such as Kishk, Ahmad al-Mahalawi, Muhammad Hassan, Walid Ghunayim, and Hassan Ayyub.

104. Richard, "Du nationalisme à l'islamisme."

105. Hizbullah, *Risala Maftuha*, 16 February 1986; *Al-Safir* (Beirut), 17 February 1986; *Al-Siyasa* (Kuwait), 26 March 1986. Cf. *Al-Anba* (Kuwait), 4 March 1987; Muhammad Husayn Fadlallah's article in *Al-Muntalaq* (Beirut), October 1986.

106. Lindsey, *Late Great Planet Earth*, chaps. 5–6; North, *Unconditional Surrender*, pp. 121, 370, 384.

107. Haggai Segal, *Ahim Yekarim* (Jerusalem, 1987); Gideon Aran, "Eretz Yisrael: Between Politics and Religion," Jerusalem, Institute for Israel Studies, no. 18 (1985).

108. Rene Girard, *La violence et le sacré* (Paris, 1972).

109. See "The Sanctity of Jerusalem," in my *Interpretations of Islam* (Princeton, 1985).

110. Hamas Covenant (in Arabic), December 1988, articles 11, 31; *Al-Dustur* (Amman), 2 November 1988; 'Abdallah 'Azzam, *Al-Difa' 'an Aradi al-Muslimin ahamm Fara'id al-A'yan* (Jedda, 1987), pp. 29–49. At times there is even an apocalyptic undertone to the argument: As'ad al-Tamimi, *Zawal Isra'il Hatmiyya Qur'aniyya* (Cairo, 1982).

111. Yoshor, *Hafetz Hayyim*, p. 525. Cf. Hafetz Haim, *Yalqut Meshalim*. A similar argument in an audiocassette by the Palestinian 'Abdallah 'Azzam, *Al-Hubb fi Allah*; and in 'Ali Belhadj audiocassettes nos. 6, 12, 27, 46. This is a recurrent theme among haredi preachers (on tape) such as Shabtai Yudelevitch, David Sicherman, Yoel Schwarz, and Mordechai Neugerschal.

112. McGuire, *Pentecostal Catholics*, pp. 30, 87–89, 103, 111, 169 ff.; North, *Unconditional Surrender*, pp. 166, 239, 255, 382; Falwell, *Listen America!*, pp. 12–16. Shaykh Kishk thundered in October 1992 that the Cairo earthquake was an omen of God's wrath about Egypt's sins (audiocassette, *al-Zilzal*). Note the argument made by Rafsanjani after the Iranian earthquake (sermon, Radio Tehran, 29 June 1990).

113. *Toda'a-'Alon le-Shabbat Qodesh*, 2 November 1990; *Le Monde*, 3 November 1990. Cf. Eliyahu Dessler, *Mikhtav me-Eliyahu*, 2d ed. (Jerusalem, 1963), 1: 183, 278; Frances Fitzgerald, "Jim and Tammy," *New Yorker*, 23 April 1990, pp. 45–47. This correlation is likewise a frequently invoked argument in audiocassettes of haredi preachers like Nissim Yagen, Emmanuel Tehila, Amnon Yitzhak, Reuven Elbaz, and Mordechai Iffargan. Gush Emunim rabbis argued in fall and winter 1993 that the recent rise in road accidents in Israel was the upshot of the "defeatist" Israel-PLO agreement.

114. Scherer, *Bi-Shtei 'Einayim,* pp. 246–49; Abraham Wolf, *Ha-Tequfa Ba'yoteha* (B'nai B'rak, 1965), pp. 90–101; Abraham Diskin in *Diglenu,* May–June 1990.

115. Tanzim al-Jihad's mentor is 'Abd al-Salam Faraj, mentioned above.

116. Two of the most prominent authorities, the Hazon Ish and the Rabbi of Brisk, never took part.

117. Yeshayhu Tuviya Director, *Da'at Torah* (New York, 1983), 2: 30, 4: 20–27, 58–65; Nissim Yagen, audiocassette, *Da'at Torah.*

118. Local notables and wealthy individuals, as distinct from the masses *(ha-moyn).*

119. Dessler, *Mikhtav me-Eliyahu,* 1: 75–77. Cf. Yoshor, *Hafetz Hayyim,* p. 685.

120. Menachem Friedman, "The Haredim and the Holocaust," *Jerusalem Quarterly* 53 (1990): 86–114. See Frances Fitzgerald's remarks in "Jim and Tammy" on how difficult it was for Bakker's groupies to acknowledge Bakker's guilt.

121. See the memoirs of Shlomo Lorincz in *Diglenu,* October, November 1990.

122. Khomeini, *Al-Hukuma al-Islamiyya* (Najaf, 1971; Arabic ed., Beirut, 1979). See the special issue on his thought, *Al-Tawhid* (Beirut) 47 (July 1990): 21–34, 59–68, 98–107.

123. *Kayhan al-'Arabi,* 16 January 1988. Due to the lower stature of his successor, Khamenei, this doctrine (which had never been implemented by Khomeini) has been held in abeyance till now. Cf. *Keyhan* (Tehran), 24 November 1990; *Resalat* (Tehran), 31 May 1990.

124. *Al-Safir* (Beirut), 17 April 1986; *Al-Siyasa* (Kuwait), 26 March 1986; Muhammad Baqir al-Sadr, *Lumha Tamhidiyya* (Beirut, 1979); Muhsin al-Hakim, *Bayan bi-Munasabat Khulul Muharram* (Tehran, 1982). Note that the Lebanese "council" was not supposed to be subject to Khomeini's authority and its mentor, Fadlallah, was rather linked with the marja' Kho'i in Najaf. After the latter's death, Fadlallah declared that this post can no more be filled by feeble nonagenarians, for it requires an activist political acumen.

125. *Kayhan al-'Arabi,* 29 July 1989, 23 September 1989. Cf. Abrahamian, *Khomeinism,* epilogue. The family-planning campaign launched in October 1991 is an example of an innovation launched after Khomeini's death.

126. Aviezer Ravitzky, "The Contemporary Lubavitch Hasidic Movement: Between Conservatism and Messianism," in Marty and Appleby, *Accounting for Fundamentalisms,* pp. 303–327.

127. Ammerman, *Bible Believers,* chap. 7; idem, *Baptist Battles* (1990), p. 171. Cf. Luigi Giussani's interview on the importance of charisma in *Trente jours dans l'église et dans le monde* (1987), p. 8.

128. See the writings of a Syrian radical, 'Abdallah 'Ulwan, *Warathat al- Anbiya'* (Beirut, 1983).

129. With a few notable exceptions: Shaykhs Abbasi Madani and 'Ali Belhadj in Algeria; Sa'id Sha'ban in Lebanon; 'Umar 'Abd al-Rahman in Egypt; Sa'id Hawwa in Syria.

130. Notable cases: Shukri Mustafa, 'Abd al-Salam Faraj in Egypt; Shaykh Ahmed Yassin in Gaza; Marwan Hadid in Syria.

131. Haredim refer to the Israelites grumbling or revolting against Moses (a classic case of charismatic leadership), especially Deuteronomy 1: 27 and Numbers 16: 3. Sunnis and Shi'ites speak, inter alia, of munafiqun (see above).

132. Hafetz Haim, *Shmirat ha-Lashon* (Warsaw, 1914); *Hovat ha-Shmira* (Warsaw, 1921).

133. In the jargon of cultural theory, high grid/low group. The enclave is low grid/high group. The relationship between these two is dubbed "negative diagonal." The best descriptions of fundamentalist groups in terms of empowerment can be found in Ammerman, *Bible Believers*, chap. 11; Abbruzzesse, *Communione e Liberazione*, chaps. 3–4.

134. E.g., Falwell, *Listen America!* p. 12 ff.; Giussani, *Il senso religioso*. (Giussani is here, as on other issues, largely indebted to the thought of Cardinal Joseph Ratzinger.) The jamaʿat argument can be read in almost any monthly issue of the Egyptian *Al-Iʿtisam* and *Al-Mukhtar al-Islami*. Even among Pentecostalists the right to individual interpretation is never pushed to an extreme (low group/low grid). Groups maintain a common manner of interpretation, preferring *gemeinschaft* over individualism.

135. Amicone, *In nome del niente*, pp. 74–75; Abruzzesse, *Communione e Liberazione*, p. 169 ff. This is not to underestimate the tangible services rendered by Communione e Liberazione to its supporters (employment in its cooperatives, student canteen, help for students in their studies, etc.). Yet the most crucial dependency link is in the realm of group solidarity. The same is true of Muslim student jamaʿat, and to a lesser extent (because the material dependency is bigger, especially for yeshiva students who are married with children) with regard to haredim.

136. ʿAli Belhadj, audiocassette no. 43; his four-part cassette series *Silsilat al-Jihad*; and the seven-part cassette series *Al-Amr bi-l-Maʿruf wa-l-Nahy ʿani-l-Munkar*.

Chapter 2

1. Tu Wei-Ming, "Confucian Revival in East Asia," in Martin E. Marty and R. Scott Appleby, *Fundamentalisms Observed* (Chicago, 1991), p. 802.

2. Winston Davis, "Fundamentalism in Japan: Religious and Political," in Marty and Appleby, eds. *Fundamentalisms Observed*, chapter 14; Helen Hardacre, "The New Religions, Family, and Society in Japan, " in Martin E. Marty and R. Scott Appleby, eds., *Fundamentalisms and Society: Reclaiming the Family, Education and the Sciences* (Chicago, 1993).

3. Ehud Sprinzak, "The Great Superterrorism Scare," *Foreign Policy* 113 (fall 1998): 113, 115. By contrast, the exceedingly brutal violence perpetrated by the Armed Islamic Group (GIA) and other extremist groups in Algeria in 1997 and 1998 seemed to be an expression of rage and frustration alone. Roger Cohen, "Algeria Killings: Brutal Ritual Defies Logic," *New York Times*, January 9, 1998, A1, A3.

4. The literature on social protest movements, and the ways in which fundamentalisms both typify and modify the received definition of such movements, is discussed in Rhys H. Williams, "Movement Dynamics and Social Change: Transforming Fundamentalist Ideology and Organizations," in Martin E. Marty and R. Scott Appleby, *Accounting for Fundamentalisms: The Dynamic Character of Movements* (Chicago, 1994), pp. 785–825.

5. Richard T. Hughes, "Introduction: On Recovering the Theme of Recovery," in Richard T. Hughes, ed., *The American Quest for the Primitive Church* (Urbana, Ill., 1988), p. 3.

Chapter 3

1. Ernst Mayr, "Darwin's Impact on Modern Thought," *Proceedings of The American Philosophical Society* 139, no. 4 (1995): 317 ff. See also, Ernst Mayr, *This Is Biology* (Cambridge, Mass., 1997), chapter 2, and passim; Karl Popper, *Objective Knowledge: An Evolutionary Approach* (Oxford, 1972), p. 210 ff.; Abraham Kaplan, *The Conduct of Inquiry* (San Francisco, 1964).

2. Arend Lijphart, "Comparative Politics and the Comparative Method," *American Political Science Review* 65 (September 1971): 3; David Collier, "The Comparative Method," in Ada Finifter, ed., *Political Science: The State of the Discipline* (Washington, D.C., 1993), p. 112.

3. Alexander George and Timothy McKeown, "Case Studies and Theories of Organizational Decision-Making" in *Advances in Information Processes in Organizations,* 2: 21–58. See also Harry Eckstein, "Case Study and Theory in Political Science," in *Regarding Politics* (Berkeley, 1992).

4. David Collier quotes these observations from a personal communication from Adam Przeworski ("The Comparative Method," p. 112).

5. For a discussion of causation as it is defined in the philosophy of science, see Richard Taylor, "Causation," *The Encyclopedia of Philosophy* (New York, 1967), 2: 56 ff.

6. See the essays in part 3, "Education and Media," of Martin E. Marty and R. Scott Appleby, eds., *Fundamentalisms and Society: Reclaiming the Sciences, the Family and Education* (Chicago: Chicago University Press, 1993): Majid Tehranian, "Fundamentalist Impact on Education and the Media," pp. 313–40; Majid Tehranian, "Islamic Fundamentalism in Iran and the Discourse of Development," pp. 341–73; Michael Rosenak, "Jewish Fundamentalism in Israeli Education," pp. 374–414; Susan Rose and Quentin Schultze, "The Evangelical Awakening in Guatemala: Fundamentalist Impact on Education and Media," pp. 415–51; Susan Rose, "Christian Fundamentalism and Education in the United States," pp. 452–89; Quentin Schultze, "The Two Faces of Fundamentalist Higher Education," pp. 490–535; Krishna Kumar, "Hindu Revivalism and Education in North-Central India," pp. 536–57.

7. Chadwick F. Alger, "Transnational Social Movements, World Politics, and Global Governance," in Jackie Smith, Charles Chatfield, and Ron Pagnucco, eds., *Transnational Social Movements and Global Politics: Solidarity Beyond the State* (Syracuse, N.Y., 1997), pp. 260–78; David Held, Anthony McGrew, David Goldblatt, and Jonathan Perraton, *Global Transformations: Politics, Economics and Culture* (Stanford, Calif, 1999), pp. 327–75.

8. Kenneth L. Grasso, "Beyond Liberalism: Human Dignity, the Free Society, and the Second Vatican Council," in Kenneth L. Grasso, Gerard V. Bradley, and Robert P. Hunt, *Catholicism, Liberalism and Communitarianism: The Catholic Intellectual Tradition and the Moral Foundations of Democracy* (Lanham, Md., 1995), pp. 29–58.

9. Benton Johnson, "The Denominations: The Changing Map of Religious America," in Roper Center, *The Public Perspective* (Storrs, Conn.: University of Connecticut Press, 1993), p. 3 ff.; Andrew Greeley, *Religious Change in America* (Cambridge: Harvard University Press, 1989), chapter 3, reports similar denominational trends up to 1985.

10. Ted Jelen and Clyde Wilcox, "The Christian Right in the 1990s," in Roper Center, *Public Perspective*, pp. 10, 11.

11. Nancy Ammerman, *Baptist Battles: Social Change and Religious Conflict in the Southern Baptist Convention* (New Brunswick, N.J., 1990), p. 132.

12. Ammerman, *Baptist Battles*, p. 142.

13. Ammerman, *Baptist Battles*, p. 146.

14. Mark Juergensmeyer, *The New Cold War? Religious Nationalism Confronts the Secular State* (Berkeley: University of California Press, 1993).

15. But while leadership is of great importance in the explanation of fundamentalism, there are cases in which the factor of choice, necessary as it is to all social movements, is expressed not so much through leadership as through the impulses, the knee-jerk behaviors, of groups and masses. Consider, for example, the incandescence of mobs and riots in Ayodhya or Bombay, the massacre at the Golden Temple in Amritsar, the Dry Zone of Sri Lanka, the revolver shots of anonymous assassins. On this point, cf. Stanley J. Tambiah, *Leveling Crowds: Ethnonationalist Conflicts and Collective Violence in South Asia* (Berkeley, 1996).

16. Christophe Jaffrelot, *The Hindu Nationalist Movement in India* (New York, 1996).

17. John F. Burns, "Sworn in as India's Leader, Ambiguity in His Wake: Atal Bihari Vajpayee," *New York Times*, March 20, 1998, A3.

18. Gideon Aran, "Jewish Zionist Fundamentalism: The Bloc of the Faithful in Israel (Gush Emunim)," in Martin E. Marty and R. Scott Appleby, eds., *Fundamentalisms Observed* (Chicago, 1991), pp. 265–344.

19. Aran, "Jewish Zionist Fundamentalism," pp. 268–69.

Chapter 4

1. See Susan Harding, "Imagining the Last Days: The Politics of Apocalyptic Language," in Martin E. Marty and R. Scott Appleby, eds., *Accounting for Fundamentalisms* (Chicago, 1994), pp. 57–78.

2. The Adi Granth is the sole object of worship in the Sikh ritual. Personified, it is "awakened" in the morning, revered during the day, and put to rest during the night.

3. In the years following the Golden Temple massacre, it has been impossible to eliminate large-scale violence and terrorism in Punjab. Simranjeet Singh Mann, a relatively moderate Sikh leader, has brokered the major factions of the Akali Dal into a loose coalition in order to arrive at a modus vivendi with the Indian government. The radical "fundamentalists," however, in Bhindranwale's spirit of defiance, will settle for nothing less than Khalistan.

4. These involvements with the world and borrowings from other religions triggered a purist movement among the Buddhist clergy and laity, which James Manor and Gananath Obeyesekere suggest may be more deserving of the fundamentalist label than the extremist ethnonationalist trends, which we are considering here. These "purists" are attempting to rid Sri Lankan Buddhism of Hindu accretions, magical practices, astrology, sorcery, and the like, returning it to the path of the Buddha and the original Pali canon. But the purists have been marginalized by the syncretizers, on the one hand, and by the Buddhist nationalists, on the other.

5. Other revivalist and defensive movements formed in these decades were more moderate and less in conflict with classical Theravada Buddhism. These included the Young Men's Buddhist Association (1891) and the All-Ceylon Buddhist Congress (1919).

6. James Manor, "Organizational Weakness and the Rise of Sinhalese Buddhist Extremism," in Marty and Appleby, eds., *Accounting for Fundamentalisms*, pp. 770–84.

7. In 1971, the uprising led by the Maoist People's Liberation Front was triggered by another export crisis and the serious economic distress and high unemployment resulting from it.

8. Quoted in Abdel Azim Ramadan, "Fundamentalist Influence in Egypt: The Strategies of the Muslim Brotherhood and the Takfir Groups," in Martin E. Marty and R. Scott Appleby, eds., *Fundamentalisms and the State: Remaking Polities, Economies, and Militance* (Chicago, 1993), pp. 152–83.

9. Ramadan, "Fundamentalist Influence in Egypt."

10. Susan Bayly, "Christians and Competing Fundamentalisms in South Indian Society," in Marty and Appleby, eds., *Accounting for Fundamentalisms*, p. 732.

Chapter 5

1. Severine Labat, *Les Islamistes Algériens* (Paris, 1995); Rémy Leveau, *Le Sabre et le Turban* (Paris, 1993).

2. David Stoll, *Is Latin America Turning Protestant?* (Berkeley and Los Angeles, 1993).

3. William D. Dinges and James Hitchcock, "Roman Catholic Traditionalism and Activist Conservatism in the United States," in Martin E. Marty and R. Scott Appleby, *Fundamentalisms Observed* (Chicago, 1991), p. 68.

4. Luigi Giussani, *Communion et Liberation* (Paris, 1988), idem, *Why the Church?* trans. Viviane Hewitt (Montreal, 2001).

5. Arieh Surasky, *Marbitzei Tora u-Musar* (Bnai Brak, 1973), vols. 2 and 3.

6. Mumtaz Ahmad, "Islamic Fundamentalism in South Asia: The Jama'at-i-Islami and the Tablighi Jamaat," in Martin E. Marty and R. Scott Appleby, eds., *Fundamentalisms Observed* (Chicago, 1991), especially pp. 510–24.

7. Harjot Oberoi, *The Construction of Religious Boundaries: Culture, Identity and Diversity in the Sikh Tradition* (Chicago, 1994), p. 190. Cynthia Keppley Mahmood, *Fighting for Faith and Nation: Dialogues with Sikh Militants* (Philadelphia, 1996), pp. 40–42, 196. T. N. Madan, "The Double-Edged Sword: Fundamentalism and the Sikh Religious Tradition," in Marty and Appleby, *Fundamentalisms Observed*, pp. 599, 601, 613.

8. Steve Bruce, "Fundamentalism, Ethnicity and Enclave," in Martin E. Marty and R. Scott Appleby, eds., *Fundamentalisms and the State: Remaking Polities, Economies and Militance* (Chicago, 1993), pp. 50–67.

9. Ehud Sprinzak, *The Ascendancy of the Religious Right in Israel* (Oxford, 1998), pp. 98–101.

10. Peter van der Veer, *Religious Nationalism: Hindus and Muslims in India* (Berkeley, 1994).

11. Emmanuel Sivan, "Illusions of Change," *Journal of Democracy* 11, no. 3 (July 2000): 69–83.

12. Rémy Leveau, *L'Algerie dans la Guerre* (Brussels, 1993); idem, "The Holy War Tradition in Islam," *Orbis* (spring 1998): 187 ff.

13. Joel A. Carpenter, *Revive Us Again: The Reawakening of American Fundamentalism* (New York, 1997), pp. 187–246; Michael Lienesch, *Redeeming America: Piety and Politics in the New Christian Right* (Chapel Hill, 1993), pp. 139–94.

14. Samuel C. Heilman, *Defenders of the Faith: Inside Ultra-Orthodox Jewry* (New York, 1992), pp. 83–93; Samuel C. Heilman and Menachem Friedman, "Religious Fundamentalism and Religious Jews: The Case of the Haredim," in Marty and Appleby, eds., *Fundamentalisms Observed*, pp. 197–255.

15. Sencer Ayata, "Patronage, Party and the State: The Politicization of Islam in Turkey," *Middle East Journal* 50, no. 1 (winter 1996): 40–56; M. Hakan Yavuz, "Towards an Islamic Liberalism?: The Nurcu Movement and Fethullah Gülen," *Middle East Journal* 53, no. 4 (fall 1999): 584–605; Haldun Gülalp, "Political Islam in Turkey: The Rise and Fall of the Refah Party," *Muslim World* 89, no. 1 (January 1999): 22–41; Ugur Akinci, "The Welfare Party's Municipal Track Record: Evaluating Islamist Municipal Activism in Turkey," *Middle East Journal* 53, no. 1 (winter 1999): 75–94; Gokhan Cetinsaya, Rethinking Nationalism and Islam: Some Preliminary Notes on the Roots of Turkish-Islamic Synthesis in Modern Turkish Political Thought," *Muslim World* 89, nos. 3–4 (July–October 1999): 350–76; M. Hakan Yavuz, "The Assassination of Collective Memory: The Case of Turkey," *Muslim World* 89, nos. 3–4 (July–October 1999): 350–76.

16. Gideon Aran, "Jewish Zionist Fundamentalism: The Bloc of the Faithful in Israel," in Marty and Appleby, *Fundamentalisms Observed*, pp. 265–344; idem, "The Father, the Son and the Holy Land: The Spiritual Authorities of Jewish-Zionist Fundamentalism in Israel," in R. Scott Appleby, ed., *Spokesmen for the Despised: Fundamentalist Leaders of the Middle East* (Chicago, 1997), pp. 398–413.

17. Ziad Abu Amr, "Shaykh Ahmad Yasin and the Origins of Hamas," in Appleby, *Spokesmen for the Despised*, pp. 225–53.

18. Sivan, "Illusions of Change," p. 80.

Chapter 6

1. José Casanova, *Public Religions in the Modern World* (Chicago, 1994); Daniel Bell, *The Winding Passage* (Cambridge, Mass., 1980), pp. 331 ff.

2. Gabriel Almond, et al., *Comparative Politics Today*, 7th ed. (New York, 2000), pp. 224–25, 296.

3. *Proceedings of the American Philosophical Society* 143, no. 2 (March 1999).

4. Christian De Neuve, "Constraints on the Origin and Evolution of Life," *Proceedings of the American Philosophical Society* 142, no. 4 (December 1998): 525 ff.

5. John Horgan, *The End of Science: Facing the Limits of Knowledge in the Twilight of the Scientific Age* (Reading, Mass., 1996), p. 214.

6. Stephen Jay Gould, "Afterword: The Truth of Fiction" in George Gaylord Simpson, *The Dechronization of Sam Magruder* (New York, 1996), p. 118.

7. Steven Weinberg, *The First Three Minutes* (New York, 1977), pp. 154–55.

8. Steven Weinberg, *Dreams of a Final Theory* (New York, 1992), p. 253.

9. Horgan, *The End of Science*; John Maddox, *What Remains to Be Discovered: Mapping the Secrets of the Universe, the Origins of Life, and the Future of the Human Race* (New York, 1998).

10. Maddox, *What Remains to Be Discovered*, xiii.

11. The dominant world politico-economic trends of the last two decades have been the spread of democracy and of the market economy. Samuel Huntington writes of three historic waves of democratization: a relatively long and low wave from 1828 to 1926 (the playing out of the American and French Revolutions); a second one from 1943 to 1964 (playing out of the consequences of World War II), and a third wave beginning in 1974 and continuing into the present. The first two waves were followed by reverse waves in which some of the democracies collapsed, though there was a net democratic increase. In *Is the Third Wave Over?* Larry Diamond brings us up to date on contemporary democratic trends. As of 1995, 117 out of 191 independent countries (a little over 60 percent) were rated as formally democratic, contrasting with the situation in 1974 when only 39 out of 142 (27.5 percent) were so rated. But out of these 117 "electorally" democratic countries in 1995, only 76, or a little over one half of the total number of countries, were judged to be "liberal democracies" in the sense that political rights and civil liberties were protected.

Whether a new reverse wave has set in is still not clear. Contemporary conditions differ in three ways from those associated with the first and second waves. First, professional militaries are more reluctant to intervene in the light of their costly experiences in the 1960s and 1970s. Second, with the possible exception of the regionally specific case of Islamic fundamentalism, the nondemocratic ideologies struggle for legitimation. And third, again because of the remembered heavy costs of fascism and authoritarianism, there is little public support for antidemocratic coups and regimes. Instead of democratic breakdowns characteristic of the reverse phases of the first and second waves, Diamond points to a more limited kind of erosion setting in among the more recent democratic arrivals in which the quality of democracy deteriorates. Rather than reversing, the third wave seems to be leveling off. But democracy is still the only game in town.

12. Jason DeParle, "A Fundamental Problem," *New York Times Magazine*, July 14, 1999, p. 20.

13. "Second Waco Church Severs Ties with Southern Baptist Convention," Associated Press, December 8, 2000.

14. James Gwartney, Robert Lawson, and Walter Block, *Economic Freedom of the World, 1975–1995* ([Vancouver], 1996), chapters 2 and 4.

15. See the essays on "Economies" in Martin E. Marty and R. Scott Appleby, eds., *Fundamentalisms and the State: Remaking Polities, Economies, and Militance* (Chicago: University of Chicago Press, 1993): Timur Kuran, "Fundamentalisms and the Economy," pp. 289–301; Timur Kuran, "The Economic Impact of Islamic Fundamentalism," pp. 302–41; Laurence R. Iannoccone, "Heirs to the Protestant Ethic? The Economics of American Fundamentalists," pp. 342–66; Charles F. Keyes, "Buddhist Economics and Buddhist Fundamentalism in Burma and Thailand," pp. 367–409; Deepak Lal, "The Economic Impact of Hindu Revivalism," pp. 410–26.

For more detailed analysis of the problems of the political economy of development, see Stephen Haggard and Steven B. Webb, eds., *Voting for Reform: Democracy, Political Liberalization, and Economic Adjustment* (New York, 1994); Stephen Haggard and Robert Kaufman, *The Political Economy of Democratic Transitions* (Princeton, N.J., 1995); Adam Przeworski, *Democracy And the Market: Political and Economic Reform in Eastern Europe and Latin America* (Cambridge, 1991); Juan Linz and Alfred Stepan, *Problems of Democratic Transition and Consolidation* (Baltimore, Md., 1996).

16. Philip Slater, *The Pursuit of Loneliness: American Culture at the Breaking Point* (Boston, 1971).

17. The wide-ranging cultural response to this sociomoral crisis included the attempted retrieval and gilding, by social critics and liberal intellectuals, of communitarian values, the notion of the "common good," and practices of social solidarity that Tocqueville had famously described as "American habits of the heart"; and, on a popular level, the rise of "soft evangelical" megachurches as well as an array of self-help and small group spiritual movements that qualify as "revivalist" rather than "fundamentalist." See Robert Bellah et al., *Habits of the Heart: Individualism and Commitment in American Life* (New York 1985).

18. Peter Berger, *The Heretical Imperative: Contemporary Possibilities of Religious Affirmation* (Garden City, N.Y., 1979). A series of sociological studies of the religious individualism of the baby boomer generation followed Berger's trenchant analysis. Born between 1946 and 1964 and numbering approximately 75 million, the boomers transformed the most intimate realms of life, extending to gender roles, personal lifestyle, and family structures "the very same operative principles that have long characterized the public spheres." See Wade Clark Rood and Lyn Gesch, "Boomers and the Culture of Choice: Changing Patterns of Work, Family, and Religion," in Nancy Tatom Ammerman and Wade Clark Roof, eds., *Work, Family, and Religion in Contemporary Society* (New York and London, 1995), p. 62.

19. Arlene Skolnick, *Embattled Paradise: The American Family in an Age of Uncertainty* (New York, 1991); Ammerman also cites, inter alia: Mary Y. Morgan and John Scanzoni, "Religious Orientations and Women's Expected Continuity in the Labor Force, *Journal of Marriage and the Family* 49 (1987): 367–79; William V. D'Antonio, "Family Life, Religion, and Societal Values and Structures," and Barbara Hargrove, "The Church, the Family, and the Modernization Process, in William V. D'Antonio and Joan Aldous, eds., *Families and Religions: Conflict and Change in Modern Society* (Beverly Hills, 1983).

20. Robert N. Bellah, Richard Madsen, William M. Sullivan, Ann Swidler, and Steven M. Tipton, "Individualism and the Crisis of Civic Membership," *Christian Century* (May 8, 1996): 510–16.

21. Wade Clark Roof, *A Generation of Seekers: The Spiritual Journeys of the Baby Boom Generation* (New York,, 1993), pp. 214, 276. "Whether Catholic, Protestant, Jewish or whatever, the highly privatized, personally expressive mode of religion is a contemporary American cultural form." Roof and Gesch, "Boomers and the Culture of Choice," p. 63. The implications for conventional modes of religious education were startling: even children should be free to choose their faith. A majority of those questioned agreed that "Church is something freely chosen by each person rather than passed on from generation to generation" (pp. 64–65). By 1995, the

link between family and organized religion was still alive and well "only for a specific segment of the population with traditional views about family participation and traditional family structures to match." Nancy Tatom Ammerman and Wade Clark Roof, "Introduction: Old Patterns, New Trends, Fragile Experiments," in Ammerman and Roof, *Work, Family, and Religion in Contemporary Society*, 9.

22. "Jihad against Jews and Crusaders," World Islamic Front Statement, 23 February 1998. Available on the World Wide Web at www.fas.org/irp/world/para/docs/980223-fatwa.htm.

23. W. Montgomery Watt, *Islamic Fundamentalism and Modernity* (London, 1988), p. 29.

24. Gustav Niehbuhr, "Iranian Contrasts Faith and Nihilism," *New York Times*, 17 November 2001, A10.

INDEX

ABC News, 3
Accounting for Fundamentalisms, 13
Adi Granth, 157
Advani, Lal Krishna, 139, 176
Agudat Yisrael, 39, 46, 77, 104, 108, 186
  split of extreme wing, 188
  world creator phase, 187
Ahmad, Jalal Al-e, 28–29
Ahmadiyya, 42
al-Asad, Hafiz, 42
Al Qaeda, 1, 2, 30, 151, 241
American Academy of Arts and Sciences, 9
American Philosophical Society, 222
American Theosophical Society, 163, 167, 188
Ammerman, Nancy, 53–54, 127–28
Amritsar, 158
"apostate" regimes, 82
Aran, Gideon, 140
Armed Islamic Group in Algeria (GIA), 1, 241
Arya Samaj, 184–85
Asahara, Shoko, 91
Ashcroft, John, 3
'Ashura, 66
"Assimilation Mania" (*Assimilationgesucht*), 28
Atta, Mohamed, 3
Aum Shinrikyo, 91
Aviner, Rabbi Shlomo, 70

Babri Masjid, 124, 139
Baha'is, 42
Bakker, Jim, 74, 75
Bakker, Tammy Faye, 74
Balfour Declaration (1917), 61
Balthasar, Hans Urs von, 27
Bandaranaike, S. W. R. D., 164
al-Banna, Hasan, 46, 103, 153, 177
Baptists, 96, 103
Barth, Karl, 170
Ba'th Party, 25
Bayly, Susan, 183
Belhadj, 'Ali, 74–75, 88–89
Bell, Daniel, 220–21
Betrayal of Buddhism, The, 164
Bharatiya Janata Party (Indian People's Party), 13, 131, 137–38, 172–75
Bhindranwale, Jarnail Singh, 159
bin Laden, Osama, 2, 6, 30, 151, 238–39, 241
Birnbaum, Dr. Nathan, 23–28, 82
Blanchard, Jonathan, 29
Bnei Akiva, 161
Bob Jones University, 34, 51, 86
Bolshevism, 5
Branch Davidians, 91
Bright, Bill, 171
Bruce, Steve, 154–55
Buddhism, 90, 102
Buddhist Philosophical Society, 163

Burke, Edmund, 5
Bush, George W., 3, 6, 51

caliphate, 24
Carter, Jimmy, 121
Carver, Raymond, 33
Casanova, José, 220–221
Chechnya, 1
Christian Coalition, 156–57
Christian Democratic Party, 79, 196
Christian Democrats, 196
clerico-authoritarianism, 5
Cold War, 3
Collier, David, 117–18
Comunione e Liberazione, 25, 34, 45, 55, 71, 84–85, 95
    Barthian theology, 95
    Compagnia delle Opere, 55, 170
    historical perceptions, 60
    impact of migration on the rise of, 129
    lay authority, 79
    Movimento Popolare, 55, 170
    overview, 106, 170–71
    Scuola di Communità, 55
Concerned Yeshiva Students, 29
Congress Party (Hindu), 13, 136, 138
Congress Party (Sikh), 159
Council of Torah Sages, 77
Couscous Riots, 74

Dagestan, 1
Darby, John Nelson, 57
Darwin, Charles, 117, 221
Darwinism, 38, 221–22
Dayananda, Swami, 184, 188
Deoras, Balasaheb, 176
Dessler, Rabbi E., 24
al-Dhahabi, Shaykh Muhmmad Husayn, 18
Dharmapala, Anagarika, 164–67, 184
Douglas, Mary, 7, 31, 103

Eckstein, Harry, 117
Ecuadorian Puruha, 114
'Eda Haredit, 44, 78
Edwards, Jonathan, 46
Episcopalians, 127

"enclave," 24, 30, 35, 36, 43, 47, 75–85
    as alternative to governmental subordination, 83–85
    and antinomian tendencies, 49
    apocalyptic worldview of, 64–65
    and apostasy, 42
    behavioral standards, 46, 48–52, 75
    as "Believing Remnant," 35
    body language, 47
    code names, 66–67
    control of behavior via religious law, 51
    cosmological space, 71–75
    cosmology, 56–70
    decentralization/compartmentalization as threat, 88
    dualistic mentality of, 36–37, 38, 40, 42, 43
    enemies of, 37–38
    fear of novelty, 51, 52, 58
    "feedback" from reality, 70
    as function of the past, 61–62
    historical perception, 58–62
    historical time, 57
    loss of members, 32–33
    material success as threat, 86–87
    messianism and eschatology, 62–71
    organization of time, 52–54
    and separatism, 40–41, 44, 46–47
    social groupings, 53–56
    societal accommodation as threat, 85–86
    space, 46–47, 52–54
    splits, 82–83
    survival of, 68
    theory of, 7, 30–33
    tradition, 57–60
    voluntary membership, 34, 48
    vulnerability, 67
    "wall of virtue," 34, 86
    and zealotry, 35–36
Enlightenment, 4–5, 25, 27. See also modernity; secularization
ethnonationalism
    as component of Abrahamic fundamentalisms, 90
    as movements against minorities, 112
    as reactivity, 99–101
ethnoreligion, 94, 101
ethnoreligious confrontation, 198–202

Fadlallah, Shaykh Muhammad Husayn, 25, 51, 72

Falwell, Rev. Jerry, 18, 26, 70, 88, 156
    and cosmological space, 71–72
    establishment of Moral Majority, 156
    and premillennialism, 62
    and Religious Round Table, 156
    and separatism, 48

fascism, 5

France, 60, 129

Free Presbyterian Church, 155

Front Islamique Du Salut (FIS), 69–70, 75

"fundamentalism," 94
    definition of, 17
    popular usage, 1–2
    problems with term, 14
    proper word usage, 16–17

Fundamentalism Project, 5, 6, 9, 15, 116

Fundamentalisms Comprehended, 14, 118

Fundamentalisms Observed, 9

Fundamentalisms and Society, 11

fundamentalist movements
    in democratic states, 225–228
    dynamics of, 9–10
    and globalization, 6
    and modern science, 5, 11
    as political movements, 4
    as reaction to modern state, 20
    secular myopia toward, 2, 4, 6
    and tradition, 92–93
    and violence, 17, 234–37

fundamentalists
    within Asian religions, 15–16, 91
    and education, 12
    envy of West, 29
    as "hypothetical family," 14
    ideological characteristics of, 93–104
    and media, 12
    and premillennialism, 62
    women and family, 11–12

Gaebelein, A. C., 46

Gandhi, Indira
    assassination of, 139
    attempt to form counterpart to Akali Dal, 159, 177
    support of Sikh militants, 176
    suspension of Indian constitution, 182

Garden of Pious Believers, The, 76

Gell-Mann, Murray, 222–23

George, Alexander, 117

Germany, 221

Girard, Rene, 73

Giussani, Luigi, 25–26, 77
    and behavioral standards, 46
    blend of ideologies and philosophies, 170–71, 197
    as charismatic leader, 197
    as founder of Comunione e Liberazione, 106–7, 135, 188
    "Remnant of Israel," 35

global fundamentalism, 2

globalization, 125

Gobind, 157

Golden Temple of Amritsar, 159

Golwarkar, M. S., 135, 139, 176. *See also* Hindu fundamentalism

Gould, Steven Jay, 223

Granth Sahib, 109–10

Green Revolution, 133, 158, 176–77

Guatemalan Pentecostalists
    Catholic decline, 171
    as competing religion, 100
    contingency of, 194
    involvement and goals of, 171–72
    overview, 111
    triggers of, 194

Gush Emunim (Bloc of the Faithful), 55, 58
    authority, 81, 104
    behavioral standards, 50
    cosmological space, 53, 73
    dress, 47
    emergence, 160–61
    fear of novelty, 52
    formation of, 140–42
    historical perceptions, 60
    messianism and eschatology, 63–64, 68, 70, 73
    overview, 109
    Pioneer Torah Scholars' Group, 141–42
    secular opponents, 38
    and separatism, 40–41
    as "world conqueror," 148, 187–88

Habad. *See* Lubavitcher Hasidism
Haim, Hafetz (Rabbi I. M. HaCohen), 24, 29, 52, 74, 83
Ha-Mahane ha-Haredi, 24
Hamas, 108
and bureaucracy, 88
cosmological space, 73–74
enemies of, 100, 101
as ethnoreligious group, 199–200
triggers, 179
Haredim (Jewish Ultra-Orthodox), 34, 37–38, 54–55, 57–58, 108–9
"affinity groups," 186
and age of exile, 63
authority, 77
behavioral standards, 50
as "Believing Remnant," 35
cosmological space, 53, 75, 97–98
da'as Torah, 77, 78, 79
dualistic views of, 39
emergence of, 18–19
encouragements for memberships, 34
"foundation myths," 60
historical perceptions of, 58
impact of Holocaust, 188
leadership, 186
messianism and eschatology, 62–63, 67–68
multigenerationalism, 186–187
political aspirations of, 27–28
sense of exile, 24, 44, 67
separatism, 40, 44–45, 48
and state of Israel, 63
threat of material success, 87
"Torah for its own sake," 54
as world renouncers, 148, 187
Haredit, Eda, 188
Hargobind, 157, 159
Hasidim, Satmar, 188
Hazm, Ibn, 57
Hedgewar, K. B., 135, 139, 175
Hidden Imam, 65–66, 80, 81, 97
Hinduism, 90
and ethnonationalism, 101
inerrancy of religious text, 96, 102
as syncretic movement, 90
use of media, 201–2
Hindu fundamentalism, 200
Hindutva ("Hinduness"), 16, 173, 200

impact of chance, 139
internal unity, 200
militant Hindu Nationalism, 135–40, 172–75
political parties (*see individual parties*)
political success, 138–40
structural variables, 138
Hizbullah
cosmological space, 72
enemies of, 100, 101
and messianism, 66, 69
Holocaust, 78
effect on Haredi activists, 24
effect on religious practice, 19
migration of survivors, 129
sense of exile, 67
and Zionism, 188–89
Horgan, John, 223
Husayn, Imam, 61, 66
Hussein, Saddam, 42

ijtihad, 51
Ilyas, Maulana, 112
inerrancy (of religious texts), 14, 96, 75–76
infidels (*kuffir*), 42
Intifada, 73
Iranian revolution, 27, 72
Ish, Hazon, 28
and behavioral standards, 49, 50, 52
as ideologist, 186
Islam, 18, 24, 41, 42, 82
enclave tendencies, 41–45
guiding principles of, 49, 50
Hanbalism, 102, 107
inerrancy of religious text, 102
jahiliyya (pre-Islamic Arabia), 25, 38, 69
Kharijites, 57
messianism, 64
nationalism as threat, 41
role of Qur'an, 76, 113
sense of exile, 25
traditional roots, 57
Islamic Government, 65, 76
Islamic movements in South Asia, 114
Islamic Salvation Front (FIS) of Algeria, 13, 97
Islamist Refah Party, 132

Israel, 131
    Knesset, 24, 27, 40

Jamaʿat al-Takfir wal-l-Hijra, 44, 49, 54, 64
Jamaʿat-i-Islami, 101, 107
Jewish Defense League. See Kach, Meir Kahane
Jewish Underground
    crisis of leadership, 81
    dismantling of, 70
    and messianism, 63
    sense of exile, 67
Jews, Orthodox. See Gush Emunim; Haredim
jihad, 2, 74
Jihad Organization, 69
John XXIII (pope), 134
John Paul II (pope), 170–71
Jones, Bob, Sr., 40, 44
Jonestown, 91
Joshi, M. M., 174
Joseph, Ovadia, 135
Judaism, 19, 76
    Diaspora, 39, 57, 60
    disparity between law and practice, 19
    enclave tendencies, 39–41
    role of Halakhah, 19, 49, 52, 70
    inerrancy of religious texts, 102
    Khug, 78, 79
    messianism, 64
    Three Oaths (in Talmud), 67

Kach, 111–12
    authority, 104
    enemies of, 99, 100
    ethnic group identity of, 199
Kahane, Rabbi Meier, 88, 128, 200
Kahaneman, Rabbi Shlomo, 186, 197
Kaplan, Abraham, 117
Khaldun, Ibn, 64
Khalsa, 158, 160
Khamanei, Ali, 66, 80–81
Khatami, Mohammad, 41
Khomeini, Ayatollah
    and anti-activism, 65–66
    as charismatic leader, 107, 121
    dependence on, 104
    doctrine of wilayat al-faqih, 79–80

as intellectual, 76
    role in Shiʿite movement, 133, 152–53
    and tradition, 58
    use of media technology, 119
    as world conqueror, 188
Khomeinism, 12, 27, 147
Kishk, Shaykh ʿAbd al-Hamid, 43–74
Klal Yisrael (community of the Jews), 39
Kook, Rabbi Avraham
    historical perceptions of, 61
    "Kookism," 140
    and separatism, 40
Kook, Rabbi Zvi Yehuda, 58
    Bnei Akiva disciples of, 141
    as charismatic leader, 81
    dependence on, 104
    establishment of state of Israel, 63
    head of Merkaz Harav yeshiva, 161
    sermons of, 140
Koresh, David, 91
Kottler, Aharon, 197

LaHaye, Timothy, 27, 70. See also Moral Majority
Late Great Planet Earth, The, 77
Le Pen, Jean Marie, 186
Lefebvre, Marcel (archbishop)
    dualistic ideas of, 39
    fight against corruption, 186
    and novelty, 58
    and secularization, 25–26, 28, 29
    and separatism, 45
    as world renouncer, 188
    and zealotry, 35
Lefebvrists
    behavioral standards of, 52
    cosmological space, 72
    dependence on founder, 77
    goals of, 185–86
    historical perceptions, 60
    lay authority, 79
    organization of, 186
    social groupings, 55
    social life, 53
    traditionalism, 57
Leo XIII (pope), 60
Levin, I. M., 186
Liberty University, 51, 71
Lijphart, Arend, 11

Lindsay, Hal, 77
Longowal, Sant Harchand Singh, 159
de Lubac, Henri, 27
Lubavitcher Sect (Habad), 56, 109
  authority, 78, 81
  charismatic leadership, 88
  effect of Bolshevik Revolution, 180
  factors of growth, 180–81
  and messianism, 64, 68
  missionary zeal, 197–98
  threat of material success, 87
Lubavitcher Hasidism, 13, 63

Maddox, John, 223
Mahavamsa, 164, 166
Mahdi, 64, 65, 66, 69
Maistre, Joseph de, 5
Manor, James, 166
Maritain, Jacques, 25
Marty, Martin E., 17
martyrdom, 2
Marxism, 15
Matsumoto, Shoko. See Asahara, Shoko
Maududi, Maulana, 24–25, 82, 107, 153
Mayr, Ernest, 117
messianism
  in enclave, 66–71
  in Gush Emunim, 58, 68, 73
  in haredim, 67–68
  in Lubavitchers, 68
  in Protestant Christians, 68
migration, 128–29
"mimetic desire effect," 73–74
Mishna Berura, 29
modernity/modernization
  exile as response, 30
  as opposed by enclave, 37–38
  selectivity toward/by enclave, 94–95
  as threat to apocalyptic activism, 64–65
Montt, Ríos, 100, 111, 194, 194
Moral Majority, 27, 48, 70, 156
mujtahidun, 80
Muslim Brotherhood, 177–79
  authority, 103
  disbandment of, 179
  of Egypt, 153
  goals of, 178
  Hamas as offshoot of, 154
  logic of, 46

of Syria, 86
  from world creators to world transform-
    ers, 189, 193
Mustafa, Shukri Ahmad, 18, 189
Mutahhari, Ayatollah Murtaza, 18

Nanak, Guru, 157
Nasser, Abdel, 153, 179, 189
"National Union of Volunteers." See Rash-
  triya Sangh (RSS)
Nature, 223
Nazism, 5
Neturei Karta ("The Wall"), 34
  as extreme separatists, 40, 44
  as pure world renouncer, 187
  tradition, 57–58
New Christian Right, 127, 157, 195
  nondemocratic structures, 192–194
Norris, Rev. Frank, 135
North, Gary, 27, 54, 157

Olcott, Henry Steele, 163, 167
Operation Blue Star, 201
"Operation Infinite Justice," 3
Operation Rescue, 77
Origin of Species, On the, 221
Oslo Accords of 1993, 154
Ottoman Empire, 24, 61

Paisley, Rev. Ian, 154–55
Pahlavi, Reza Shah, 107
Palestine, 73
Paul VI (pope), 37
Penados (archbishop), 171
Pentecostalists
  Catholic Pentecostalists, 27
  increase in membership, 127
  irrelevance of intellectualism, 82
  reliance on Holy Spirit, 93
  See also Guatemalan Pentecostalists
Pentagon, 2, 151
Pius V (pope), 60
Pius X (pope), 60
Popper, Karl, 117
postmillennialism, 69, 156
"postmillennial window," 70
premillennialism, 62, 66, 156
pretribulationism. See premillennialism

Protestant Christian fundamentalists, 16,
    122
  components of, 169–70
  distinction with Pentecostals, 93
  enclave tendencies, 45–46
  fear of Romanism, 26
  first public emergence of, 168–70
  growth of, 169
  historical perceptions of, 58, 61
  and inerrancy (of Bible and Second
    Coming), 14
  and messianism, 68–69
  use of *mish-mash*, 29
  and modernity, 37
  and nationalism, 198–99
  and patriotism, 45
  and premillennialism, 62
  religious law, 51
  "sacred desk," 81
  second public emergence of, 155–57
  and separatism, 44
  special language, 46–47
  triggers of, 168–69
  and violence, 1
  vision of America, 45, 73
  as world transformer, 187
  and xenophobia, 45
Przeworski, Adam, 118

Qutb, Sayyid, 82
  effect of imprisonment, 179
  ideology of, 153–54, 189
  prison writings of, 153
  as Qur'anic scholar, 76
  reinterpretation of political theory, 58
  and "sense of exile," 25
  as world conqueror, 188

Ramadan, Abdel Azim, 177–78
Rashid, Rida, 24–26, 46, 49
Rashtriya Svayamsevak Sangh (RSS), 100,
    111, 136–37
  ethnonationalist reactivity, 99
  Hindu nation-building, 181
  involvement in Hindu nationalism,
    172–75
Reconstructionists, 64, 69
Robertson, Pat, 70, 88, 156–57, 171
Roe v. Wade, 132

Roman Catholic traditionalists, 50, 133–
    34
Roman Catholicism, 59–60, 102
Roncalli, Angelo. *See* John XXIII (pope)
Rosenheim, J., 186
Rushdie, Salman, 41
Rushdoony, Rousas John, 157

Sadat, Anwar, 42
al-Sadr, Muhammad Baqir, 25
Samawiya, 187, 189
Sarasvati, Swami Dayananda, 175
Satanic Verses, The, 41
Savarkar, V. D., 136, 139, 175, 188, 199
Saudis, 34
Schach, Rabbi E. M., 28, 43, 77, 104, 135
Scheinfeld, Moshe, 82
Schneerson, Rabbi Menachem Mendel,
    13, 56, 64, 104
Schmidberger, Father Franz, 77
science, 5, 221–23
  "big bang," 222
  Darwinism, 221–222
  evolution, 26
  effect on faith, 224
  fading of scientific revolution, 223
  impact on secularization, 220–24
  new demeanor of, 224
  and technology, 224
Scientific American, 223
Shamir, Yitzhak, 27
Shari'a (Islamic law), 76, 102, 107
  as behavioral standard, 50
  organization of membership, 113
Shi'ite radicals, 37, 41, 42, 57, 77, 80, 81,
    100, 107–8
  role of clergy, 152
  dualism, 96
  hierarchy, 79
  historical perceptions, 58–59, 60
  Imamite sect, 65
  Iraqi Shi'ite Muslims, 86
  maraji', 79, 80
  messianism, 65, 69
  opposition to Khomeini's appeal, 27
  origin and emergence, 151–53
  role of *mujtahid*, 38
  selectivity, 95
  Shi'ite revolution (in Iran), 3

Shi'ite radicals (continued)
enemies with Sunni Islam, 122
triggers of movement, 152
U.S. hostages, 147
"world" of, 147–48
Shiromani Akali Dal, 158
Shulkhan 'Arukh, 76, 102, 108
Sikh militants, 15, 109–10, 157–60, 177
All India Sikh Student Foundation, 159
apocalyptic views, 16
goals of, 101
effect of government policies, 176
and inerrancy (of religious texts), 102
Khalistan, 159
means to attain goals, 183–84
and nationalist exclusion, 200
political parties, 157–59, 176 (see also
individual parties)
under Sant Fateh Singh, 183–84
and violence, 1, 201
Sinhala Maha Sabha, 164, 177
Singh, Amrit, 159
Singh, Sant Fateh, 159, 183
Sinhala Buddhists. See Sri Lankan Buddhist extremism
Six Day War (1967 War)
effect on Arabs, 133
effect on Israelis and Baptist fundamentalists, 133
trigger of formation of Gush Emunim,
63, 109, 140, 160
Sofer, Hatam, 23, 39, 46, 49
Soloveitchik, Haym, 19
Southern Baptists
education as leading influence, 128
gender roles, 29
increase in numbers, 127
influence of urbanization, 128
lack of charismatic leader, 88
social structure within church, 127
South Indian Christians
comparison to Christians/Muslims/
Hindus, 183
comparison to Guatemalan cases, 181
economic triggers, 182–83
religious diversity, 181–82
threats to, 111
Soviet Union, 3
and Sputnik, 124

Sunni radicals, 57, 82, 107
authority, 81–82
behavioral standards, 49
dualism, 96
emergence, 153–54, 177–78
ghatrasa (arrogance), 38
historical perceptions, 60
jahiliyya, 153
messianism, 64, 65
modernity as threat, 37
role of Muslim brotherhood, 177–79
opposition to Khomeini's appeal, 27
shaykhs, 82
takfir wal hijra cells, 153
threat of novelty, 51
Sri Lankan Buddhist extremism, 16, 111
economic crisis, 177
effect of imperialism on Buddhist revival, 163–64
ethnonationalism as reactivity, 99
Four Noble Truths and the Eightfold
Path, 165, 184
growth of, 177
impact of Ministry of cultural affairs,
164
influence of American Theosophical Society, 188
Mahavamsa, 164
origins, 184–85
"Protestant Buddhism," 184
"purification" of society, 101
rise of Buddhist fundamentalism, 166–
67
Sri Lankan political scene, 164–65
triggers of chance and contingency, 167
Sri Lankan Freedom Party (SLFP), 164–65
St. Pius X Fraternity, 55
"strong religion," 2, 7, 9, 17–20
Sufis, 64, 93, 189

Tablighi Jama'at, 43, 56, 76, 82, 90, 112–
13
missionary zeal, 198
"purification" campaign, 198
Takfir wal-Hijra, 189
Taliban, 29
Tamil Separatist Movement, 111, 163–68.
See also Sri Lankan Buddhists

Tamil United Liberation Front (TULF),
    165
Tanzim al-Jihad, 77
Taymiyya, Ibn, 57, 58, 72
Teilhard de Chardin, Pierre, 25
Temple Mount, 70, 73
Temple Mount Faithful, 67
Terry, Randall, 70
Theravada Buddhists. *See* Sri Lankan Bud-
    dhist extremism
Third Temple, 73
Tribulation, 70
Twelfth Imam, 65, 80, 81

Ulster Protestants, 110–11
    emergence and growth, 154–55
United Methodists, 127
United National Party (UNP), 164
urbanization (as trigger of fundamental-
    ism), 128

Vajpayee, Atal Bihari, 137, 139, 176
Vatican II, 58, 113, 134
vigilantism, 43
Vishwa Hindu Parishad (World Hindu
    Party), 13, 137, 181

Waco, 91
"wall of virtue," 33–37, 86
Wasserman, Rabbi E., 24
Watchman-Examiner, 1
Watergate scandal, 121
Weinberg, Steven, 222–23
Westoxication *(gharbzadagi)*, 29, 42, 103
Woodward, Bob, 3
world conqueror (model of fundamental-
    ism), 151–68
world creator (model of fundamental-
    ism), 179–85
World Hindu Society (VHP), 172–76
world renouncer (model of fundamental-
    ism), 185–87
World Trade Center, 2, 151

Yagen, Rabbi Nissim, 43, 74
Yamit (evacuation of), 70
Yasin, Abd al-Salam, 82
Yassin, Shaykh, 108, 154, 179
Yom Kippur War (1973), 63–64, 109, 161

Zakariya, Muhammad, 76
Zionism, 40, 67, 74
Zvi, Shabtai, 58